DISCARDED

Kamisama Kiss

Story & Art by
Julietta Suzuki

Kamisama Kiss

Volume 23
CONTENTS

CHARACTERS

Tomoe
The shinshi who serves Nanami now that she's a tochigami. Originally a wild fox ayakashi.

Nanami Momozono
A high school student who was turned into a kamisama by the tochigami Mikage. She likes Tomoe.

Onikiri
Onibi-warashi, spirits of the shrine.

Kotetsu
Onibi-warashi, spirits of the shrine.

Mamoru
Nanami's shikigami. He can create a spiritual barrier to keep out evil.

Mikage
The kamisama who turned Nanami into a tochigami and left his shrine in her care. He doesn't like dogs. He's also a kamisama of marriage.

Mizuki
Nanami's second shinshi. The incarnation of a white snake. Used to be the shinshi of Yonomori shrine.

Yatori
An ayakashi who is infatuated with Akura-oh and wants to resurrect him.

Kirihito
A human whose body was taken over by the great yokai Akura-oh, who committed every evil he possibly could.

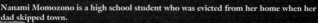

Nanami Momozono is a high school student who was evicted from her home when her dad skipped town.
She meets the tochigami Mikage in a park, and he leaves his shrine and his kami powers to her.
Now Nanami spends her days with Tomoe and Mizuki, her shinshi, and with Onikiri and Kotetsu, the onibi-warashi spirits of the shrine.
Nanami has been slowly gaining powers as kamisama by holding a festival at her shrine, attending a big kami conference, and all sorts of other adventures.
Nanami's and Tomoe's feelings for each other are finally out in the open and they have started to date!
Tomoe drinks the "water of evolution" to become human so he can live his life with Nanami, but he's transformed into a fox instead.
Meanwhile, Kirihito and Yatori are heading for the Mountain of Flames, where Akura-oh's body is interred. Nanami and company head to the Land of the Dead to stop them, but then it comes out that Nanami has very little time left to live...!

Story so far

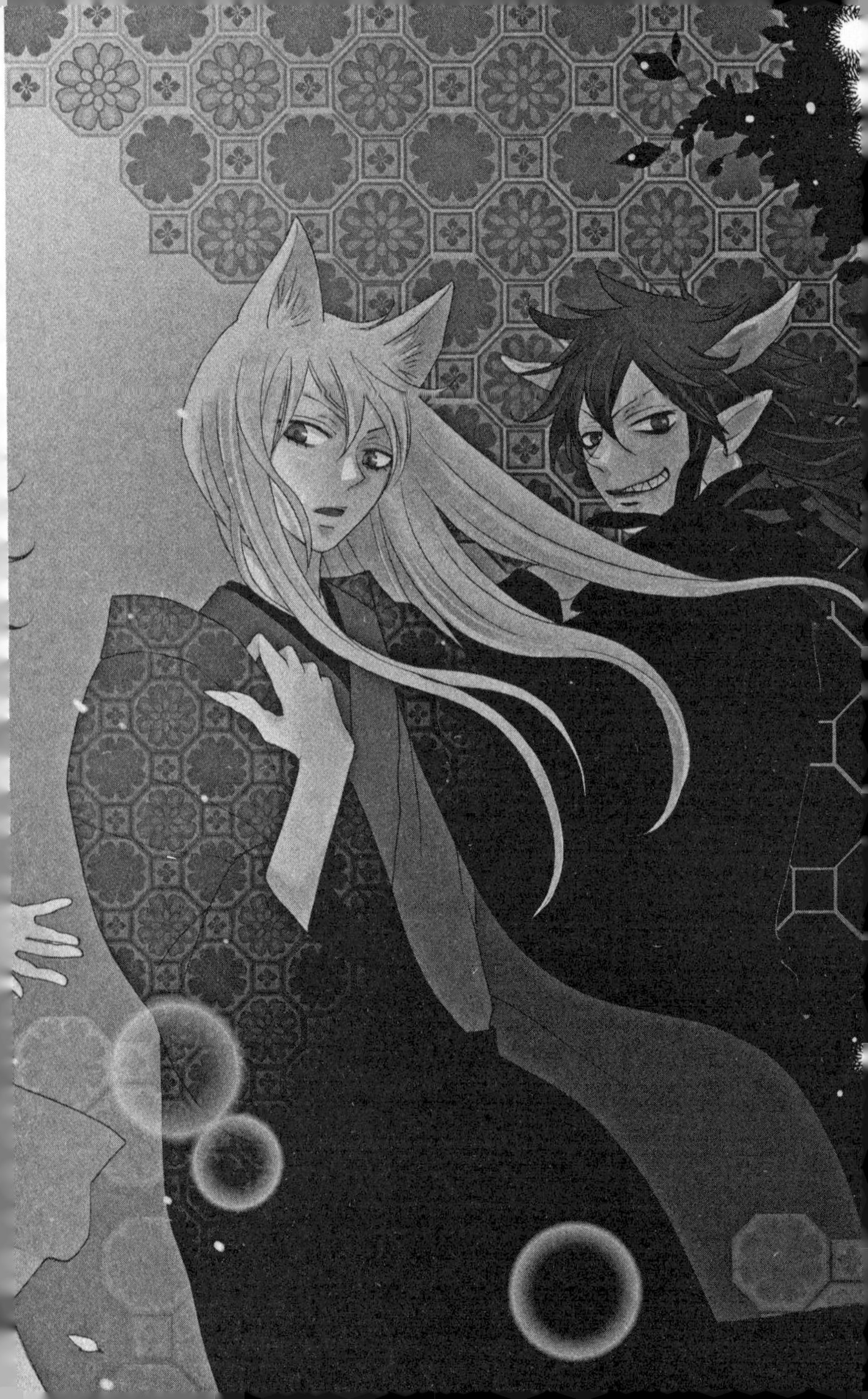

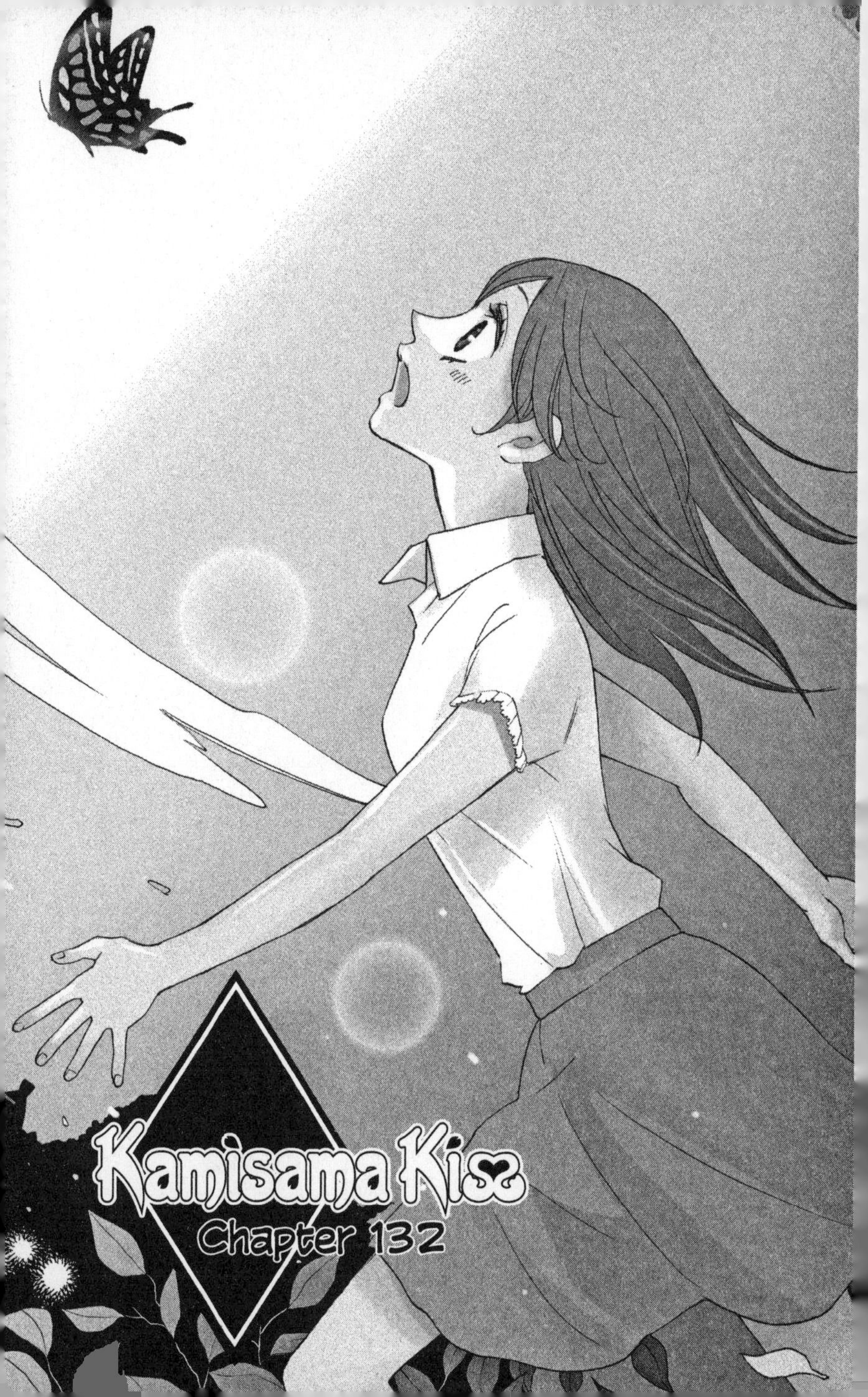
Kamisama Kiss
Chapter 132

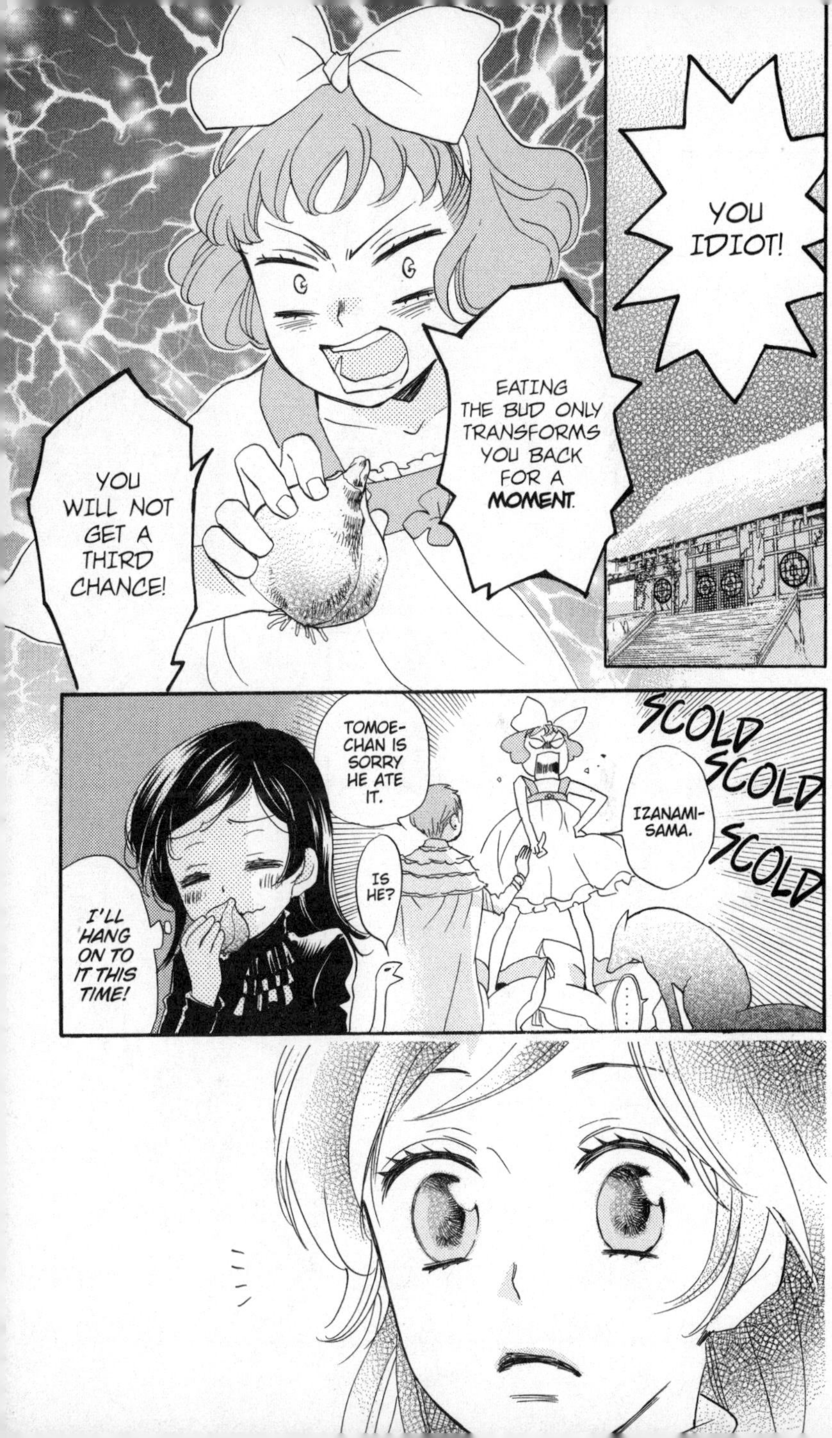
YOU IDIOT!
EATING THE BUD ONLY TRANSFORMS YOU BACK FOR A **MOMENT**.
YOU WILL NOT GET A THIRD CHANCE!
SCOLD SCOLD SCOLD
IZANAMI-SAMA.
TOMOE-CHAN IS SORRY HE ATE IT.
IS HE?
I'LL HANG ON TO IT THIS TIME!

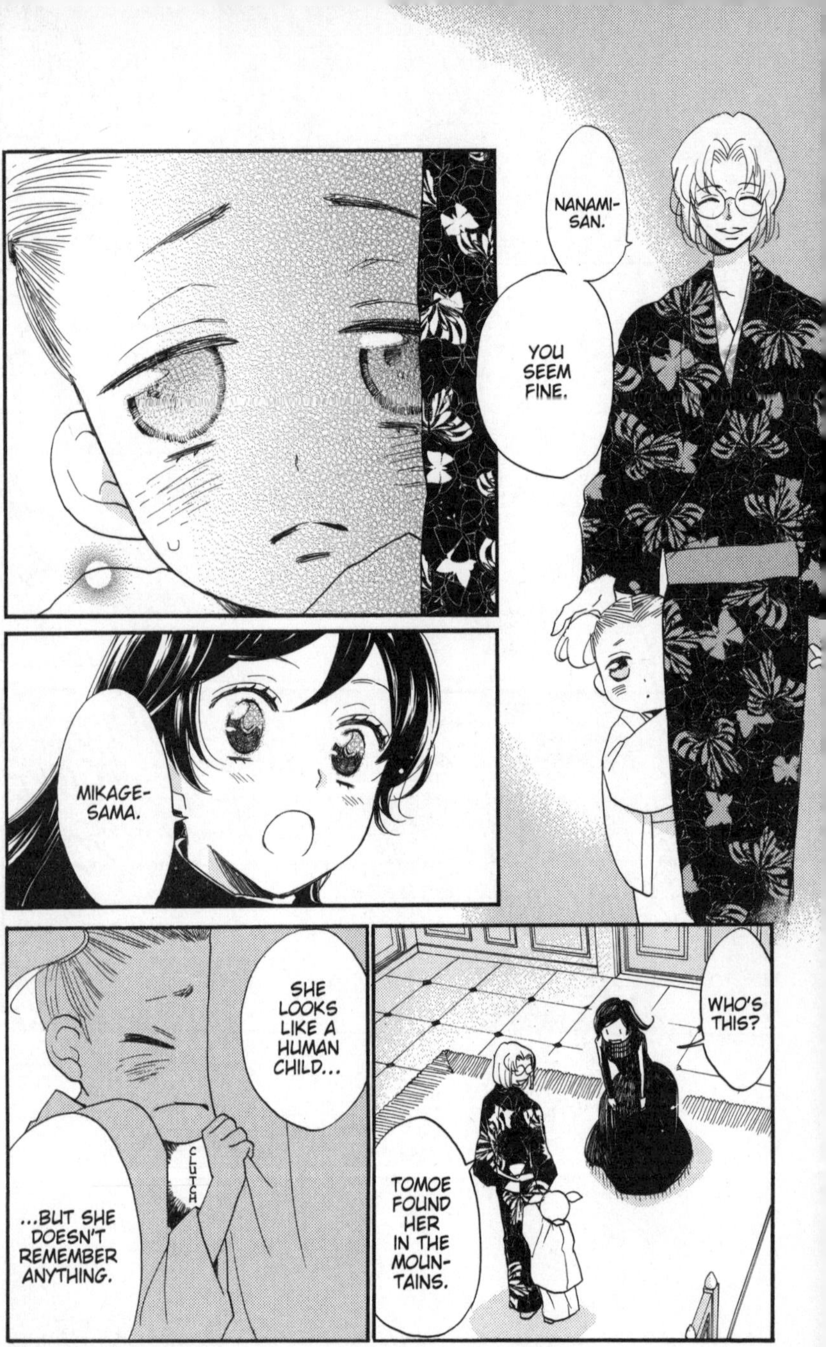
NANAMI-SAN.
YOU SEEM FINE.
MIKAGE-SAMA.
WHO'S THIS?
TOMOE FOUND HER IN THE MOUNTAINS.
SHE LOOKS LIKE A HUMAN CHILD...
CLUTCH
...BUT SHE DOESN'T REMEMBER ANYTHING.

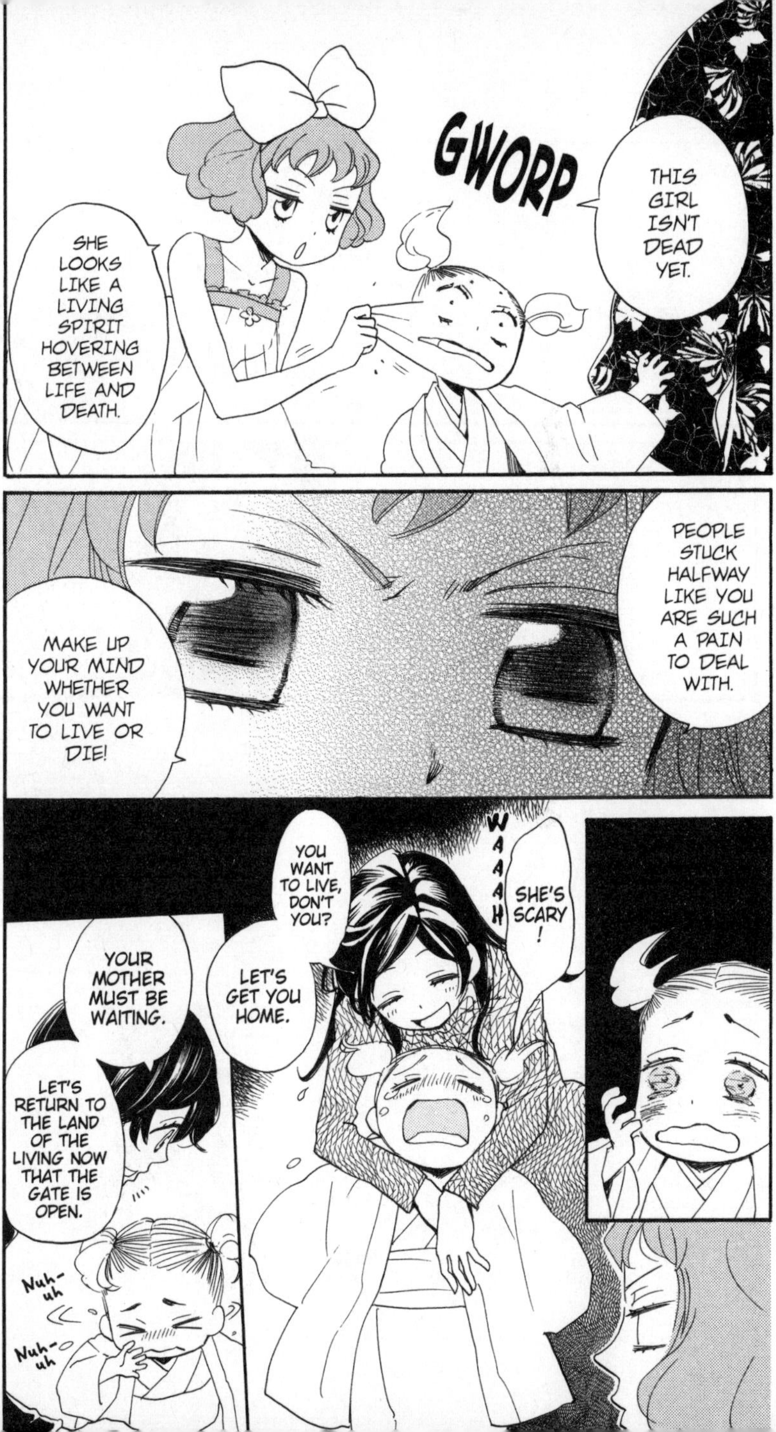
THIS GIRL ISN'T DEAD YET.
GWORP
SHE LOOKS LIKE A LIVING SPIRIT HOVERING BETWEEN LIFE AND DEATH.
PEOPLE STUCK HALFWAY LIKE YOU ARE SUCH A PAIN TO DEAL WITH.
MAKE UP YOUR MIND WHETHER YOU WANT TO LIVE OR DIE!
SHE'S SCARY!
WAAAAH
YOU WANT TO LIVE, DON'T YOU?
LET'S GET YOU HOME.
YOUR MOTHER MUST BE WAITING.
LET'S RETURN TO THE LAND OF THE LIVING NOW THAT THE GATE IS OPEN.
Nuh-uh
Nuh-uh

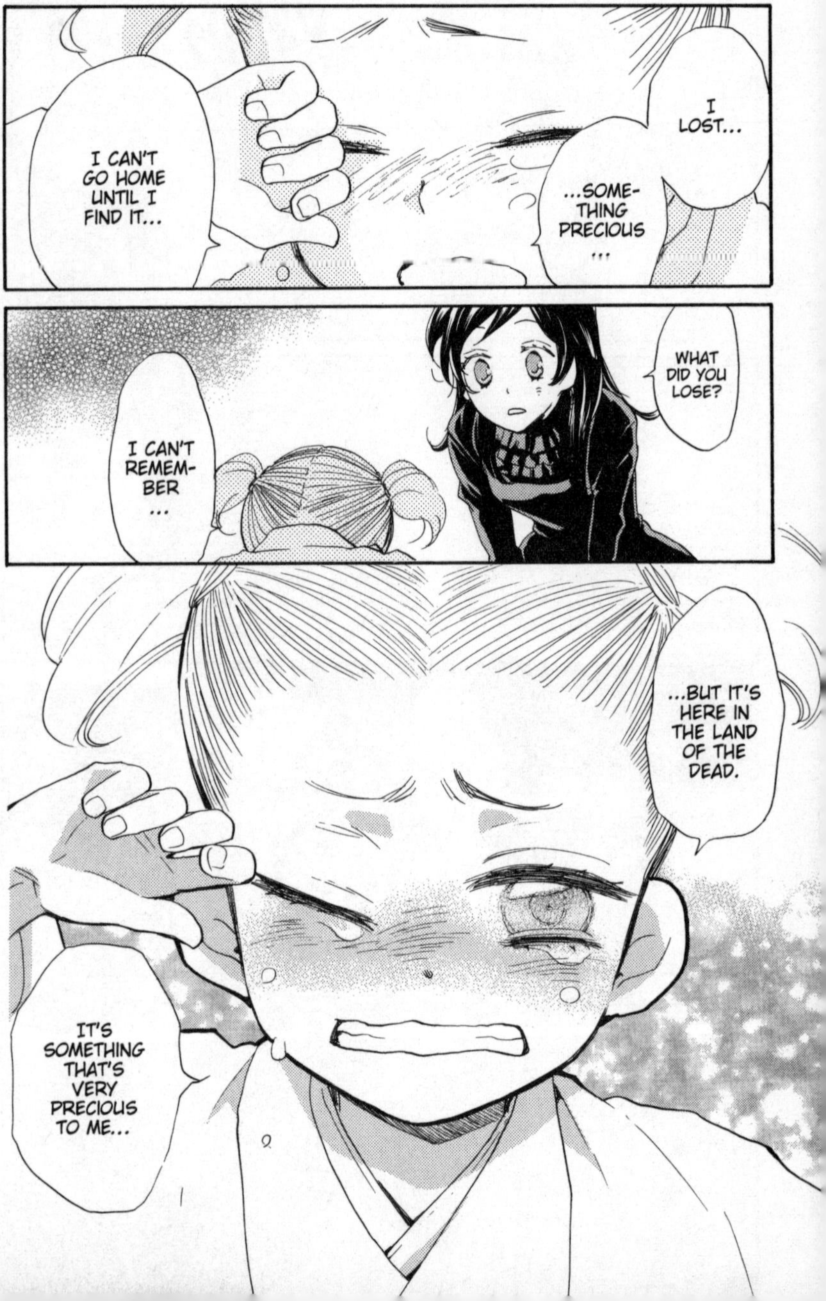
I LOST...
...SOME-THING PRECIOUS...
I CAN'T GO HOME UNTIL I FIND IT...
WHAT DID YOU LOSE?
I CAN'T REMEMBER...
...BUT IT'S HERE IN THE LAND OF THE DEAD.
IT'S SOMETHING THAT'S VERY PRECIOUS TO ME...

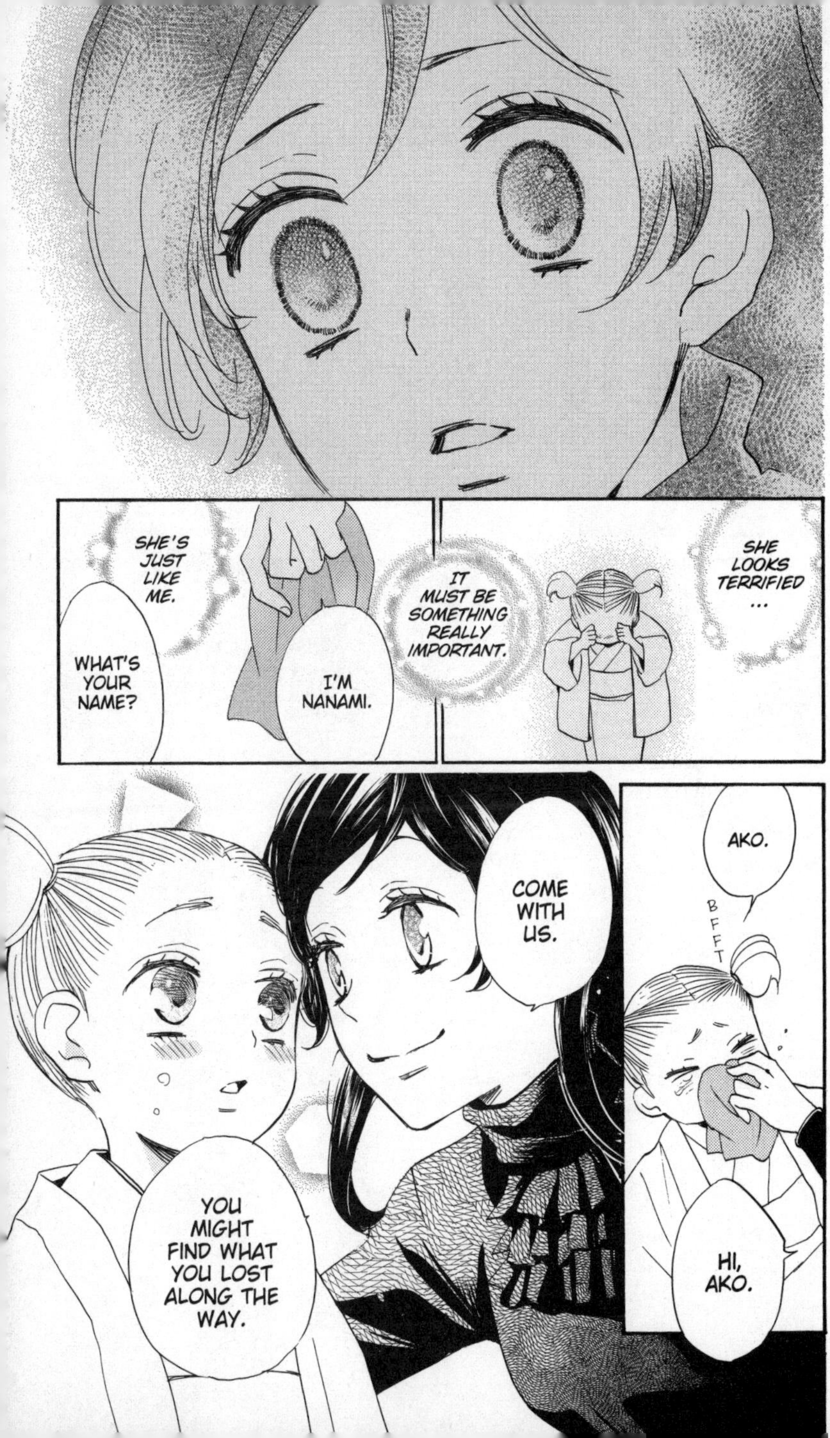
SHE LOOKS TERRIFIED...
IT MUST BE SOMETHING REALLY IMPORTANT.
SHE'S JUST LIKE ME.
I'M NANAMI.
WHAT'S YOUR NAME?
AKO.
BFFT
HI, AKO.
COME WITH US.
YOU MIGHT FIND WHAT YOU LOST ALONG THE WAY.

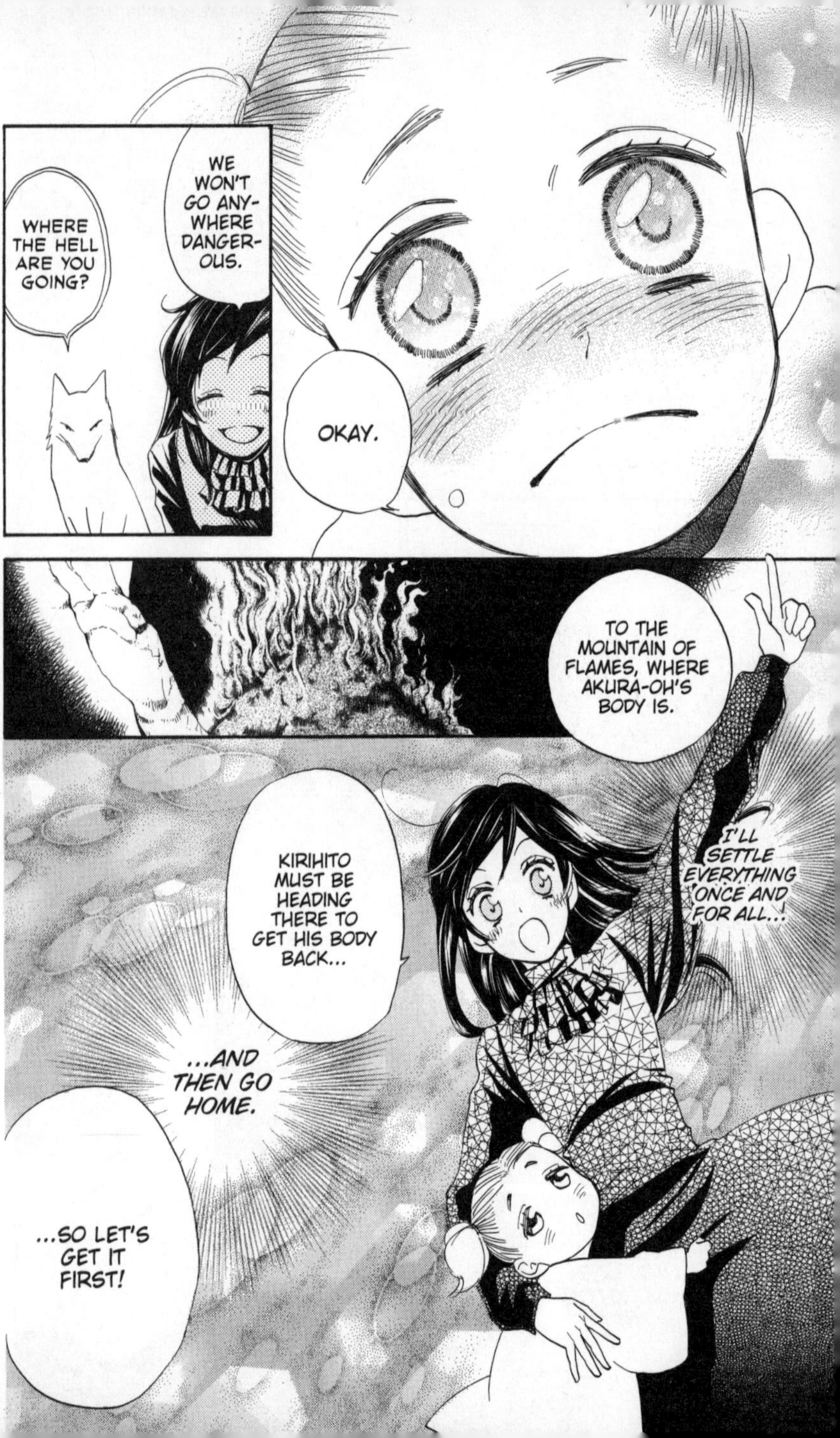
OKAY.
WE WON'T GO ANYWHERE DANGEROUS.
WHERE THE HELL ARE YOU GOING?
TO THE MOUNTAIN OF FLAMES, WHERE AKURA-OH'S BODY IS.
I'LL SETTLE EVERYTHING ONCE AND FOR ALL...!
KIRIHITO MUST BE HEADING THERE TO GET HIS BODY BACK...
...AND THEN GO HOME.
...SO LET'S GET IT FIRST!

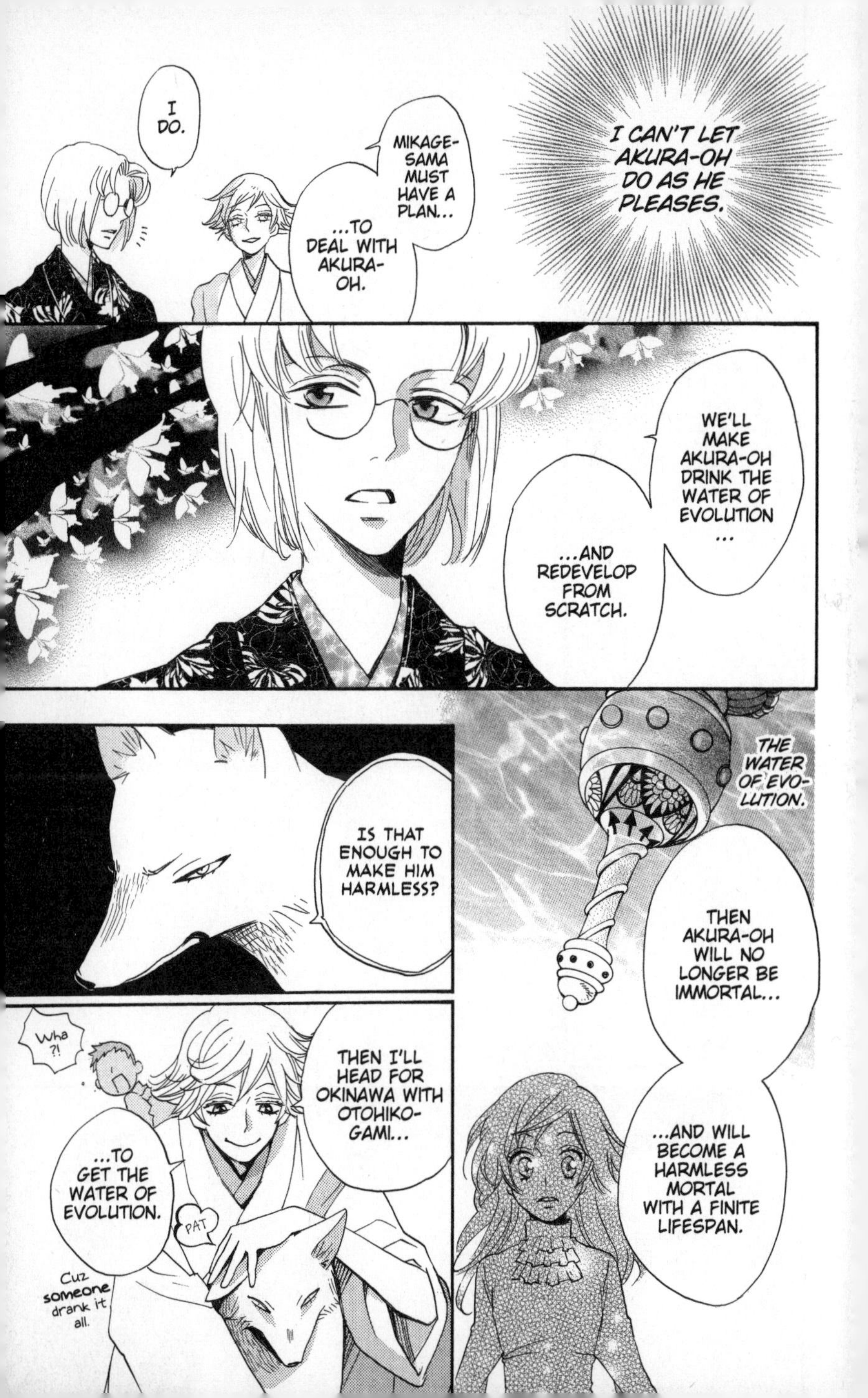
I CAN'T LET AKURA-OH DO AS HE PLEASES.
MIKAGE-SAMA MUST HAVE A PLAN...
...TO DEAL WITH AKURA-OH.
I DO.
WE'LL MAKE AKURA-OH DRINK THE WATER OF EVOLUTION ...
...AND REDEVELOP FROM SCRATCH.
THE WATER OF EVO-LUTION.
THEN AKURA-OH WILL NO LONGER BE IMMORTAL...
...AND WILL BECOME A HARMLESS MORTAL WITH A FINITE LIFESPAN.
IS THAT ENOUGH TO MAKE HIM HARMLESS?
THEN I'LL HEAD FOR OKINAWA WITH OTOHIKO-GAMI...
Wha ?!
...TO GET THE WATER OF EVOLUTION.
PAT
Cuz someone drank it all.

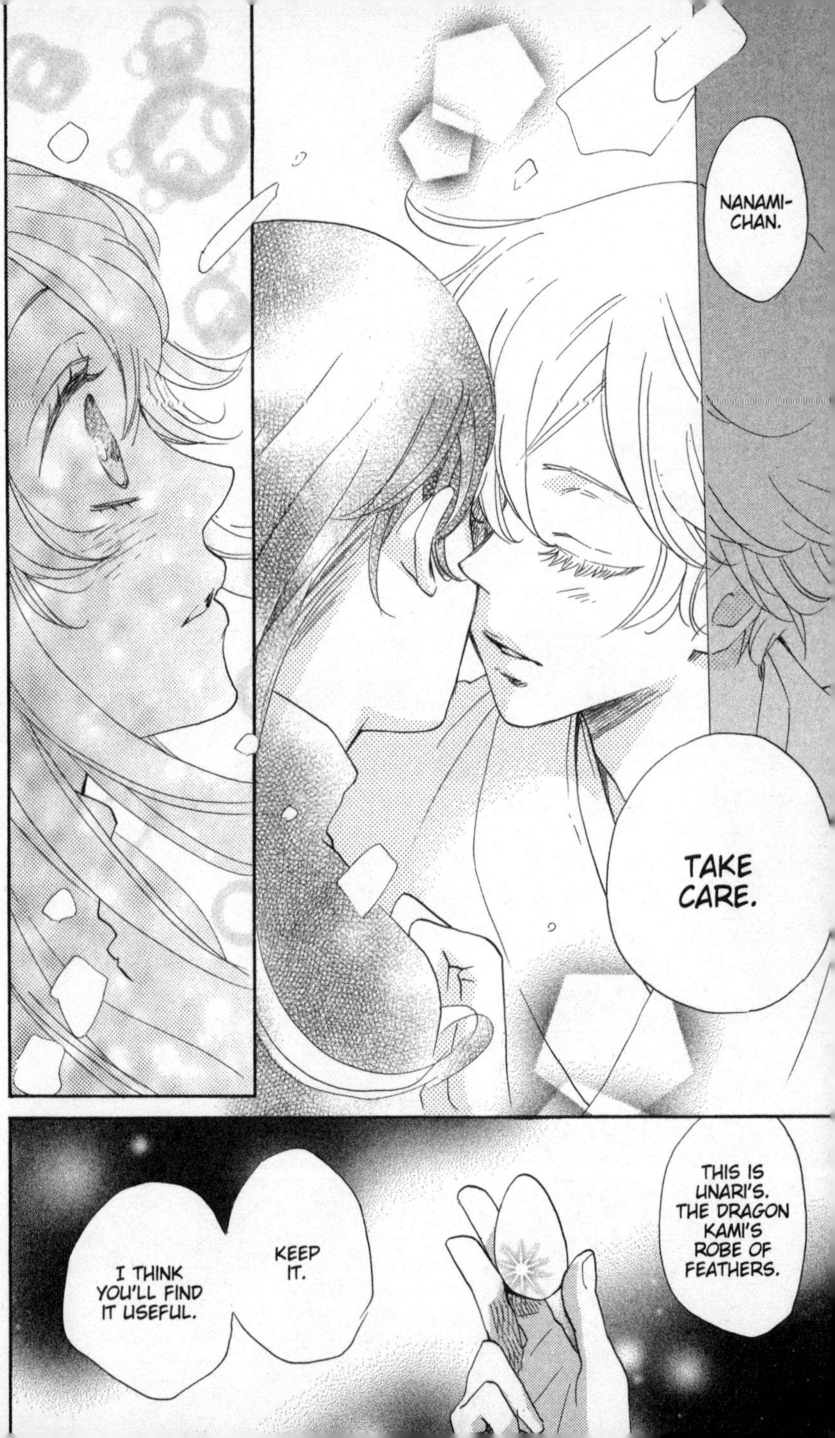
NANAMI-CHAN.
TAKE CARE.
THIS IS UNARI'S. THE DRAGON KAMI'S ROBE OF FEATHERS.
KEEP IT.
I THINK YOU'LL FIND IT USEFUL.

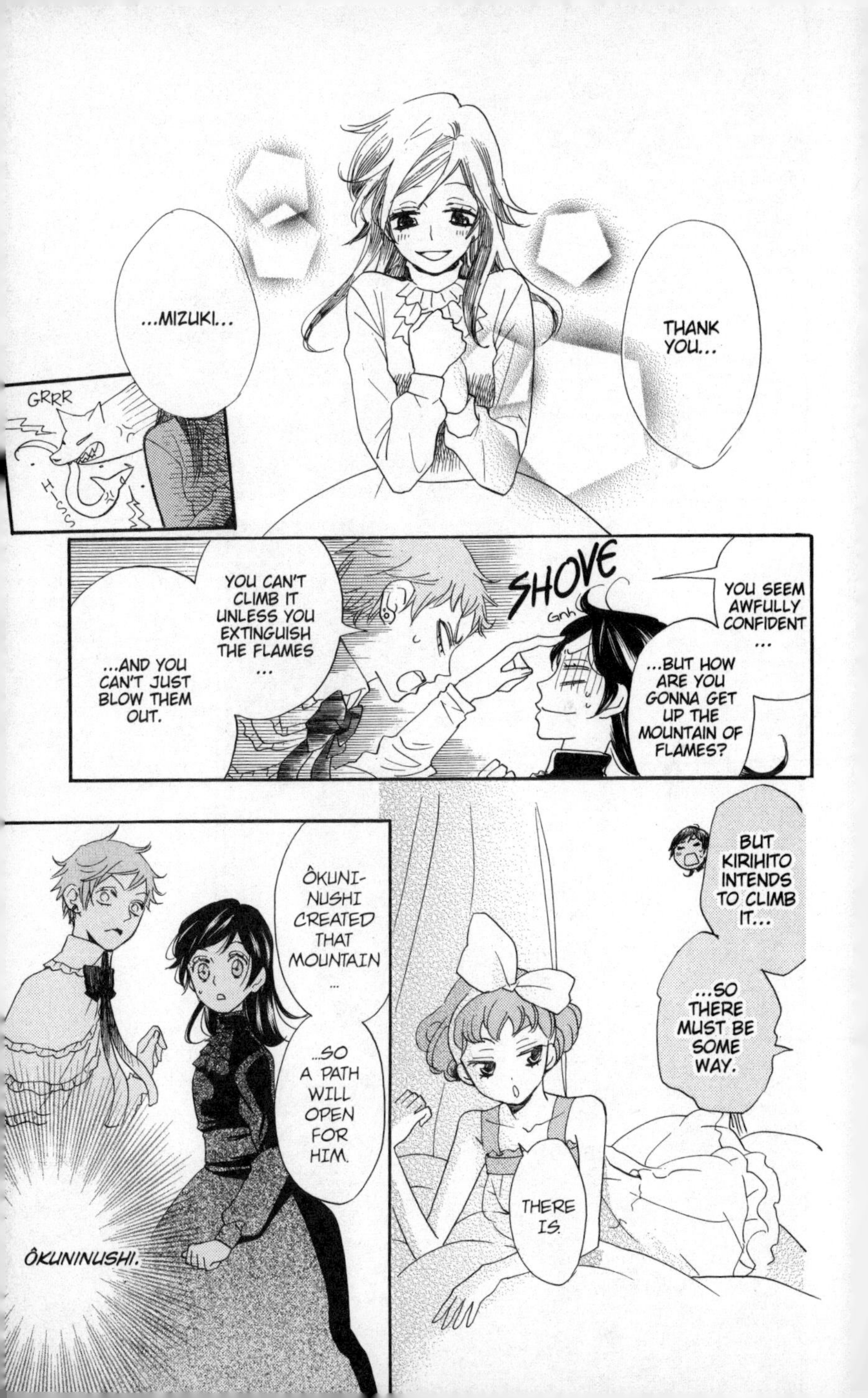
THANK YOU...
...MIZUKI...
GRRR
HISS
YOU SEEM AWFULLY CONFIDENT ...
...BUT HOW ARE YOU GONNA GET UP THE MOUNTAIN OF FLAMES?
SHOVE
Gnh
YOU CAN'T CLIMB IT UNLESS YOU EXTINGUISH THE FLAMES ...
...AND YOU CAN'T JUST BLOW THEM OUT.
BUT KIRIHITO INTENDS TO CLIMB IT...
...SO THERE MUST BE SOME WAY.
THERE IS.
ÔKUNI-NUSHI CREATED THAT MOUNTAIN ...
...SO A PATH WILL OPEN FOR HIM.
ÔKUNINUSHI.

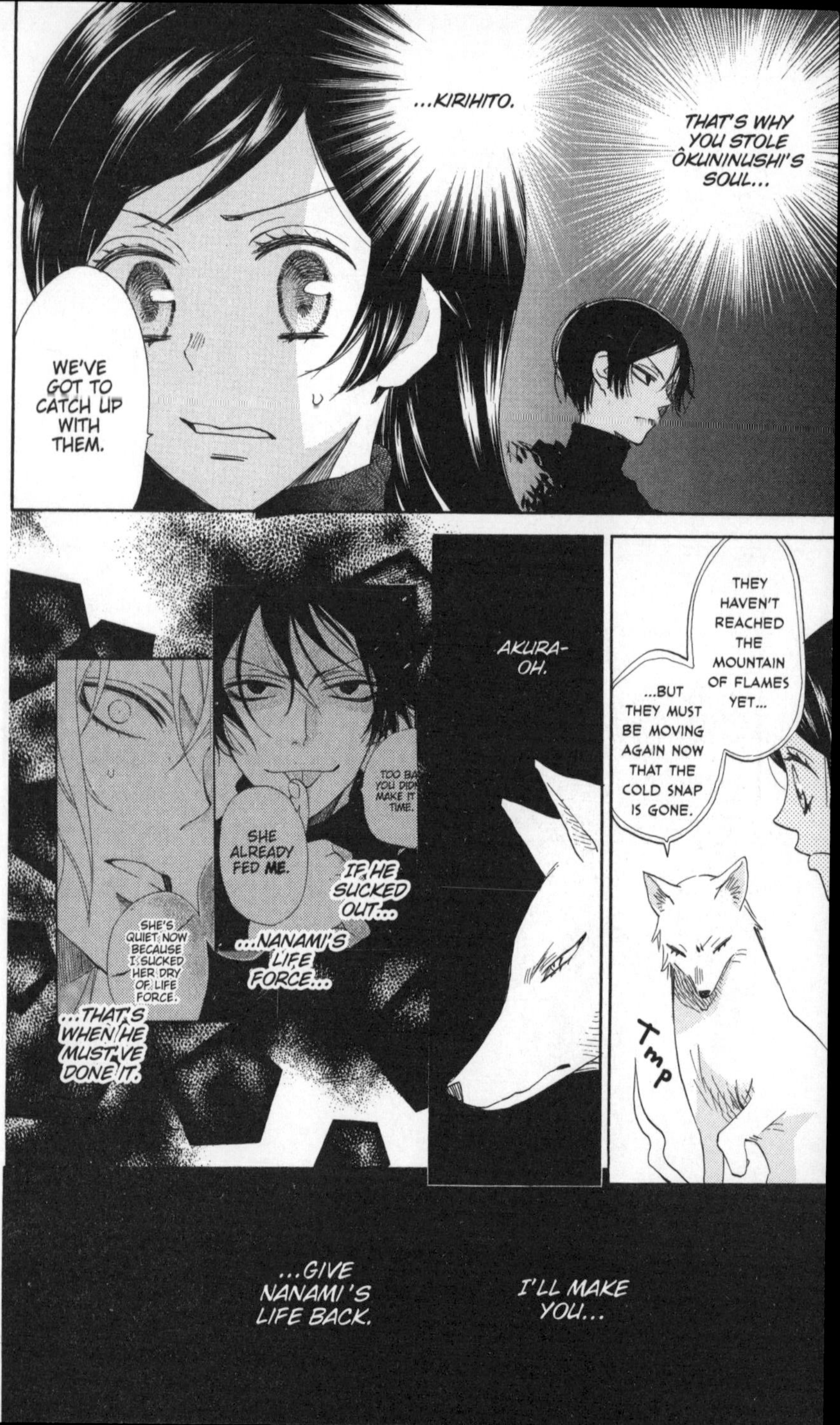
THAT'S WHY YOU STOLE ÔKUNINUSHI'S SOUL...
...KIRIHITO.
WE'VE GOT TO CATCH UP WITH THEM.
THEY HAVEN'T REACHED THE MOUNTAIN OF FLAMES YET...
...BUT THEY MUST BE MOVING AGAIN NOW THAT THE COLD SNAP IS GONE.
Tmp
AKURA-OH.
TOO BA YOU DIDN MAKE IT TIME.
SHE ALREADY FED ME.
IF HE SUCKED OUT...
...NANAMI'S LIFE FORCE...
SHE'S QUIET NOW BECAUSE I SUCKED HER DRY OF LIFE FORCE.
...THAT'S WHEN HE MUST'VE DONE IT.
I'LL MAKE YOU...
...GIVE NANAMI'S LIFE BACK.

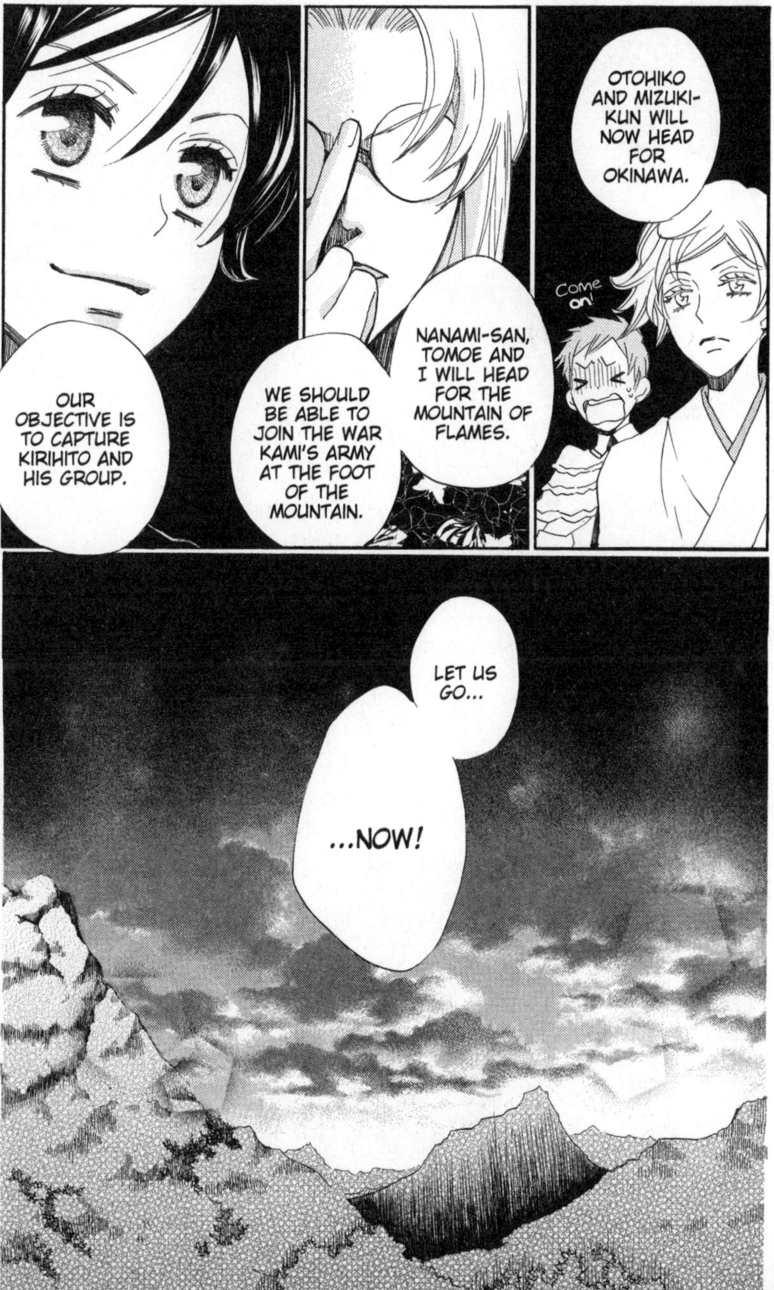

OTOHIKO AND MIZUKI-KUN WILL NOW HEAD FOR OKINAWA.
Come on!
NANAMI-SAN, TOMOE AND I WILL HEAD FOR THE MOUNTAIN OF FLAMES.
WE SHOULD BE ABLE TO JOIN THE WAR KAMI'S ARMY AT THE FOOT OF THE MOUNTAIN.
OUR OBJECTIVE IS TO CAPTURE KIRIHITO AND HIS GROUP.
LET US GO...
...NOW!

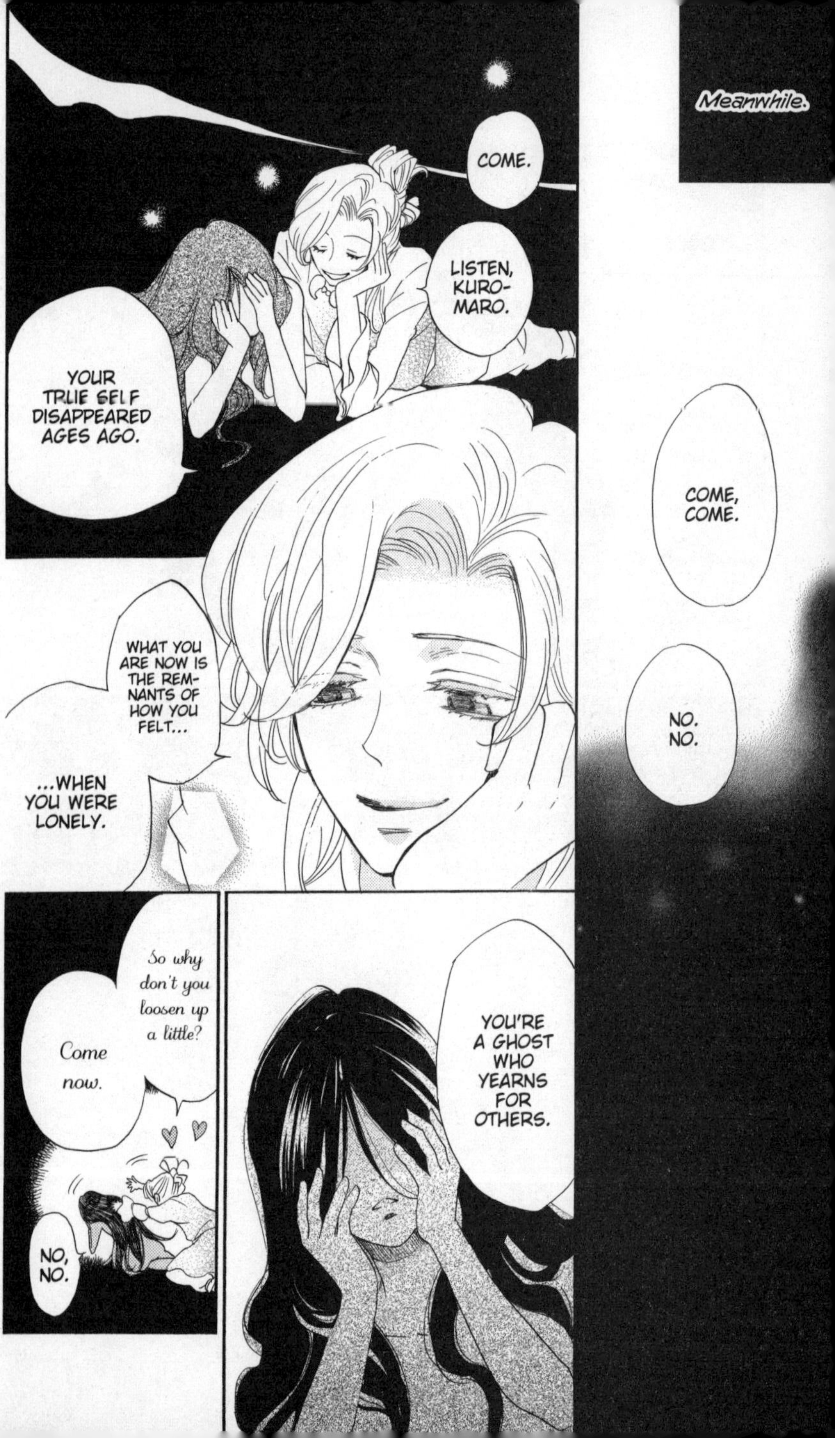
Meanwhile.
COME, COME.
NO. NO.
COME.
LISTEN, KURO-MARO.
YOUR TRUE SELF DISAPPEARED AGES AGO.
WHAT YOU ARE NOW IS THE REMNANTS OF HOW YOU FELT...
...WHEN YOU WERE LONELY.
YOU'RE A GHOST WHO YEARNS FOR OTHERS.
So why don't you loosen up a little?
Come now.
NO, NO.

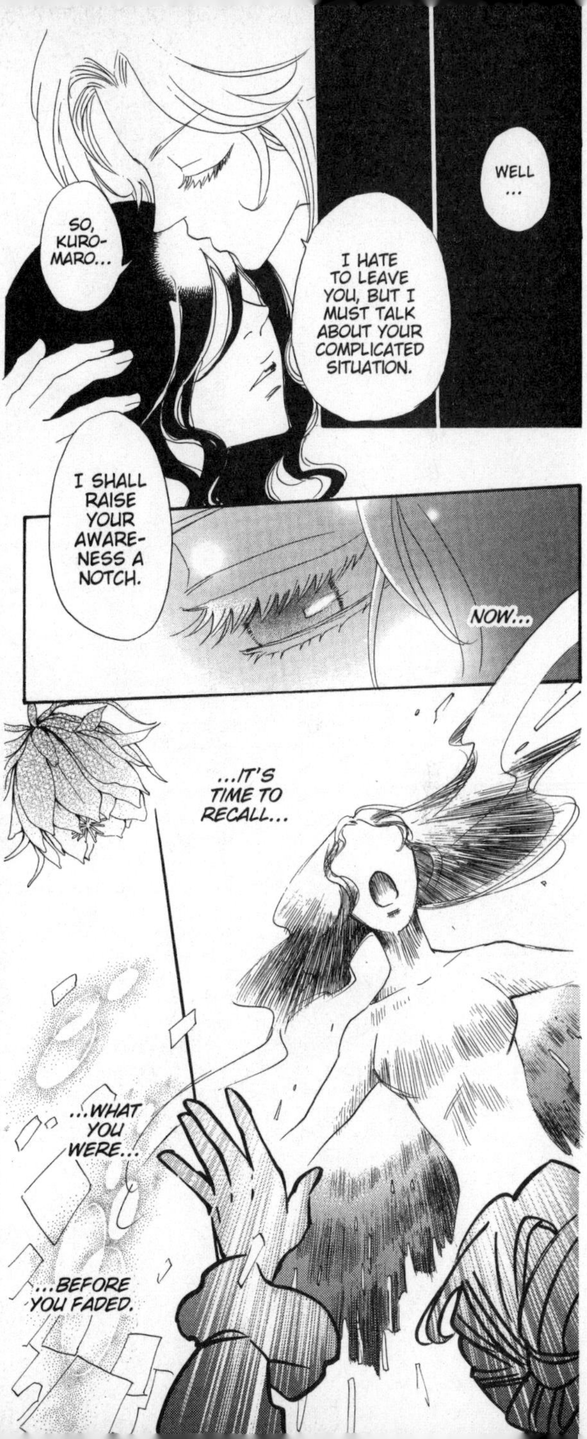
WELL ...
I HATE TO LEAVE YOU, BUT I MUST TALK ABOUT YOUR COMPLICATED SITUATION.
SO, KURO-MARO...
I SHALL RAISE YOUR AWARE-NESS A NOTCH.
NOW...
...IT'S TIME TO RECALL...
...WHAT YOU WERE...
...BEFORE YOU FADED.

Hello!

Thank you for picking up this volume of Kamisama Kiss!!

I hope you enjoy volume 23, which continues the Akura-oh arc!

Please enjoy your reading!

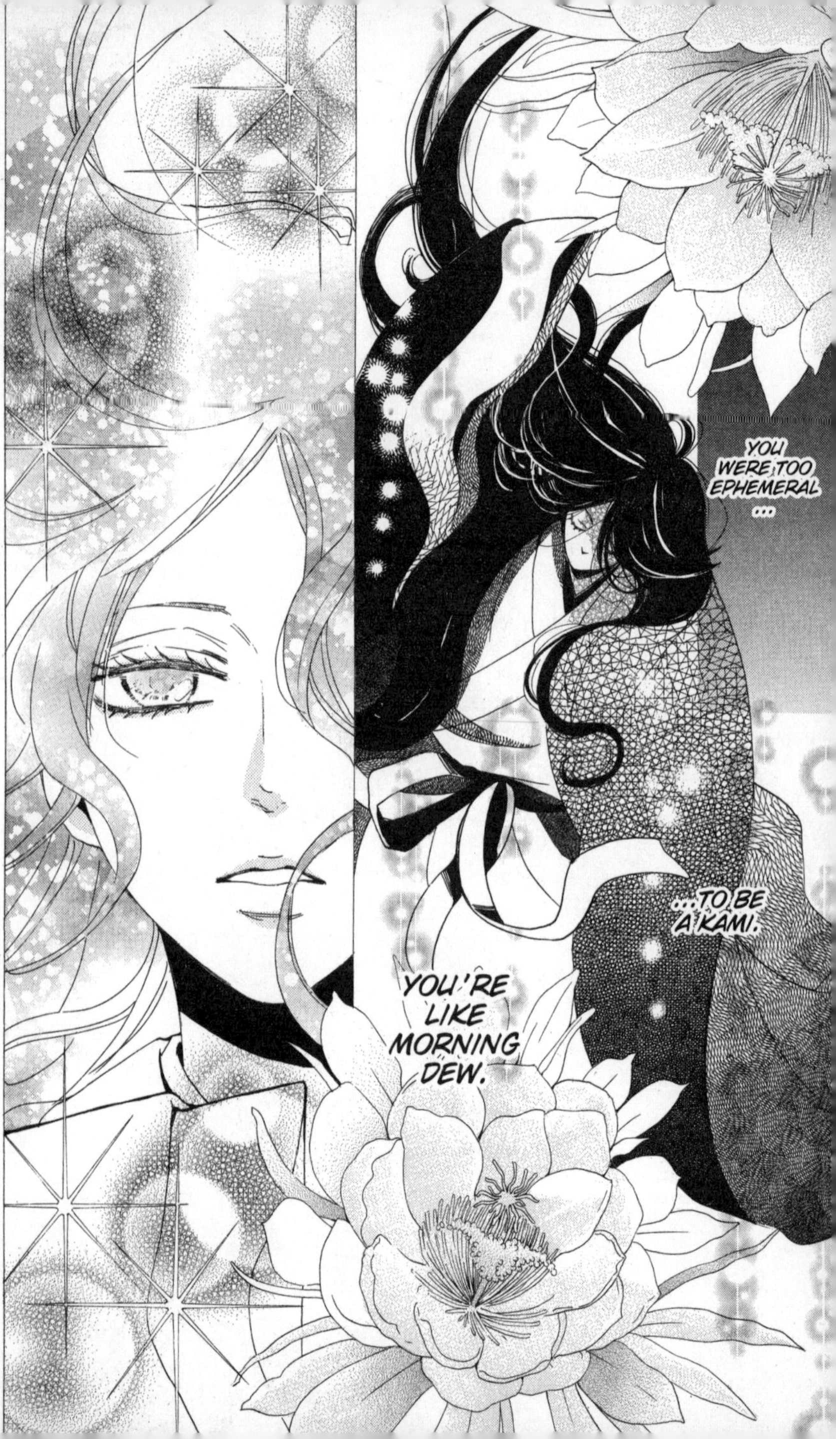
YOU WERE TOO EPHEMERAL ...
...TO BE A KAMI.
YOU'RE LIKE MORNING DEW.

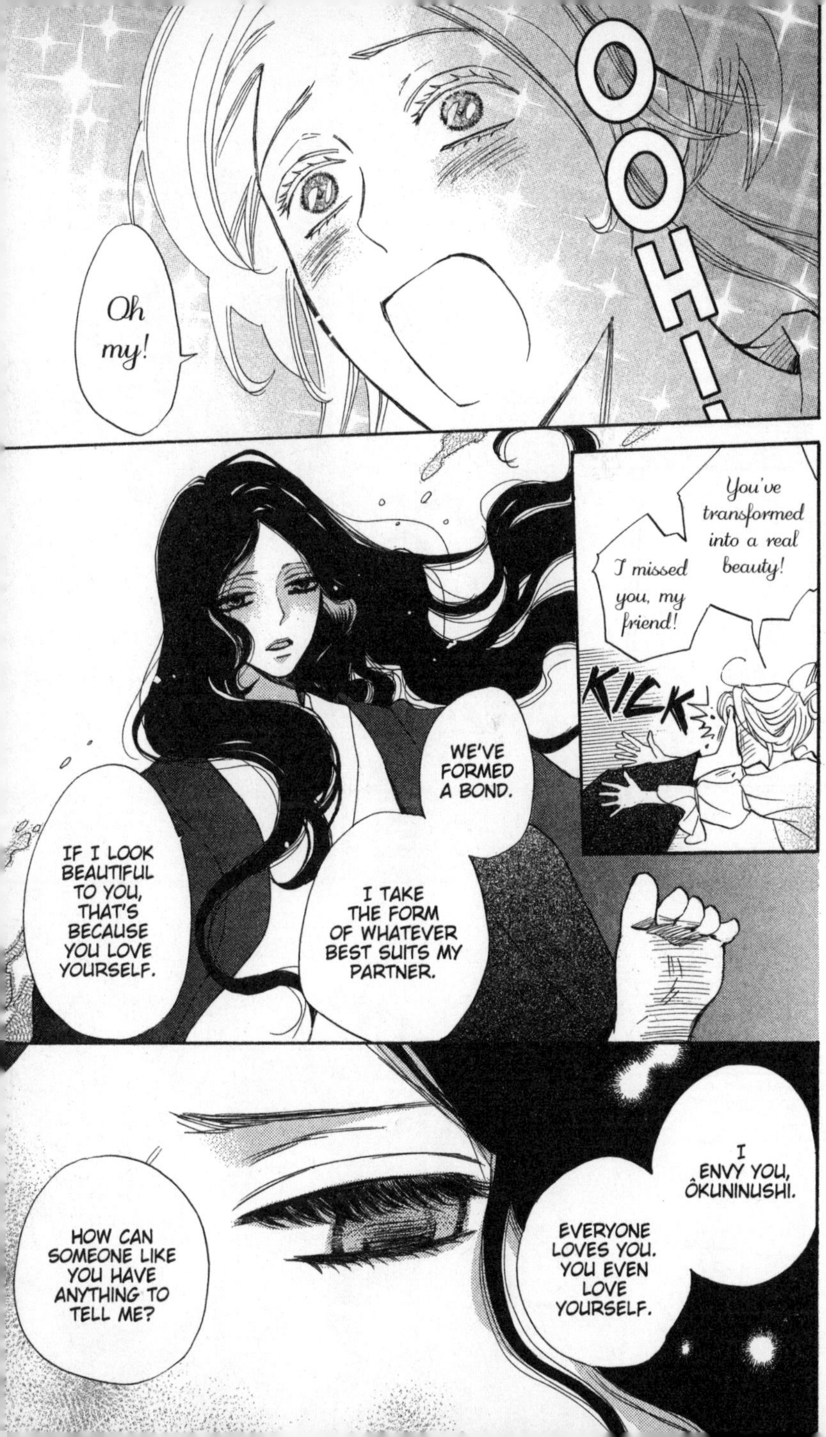
OOOH
Oh my!
You've transformed into a real beauty!
I missed you, my friend!
KICK
WE'VE FORMED A BOND.
I TAKE THE FORM OF WHATEVER BEST SUITS MY PARTNER.
IF I LOOK BEAUTIFUL TO YOU, THAT'S BECAUSE YOU LOVE YOURSELF.
I ENVY YOU, ÔKUNINUSHI.
EVERYONE LOVES YOU. YOU EVEN LOVE YOURSELF.
HOW CAN SOMEONE LIKE YOU HAVE ANYTHING TO TELL ME?

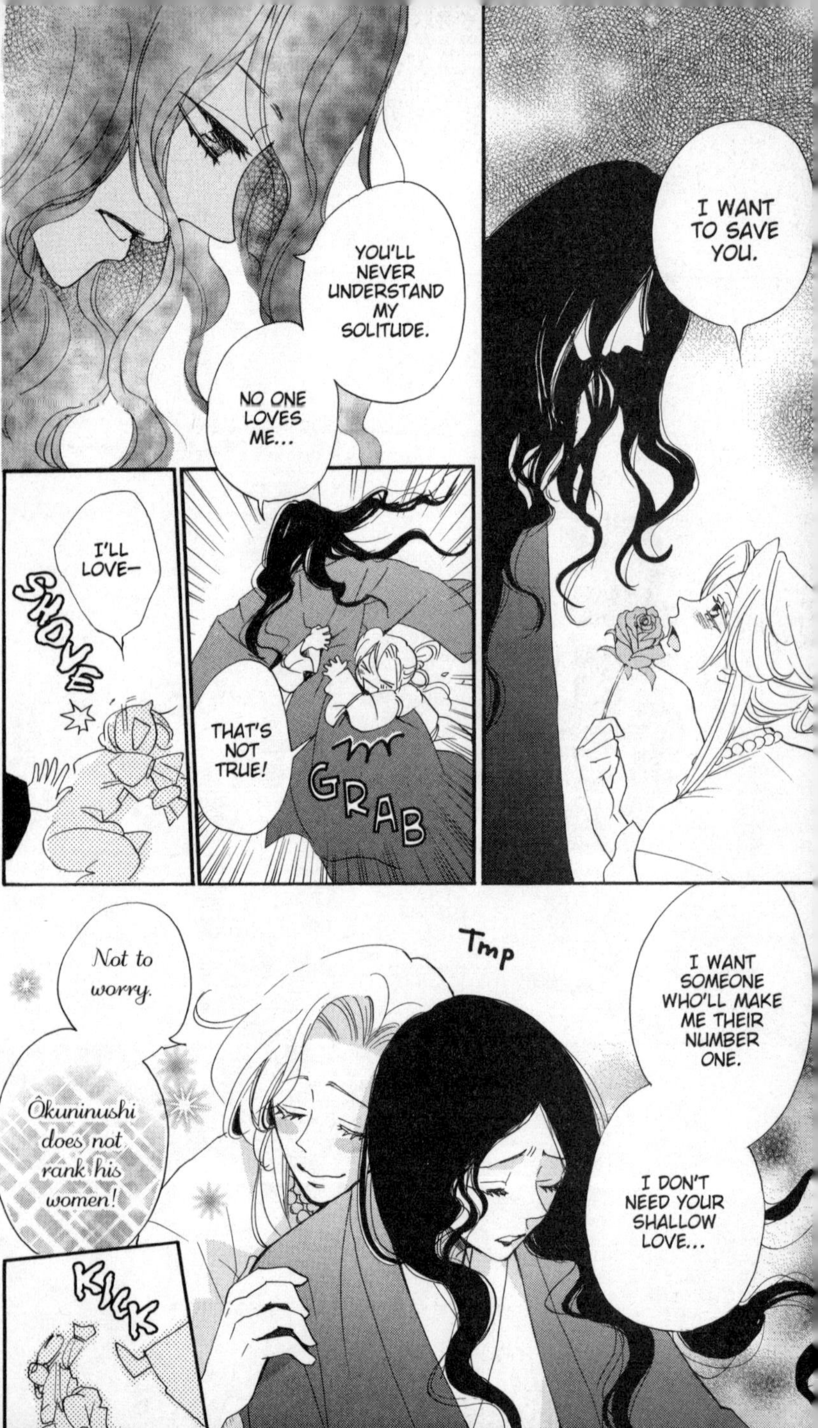
I WANT TO SAVE YOU.
YOU'LL NEVER UNDERSTAND MY SOLITUDE.
NO ONE LOVES ME...
THAT'S NOT TRUE!
GRAB
I'LL LOVE—
SHOVE
I WANT SOMEONE WHO'LL MAKE ME THEIR NUMBER ONE.
I DON'T NEED YOUR SHALLOW LOVE...
Tmp
Not to worry.
Ôkuninushi does not rank his women!
KICK

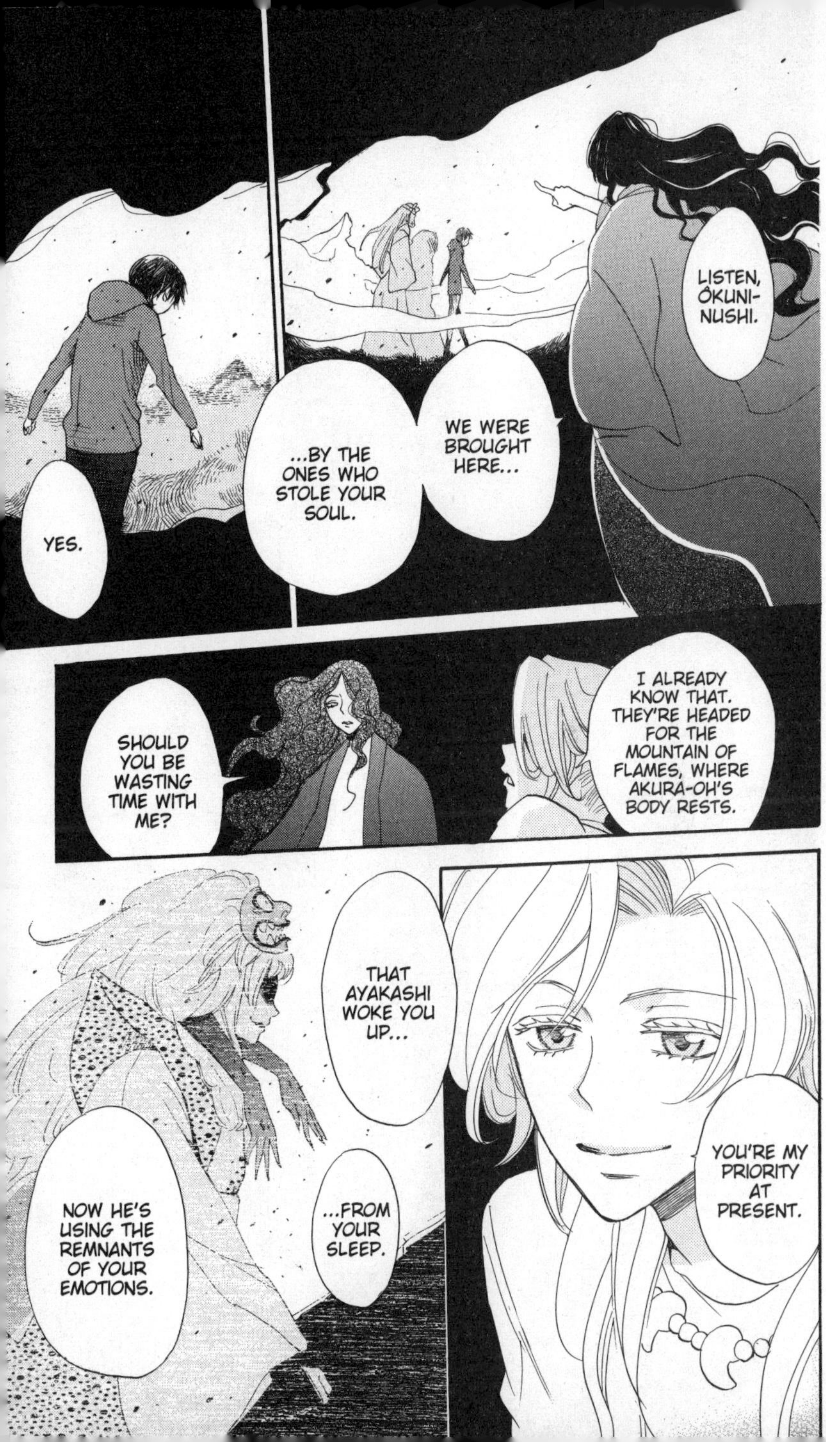
LISTEN, ŌKUNI-NUSHI.
WE WERE BROUGHT HERE...
...BY THE ONES WHO STOLE YOUR SOUL.
YES.
I ALREADY KNOW THAT. THEY'RE HEADED FOR THE MOUNTAIN OF FLAMES, WHERE AKURA-OH'S BODY RESTS.
SHOULD YOU BE WASTING TIME WITH ME?
YOU'RE MY PRIORITY AT PRESENT.
THAT AYAKASHI WOKE YOU UP...
...FROM YOUR SLEEP.
NOW HE'S USING THE REMNANTS OF YOUR EMOTIONS.

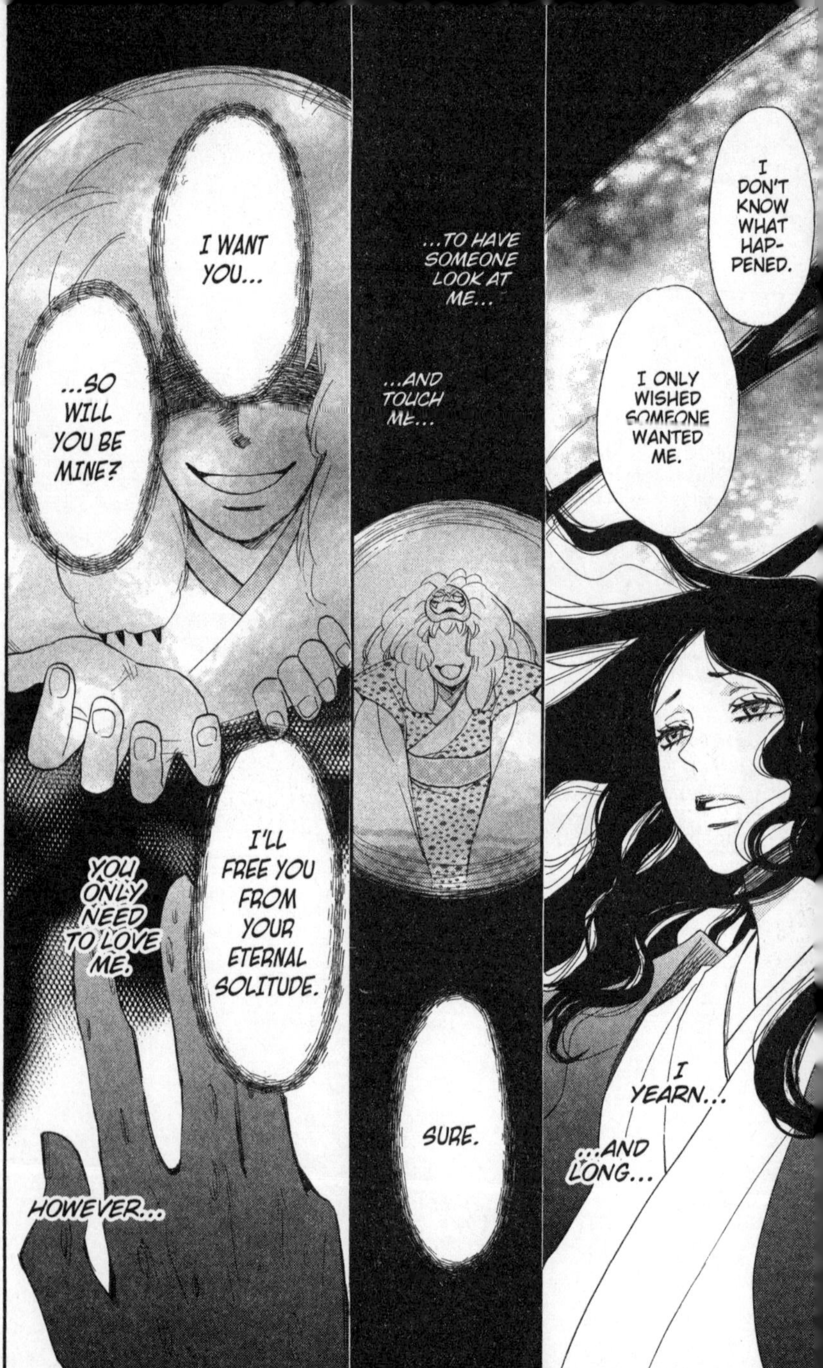
I DON'T KNOW WHAT HAP-PENED.
I ONLY WISHED SOMEONE WANTED ME.
I YEARN...
...AND LONG...
...TO HAVE SOMEONE LOOK AT ME...
...AND TOUCH ME...
SURE.
I WANT YOU...
...SO WILL YOU BE MINE?
I'LL FREE YOU FROM YOUR ETERNAL SOLITUDE.
YOU ONLY NEED TO LOVE ME.
HOWEVER...

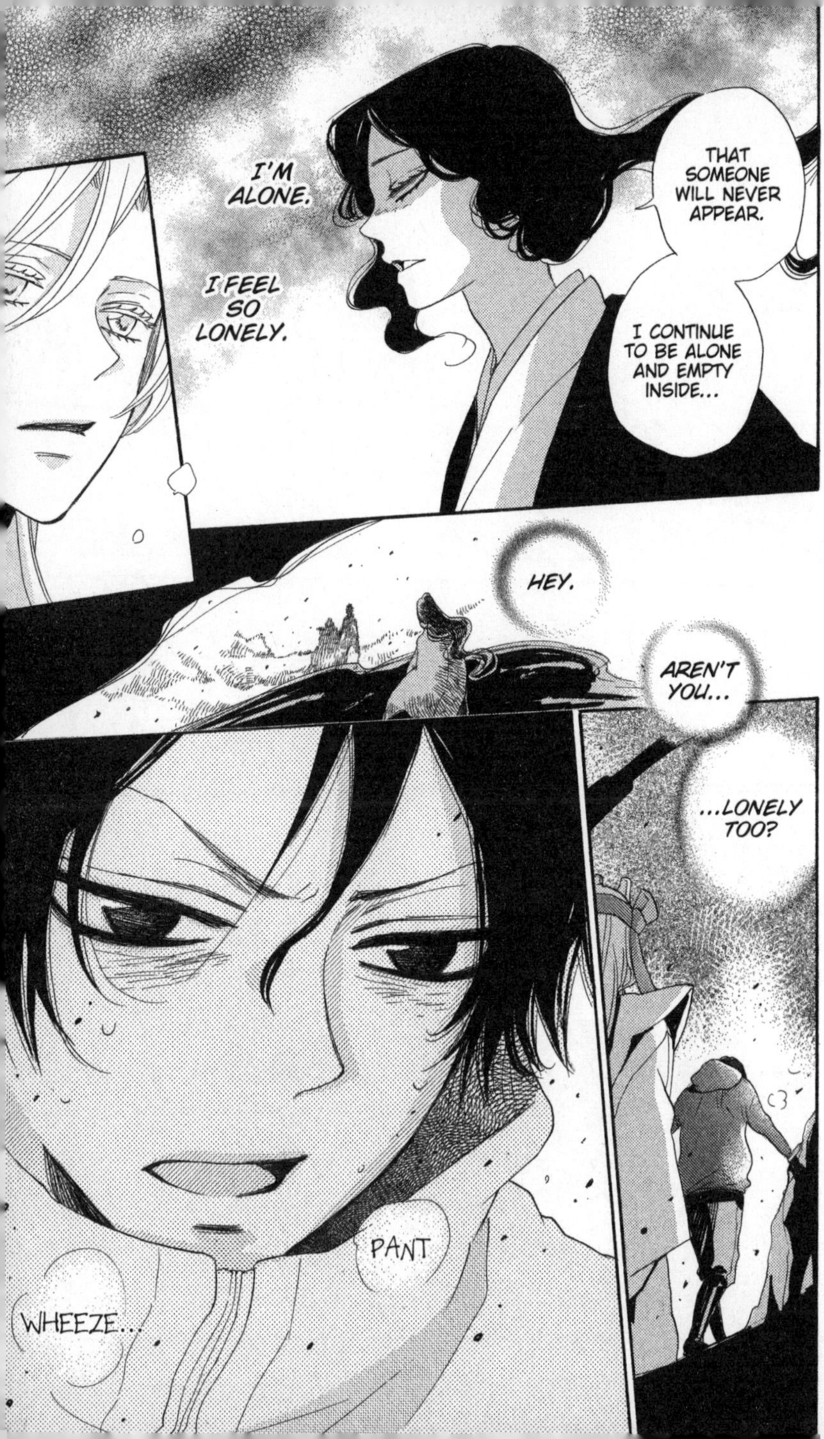
THAT SOMEONE WILL NEVER APPEAR.
I CONTINUE TO BE ALONE AND EMPTY INSIDE...
I'M ALONE.
I FEEL SO LONELY.
HEY.
AREN'T YOU...
...LONELY TOO?
PANT
WHEEZE...

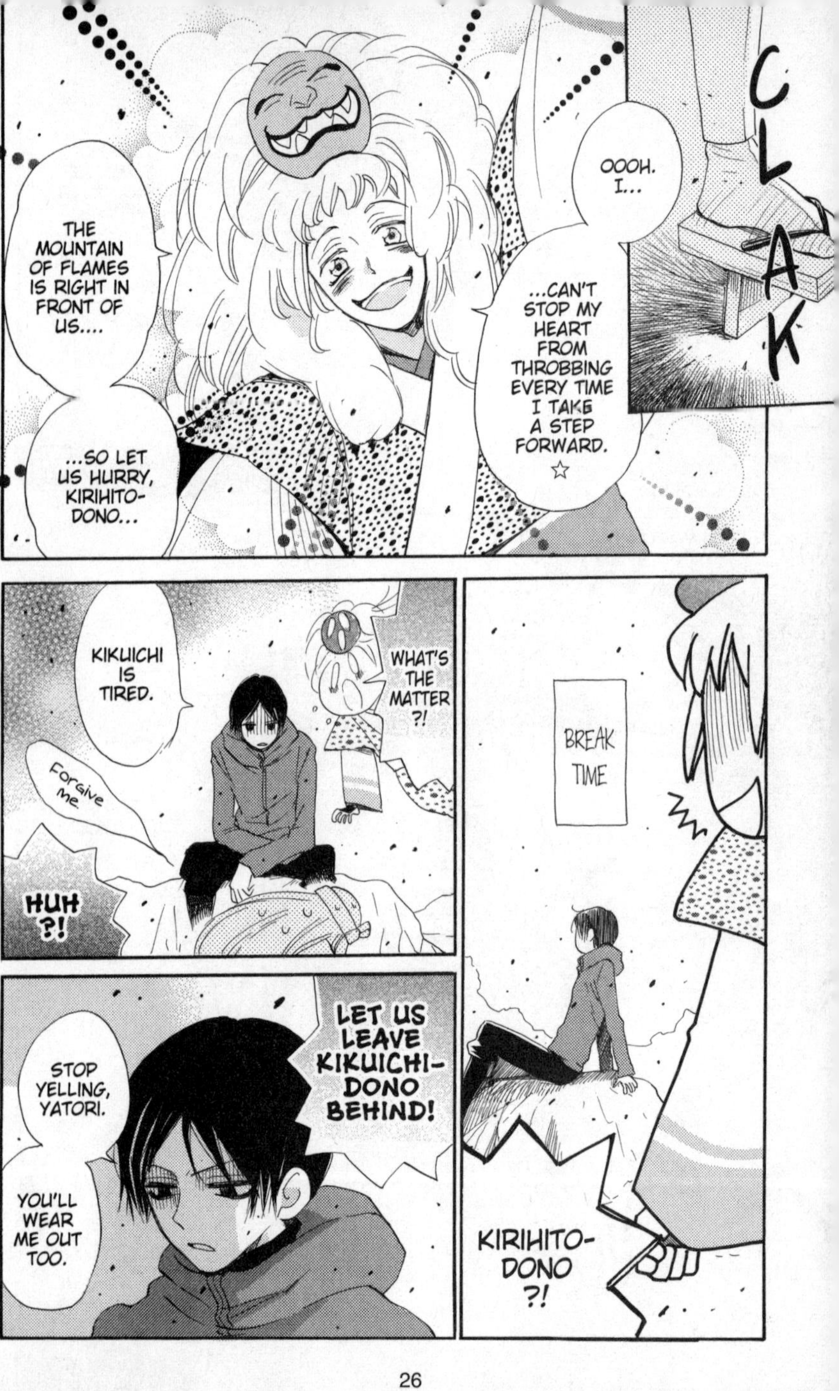
CLAK
OOOH. I...
...CAN'T STOP MY HEART FROM THROBBING EVERY TIME I TAKE A STEP FORWARD. ☆
THE MOUNTAIN OF FLAMES IS RIGHT IN FRONT OF US....
...SO LET US HURRY, KIRIHITO-DONO...
BREAK TIME
KIRIHITO-DONO ?!
WHAT'S THE MATTER ?!
KIKUICHI IS TIRED.
Forgive me.
HUH ?!
LET US LEAVE KIKUICHI-DONO BEHIND!
STOP YELLING, YATORI.
YOU'LL WEAR ME OUT TOO.

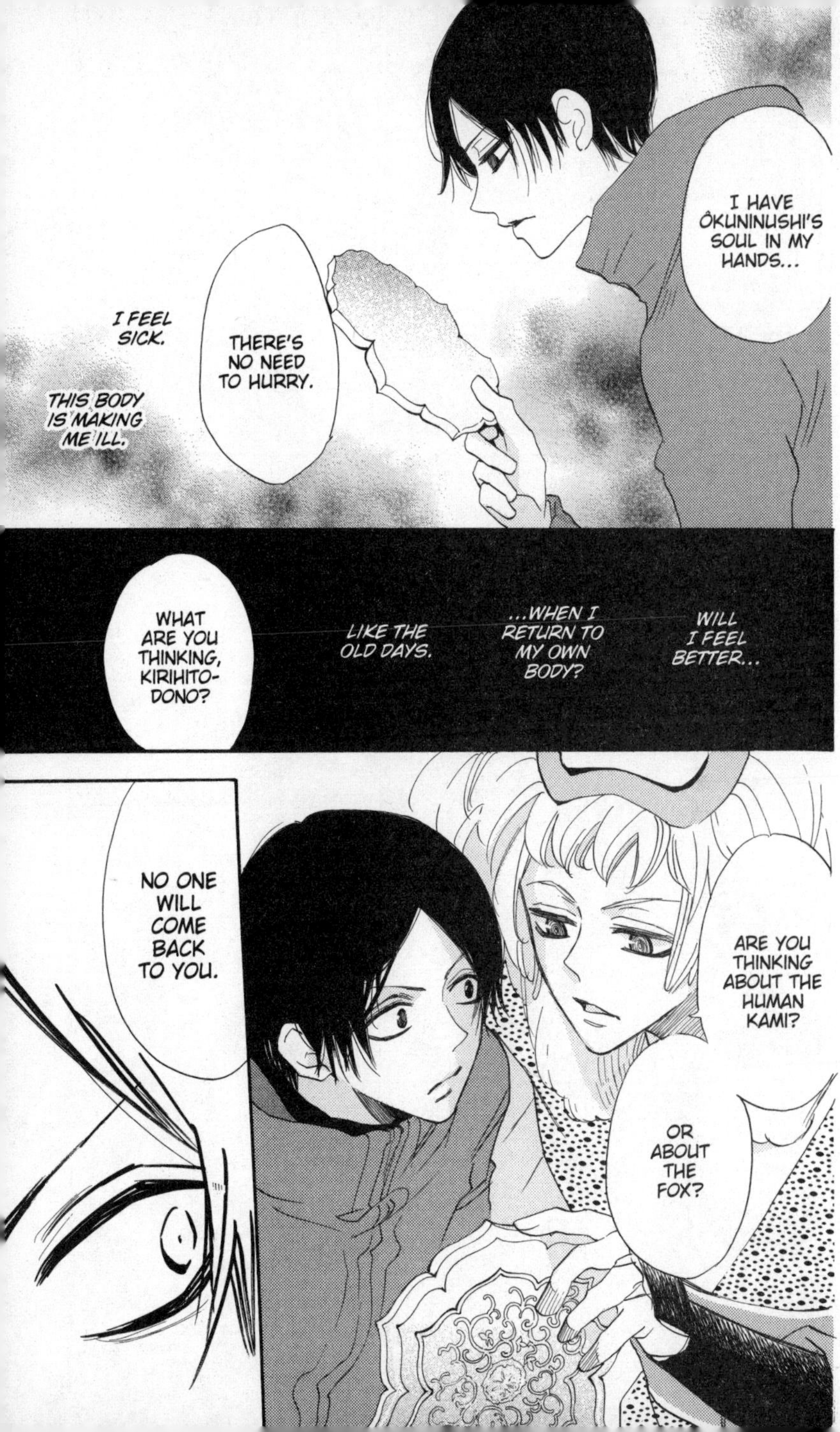
I HAVE ÔKUNINUSHI'S SOUL IN MY HANDS...
THERE'S NO NEED TO HURRY.
I FEEL SICK.
THIS BODY IS MAKING ME ILL.
WILL I FEEL BETTER...
...WHEN I RETURN TO MY OWN BODY?
LIKE THE OLD DAYS.
WHAT ARE YOU THINKING, KIRIHITO-DONO?
ARE YOU THINKING ABOUT THE HUMAN KAMI?
OR ABOUT THE FOX?
NO ONE WILL COME BACK TO YOU.

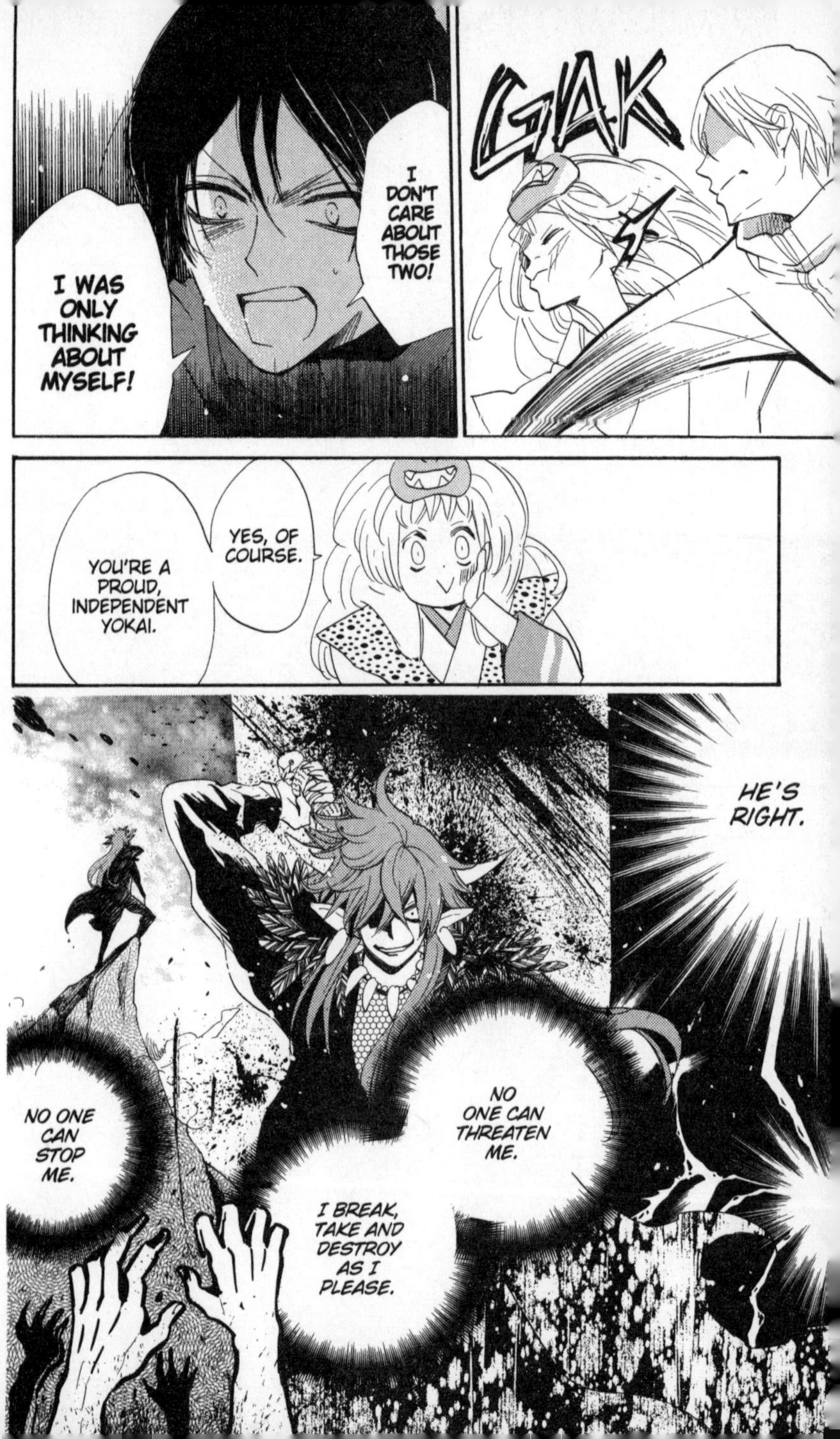
GAK
I DON'T CARE ABOUT THOSE TWO!
I WAS ONLY THINKING ABOUT MYSELF!
YES, OF COURSE.
YOU'RE A PROUD, INDEPENDENT YOKAI.
HE'S RIGHT.
NO ONE CAN THREATEN ME.
NO ONE CAN STOP ME.
I BREAK, TAKE AND DESTROY AS I PLEASE.

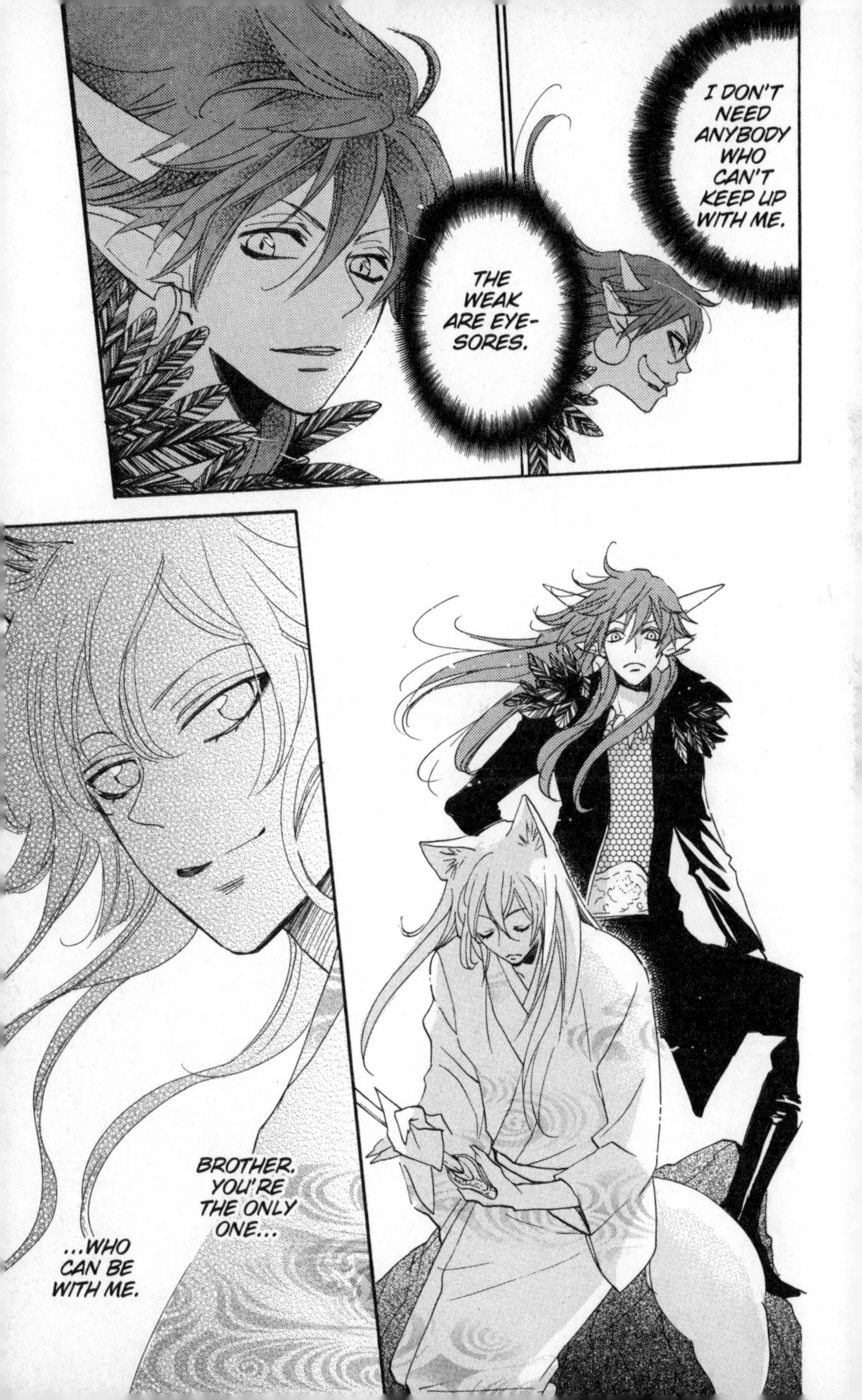
I DON'T NEED ANYBODY WHO CAN'T KEEP UP WITH ME.
THE WEAK ARE EYE-SORES.
BROTHER. YOU'RE THE ONLY ONE...
...WHO CAN BE WITH ME.

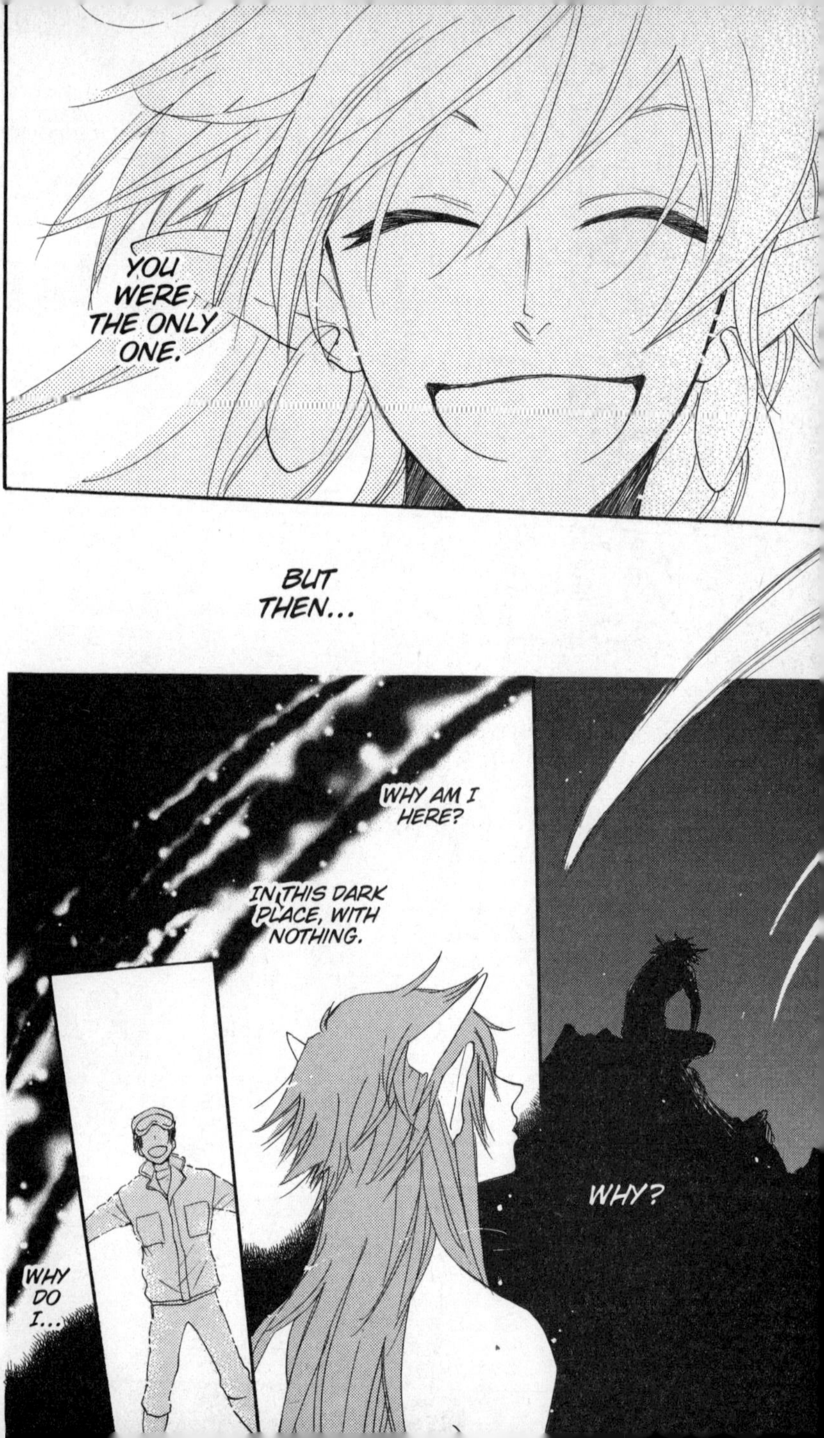
YOU WERE THE ONLY ONE.
BUT THEN...
WHY AM I HERE?
IN THIS DARK PLACE, WITH NOTHING.
WHY?
WHY DO I...

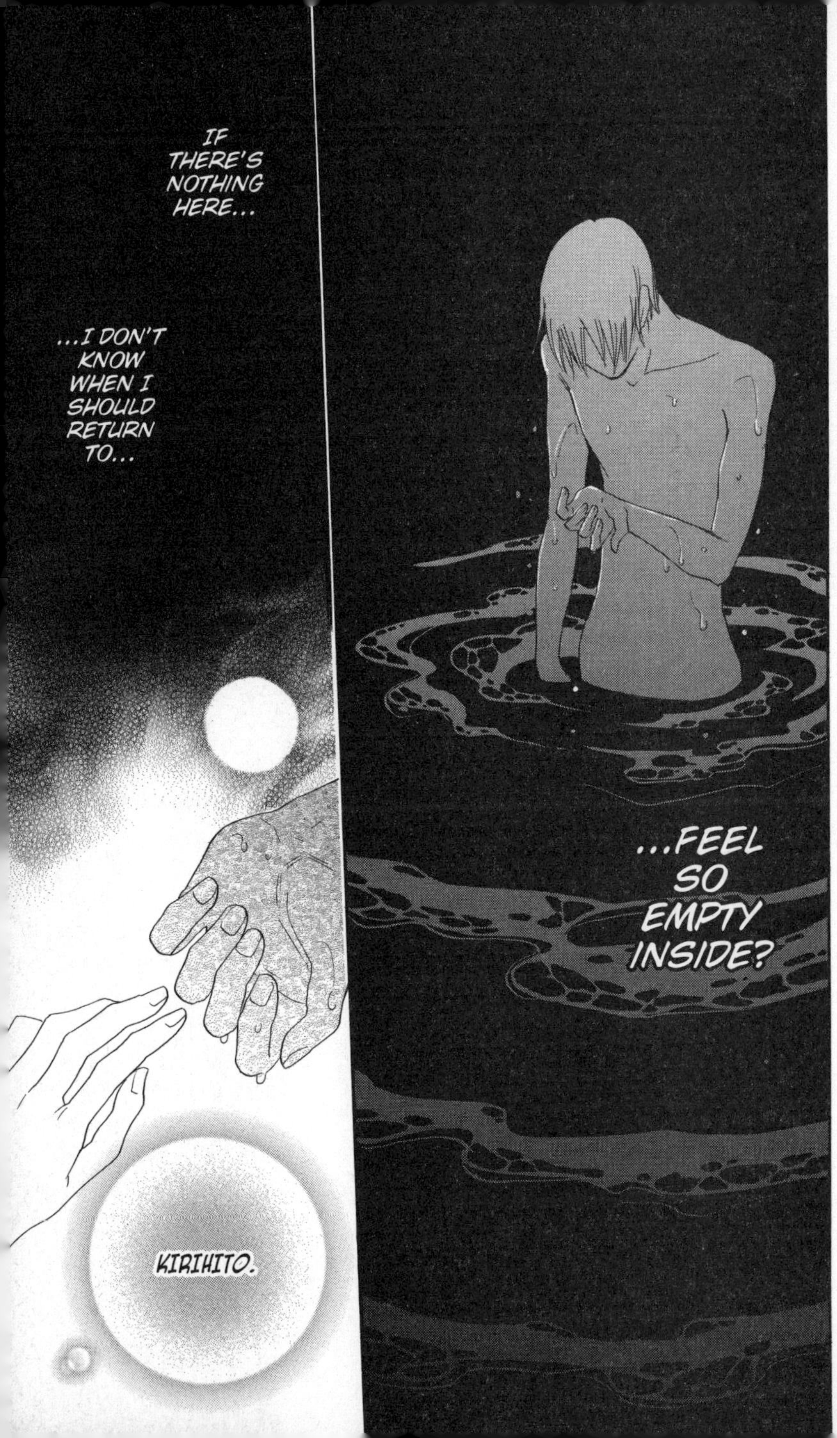
...FEEL SO EMPTY INSIDE?
IF THERE'S NOTHING HERE...
...I DON'T KNOW WHEN I SHOULD RETURN TO...
KIRIHITO.

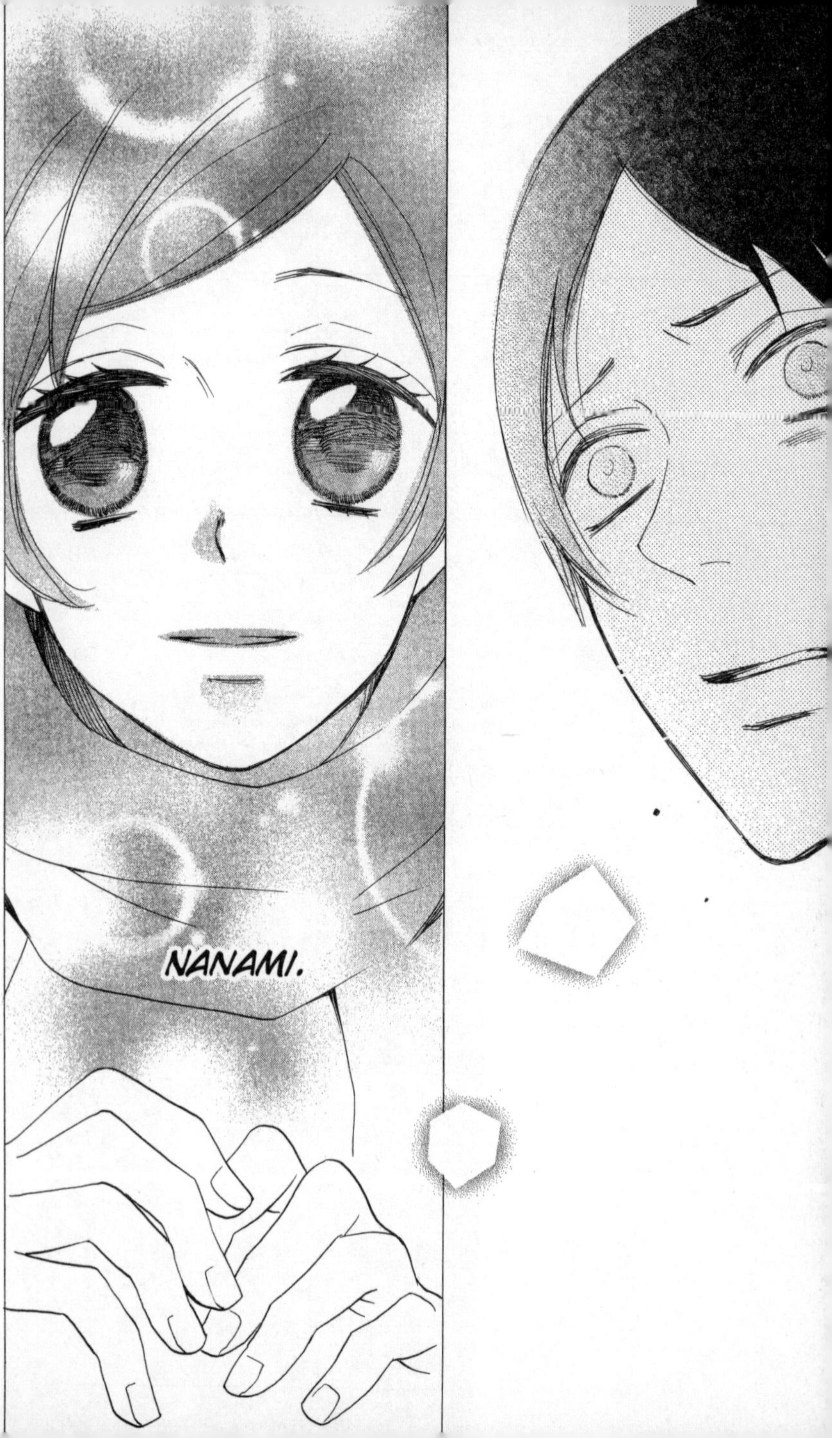
NANAMI.

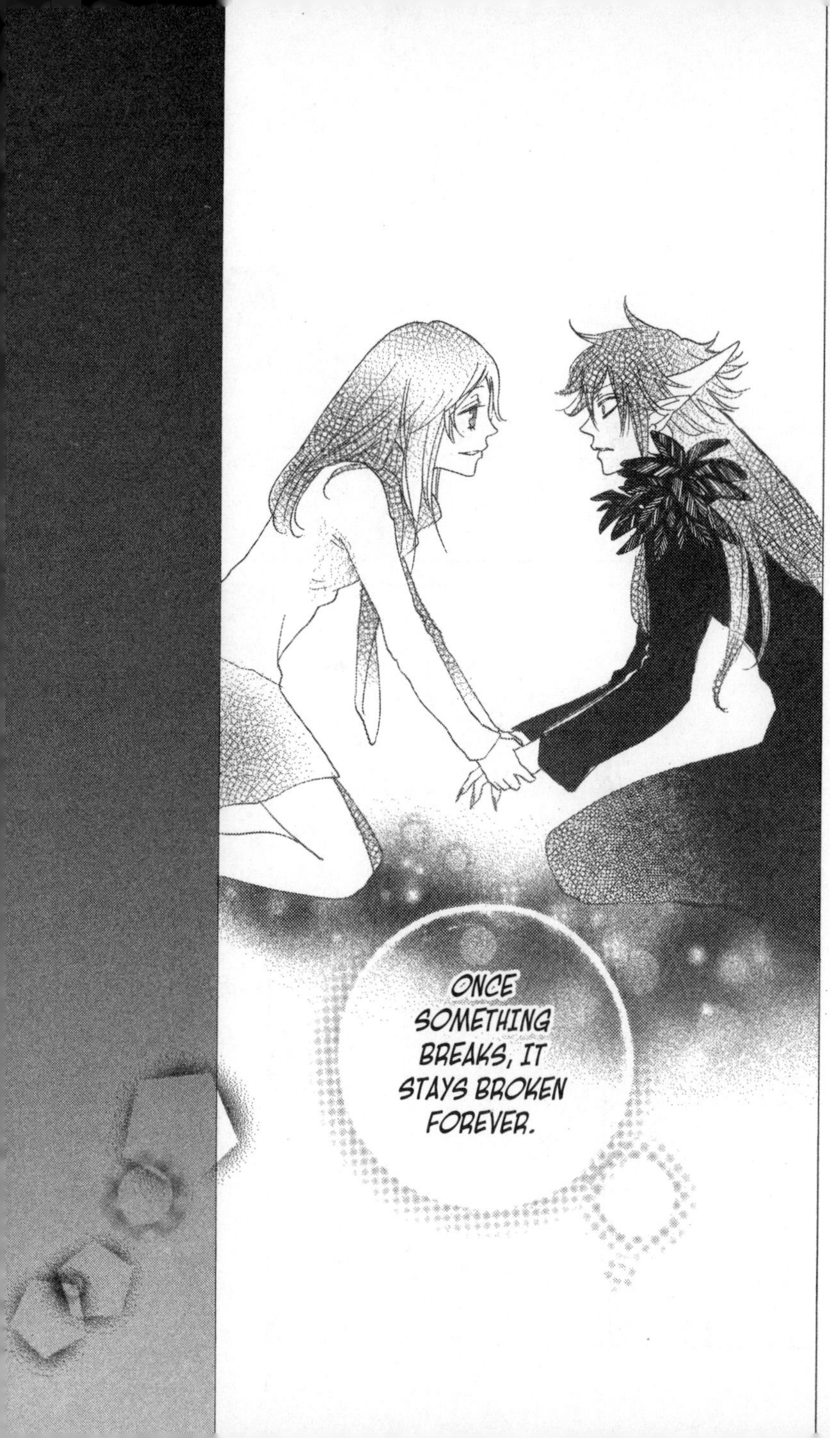
ONCE SOMETHING BREAKS, IT STAYS BROKEN FOREVER.

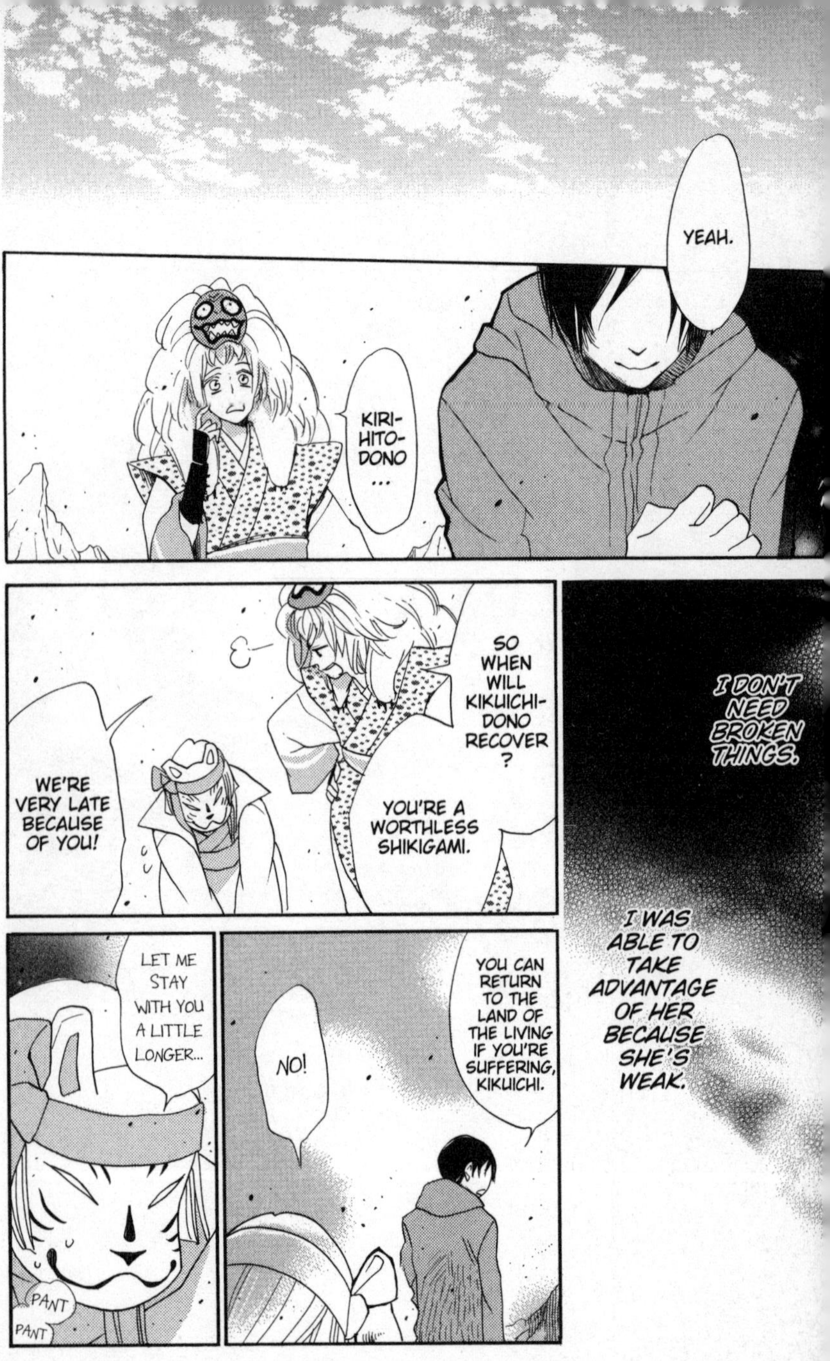
YEAH.
KIRI-HITO-DONO...
I DON'T NEED BROKEN THINGS.
I WAS ABLE TO TAKE ADVANTAGE OF HER BECAUSE SHE'S WEAK.
SO WHEN WILL KIKUICHI-DONO RECOVER?
YOU'RE A WORTHLESS SHIKIGAMI.
WE'RE VERY LATE BECAUSE OF YOU!
YOU CAN RETURN TO THE LAND OF THE LIVING IF YOU'RE SUFFERING, KIKUICHI.
NO!
LET ME STAY WITH YOU A LITTLE LONGER...
PANT
PANT

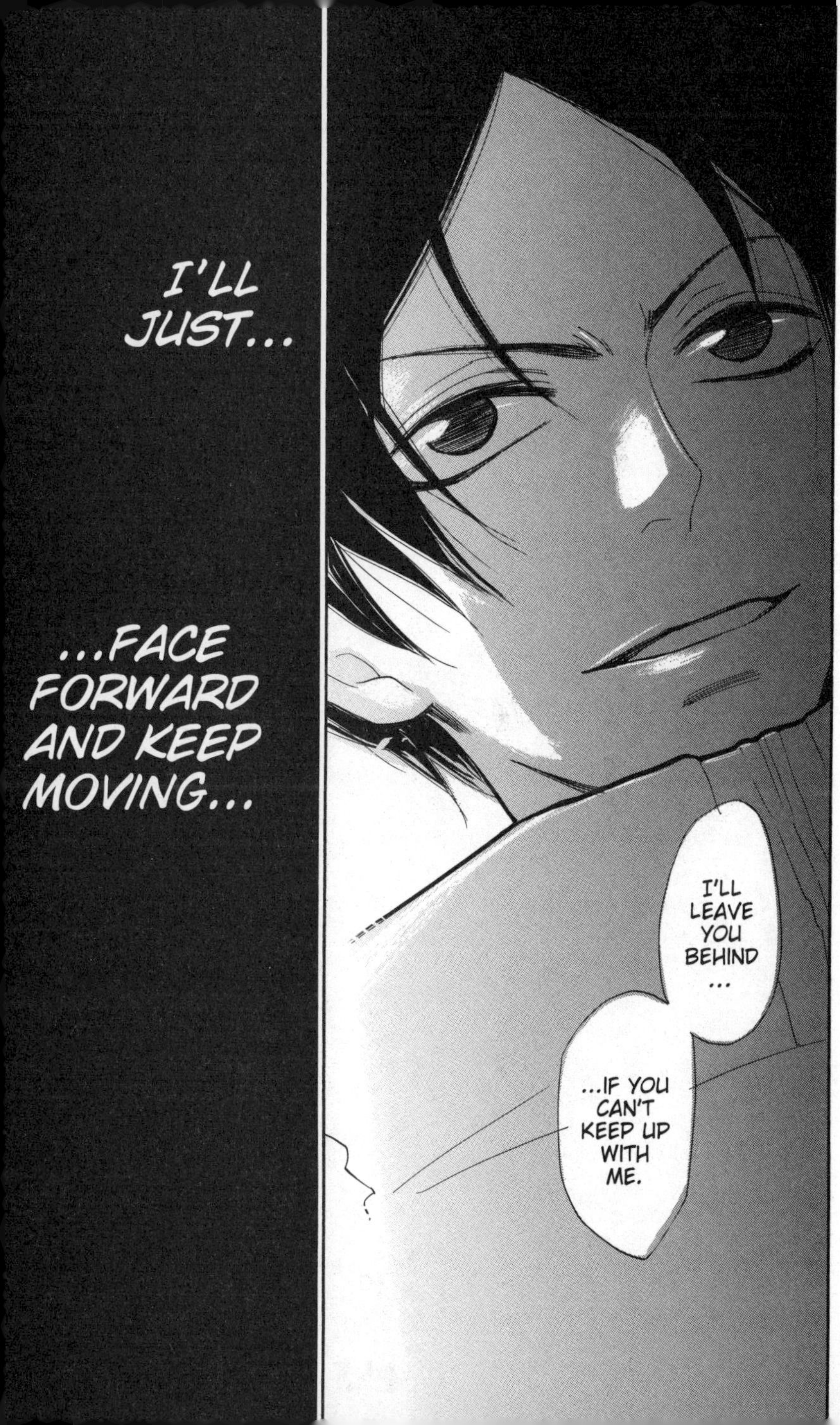
I'LL LEAVE YOU BEHIND...
...IF YOU CAN'T KEEP UP WITH ME.
I'LL JUST...
...FACE FORWARD AND KEEP MOVING...

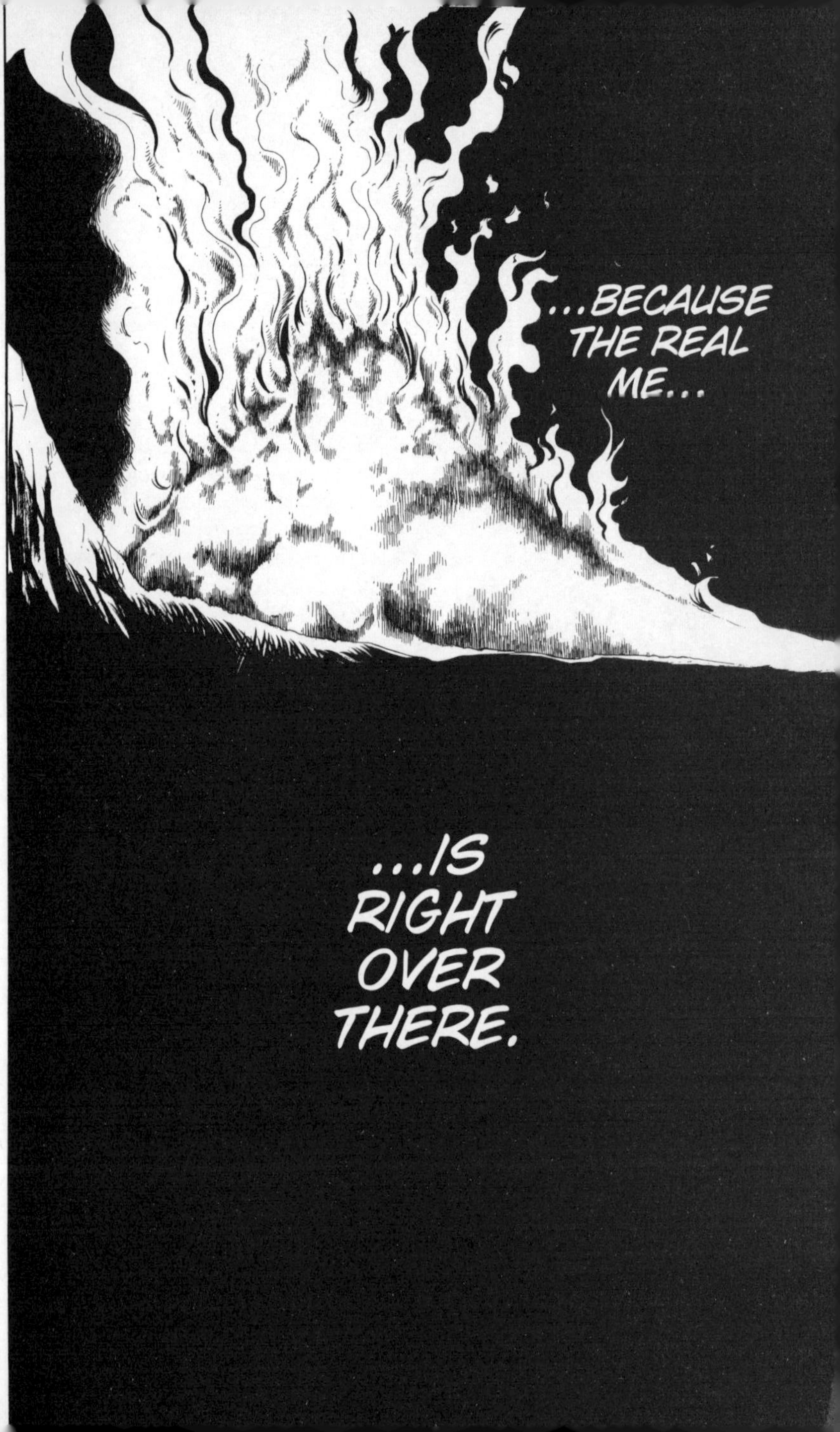
...BECAUSE THE REAL ME...
...IS RIGHT OVER THERE.

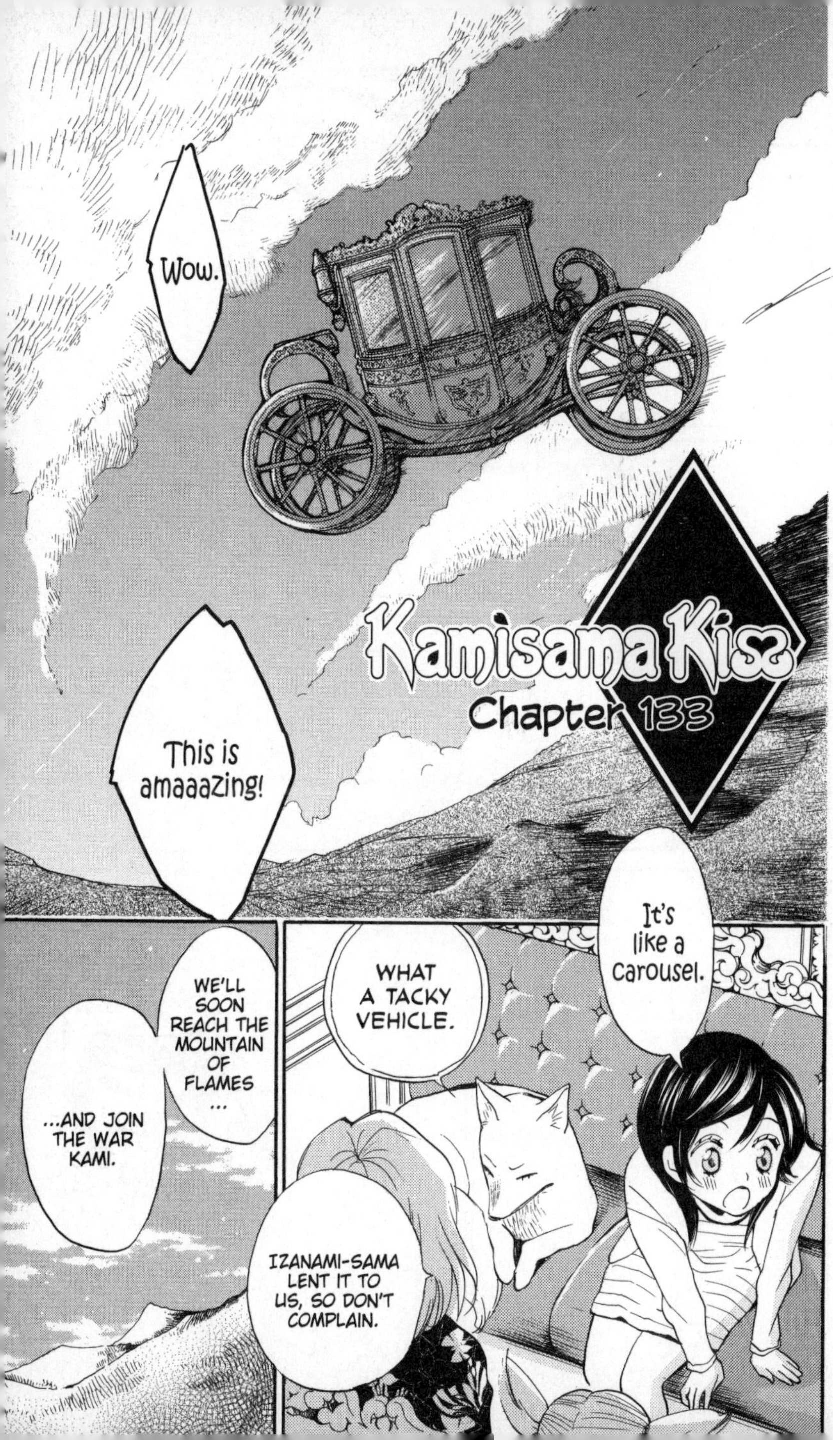
Wow.
Kamisama Kiss
Chapter 133
This is amaaazing!
It's like a carousel.
WHAT A TACKY VEHICLE.
IZANAMI-SAMA LENT IT TO US, SO DON'T COMPLAIN.
WE'LL SOON REACH THE MOUNTAIN OF FLAMES...
...AND JOIN THE WAR KAMI.

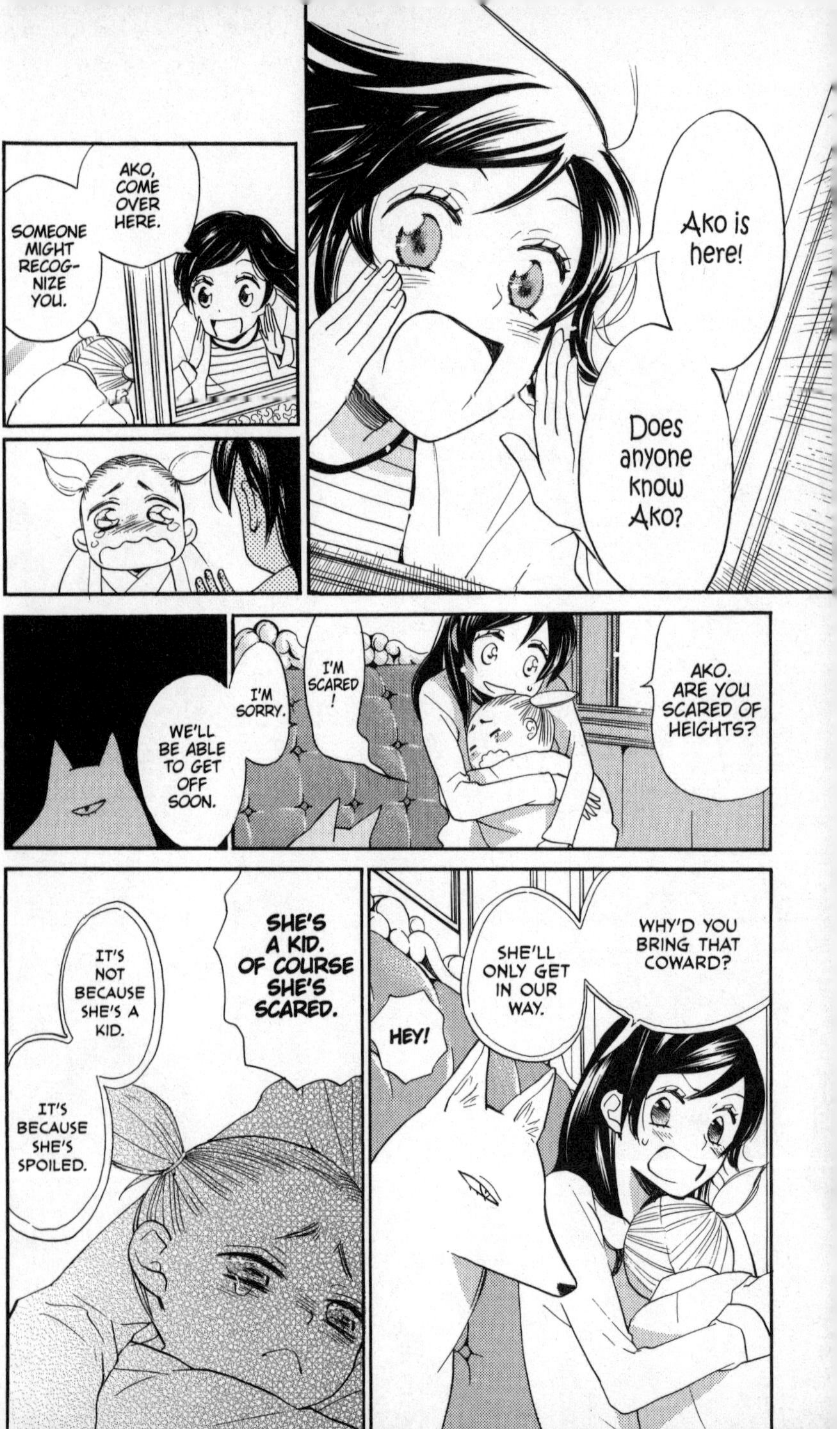
Ako is here!
Does anyone know Ako?
AKO, COME OVER HERE.
SOMEONE MIGHT RECOG-NIZE YOU.
AKO. ARE YOU SCARED OF HEIGHTS?
I'M SCARED!
I'M SORRY.
WE'LL BE ABLE TO GET OFF SOON.
WHY'D YOU BRING THAT COWARD?
SHE'LL ONLY GET IN OUR WAY.
HEY!
SHE'S A KID. OF COURSE SHE'S SCARED.
IT'S NOT BECAUSE SHE'S A KID.
IT'S BECAUSE SHE'S SPOILED.

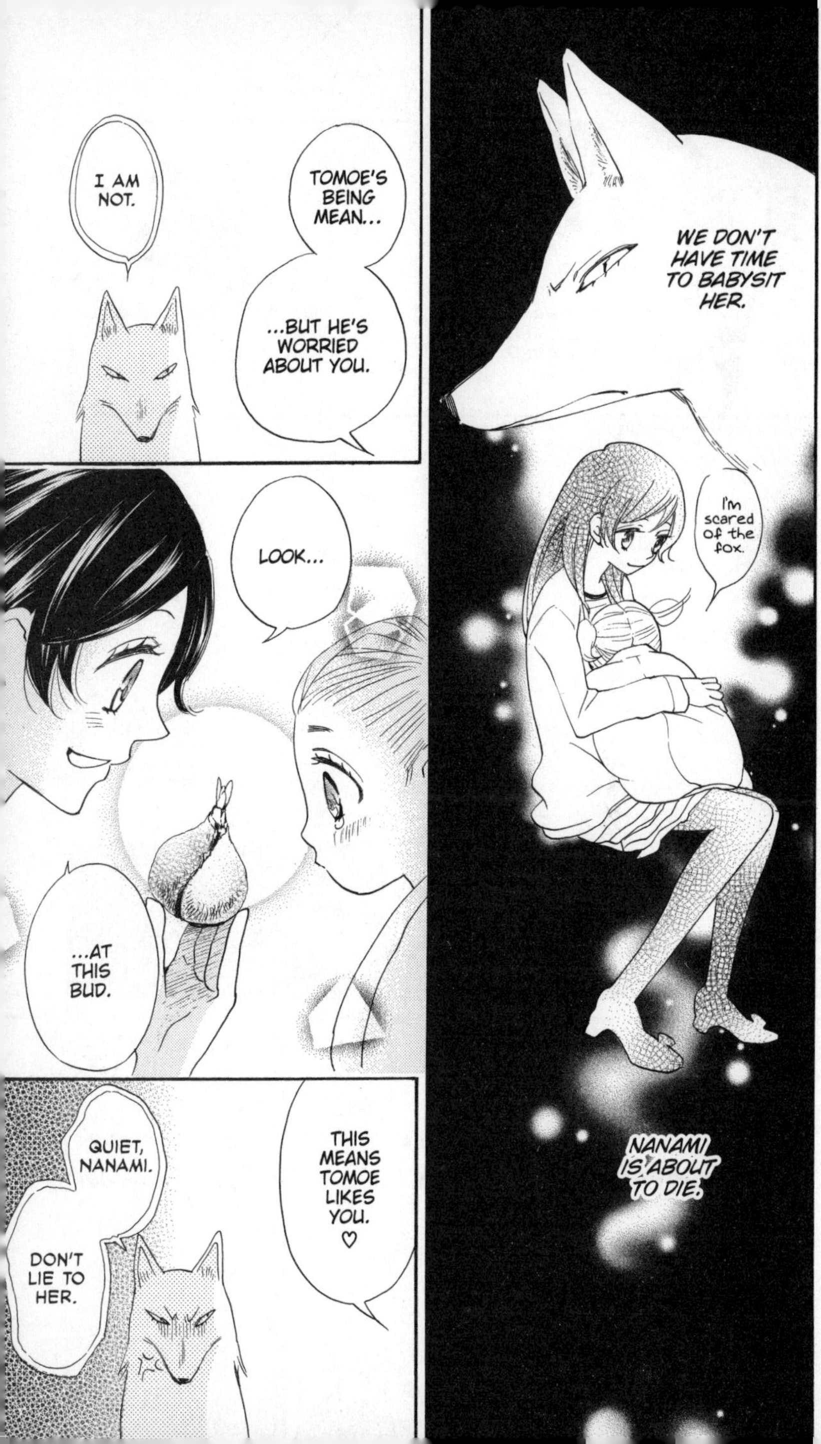
WE DON'T HAVE TIME TO BABYSIT HER.
I'm scared of the fox.
NANAMI IS ABOUT TO DIE.
TOMOE'S BEING MEAN...
...BUT HE'S WORRIED ABOUT YOU.
I AM NOT.
LOOK...
...AT THIS BUD.
THIS MEANS TOMOE LIKES YOU. ♡
QUIET, NANAMI.
DON'T LIE TO HER.

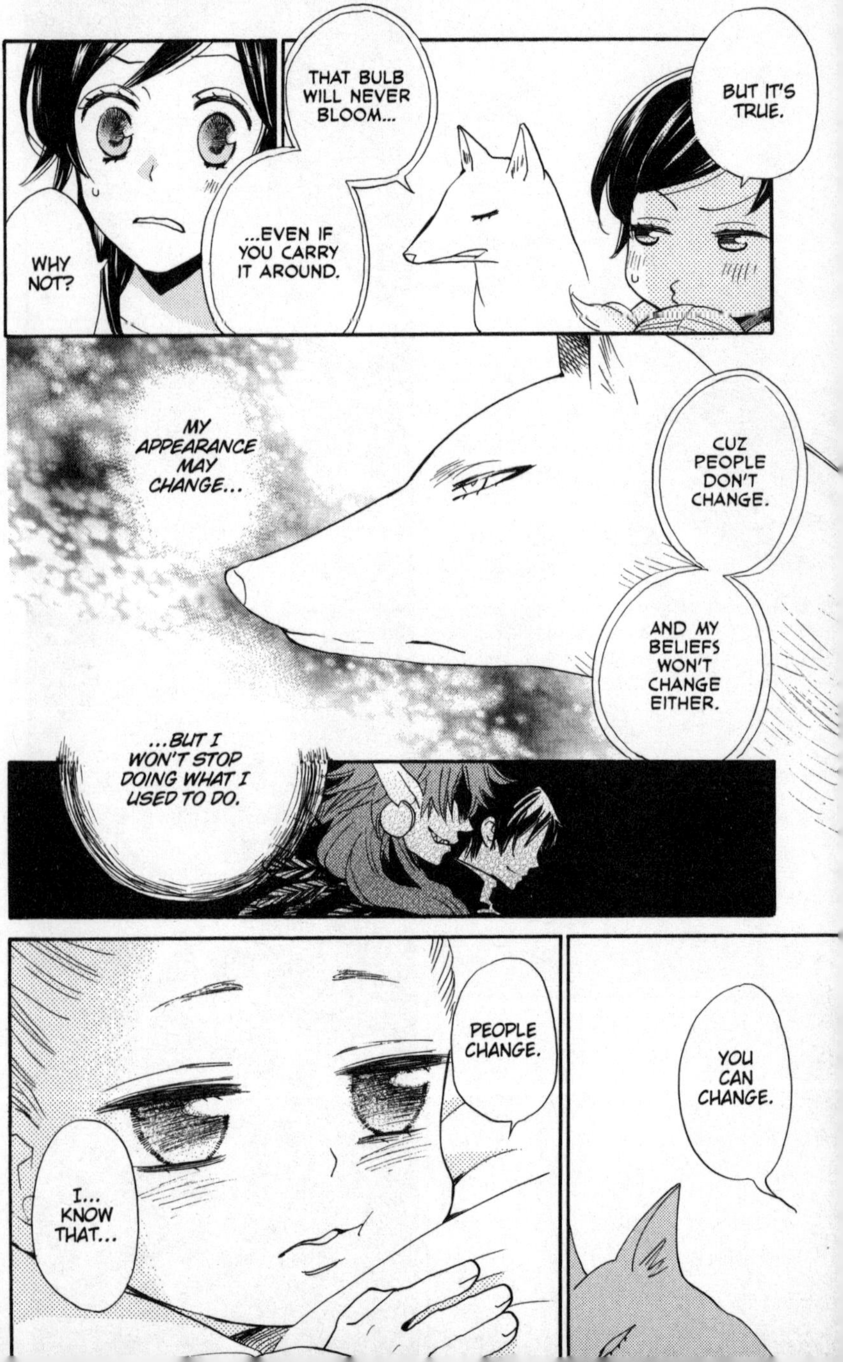
BUT IT'S TRUE.
THAT BULB WILL NEVER BLOOM...
...EVEN IF YOU CARRY IT AROUND.
WHY NOT?
CUZ PEOPLE DON'T CHANGE.
AND MY BELIEFS WON'T CHANGE EITHER.
MY APPEARANCE MAY CHANGE...
...BUT I WON'T STOP DOING WHAT I USED TO DO.
YOU CAN CHANGE.
PEOPLE CHANGE.
I... KNOW THAT...

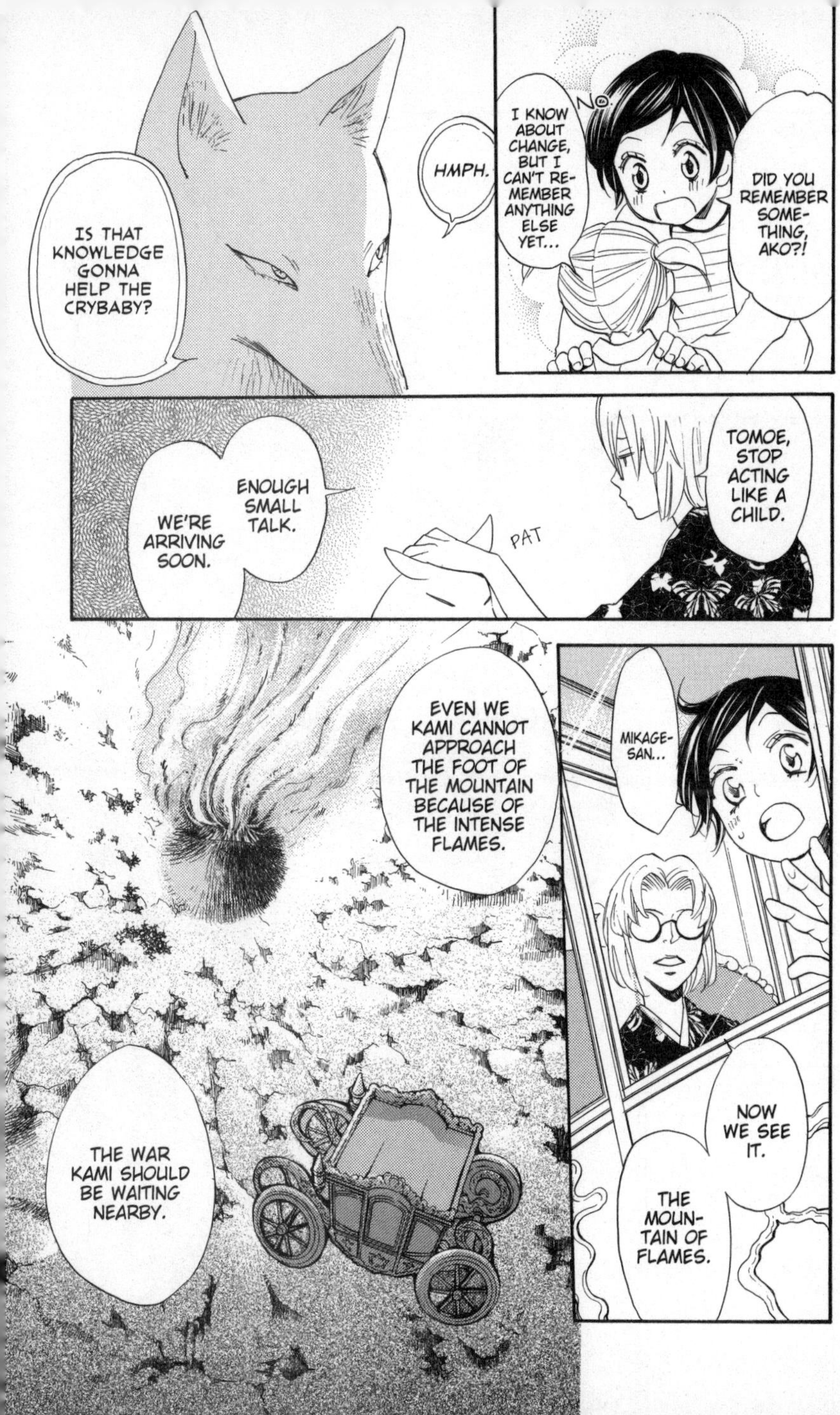
DID YOU REMEMBER SOMETHING, AKO?!
NO.
I KNOW ABOUT CHANGE, BUT I CAN'T REMEMBER ANYTHING ELSE YET...
HMPH.
IS THAT KNOWLEDGE GONNA HELP THE CRYBABY?
TOMOE, STOP ACTING LIKE A CHILD.
PAT
ENOUGH SMALL TALK.
WE'RE ARRIVING SOON.
MIKAGE-SAN...
NOW WE SEE IT.
THE MOUNTAIN OF FLAMES.
EVEN WE KAMI CANNOT APPROACH THE FOOT OF THE MOUNTAIN BECAUSE OF THE INTENSE FLAMES.
THE WAR KAMI SHOULD BE WAITING NEARBY.

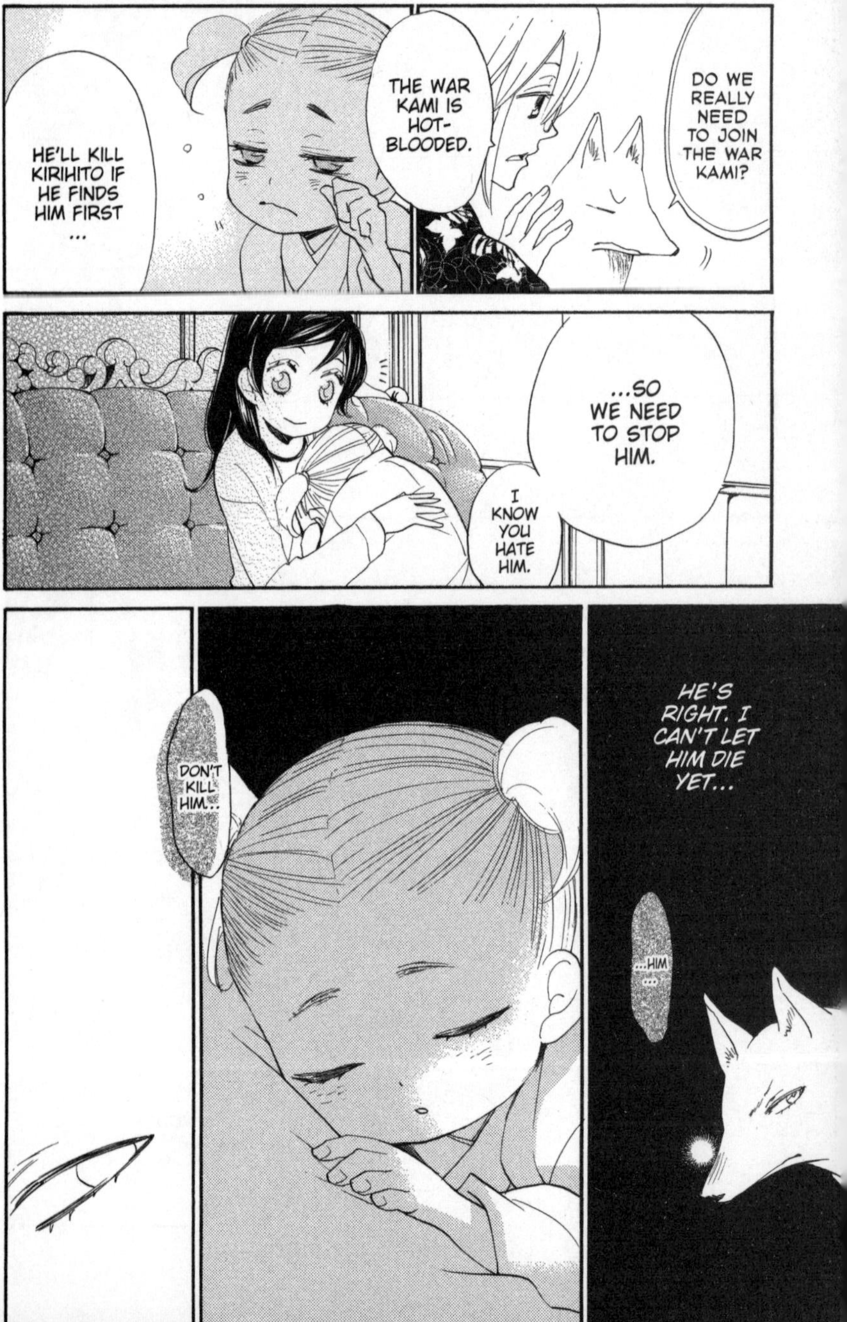
DO WE REALLY NEED TO JOIN THE WAR KAMI?
THE WAR KAMI IS HOT-BLOODED.
HE'LL KILL KIRIHITO IF HE FINDS HIM FIRST ...
...SO WE NEED TO STOP HIM.
I KNOW YOU HATE HIM.
HE'S RIGHT. I CAN'T LET HIM DIE YET...
...HIM ...
DON'T KILL HIM...

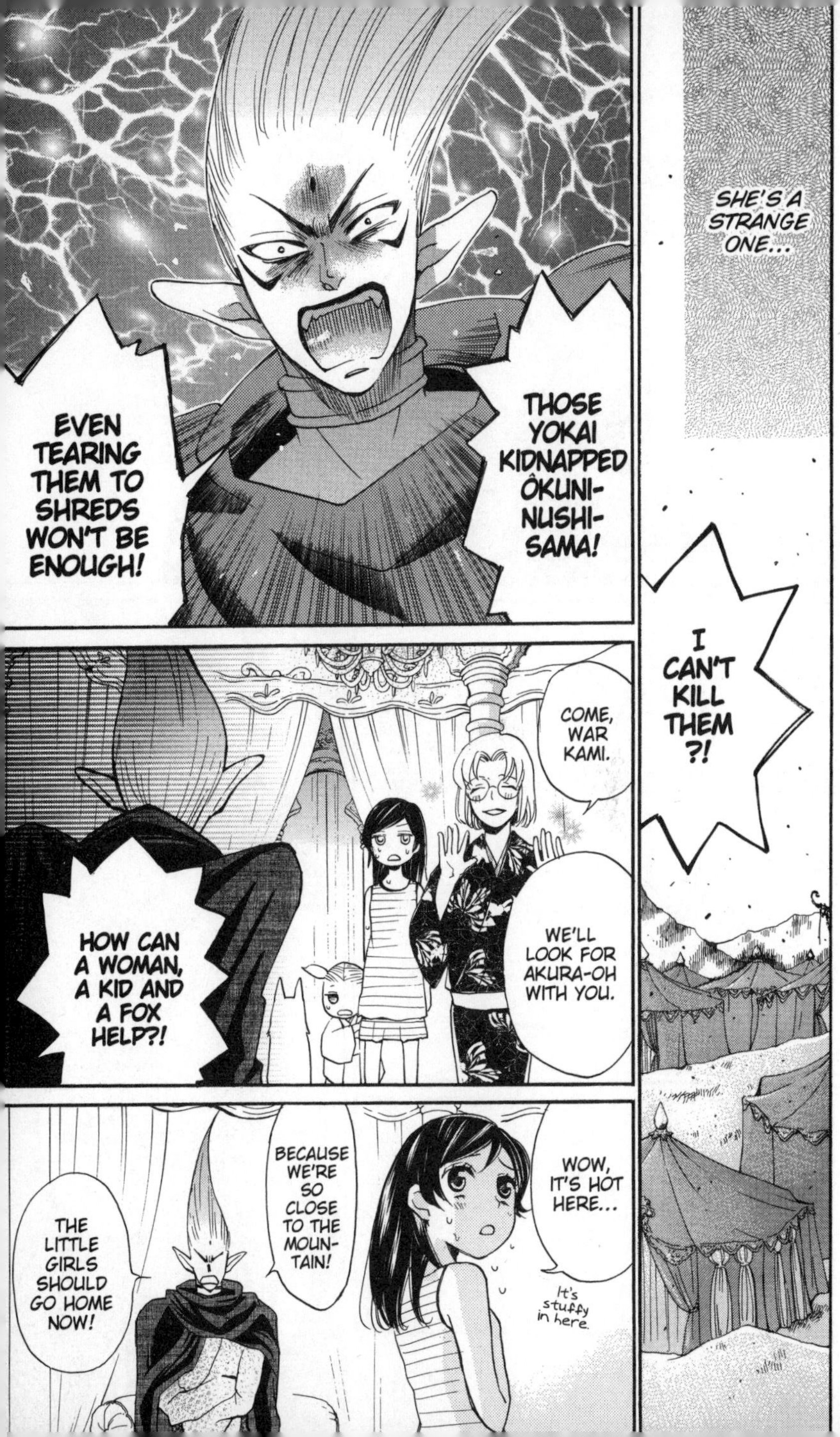
SHE'S A STRANGE ONE...
THOSE YOKAI KIDNAPPED ÔKUNI-NUSHI-SAMA!
EVEN TEARING THEM TO SHREDS WON'T BE ENOUGH!
I CAN'T KILL THEM?!
COME, WAR KAMI.
WE'LL LOOK FOR AKURA-OH WITH YOU.
HOW CAN A WOMAN, A KID AND A FOX HELP?!
WOW, IT'S HOT HERE...
It's stuffy in here.
BECAUSE WE'RE SO CLOSE TO THE MOUN-TAIN!
THE LITTLE GIRLS SHOULD GO HOME NOW!

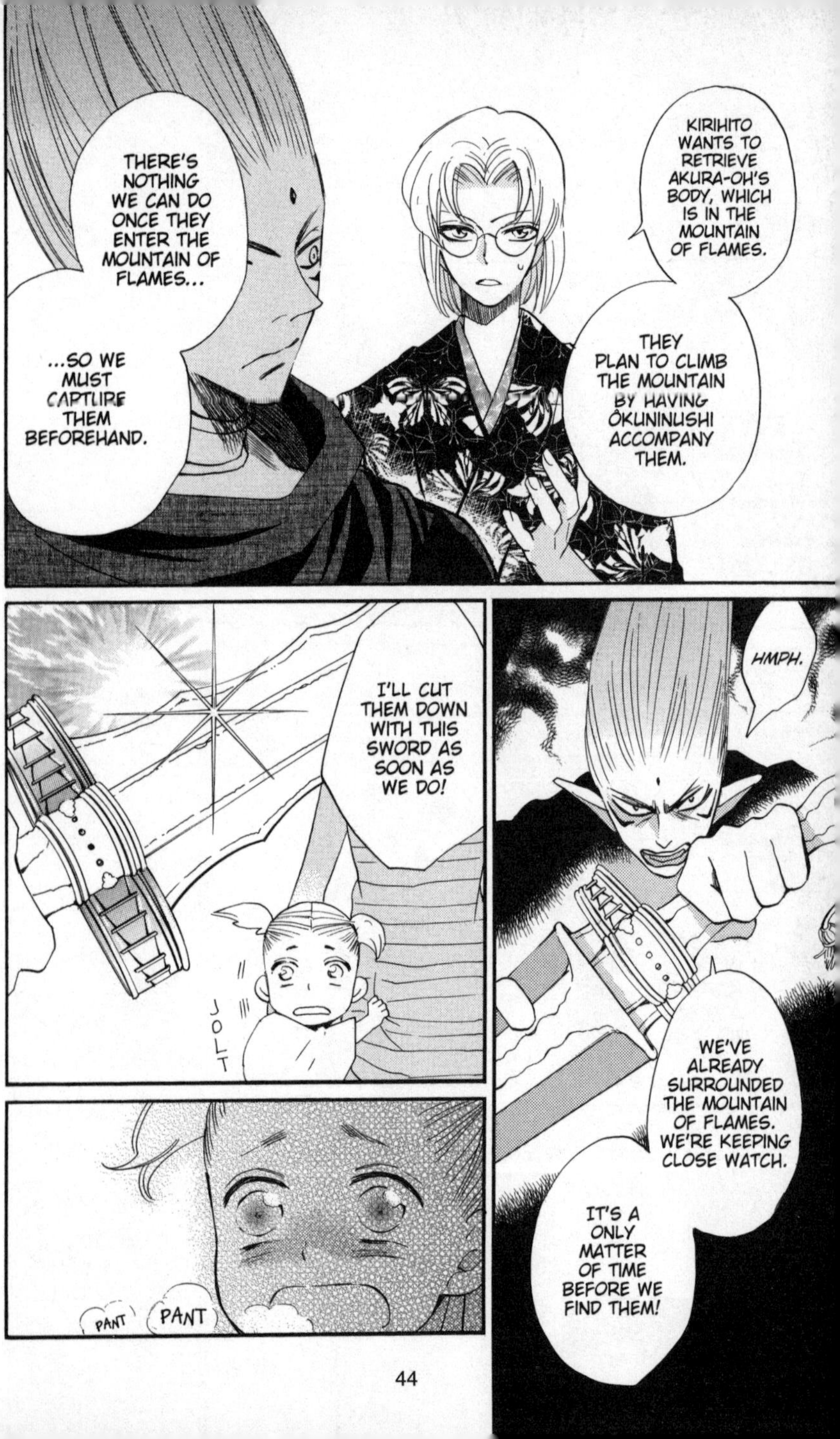
KIRIHITO WANTS TO RETRIEVE AKURA-OH'S BODY, WHICH IS IN THE MOUNTAIN OF FLAMES.
THEY PLAN TO CLIMB THE MOUNTAIN BY HAVING ÔKUNINUSHI ACCOMPANY THEM.
THERE'S NOTHING WE CAN DO ONCE THEY ENTER THE MOUNTAIN OF FLAMES...
...SO WE MUST CAPTURE THEM BEFOREHAND.
HMPH.
WE'VE ALREADY SURROUNDED THE MOUNTAIN OF FLAMES. WE'RE KEEPING CLOSE WATCH.
IT'S A ONLY MATTER OF TIME BEFORE WE FIND THEM!
I'LL CUT THEM DOWN WITH THIS SWORD AS SOON AS WE DO!
JOLT
PANT
PANT

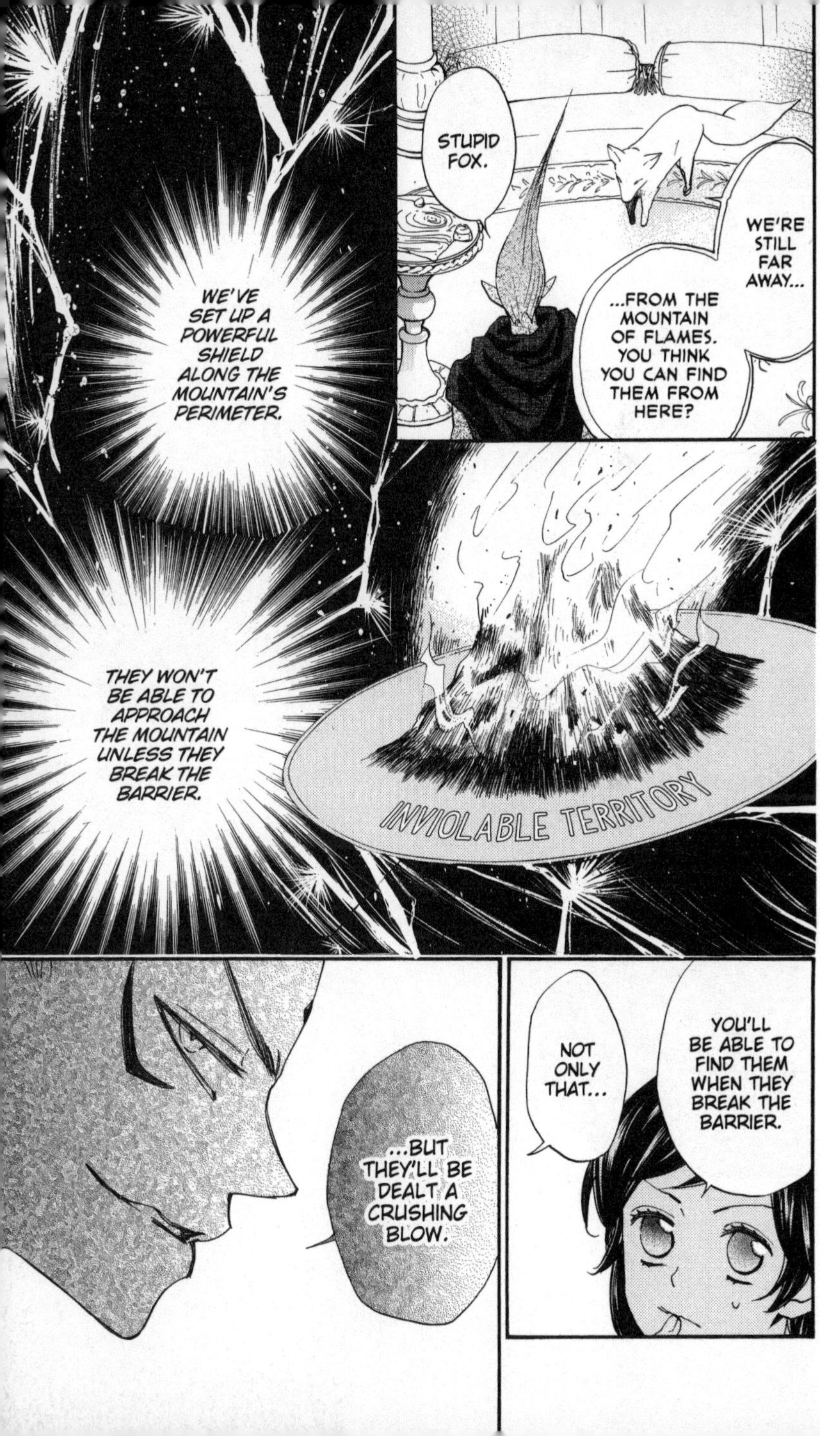
STUPID FOX.
WE'RE STILL FAR AWAY...
...FROM THE MOUNTAIN OF FLAMES. YOU THINK YOU CAN FIND THEM FROM HERE?
INVIOLABLE TERRITORY
WE'VE SET UP A POWERFUL SHIELD ALONG THE MOUNTAIN'S PERIMETER.
THEY WON'T BE ABLE TO APPROACH THE MOUNTAIN UNLESS THEY BREAK THE BARRIER.
YOU'LL BE ABLE TO FIND THEM WHEN THEY BREAK THE BARRIER.
NOT ONLY THAT...
...BUT THEY'LL BE DEALT A CRUSHING BLOW.

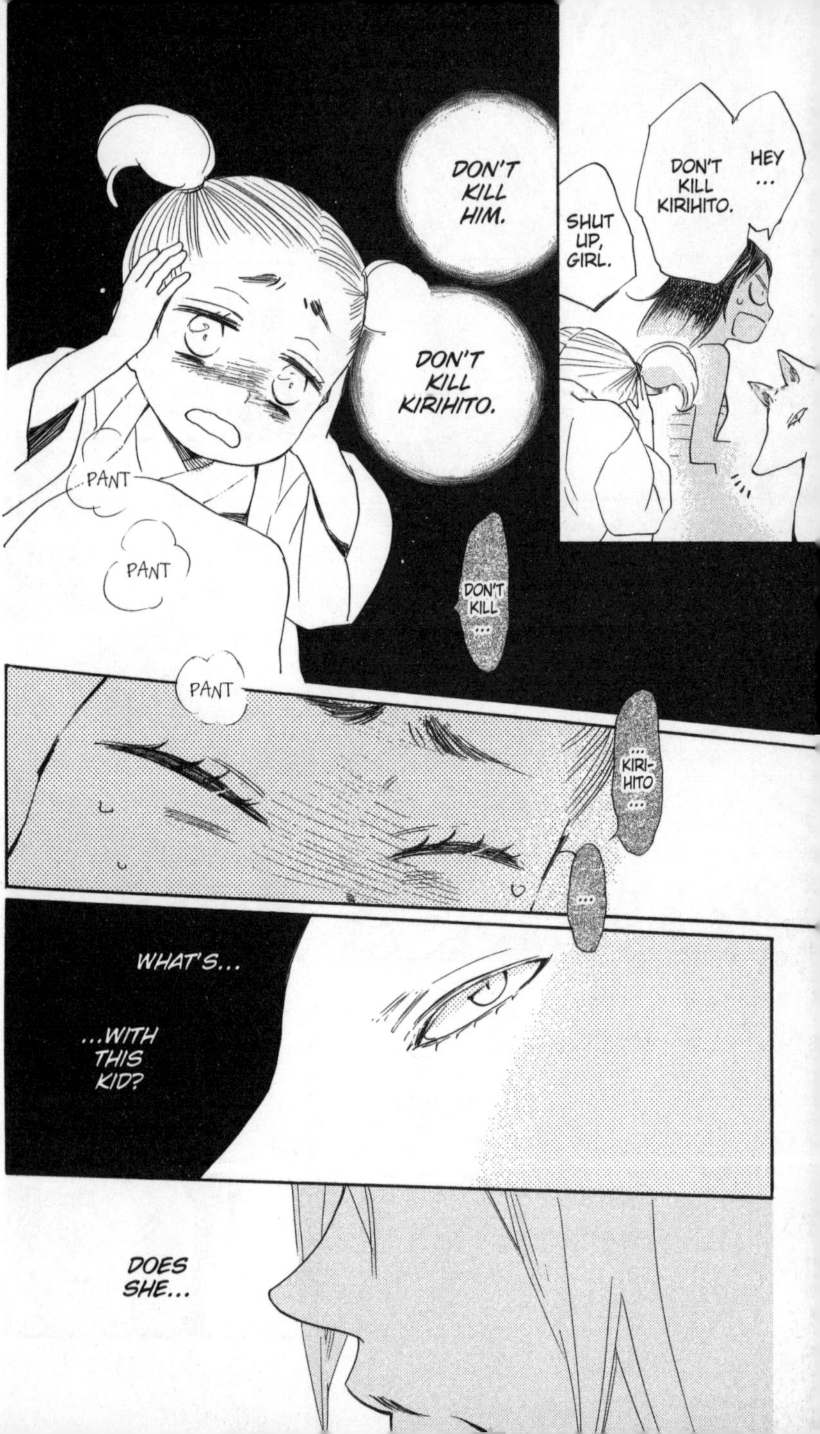
HEY...
DON'T KILL KIRIHITO.
SHUT UP, GIRL.
DON'T KILL HIM.
DON'T KILL KIRIHITO.
PANT
PANT
DON'T KILL...
PANT
...KIRI-HITO...
...
WHAT'S...
...WITH THIS KID?
DOES SHE...

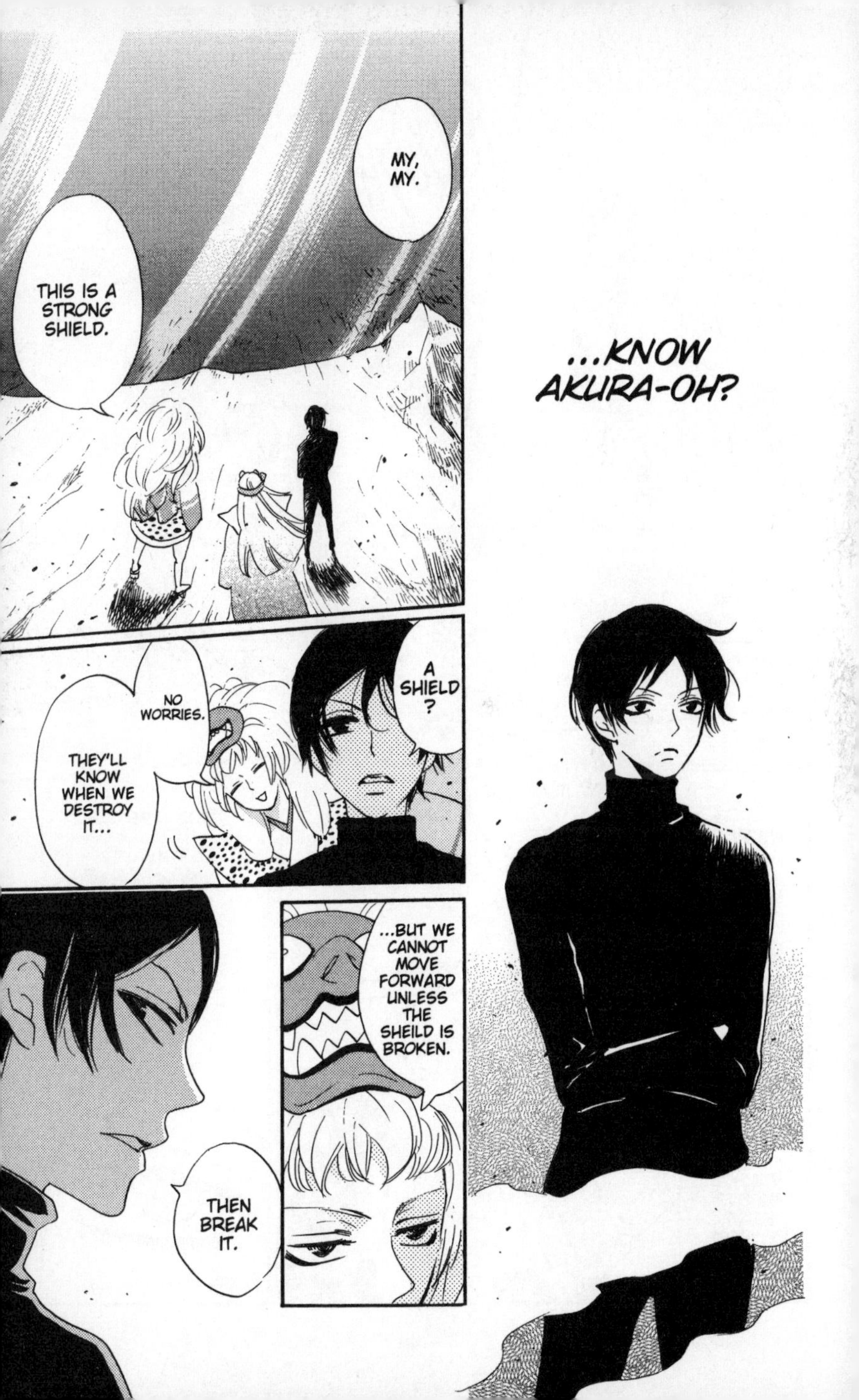
...KNOW AKURA-OH?
MY, MY.
THIS IS A STRONG SHIELD.
A SHIELD?
NO WORRIES.
THEY'LL KNOW WHEN WE DESTROY IT...
...BUT WE CANNOT MOVE FORWARD UNLESS THE SHEILD IS BROKEN.
THEN BREAK IT.

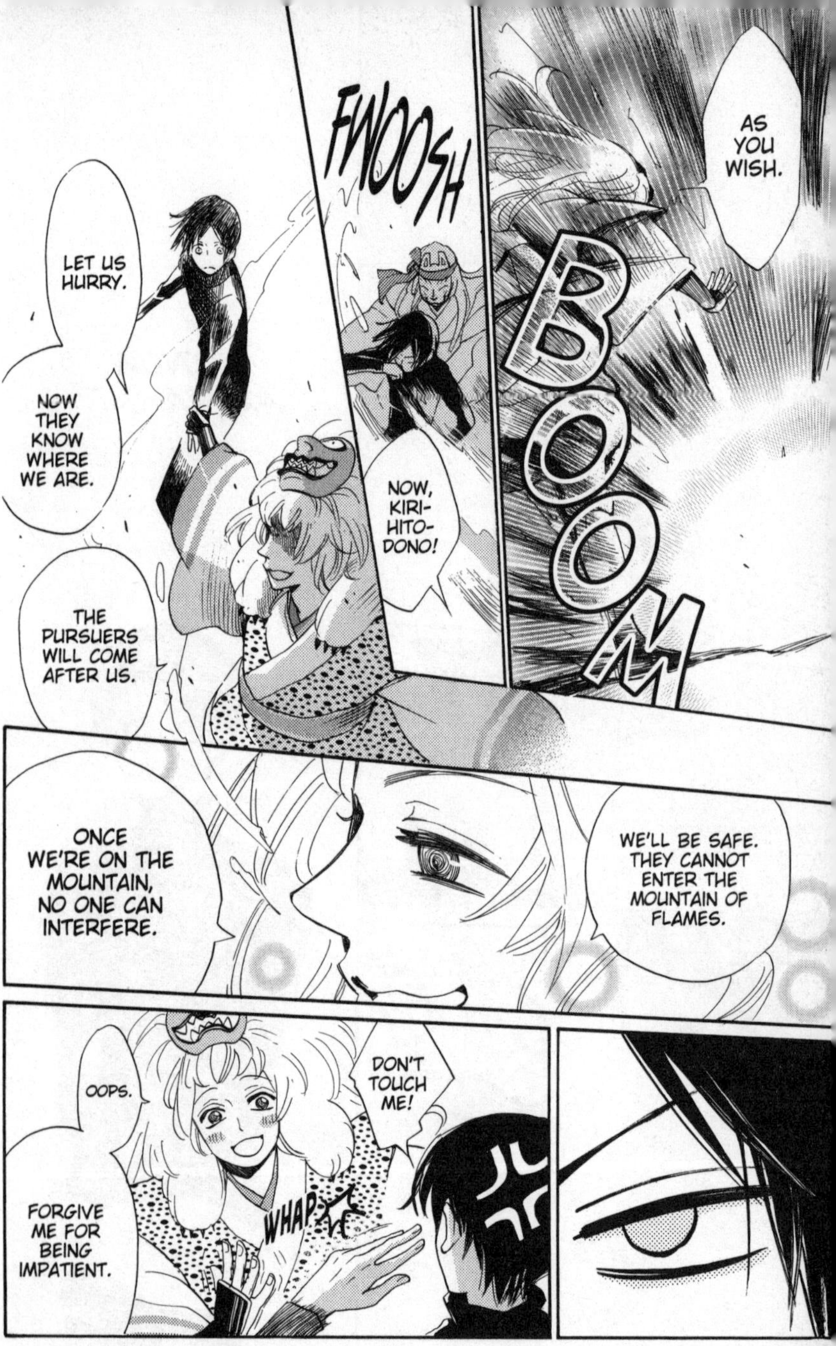
AS YOU WISH.
BOOM
FWOOSH
NOW, KIRI-HITO-DONO!
LET US HURRY.
NOW THEY KNOW WHERE WE ARE.
THE PURSUERS WILL COME AFTER US.
WE'LL BE SAFE. THEY CANNOT ENTER THE MOUNTAIN OF FLAMES.
ONCE WE'RE ON THE MOUNTAIN, NO ONE CAN INTERFERE.
DON'T TOUCH ME!
WHAP
OOPS.
FORGIVE ME FOR BEING IMPATIENT.

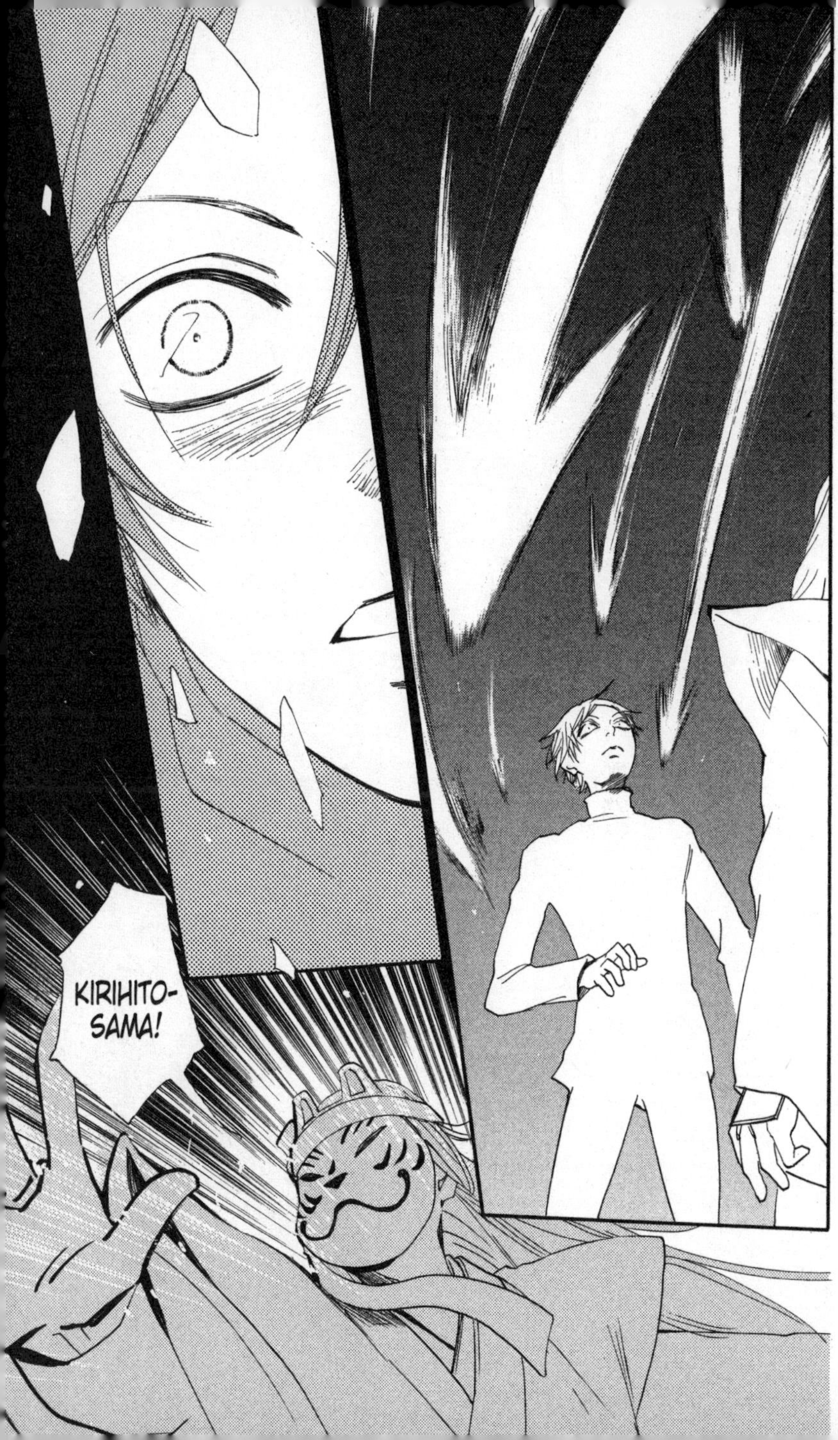
KIRIHITO-SAMA!

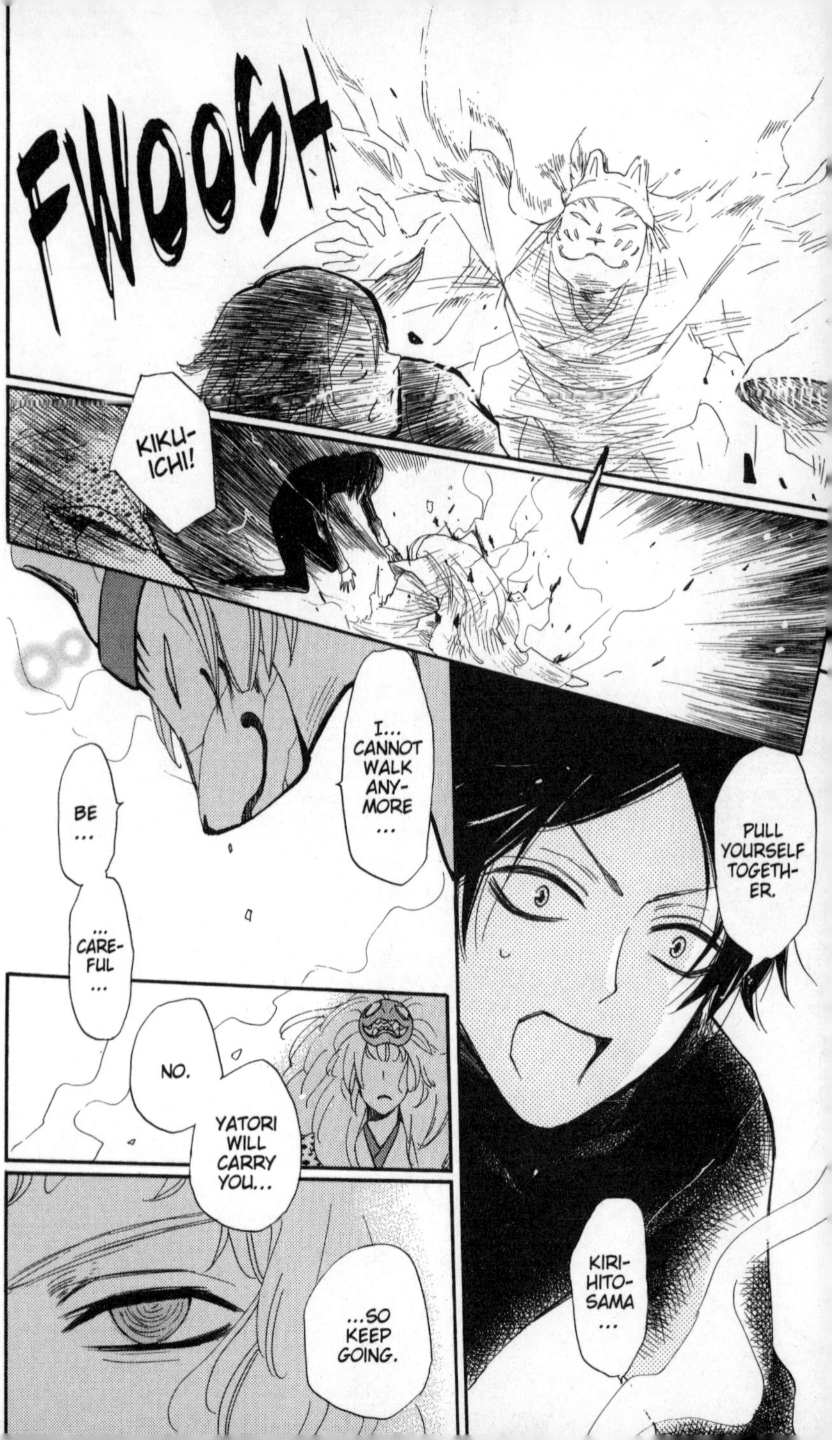
FWOOSH
KIKU-ICHI!
PULL YOURSELF TOGETH-ER.
KIRI-HITO-SAMA...
I... CANNOT WALK ANY-MORE...
BE...
...CARE-FUL...
NO.
YATORI WILL CARRY YOU...
...SO KEEP GOING.

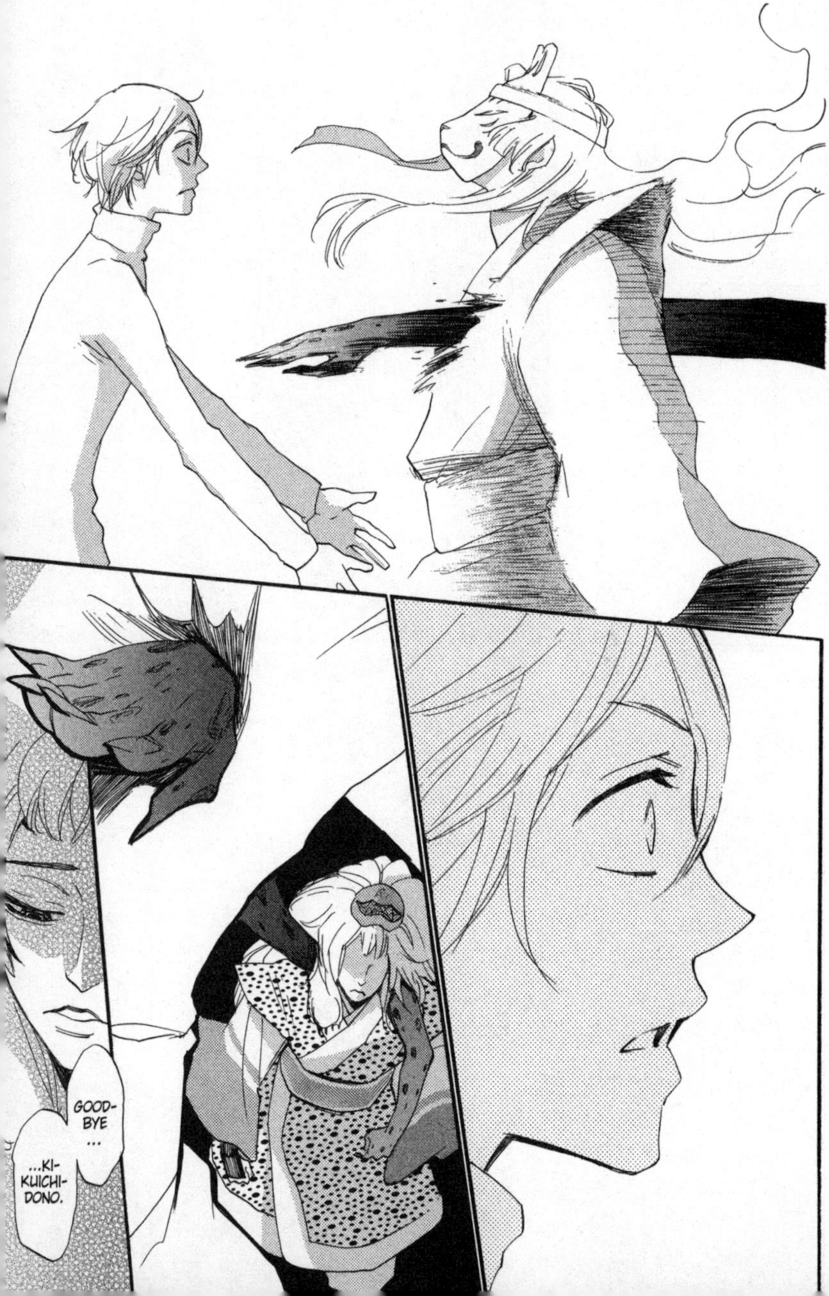
GOOD-BYE...
...KI-KUICHI-DONO.

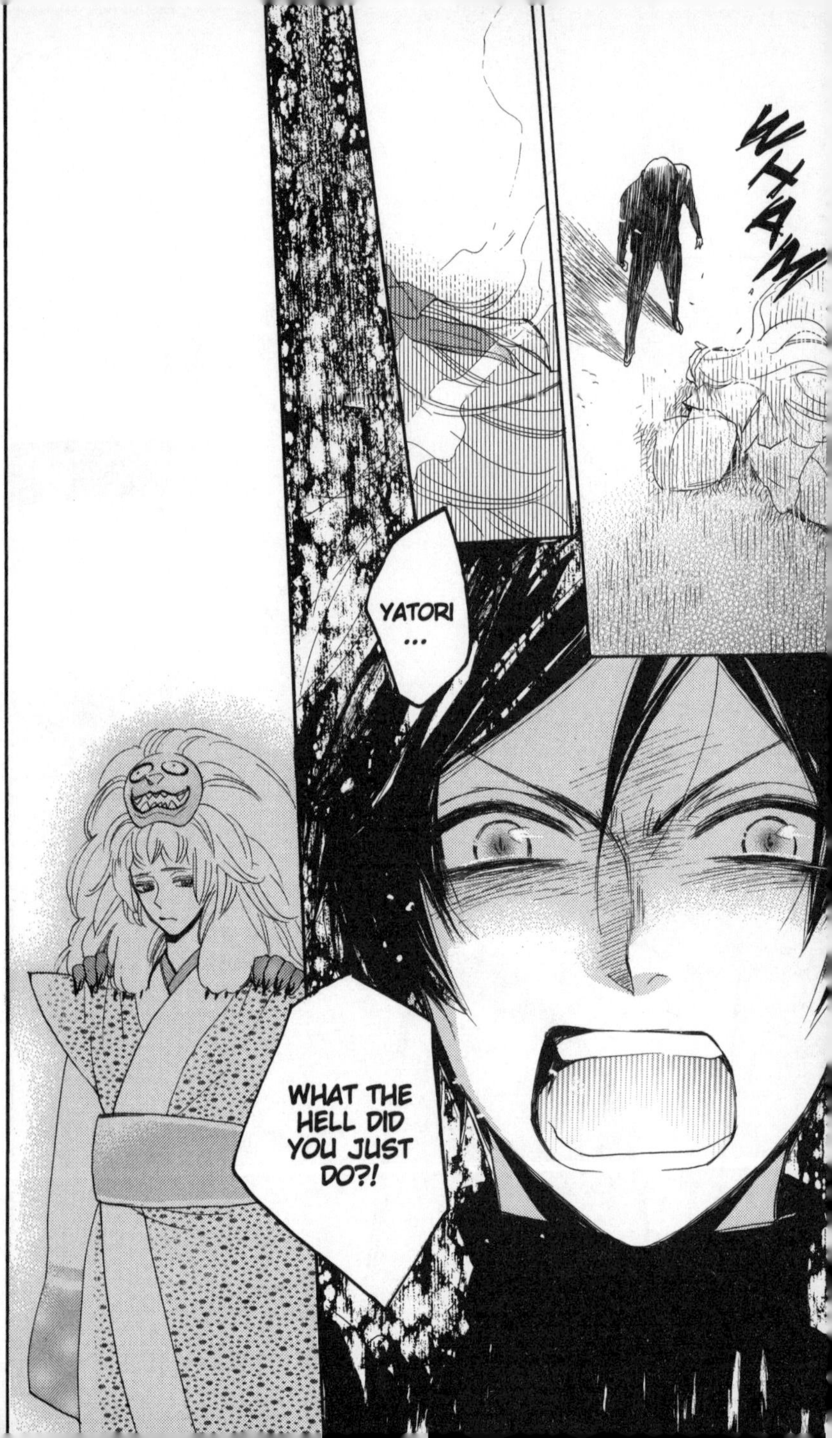
WHAM
YATORI ...
WHAT THE HELL DID YOU JUST DO?!

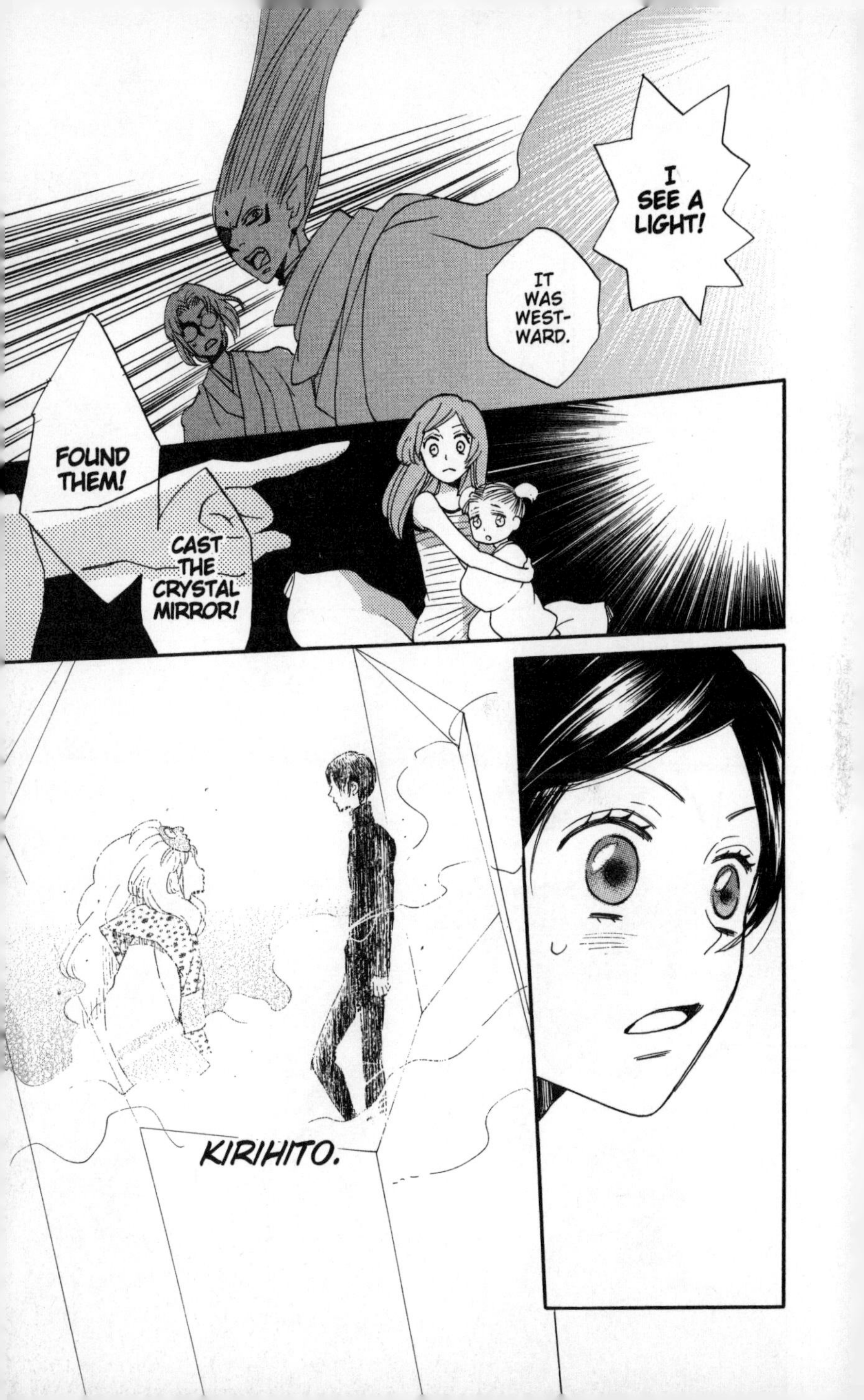
I SEE A LIGHT!
IT WAS WEST-WARD.
FOUND THEM!
CAST THE CRYSTAL MIRROR!
KIRIHITO.

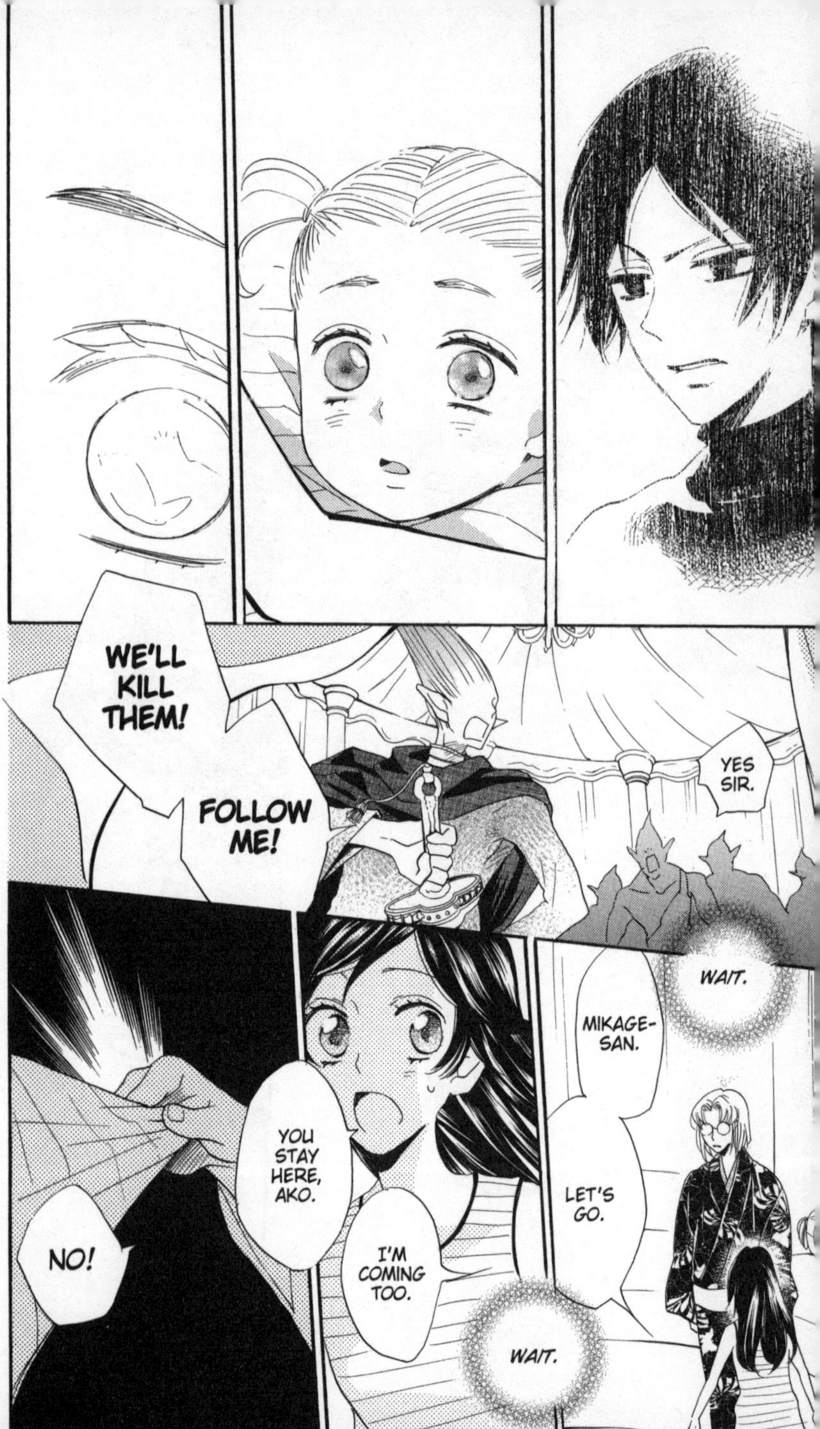
WE'LL KILL THEM!
FOLLOW ME!
YES SIR.
WAIT.
MIKAGE-SAN.
LET'S GO.
WAIT.
YOU STAY HERE, AKO.
I'M COMING TOO.
NO!

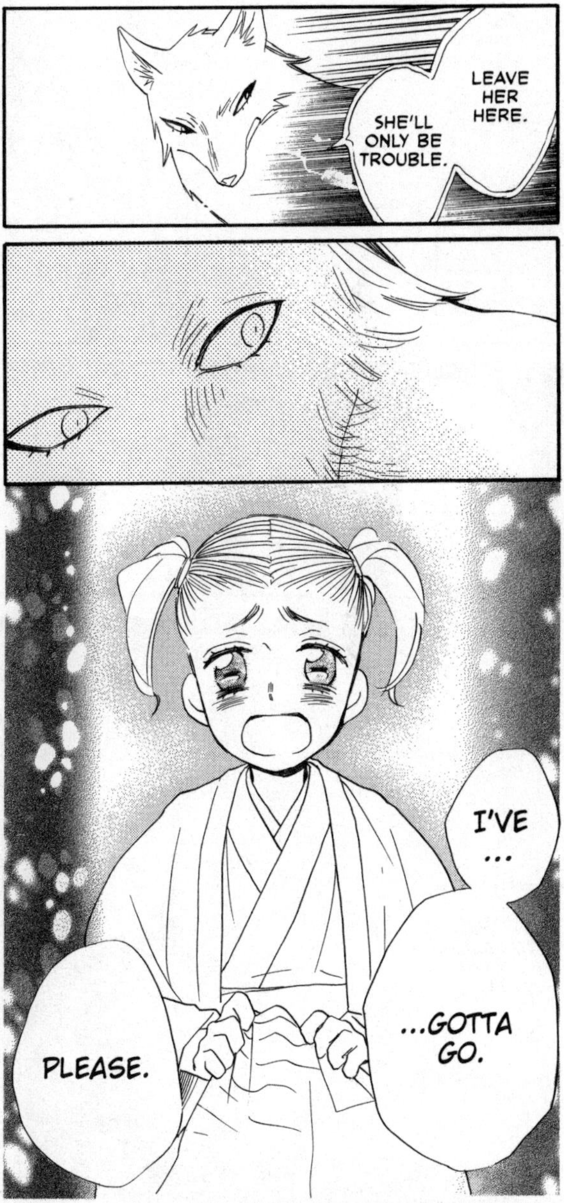
LEAVE HER HERE.
SHE'LL ONLY BE TROUBLE.
I'VE ...
...GOTTA GO.
PLEASE.

Winter is the season for nabe.

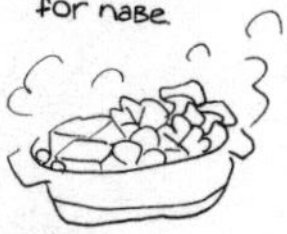

It's time to wear my favorite gloves and scarf.

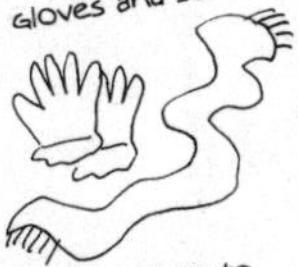

My cat comes to sleep in my bed and keeps me warm.

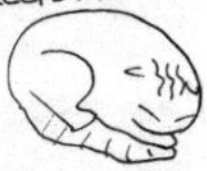

There're lots of fun events.

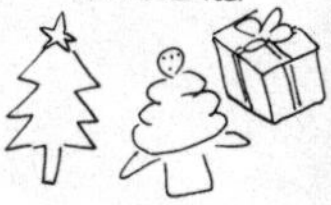

This is also the season to look back on the past year and to welcome the New Year.

So let's cherish the winter. ♡

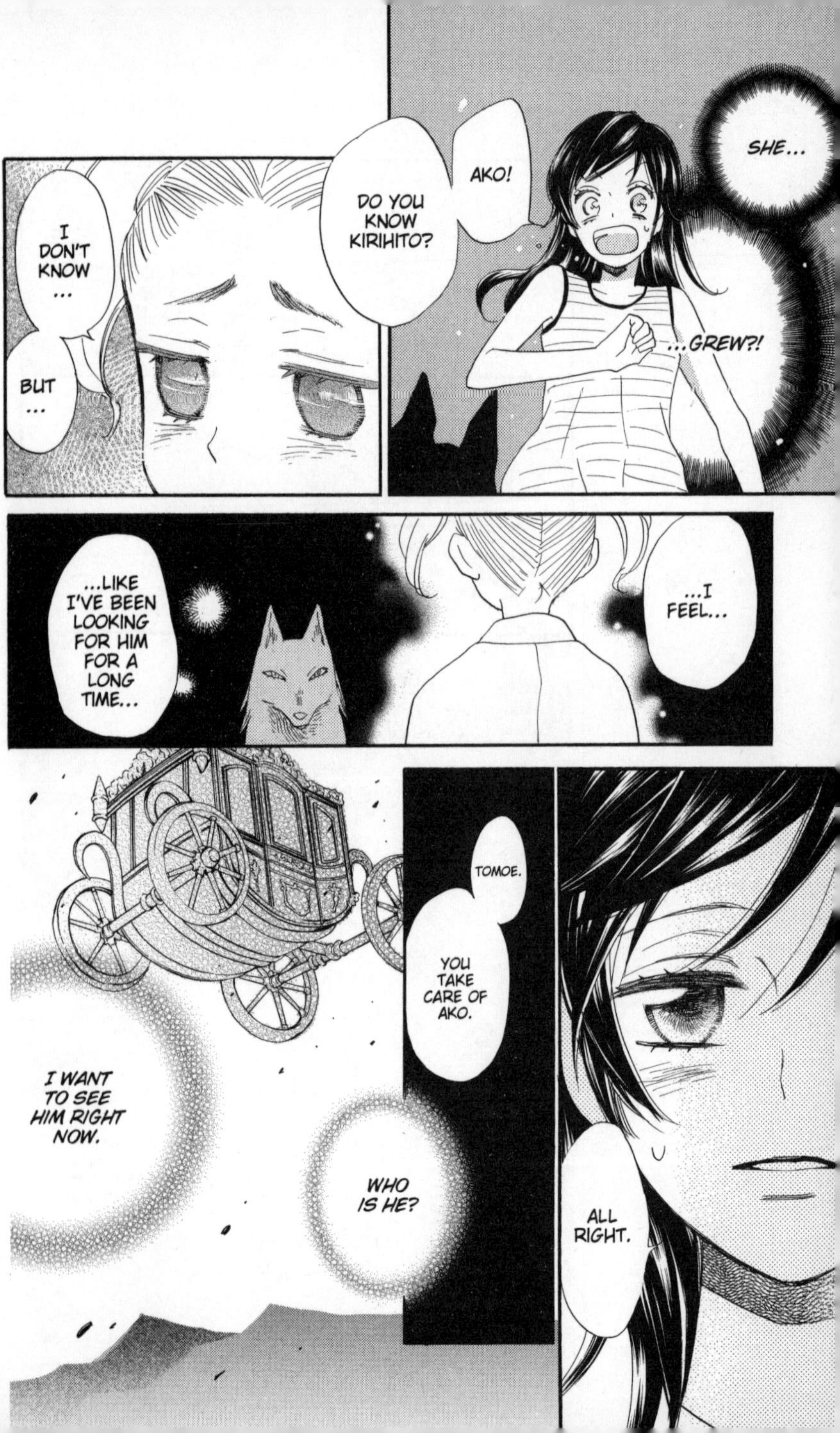
SHE...
AKO!
DO YOU KNOW KIRIHITO?
...GREW?!
I DON'T KNOW ...
BUT ...
...I FEEL...
...LIKE I'VE BEEN LOOKING FOR HIM FOR A LONG TIME...
ALL RIGHT.
TOMOE.
YOU TAKE CARE OF AKO.
I WANT TO SEE HIM RIGHT NOW.
WHO IS HE?

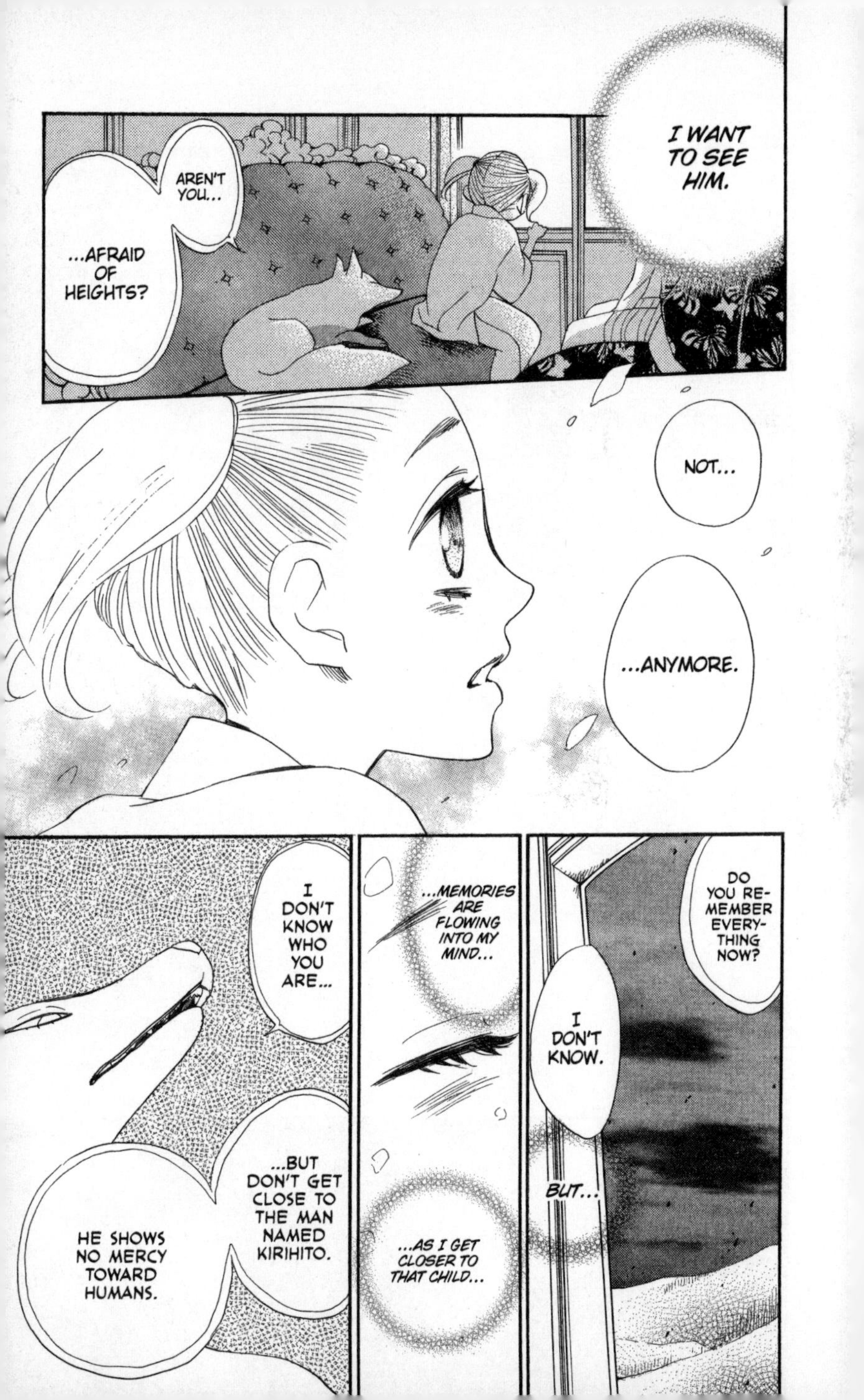
I WANT TO SEE HIM.
AREN'T YOU...
...AFRAID OF HEIGHTS?
NOT...
...ANYMORE.
DO YOU REMEMBER EVERYTHING NOW?
I DON'T KNOW.
BUT...
...MEMORIES ARE FLOWING INTO MY MIND...
...AS I GET CLOSER TO THAT CHILD...
I DON'T KNOW WHO YOU ARE...
...BUT DON'T GET CLOSE TO THE MAN NAMED KIRIHITO.
HE SHOWS NO MERCY TOWARD HUMANS.

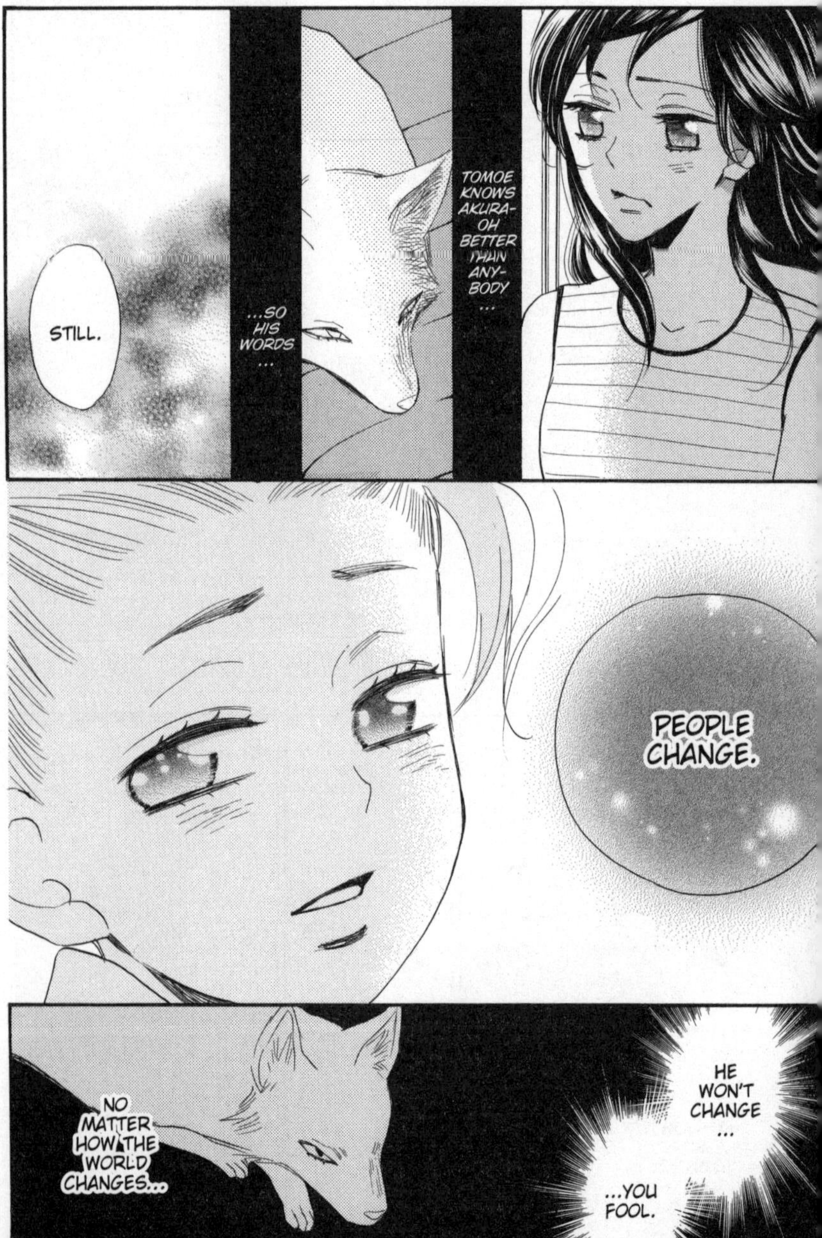

TOMOE KNOWS AKURA-OH BETTER THAN ANYBODY...
...SO HIS WORDS...
STILL.
PEOPLE CHANGE.
HE WON'T CHANGE...
NO MATTER HOW THE WORLD CHANGES...
...YOU FOOL.

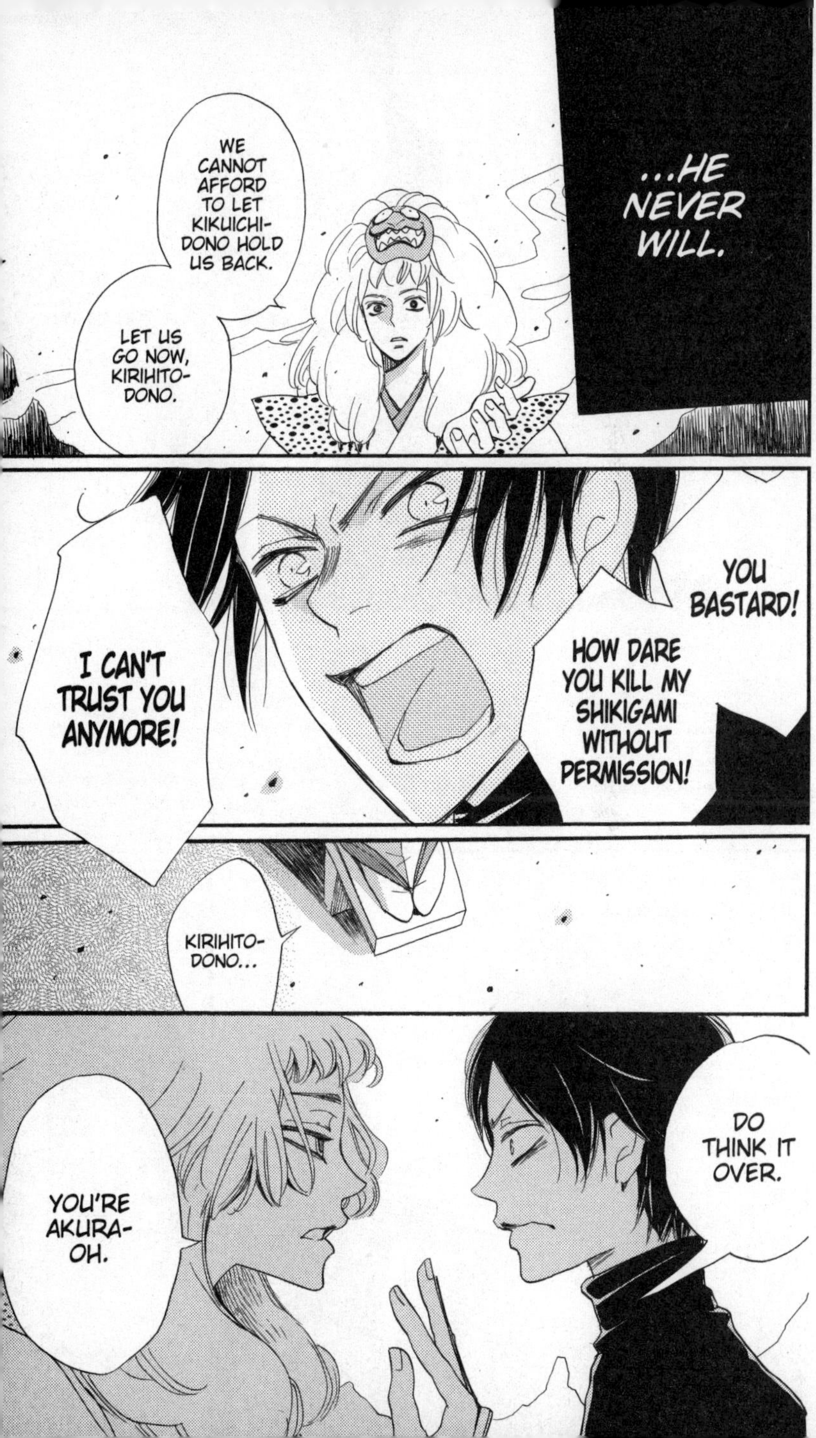
...HE NEVER WILL.
WE CANNOT AFFORD TO LET KIKUICHI-DONO HOLD US BACK.
LET US GO NOW, KIRIHITO-DONO.
YOU BASTARD!
HOW DARE YOU KILL MY SHIKIGAMI WITHOUT PERMISSION!
I CAN'T TRUST YOU ANYMORE!
KIRIHITO-DONO...
DO THINK IT OVER.
YOU'RE AKURA-OH.

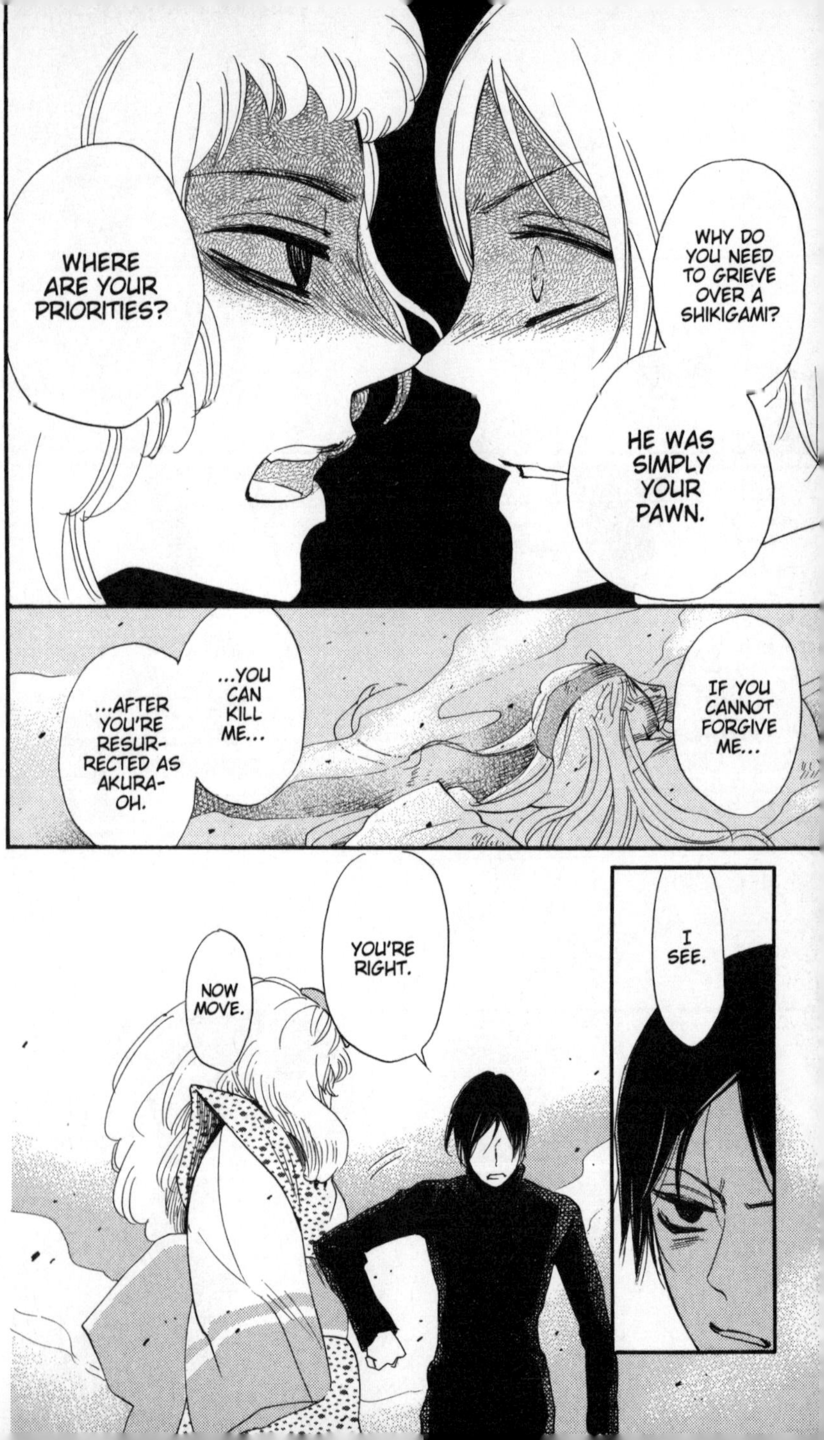
WHY DO YOU NEED TO GRIEVE OVER A SHIKIGAMI?
HE WAS SIMPLY YOUR PAWN.
WHERE ARE YOUR PRIORITIES?
IF YOU CANNOT FORGIVE ME...
...YOU CAN KILL ME...
...AFTER YOU'RE RESUR-RECTED AS AKURA-OH.
I SEE.
YOU'RE RIGHT.
NOW MOVE.

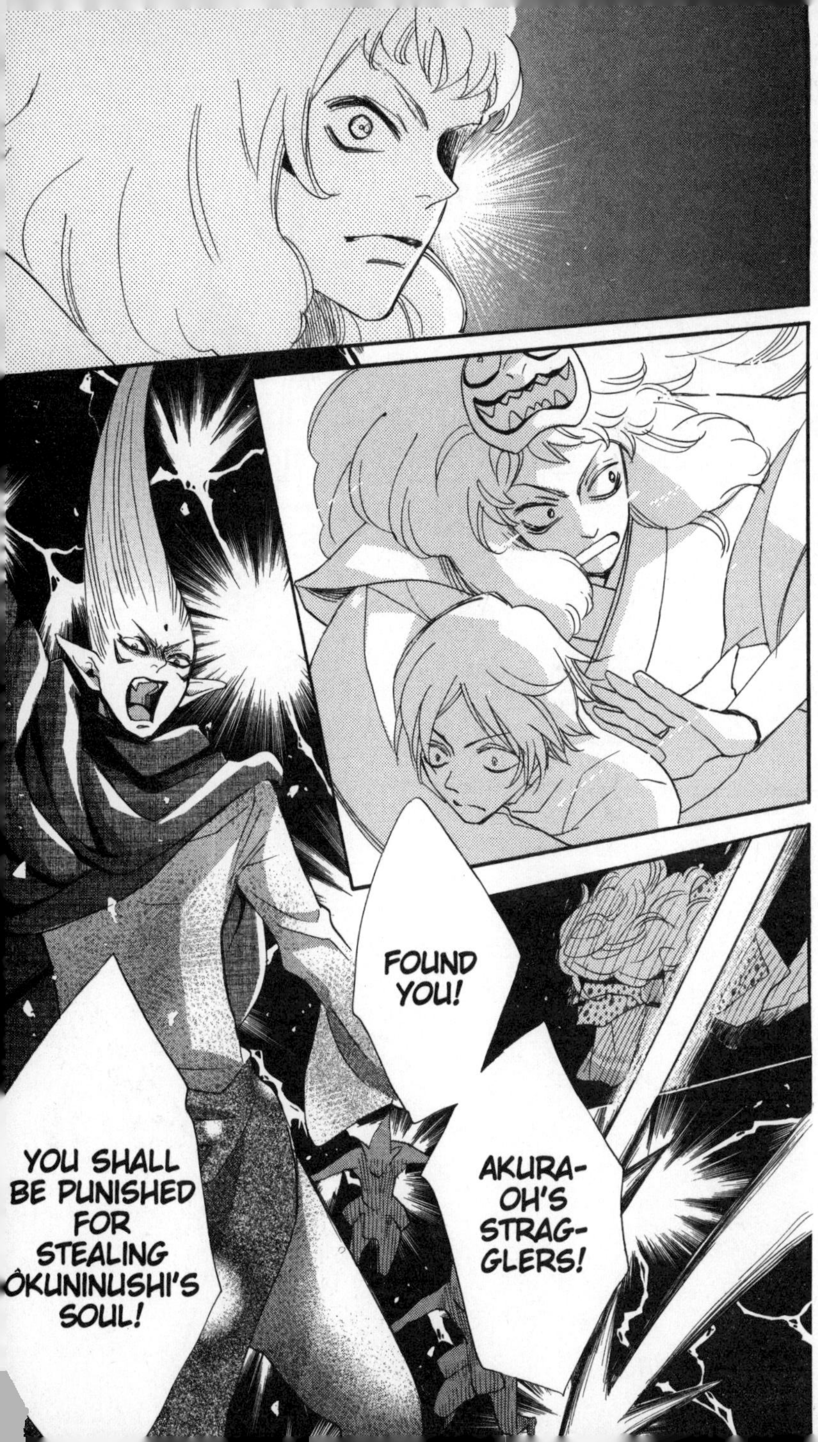
FOUND YOU!
AKURA-OH'S STRAGGLERS!
YOU SHALL BE PUNISHED FOR STEALING ÔKUNINUSHI'S SOUL!

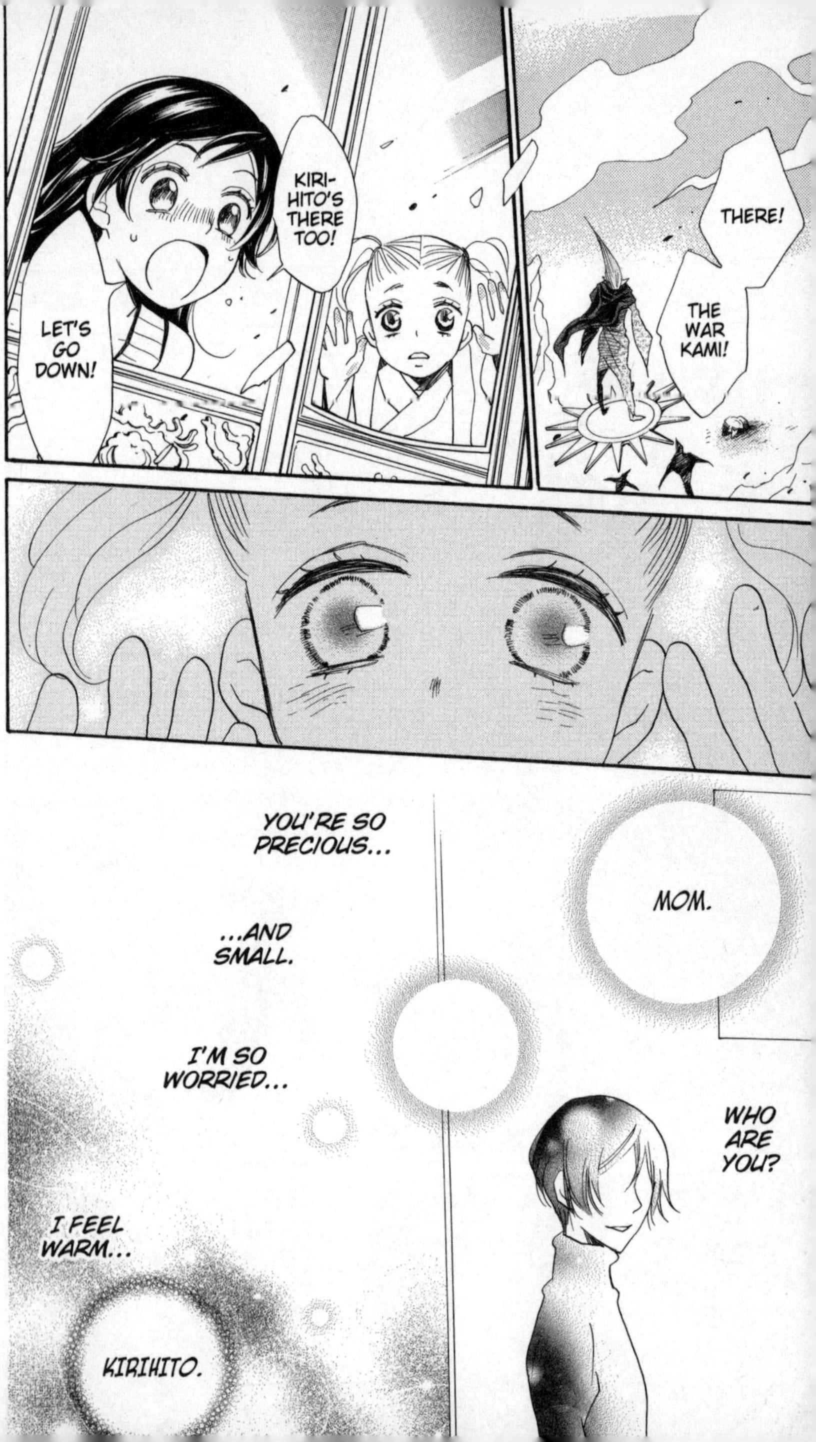
THERE!
THE WAR KAMI!
KIRI-HITO'S THERE TOO!
LET'S GO DOWN!
MOM.
WHO ARE YOU?
YOU'RE SO PRECIOUS...
...AND SMALL.
I'M SO WORRIED...
I FEEL WARM...
KIRIHITO.

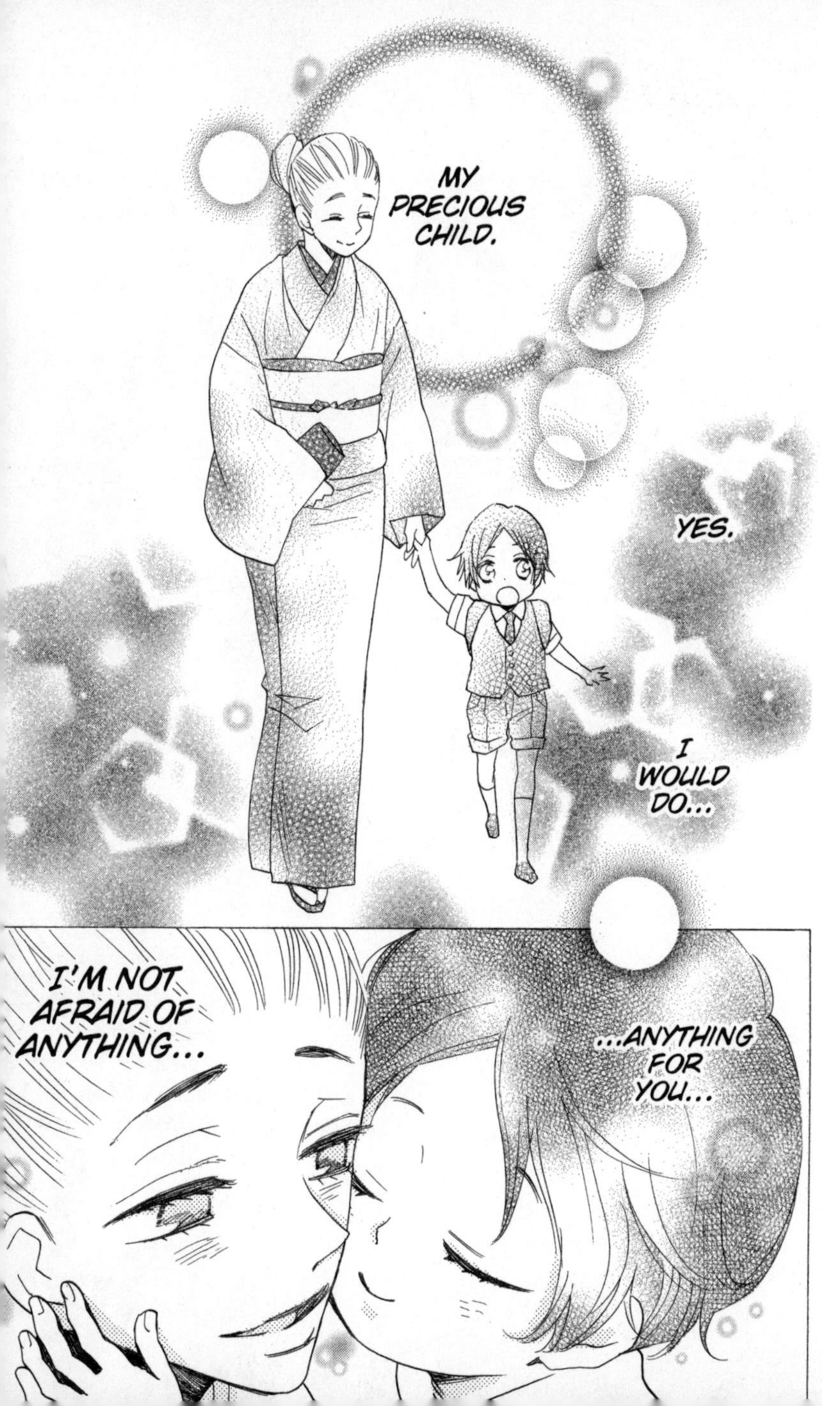
MY PRECIOUS CHILD.
YES.
I WOULD DO...
...ANYTHING FOR YOU...
I'M NOT AFRAID OF ANYTHING...

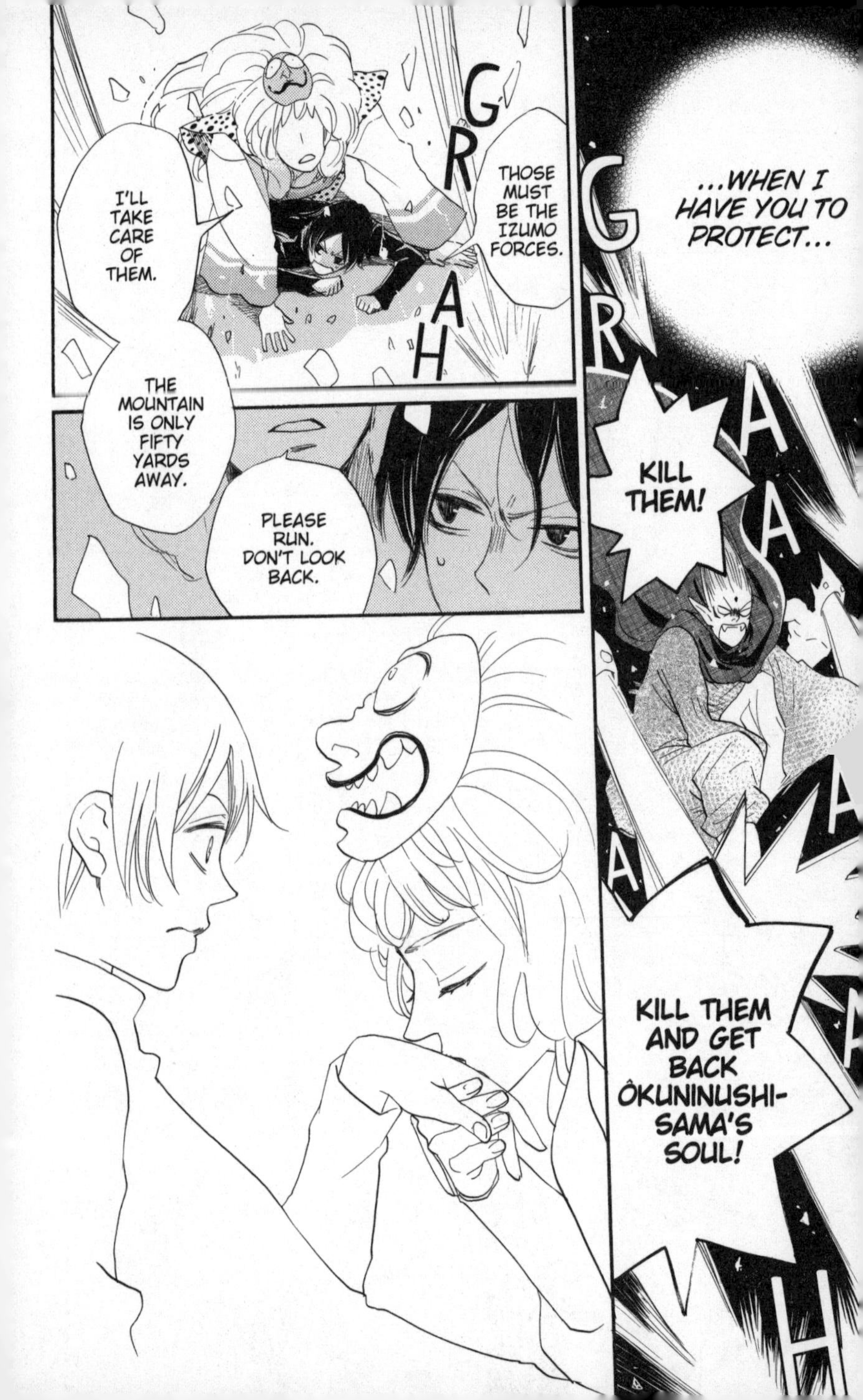
...WHEN I HAVE YOU TO PROTECT...
GRAAAAAAH
KILL THEM!
KILL THEM AND GET BACK ÔKUNINUSHI-SAMA'S SOUL!
GRAH
THOSE MUST BE THE IZUMO FORCES.
I'LL TAKE CARE OF THEM.
THE MOUNTAIN IS ONLY FIFTY YARDS AWAY.
PLEASE RUN. DON'T LOOK BACK.

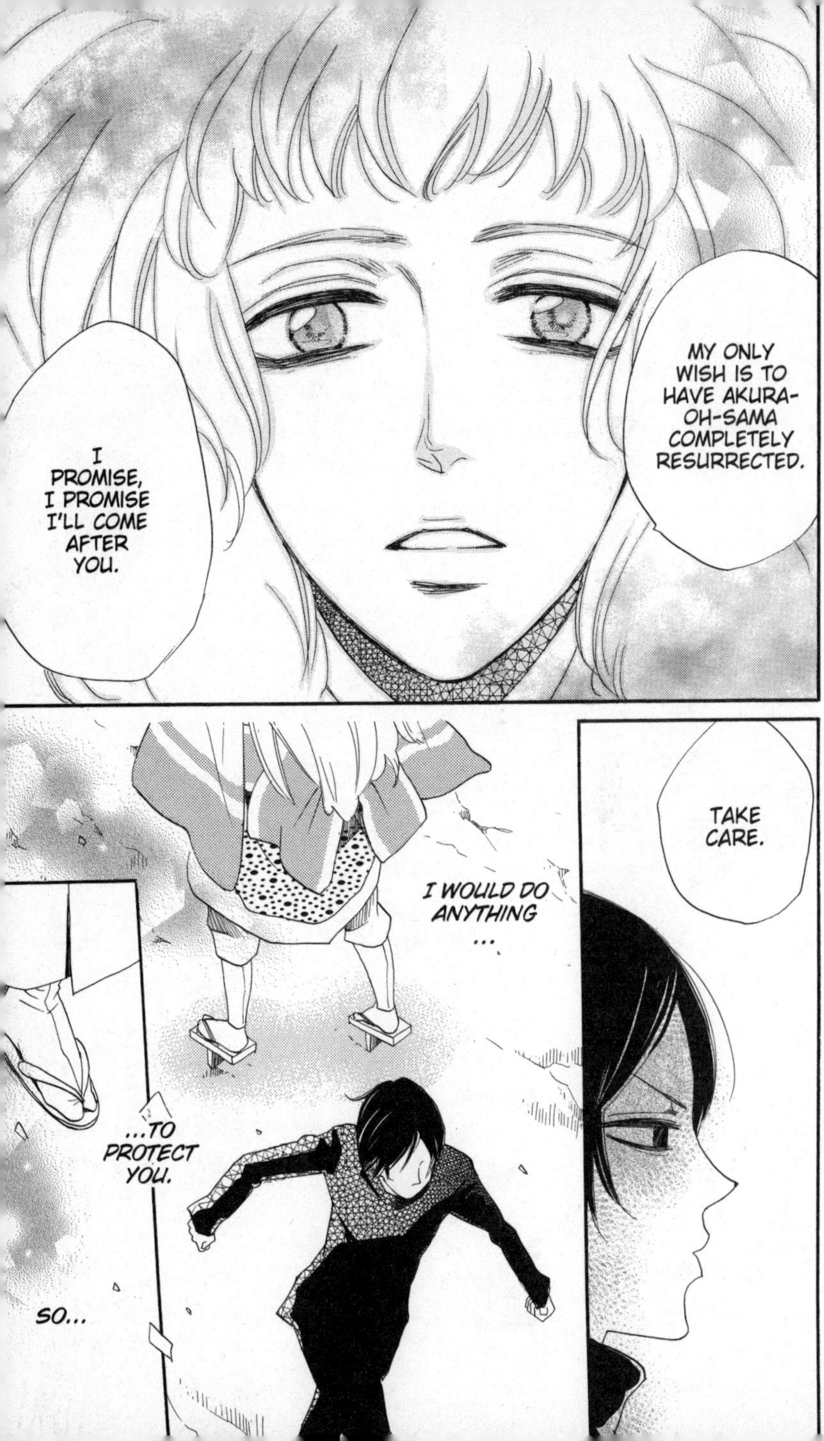
MY ONLY WISH IS TO HAVE AKURA-OH-SAMA COMPLETELY RESURRECTED.
I PROMISE, I PROMISE I'LL COME AFTER YOU.
TAKE CARE.
I WOULD DO ANYTHING...
...TO PROTECT YOU.
SO...

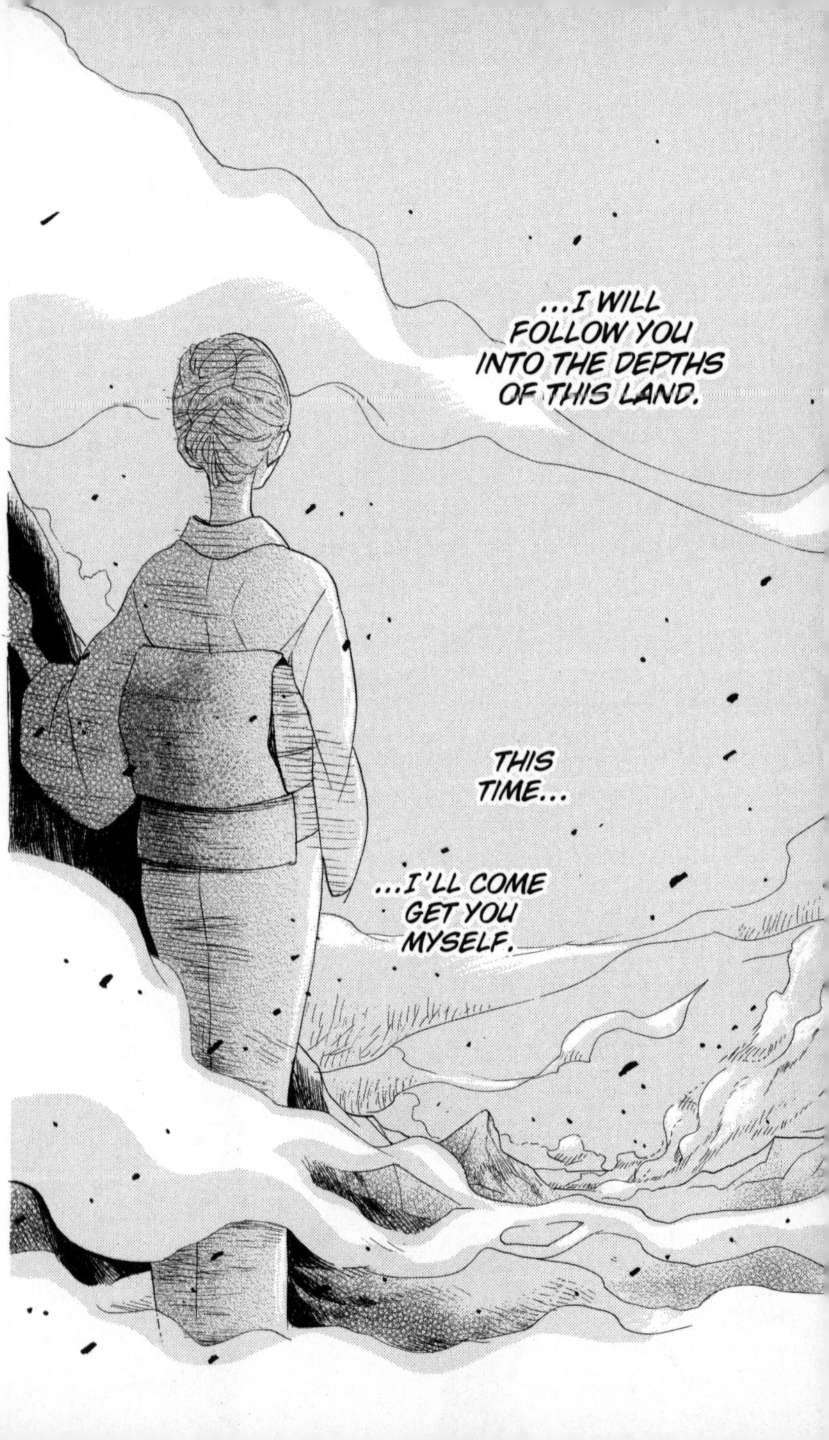
...I WILL FOLLOW YOU INTO THE DEPTHS OF THIS LAND.
THIS TIME...
...I'LL COME GET YOU MYSELF.

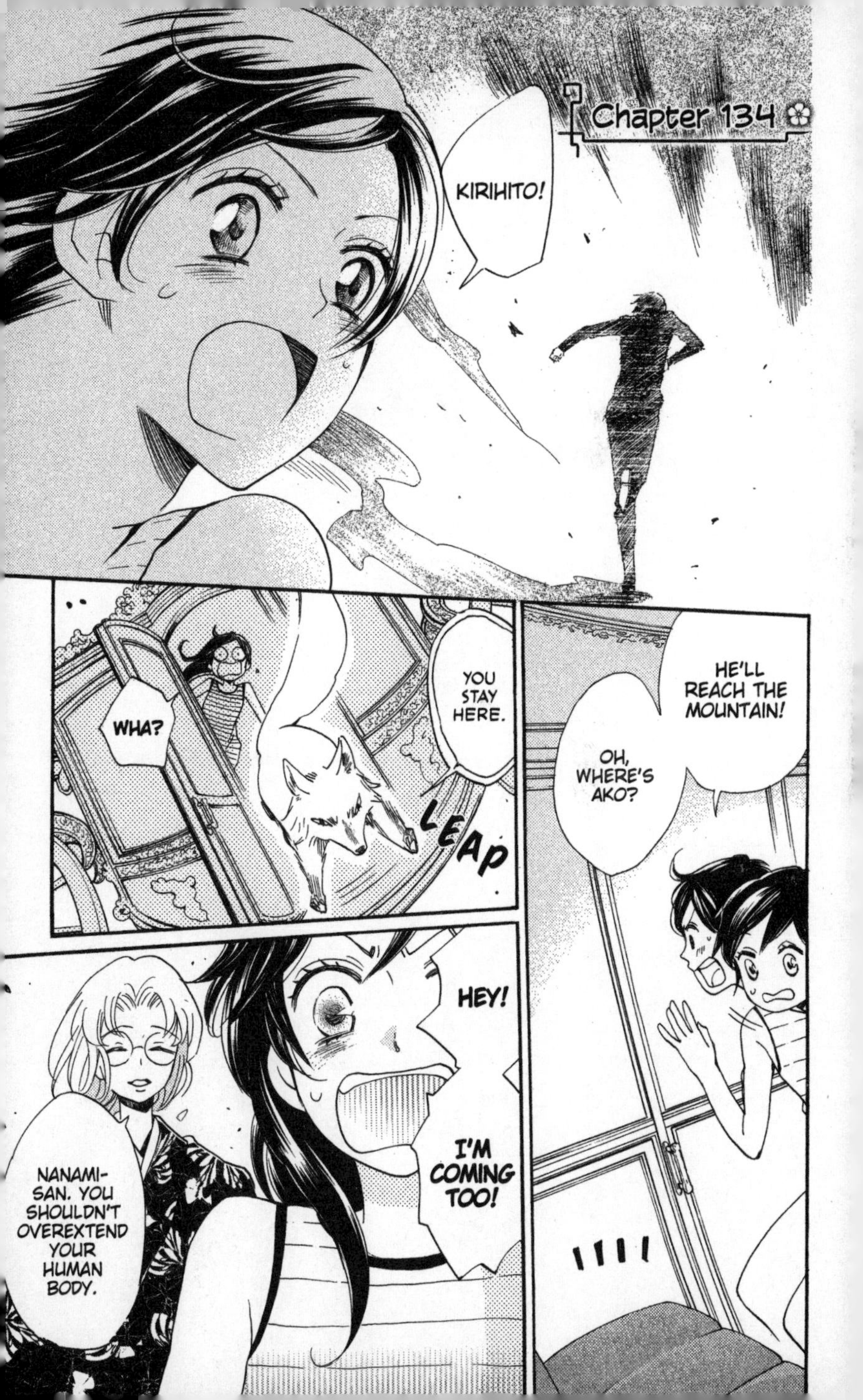

Chapter 134
KIRIHITO!
HE'LL REACH THE MOUNTAIN!
OH, WHERE'S AKO?
!!!!
YOU STAY HERE.
WHA?
LEAP
HEY!
I'M COMING TOO!
NANAMI-SAN. YOU SHOULDN'T OVEREXTEND YOUR HUMAN BODY.

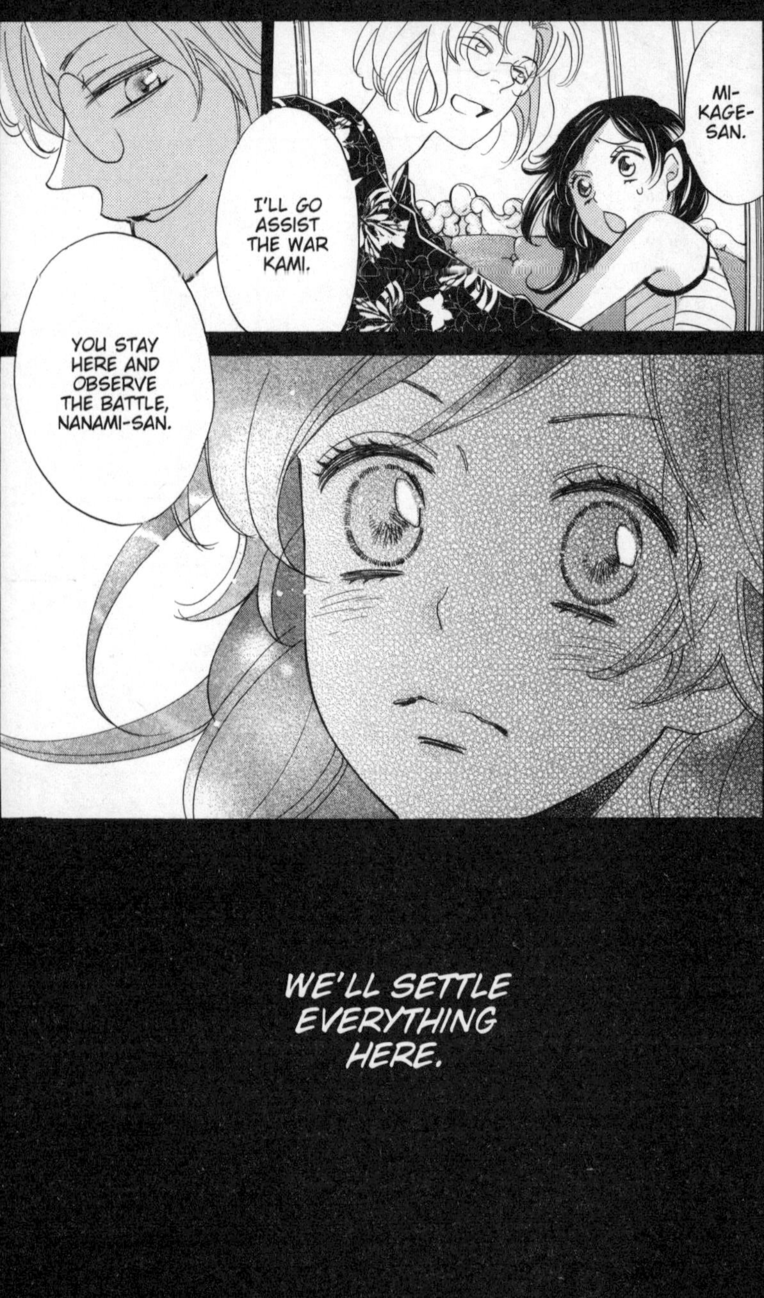
MI-KAGE-SAN.
I'LL GO ASSIST THE WAR KAMI.
YOU STAY HERE AND OBSERVE THE BATTLE, NANAMI-SAN.
WE'LL SETTLE EVERYTHING HERE.

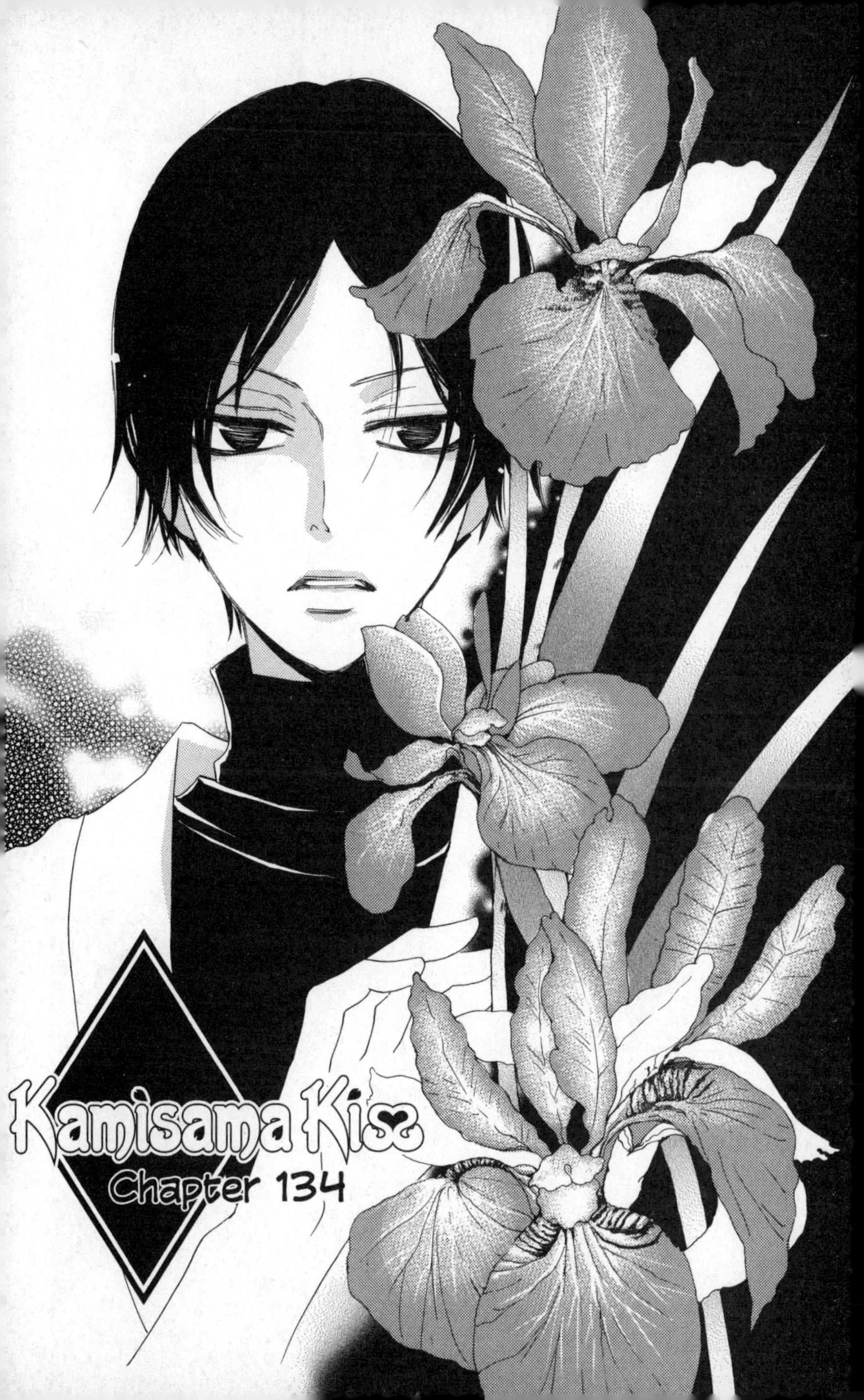
Kamisama Kiss
Chapter 134

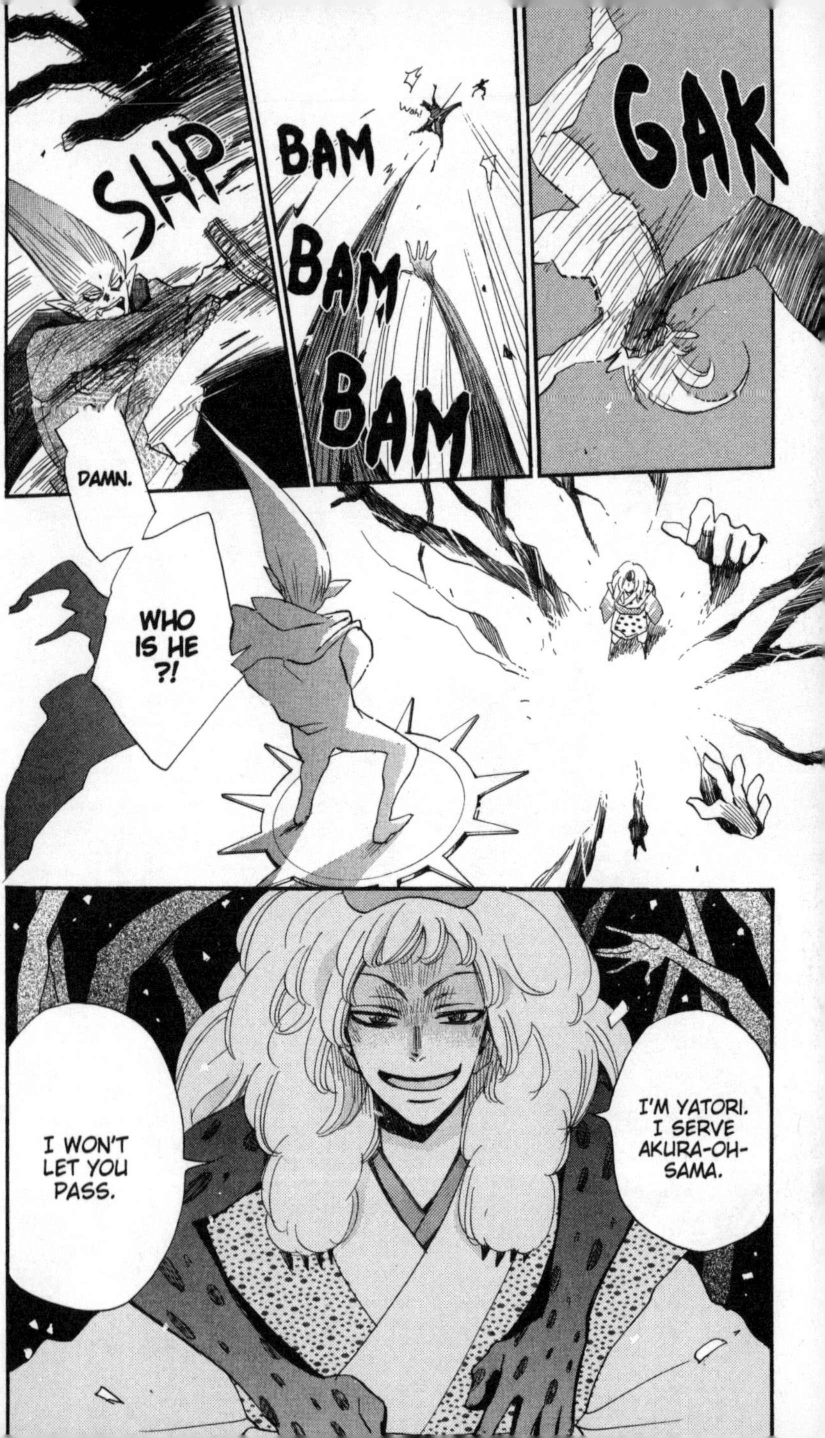
GAK
Wah!
BAM BAM BAM
SHP
DAMN.
WHO IS HE ?!
I'M YATORI. I SERVE AKURA-OH-SAMA.
I WON'T LET YOU PASS.

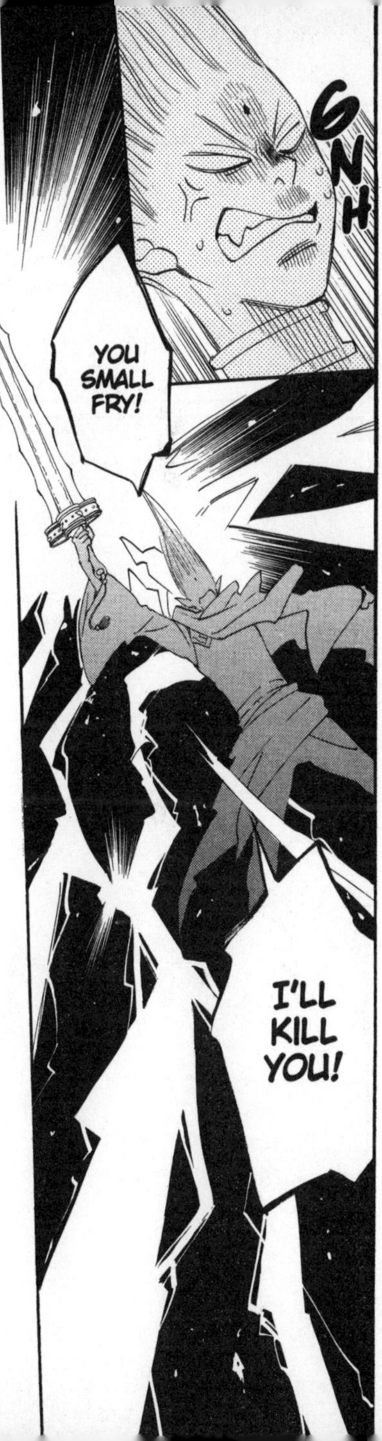
GNH
YOU SMALL FRY!
I'LL KILL YOU!

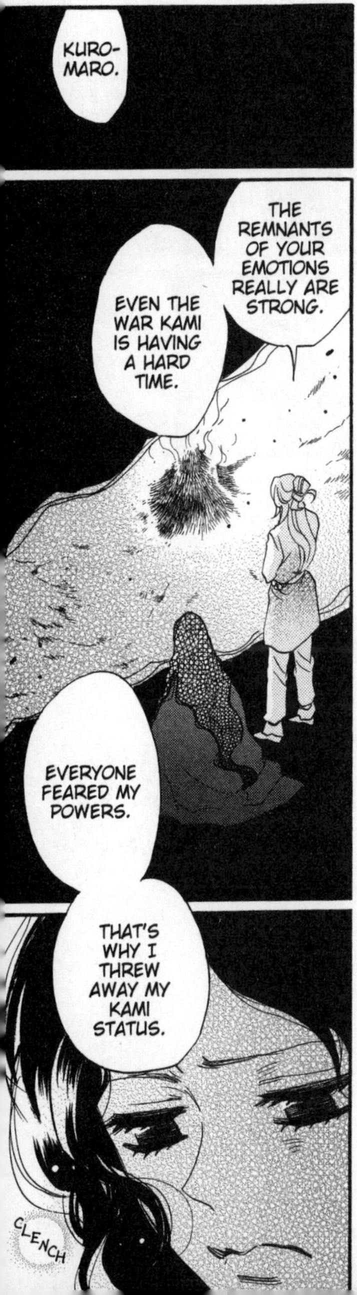
KURO-MARO.
THE REMNANTS OF YOUR EMOTIONS REALLY ARE STRONG.
EVEN THE WAR KAMI IS HAVING A HARD TIME.
EVERYONE FEARED MY POWERS.
THAT'S WHY I THREW AWAY MY KAMI STATUS.
CLENCH

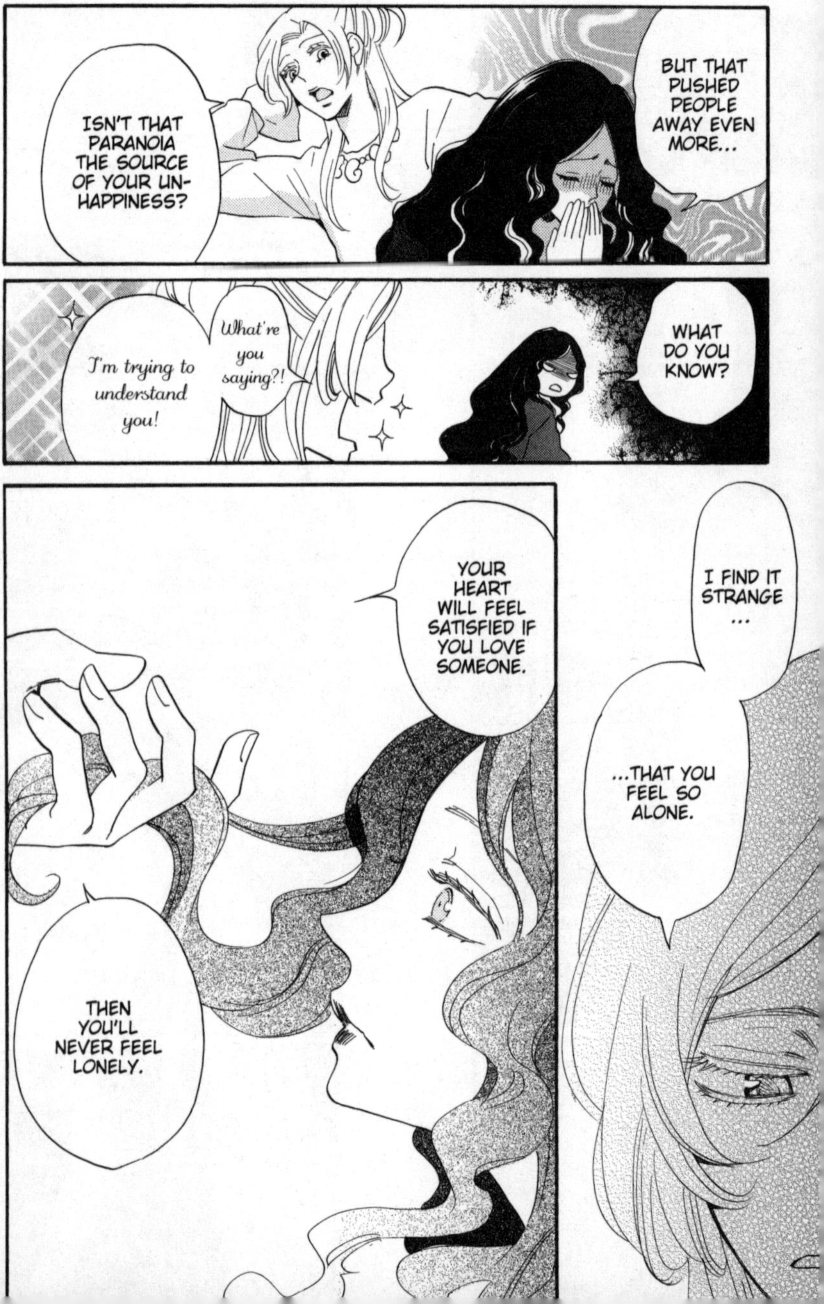
BUT THAT PUSHED PEOPLE AWAY EVEN MORE...
ISN'T THAT PARANOIA THE SOURCE OF YOUR UN-HAPPINESS?
WHAT DO YOU KNOW?
What're you saying?!
I'm trying to understand you!
I FIND IT STRANGE ...
...THAT YOU FEEL SO ALONE.
YOUR HEART WILL FEEL SATISFIED IF YOU LOVE SOMEONE.
THEN YOU'LL NEVER FEEL LONELY.

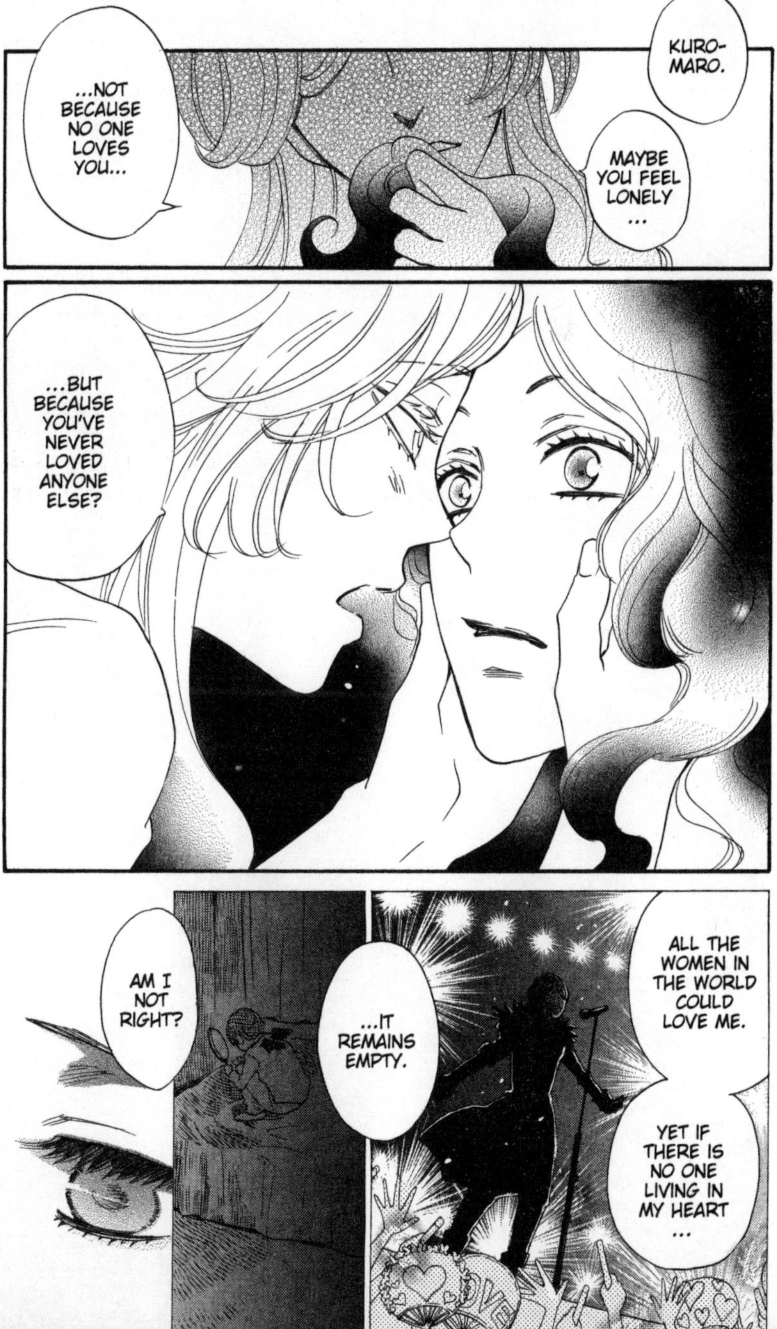
KURO-MARO.
MAYBE YOU FEEL LONELY ...
...NOT BECAUSE NO ONE LOVES YOU...
...BUT BECAUSE YOU'VE NEVER LOVED ANYONE ELSE?
ALL THE WOMEN IN THE WORLD COULD LOVE ME.
YET IF THERE IS NO ONE LIVING IN MY HEART ...
...IT REMAINS EMPTY.
AM I NOT RIGHT?

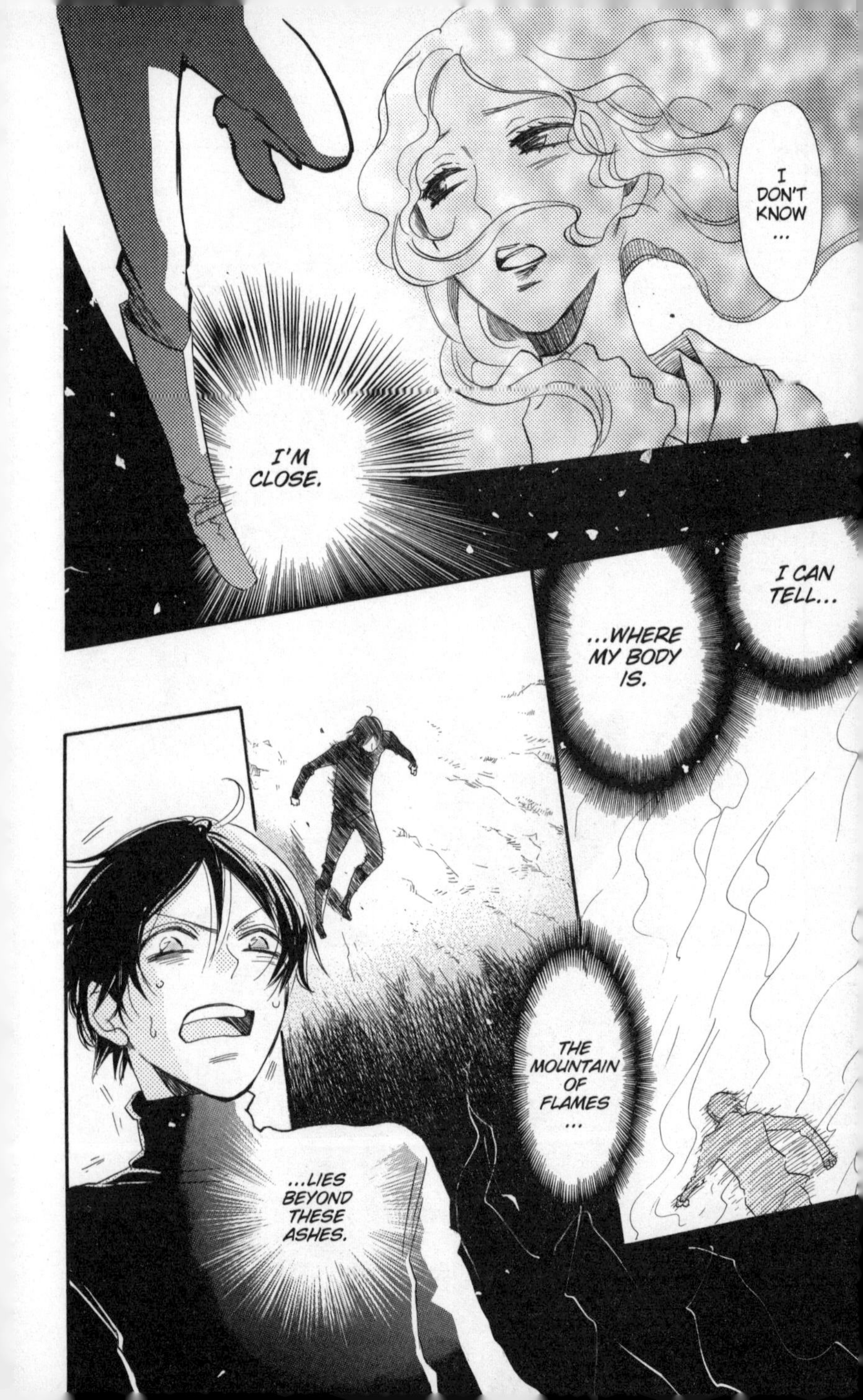
I DON'T KNOW ...
I'M CLOSE.
I CAN TELL...
...WHERE MY BODY IS.
THE MOUNTAIN OF FLAMES ...
...LIES BEYOND THESE ASHES.

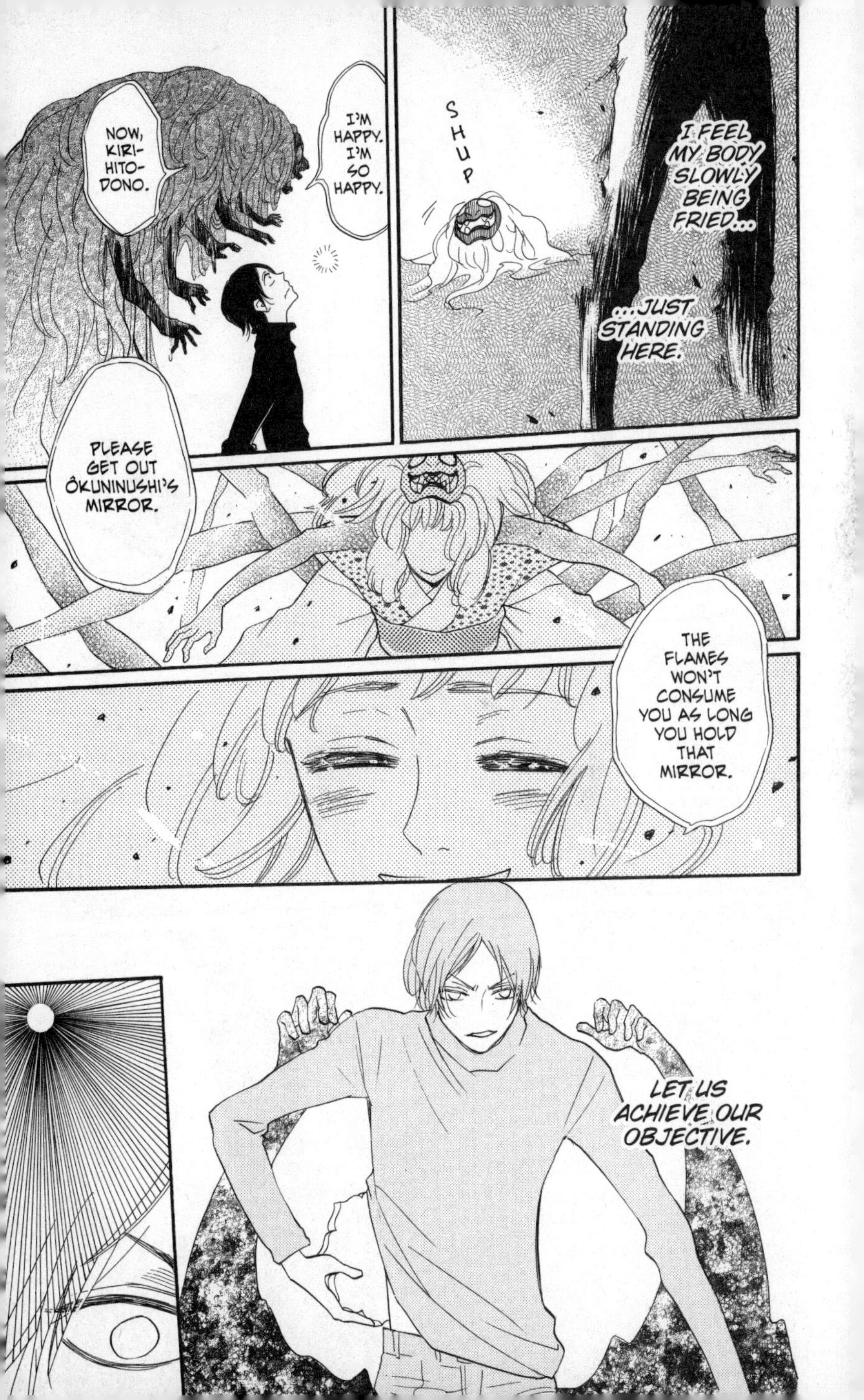
I FEEL MY BODY SLOWLY BEING FRIED...
SHUP
...JUST STANDING HERE.
I'M HAPPY. I'M SO HAPPY.
NOW, KIRI-HITO-DONO.
PLEASE GET OUT ŌKUNINUSHI'S MIRROR.
THE FLAMES WON'T CONSUME YOU AS LONG YOU HOLD THAT MIRROR.
LET US ACHIEVE OUR OBJECTIVE.

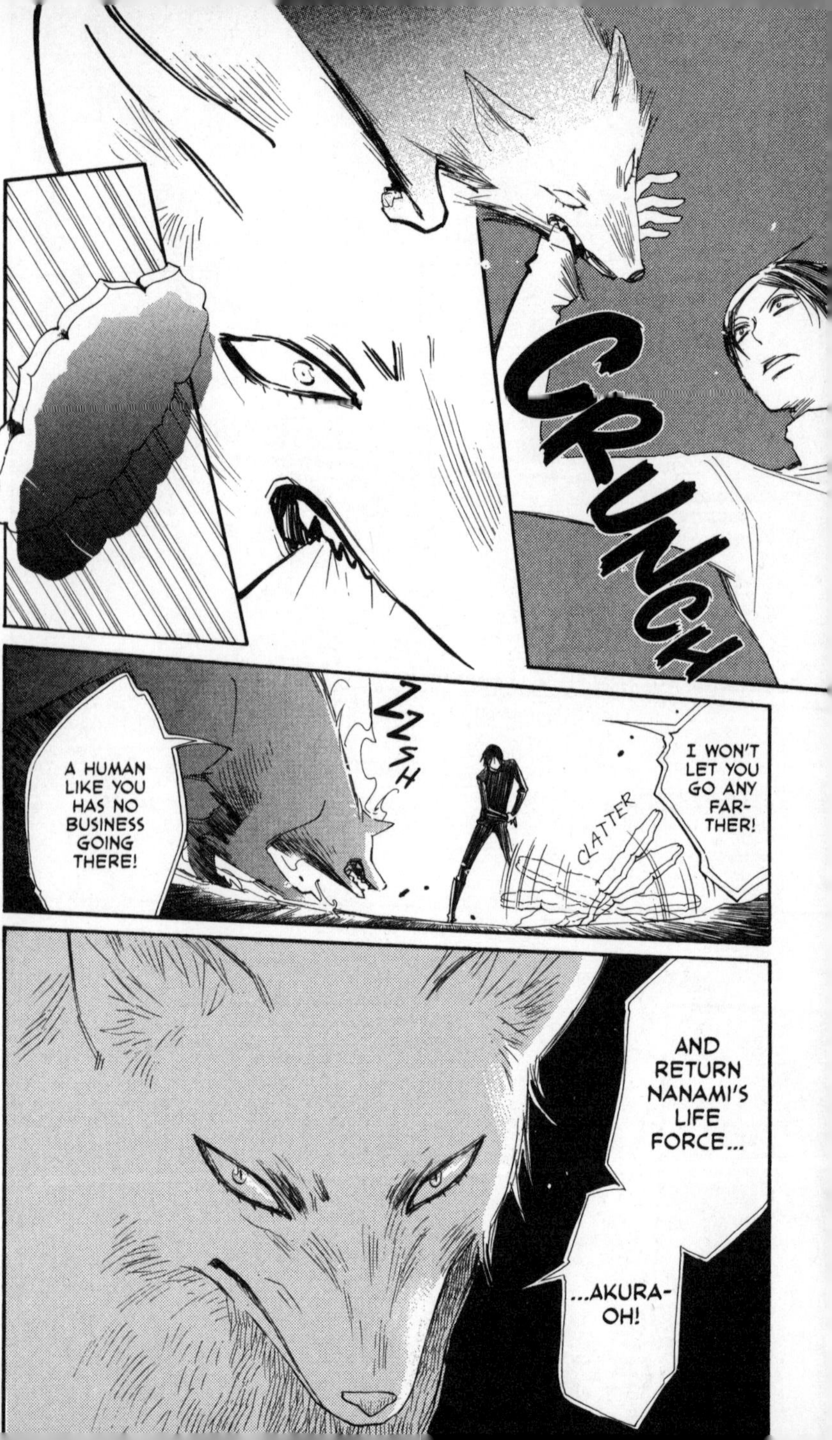
CRUNCH
I WON'T LET YOU GO ANY FAR-THER!
CLATTER
ZZSH
A HUMAN LIKE YOU HAS NO BUSINESS GOING THERE!
AND RETURN NANAMI'S LIFE FORCE...
...AKURA-OH!

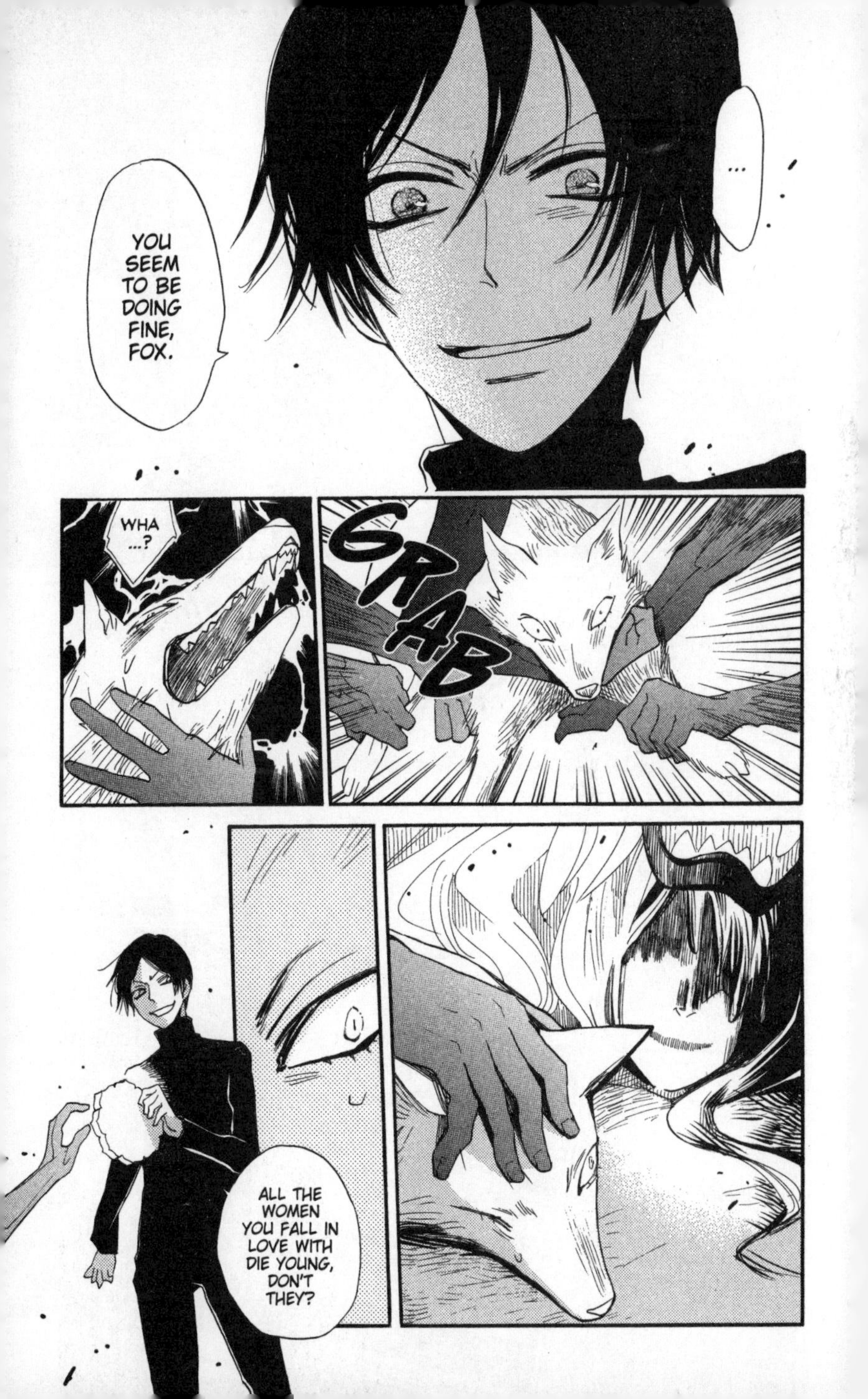
...
YOU SEEM TO BE DOING FINE, FOX.
GRAB
WHA ...?
ALL THE WOMEN YOU FALL IN LOVE WITH DIE YOUNG, DON'T THEY?

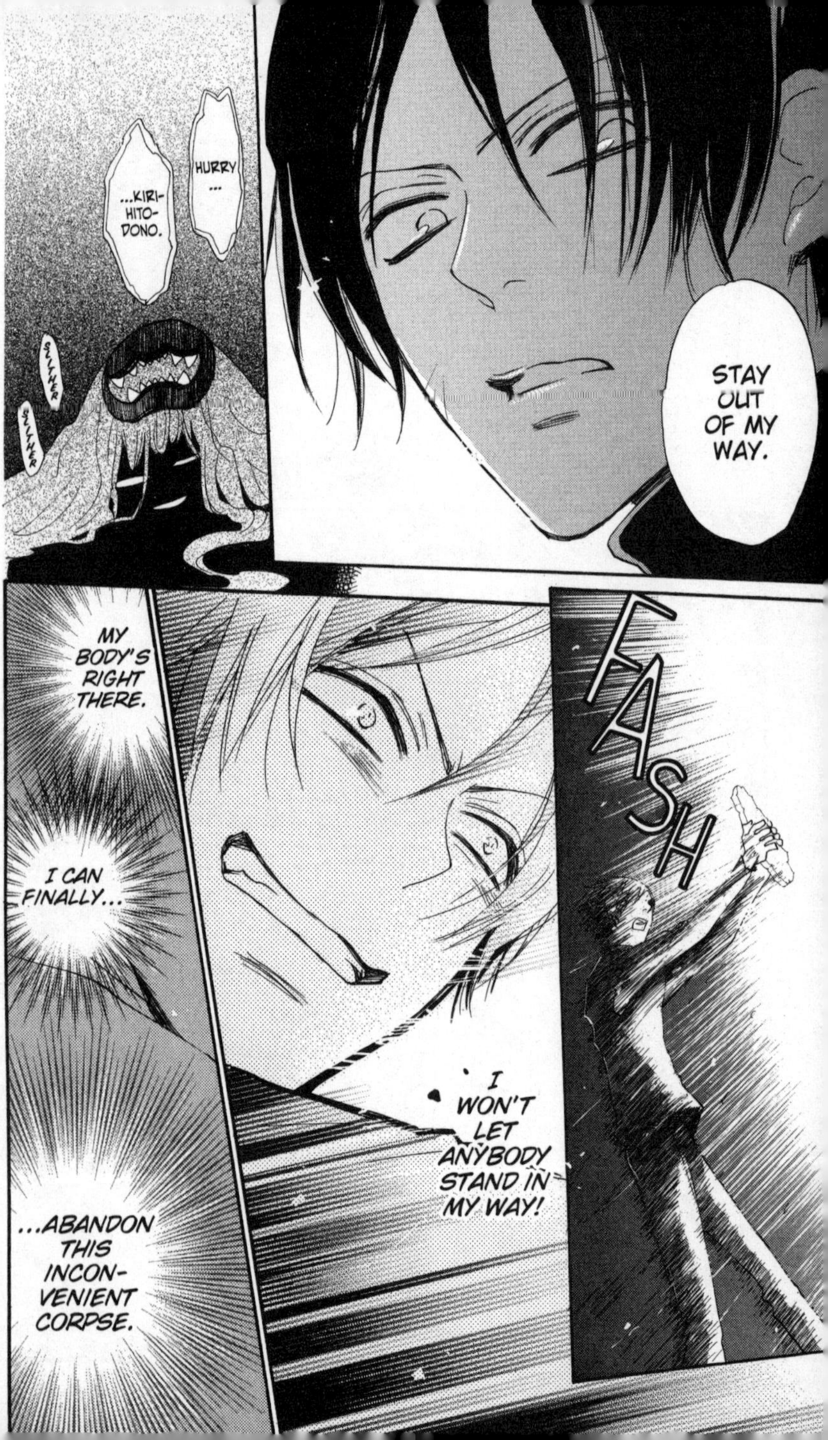
STAY OUT OF MY WAY.
HURRY...
...KIRIHITO-DONO.
SLITHER
SLITHER
FASH
I WON'T LET ANYBODY STAND IN MY WAY!
MY BODY'S RIGHT THERE.
I CAN FINALLY...
...ABANDON THIS INCONVENIENT CORPSE.

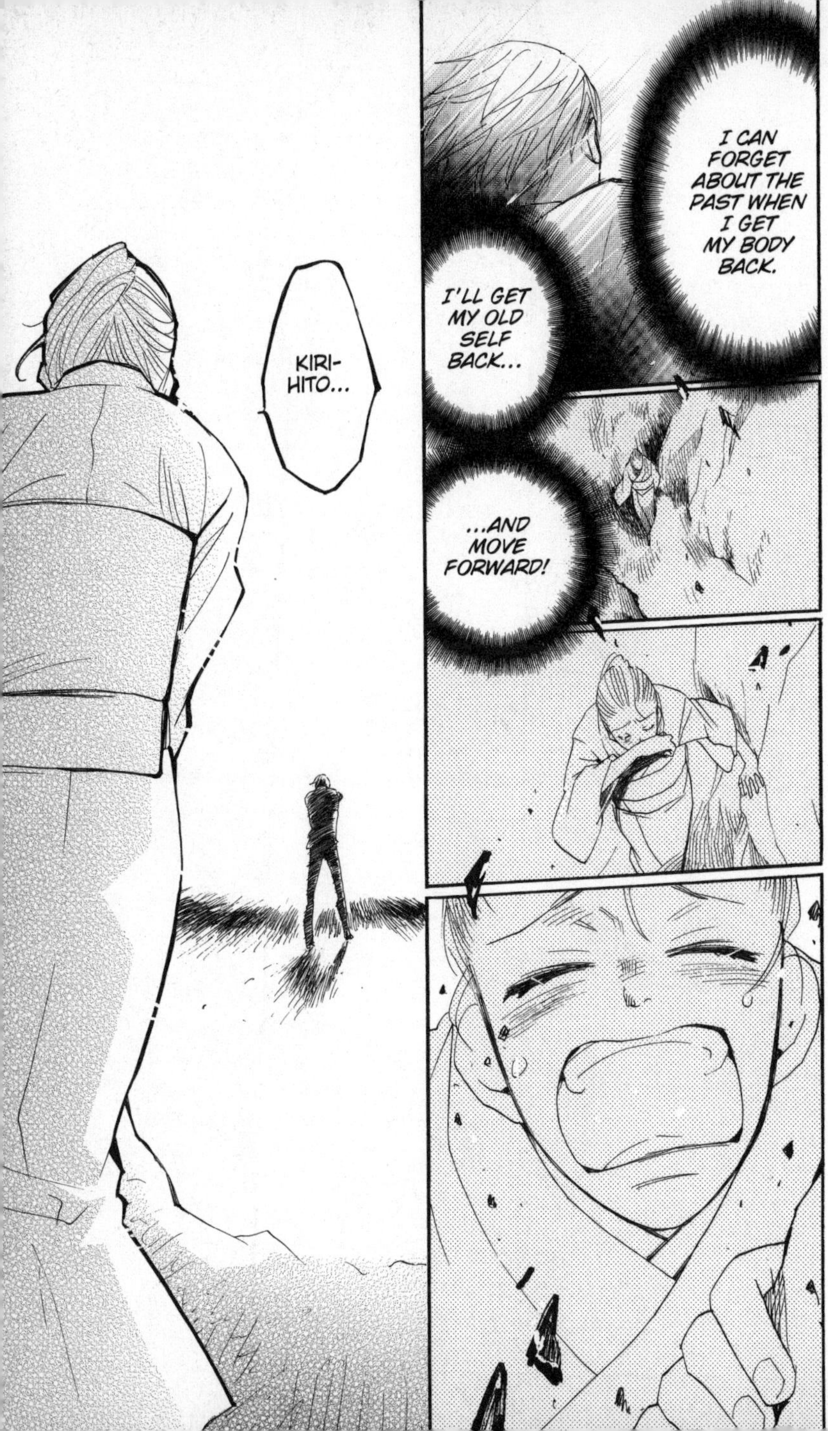
I CAN FORGET ABOUT THE PAST WHEN I GET MY BODY BACK.
I'LL GET MY OLD SELF BACK...
...AND MOVE FORWARD!
KIRI-HITO...

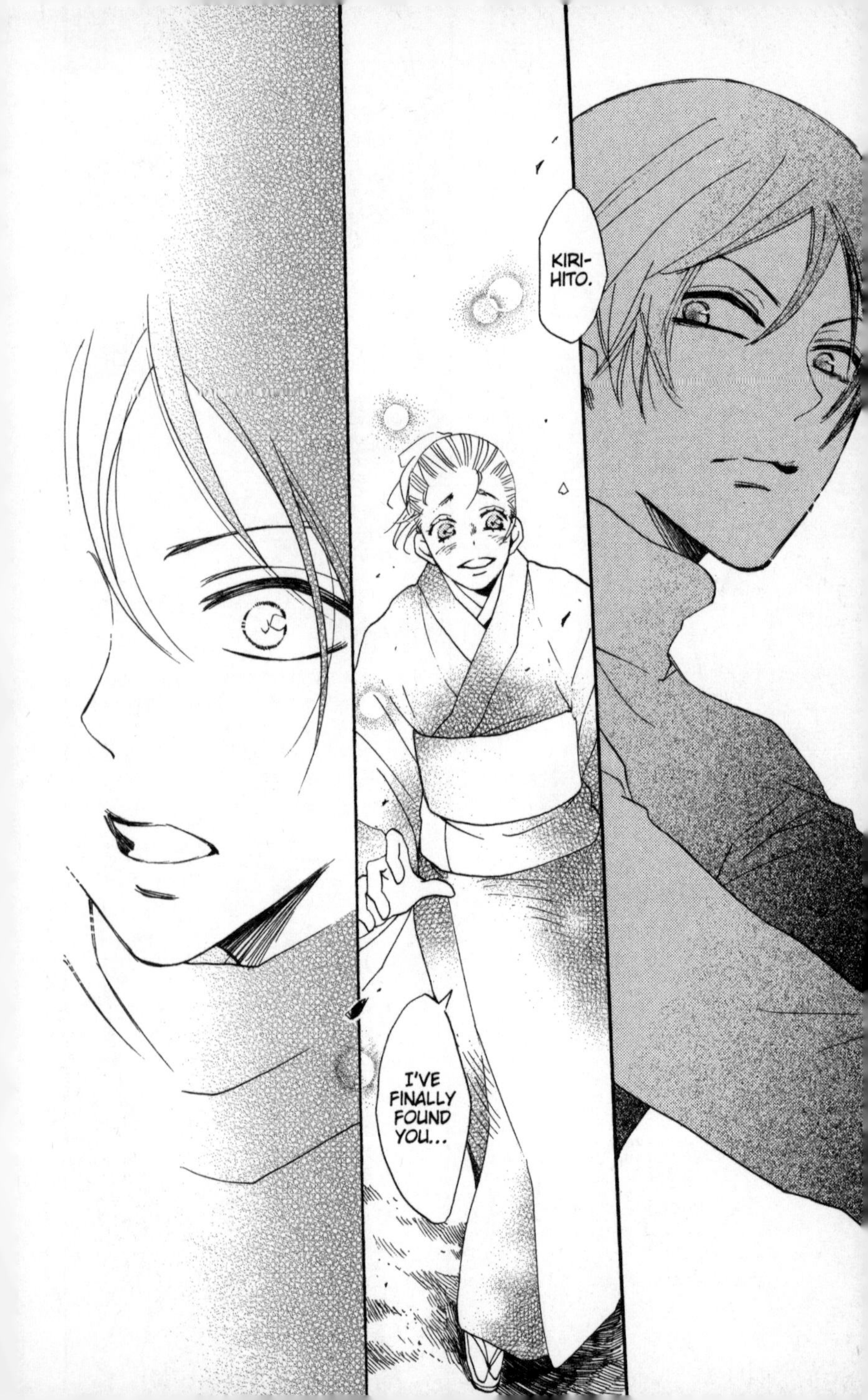
KIRI-HITO.
I'VE FINALLY FOUND YOU...

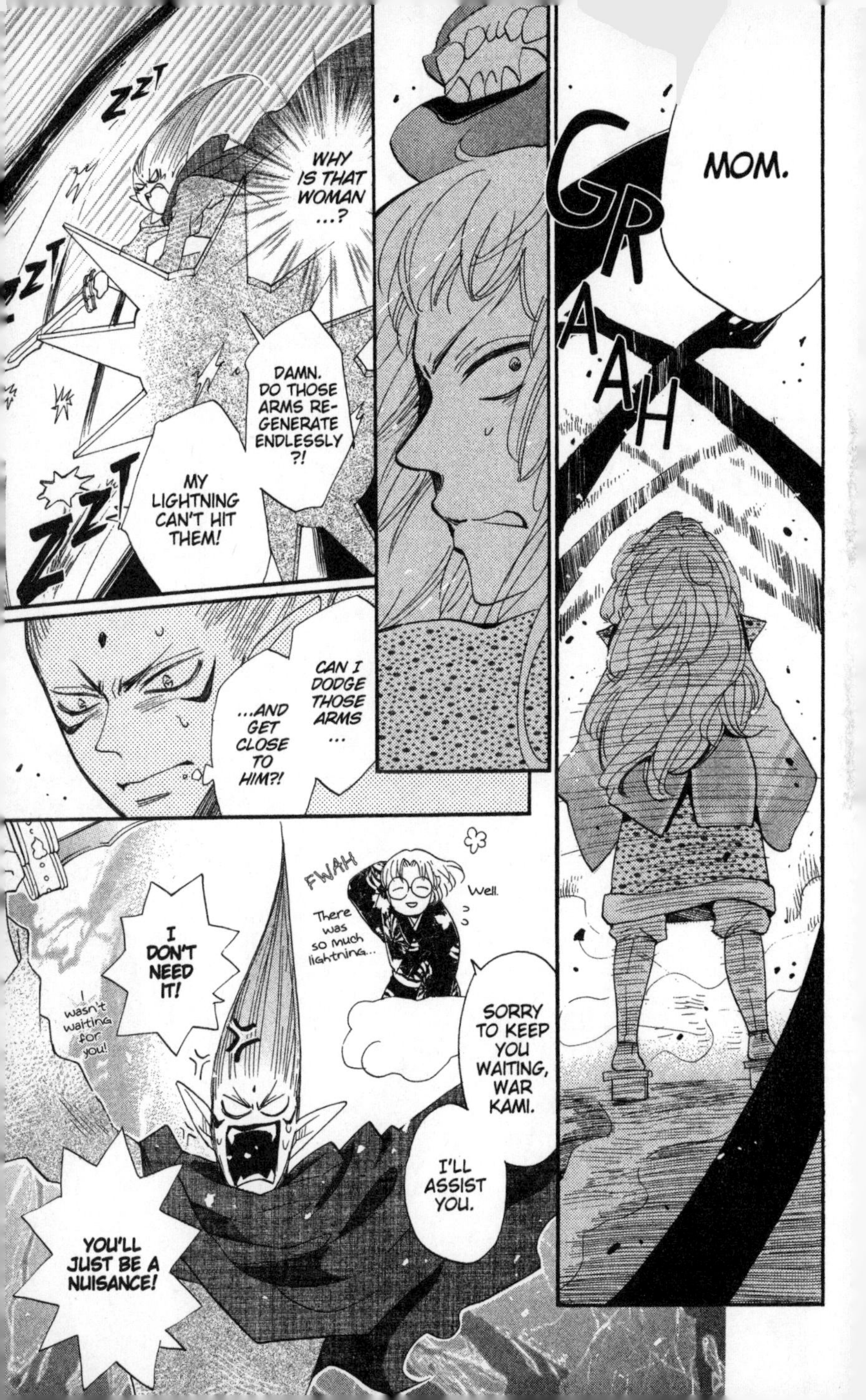
MOM.
GRAAAH
WHY IS THAT WOMAN ...?
ZZZT
ZZZT
DAMN. DO THOSE ARMS REGENERATE ENDLESSLY?!
MY LIGHTNING CAN'T HIT THEM!
ZZZT
CAN I DODGE THOSE ARMS ...
...AND GET CLOSE TO HIM?!
FWAH
Well.
There was so much lightning...
SORRY TO KEEP YOU WAITING, WAR KAMI.
I'LL ASSIST YOU.
I DON'T NEED IT!
I wasn't waiting for you!
YOU'LL JUST BE A NUISANCE!

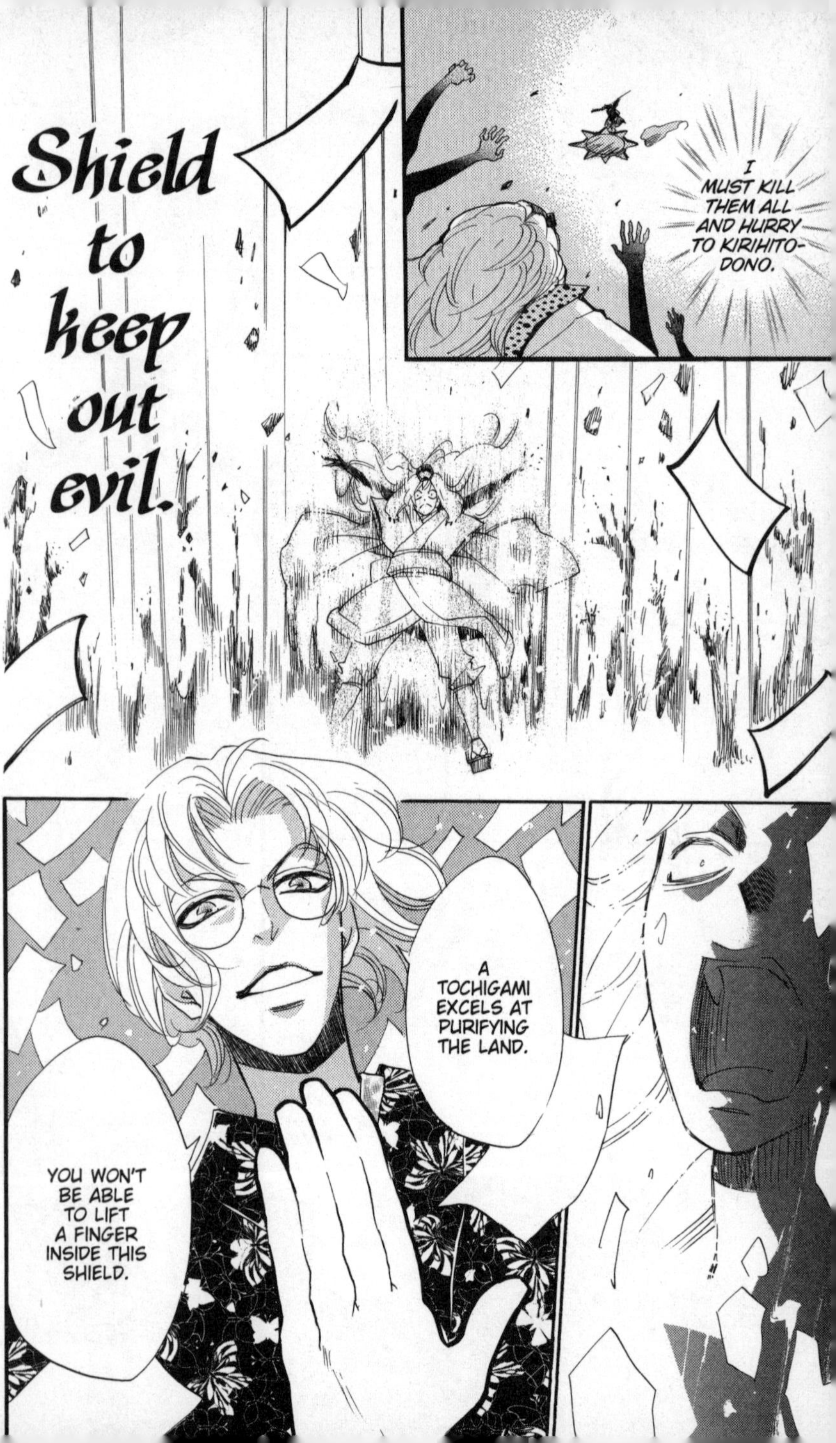
I MUST KILL THEM ALL AND HURRY TO KIRIHITO-DONO.
Shield to keep out evil.
A TOCHIGAMI EXCELS AT PURIFYING THE LAND.
YOU WON'T BE ABLE TO LIFT A FINGER INSIDE THIS SHIELD.

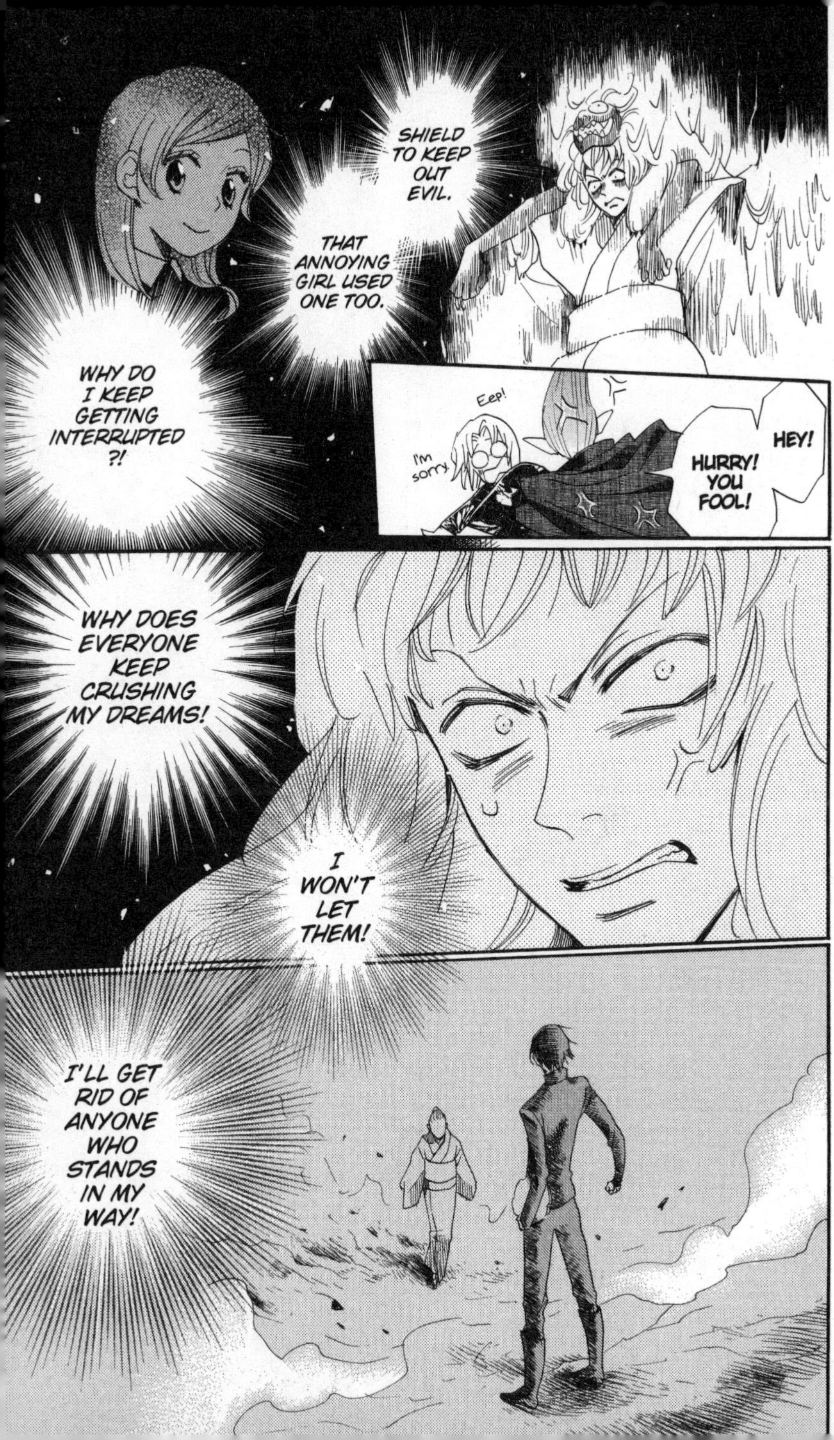
SHIELD TO KEEP OUT EVIL.
THAT ANNOYING GIRL USED ONE TOO.
WHY DO I KEEP GETTING INTERRUPTED ?!
HEY!
HURRY! YOU FOOL!
Eep!
I'm sorry.
WHY DOES EVERYONE KEEP CRUSHING MY DREAMS!
I WON'T LET THEM!
I'LL GET RID OF ANYONE WHO STANDS IN MY WAY!

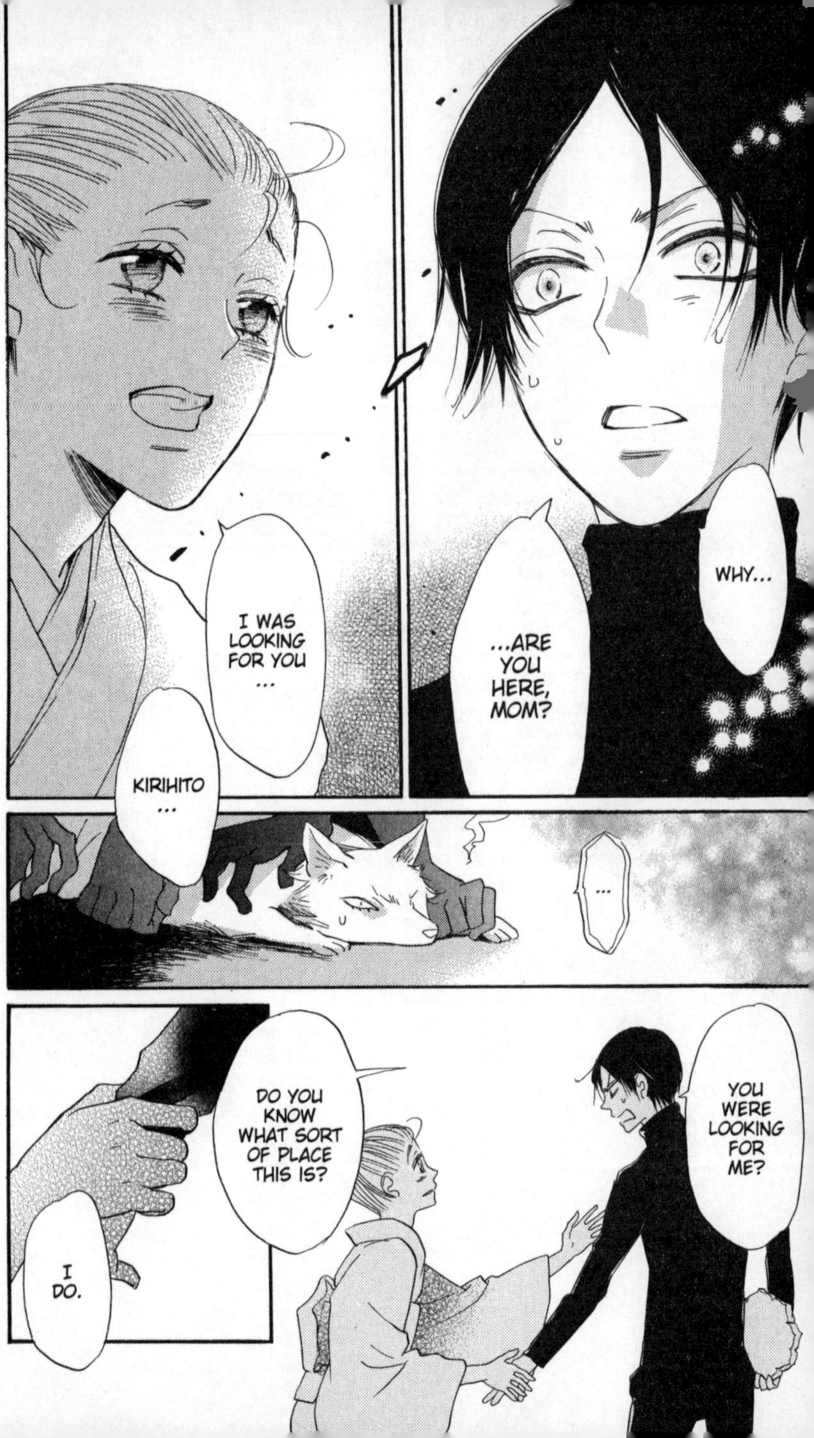
WHY...
...ARE YOU HERE, MOM?
I WAS LOOKING FOR YOU ...
KIRIHITO ...
...
YOU WERE LOOKING FOR ME?
DO YOU KNOW WHAT SORT OF PLACE THIS IS?
I DO.

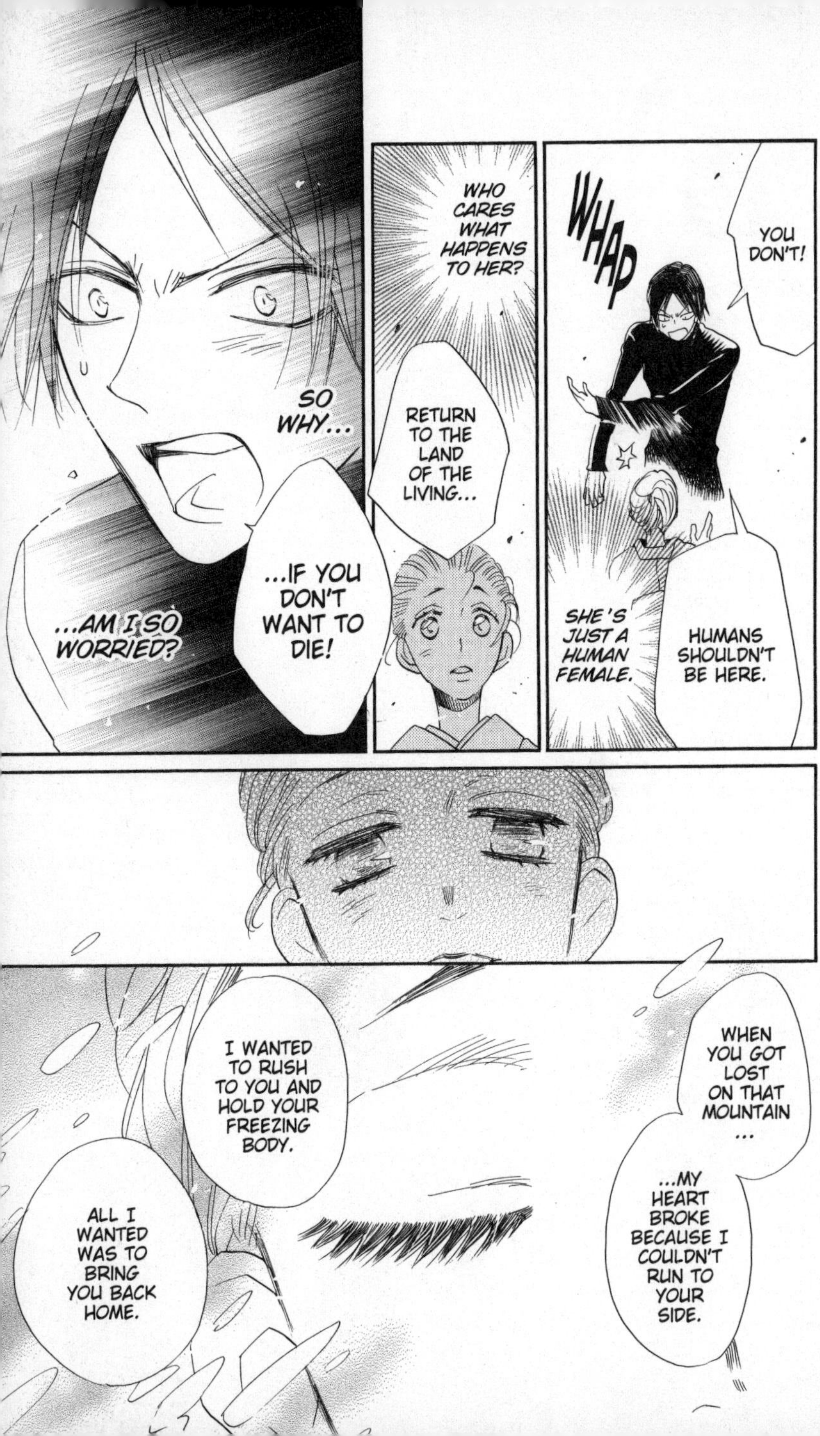
YOU DON'T!
WHAP
HUMANS SHOULDN'T BE HERE.
SHE'S JUST A HUMAN FEMALE.
WHO CARES WHAT HAPPENS TO HER?
RETURN TO THE LAND OF THE LIVING...
...IF YOU DON'T WANT TO DIE!
SO WHY...
...AM I SO WORRIED?
WHEN YOU GOT LOST ON THAT MOUNTAIN...
...MY HEART BROKE BECAUSE I COULDN'T RUN TO YOUR SIDE.
I WANTED TO RUSH TO YOU AND HOLD YOUR FREEZING BODY.
ALL I WANTED WAS TO BRING YOU BACK HOME.

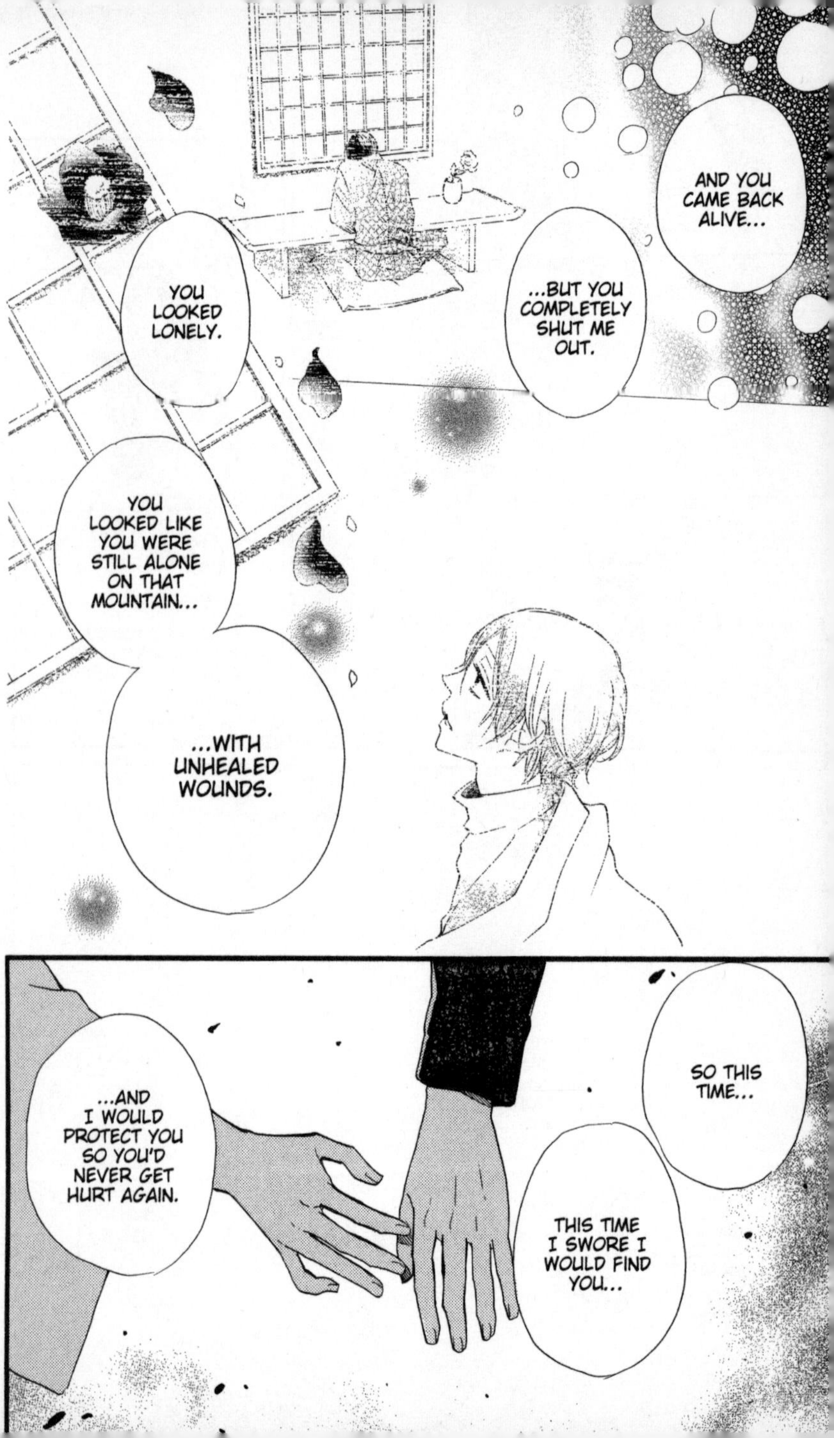
AND YOU CAME BACK ALIVE...
...BUT YOU COMPLETELY SHUT ME OUT.
YOU LOOKED LONELY.
YOU LOOKED LIKE YOU WERE STILL ALONE ON THAT MOUNTAIN...
...WITH UNHEALED WOUNDS.
SO THIS TIME...
THIS TIME I SWORE I WOULD FIND YOU...
...AND I WOULD PROTECT YOU SO YOU'D NEVER GET HURT AGAIN.

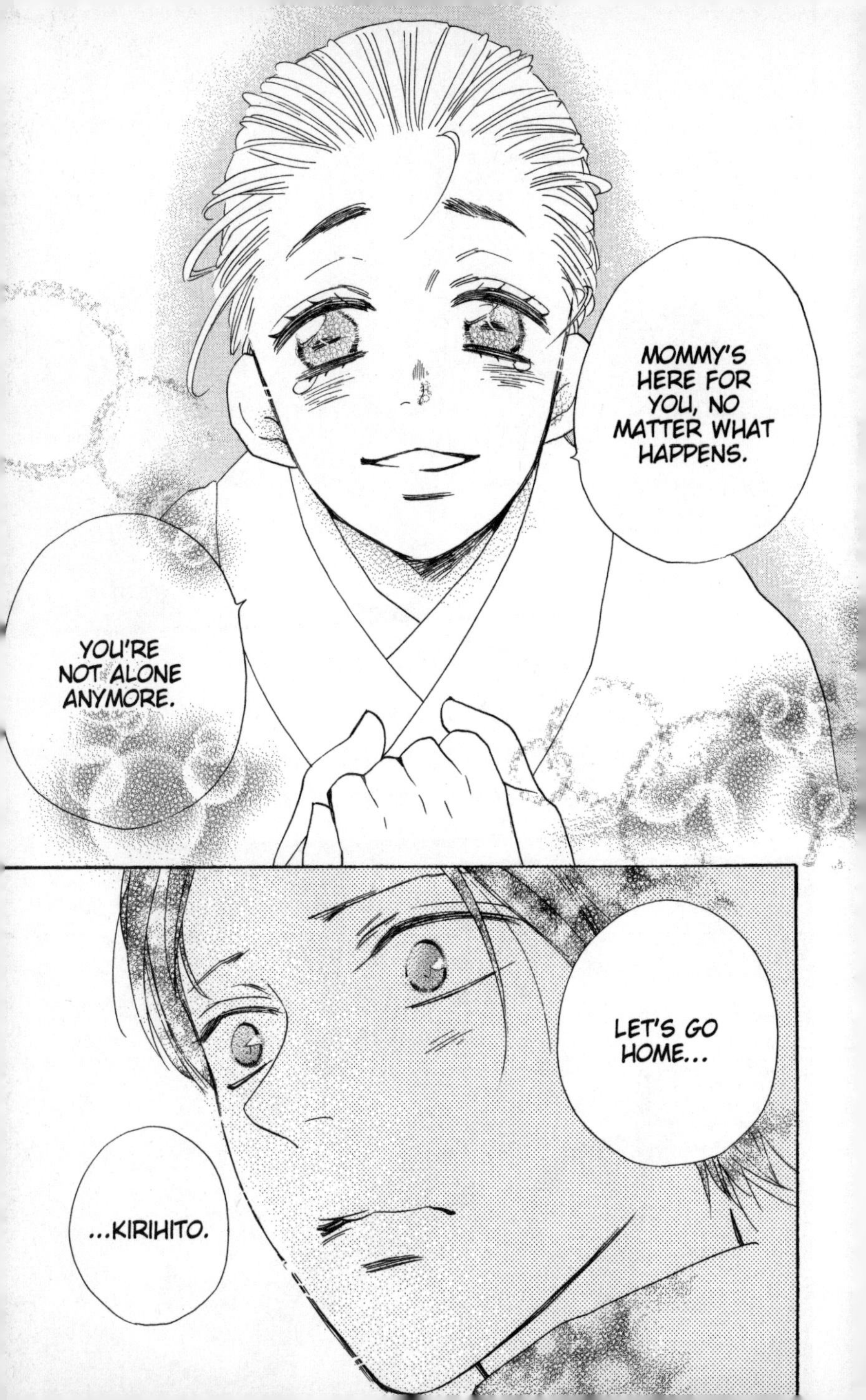
MOMMY'S HERE FOR YOU, NO MATTER WHAT HAPPENS.
YOU'RE NOT ALONE ANYMORE.
LET'S GO HOME...
...KIRIHITO.

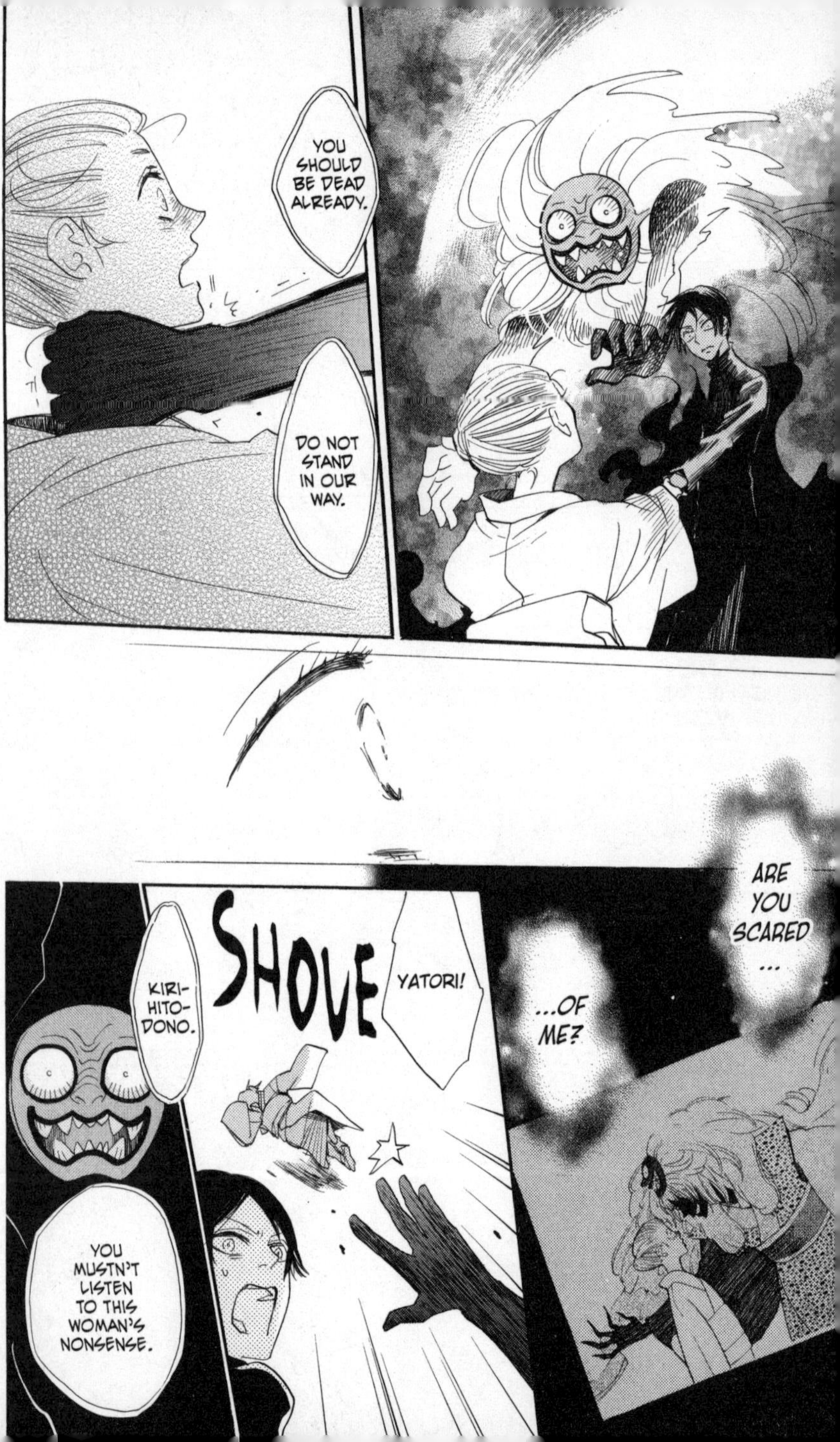

YOU SHOULD BE DEAD ALREADY.
DO NOT STAND IN OUR WAY.
ARE YOU SCARED...
...OF ME?
YATORI!
SHOVE
KIRI-HITO-DONO.
YOU MUSTN'T LISTEN TO THIS WOMAN'S NONSENSE.

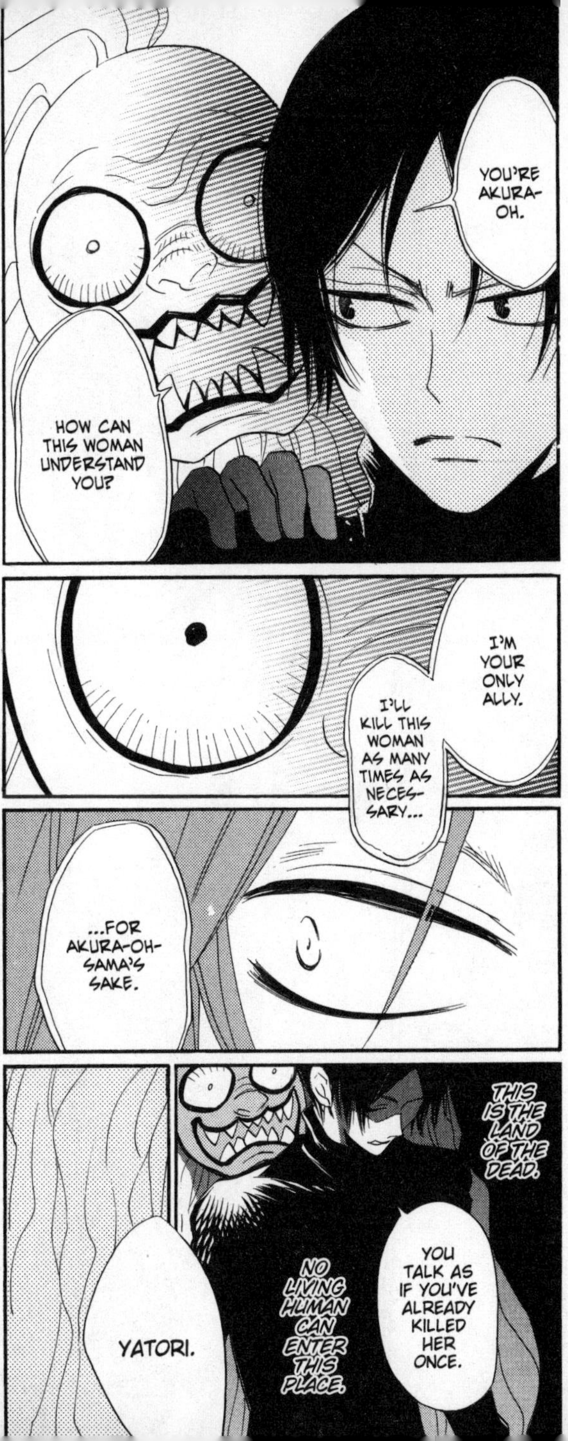
YOU'RE AKURA-OH.
HOW CAN THIS WOMAN UNDERSTAND YOU?
I'M YOUR ONLY ALLY.
I'LL KILL THIS WOMAN AS MANY TIMES AS NECES-SARY...
...FOR AKURA-OH-SAMA'S SAKE.
THIS IS THE LAND OF THE DEAD.
YOU TALK AS IF YOU'VE ALREADY KILLED HER ONCE.
NO LIVING HUMAN CAN ENTER THIS PLACE.
YATORI.

I started to pay more attention to what I eat after I was under the weather.

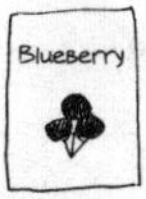
Blueberry

I use my eyes a lot more nowadays, so I've begun to take blueberry supplements in addition to using eye drops. I hope it'll help.

I'm also having problems with my jaw, so I need more calcium!

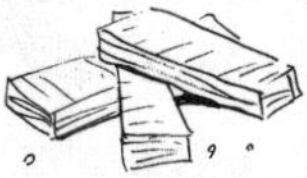

So I eat calcium-fortified wafers.

Warm milk is also a must.

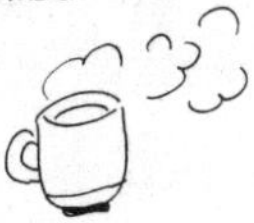

And seaweed seasoned with vinegar.

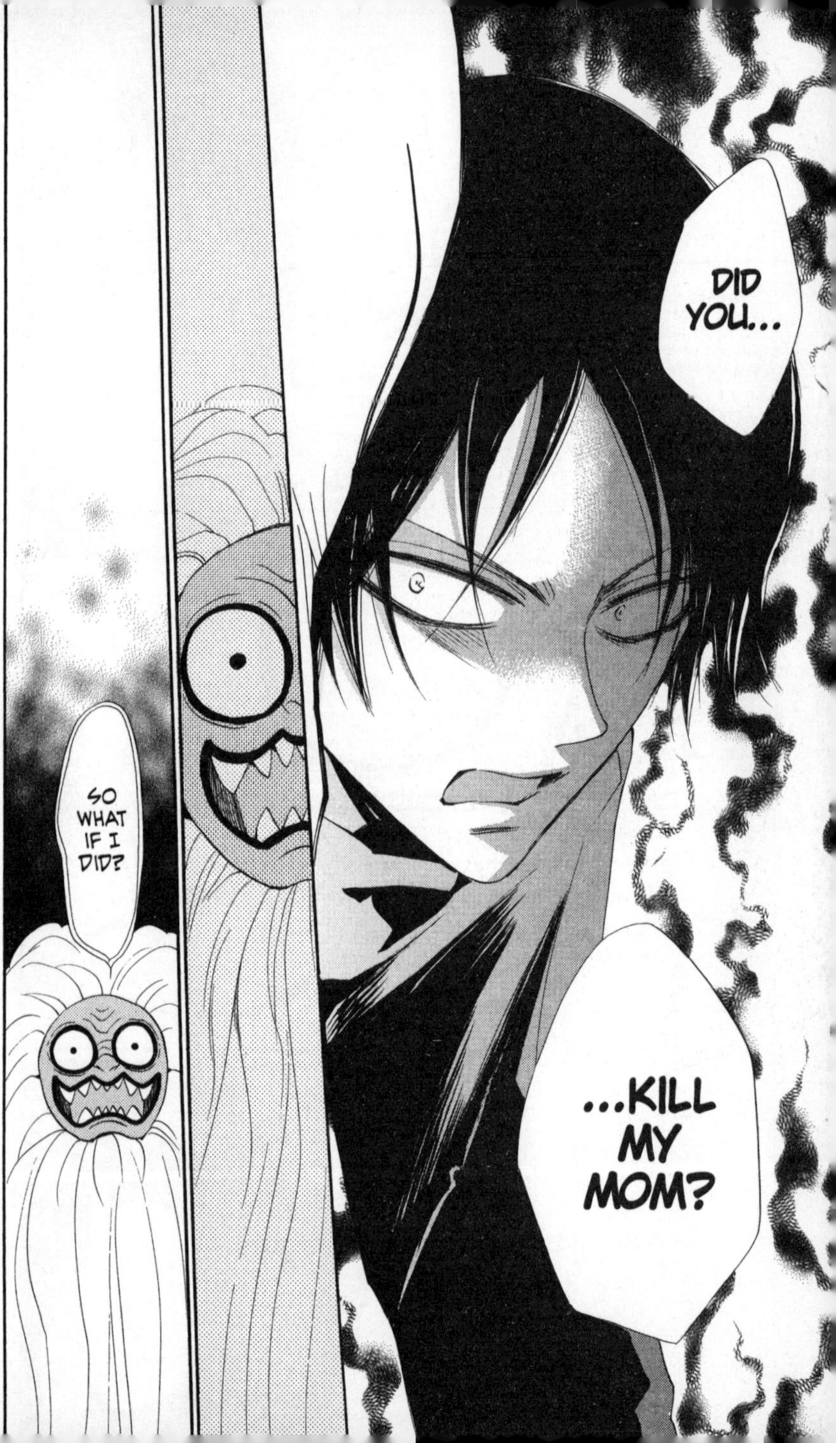
DID YOU...
...KILL MY MOM?
SO WHAT IF I DID?

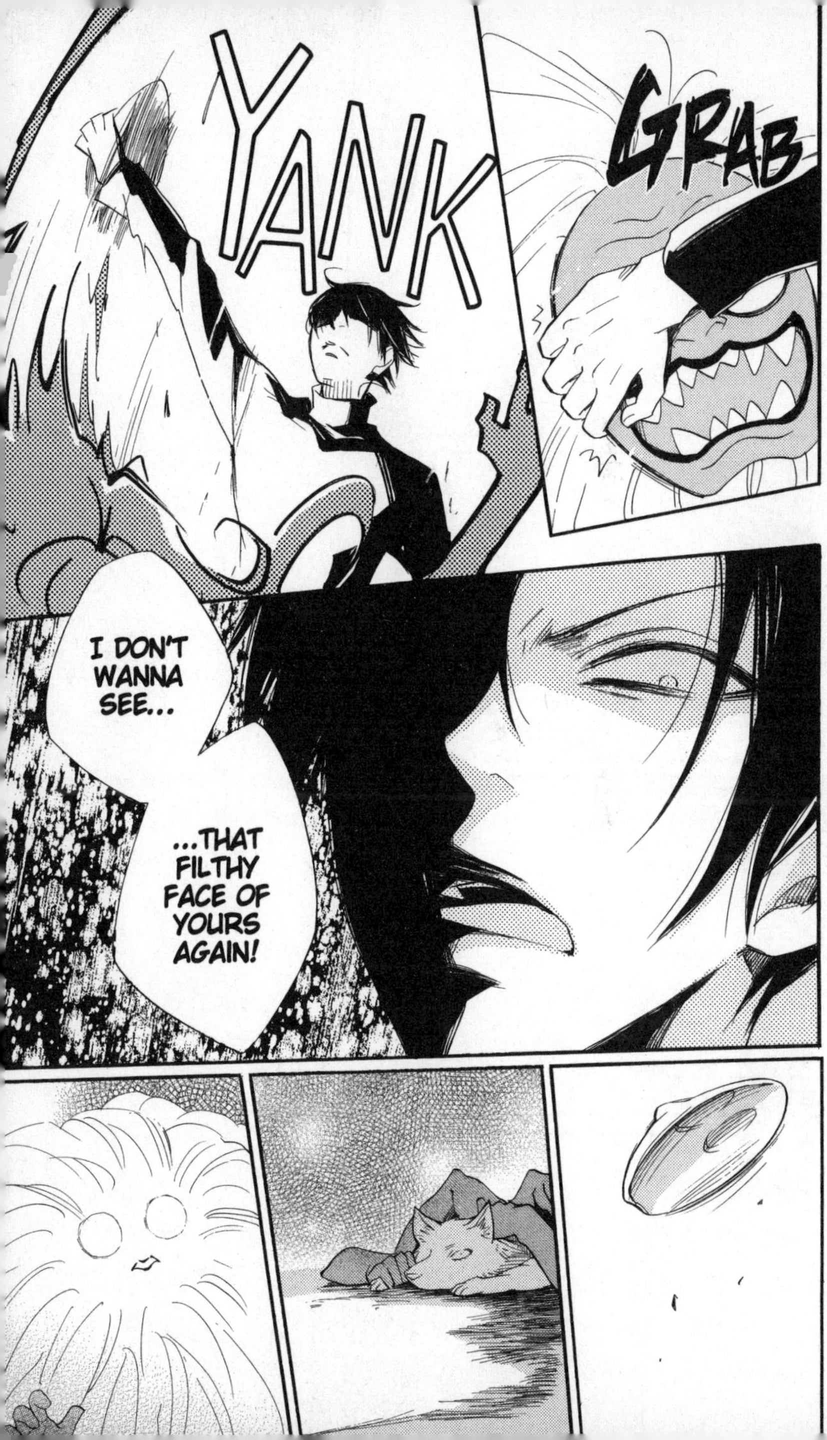
GRAB
YANK
I DON'T WANNA SEE...
...THAT FILTHY FACE OF YOURS AGAIN!

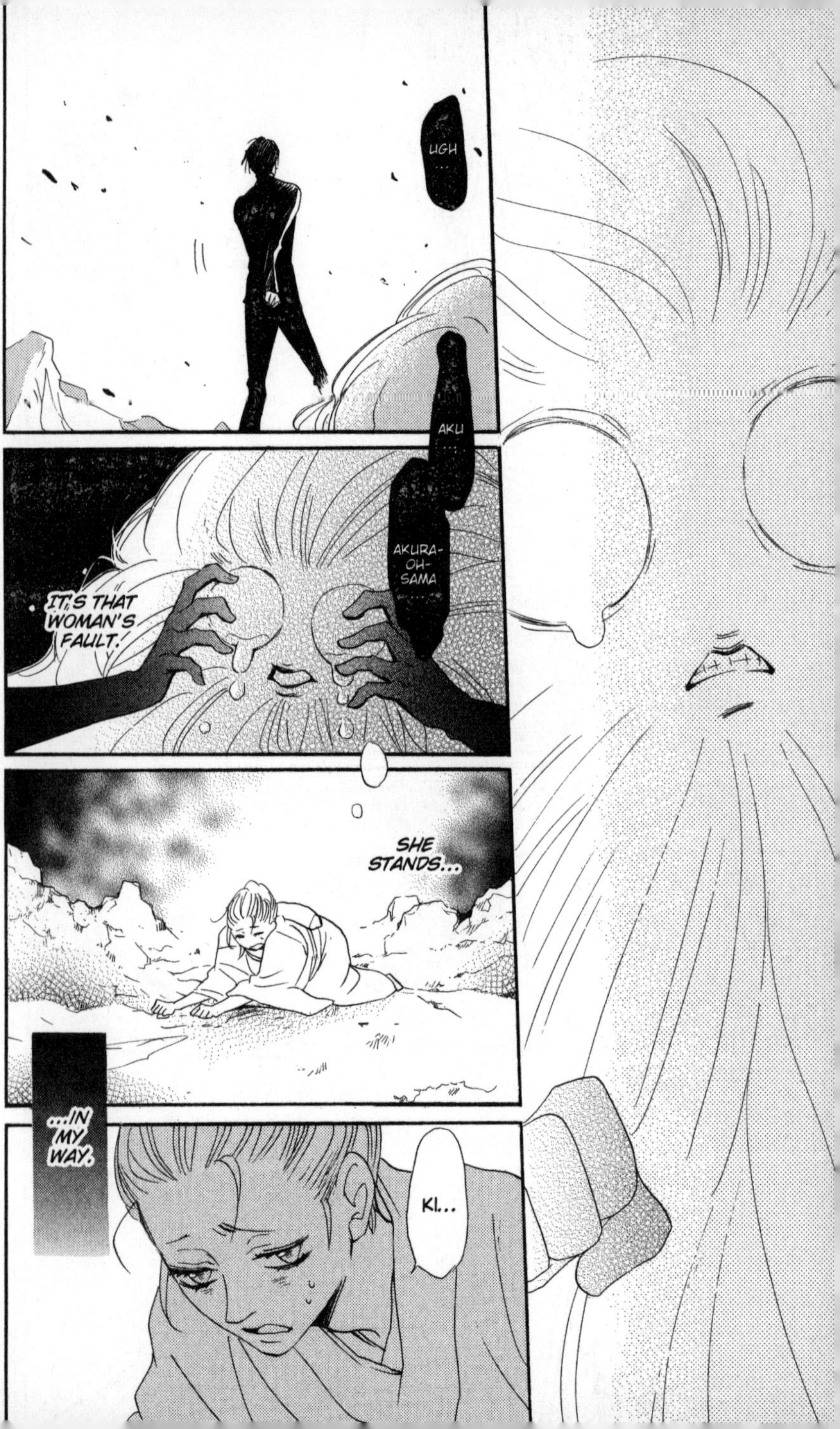
UGH...
AKU...
AKURA-OH-SAMA...
IT'S THAT WOMAN'S FAULT.
SHE STANDS...
...IN MY WAY.
KI...

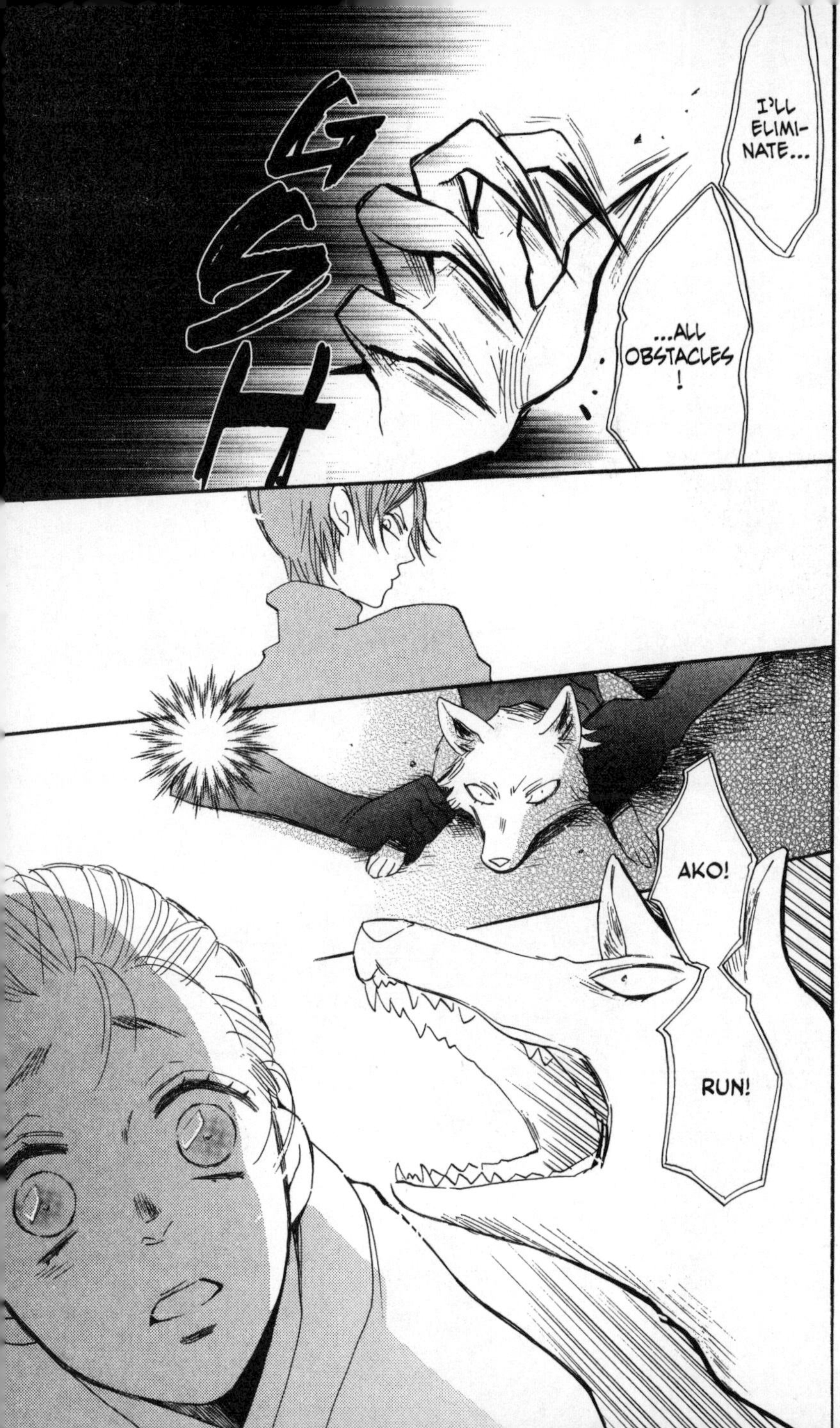
I'LL ELIMI-NATE...
...ALL OBSTACLES!
GASH
AKO!
RUN!

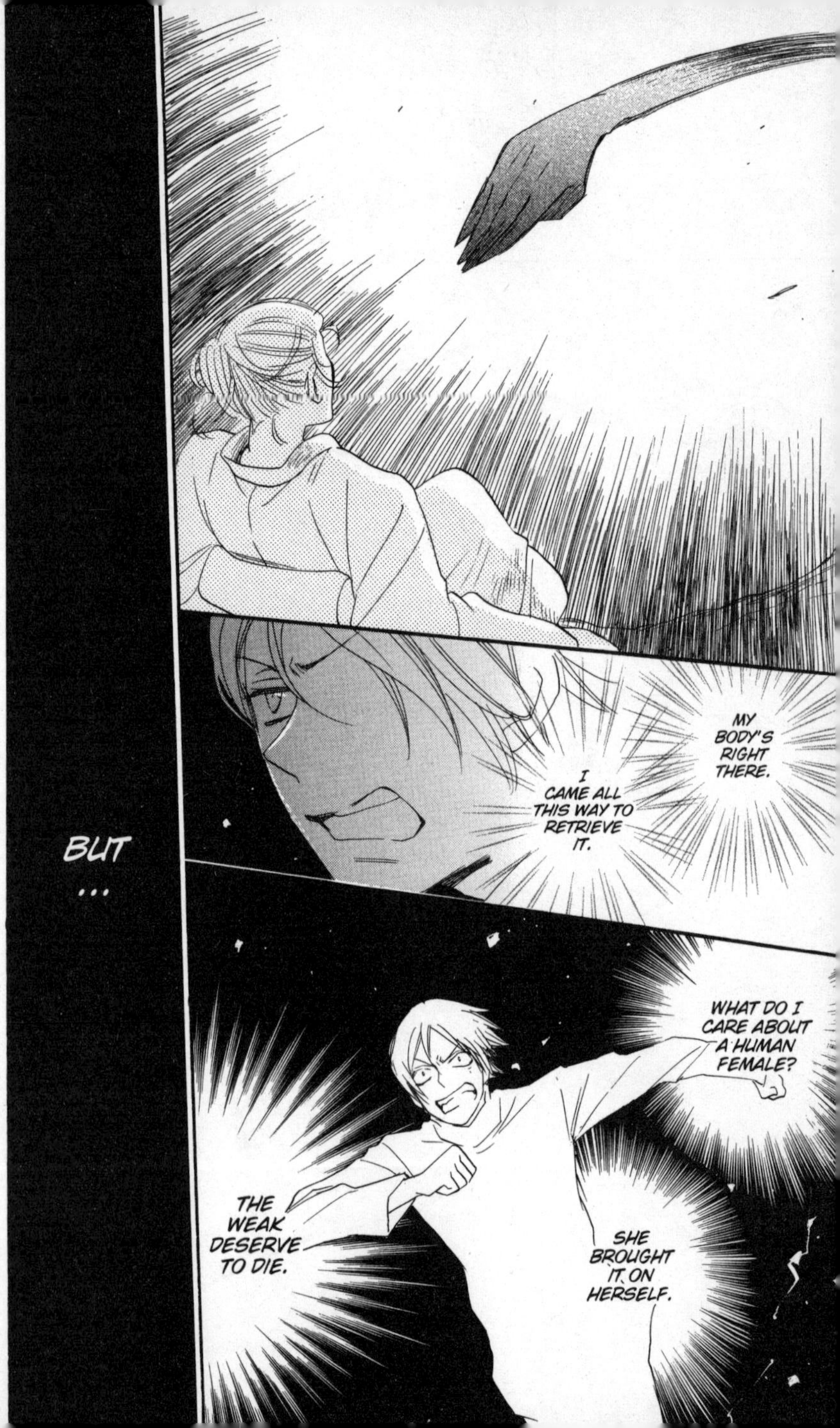
MY BODY'S RIGHT THERE.
I CAME ALL THIS WAY TO RETRIEVE IT.
BUT...
WHAT DO I CARE ABOUT A HUMAN FEMALE?
SHE BROUGHT IT ON HERSELF.
THE WEAK DESERVE TO DIE.

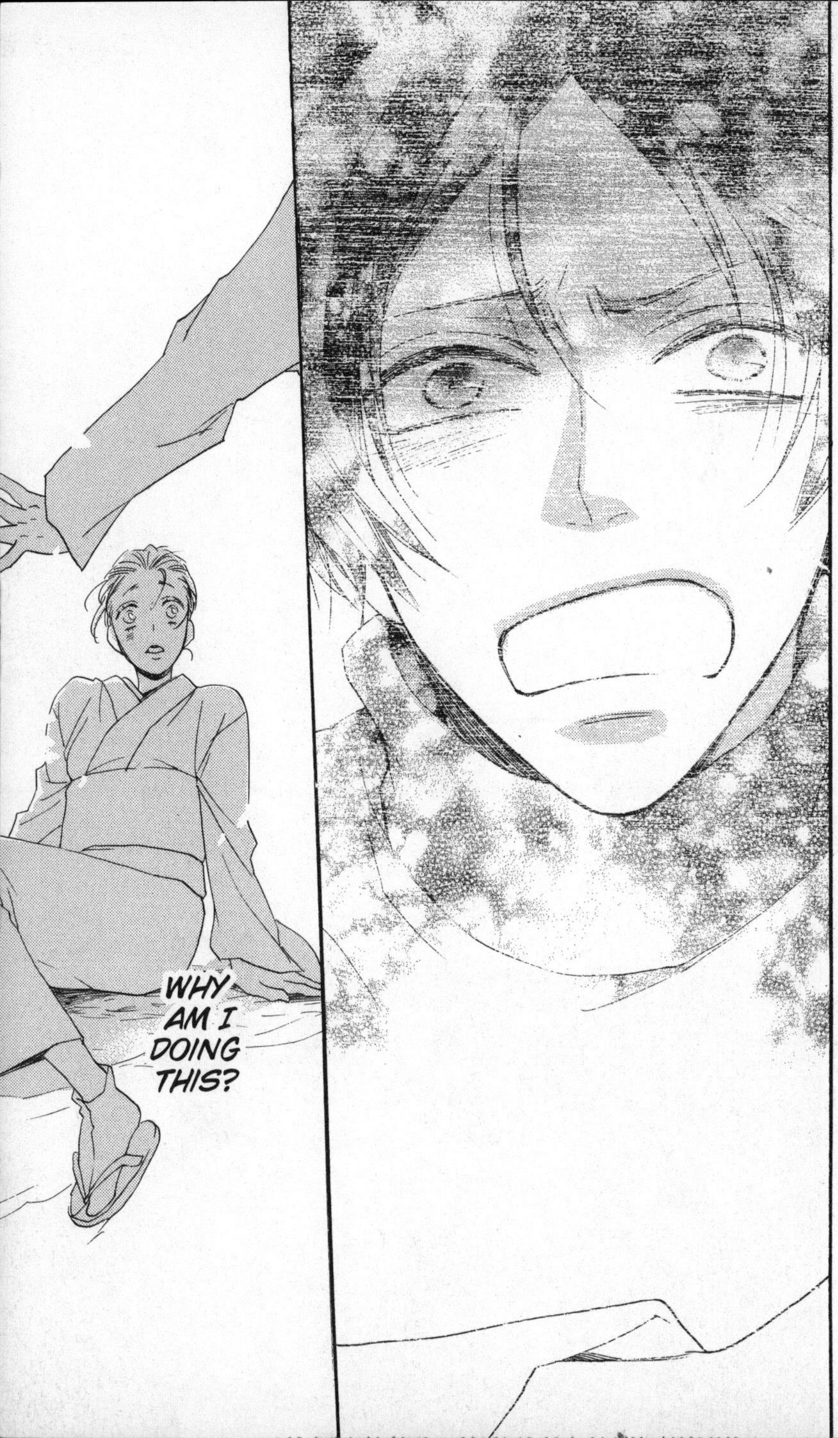
WHY AM I DOING THIS?

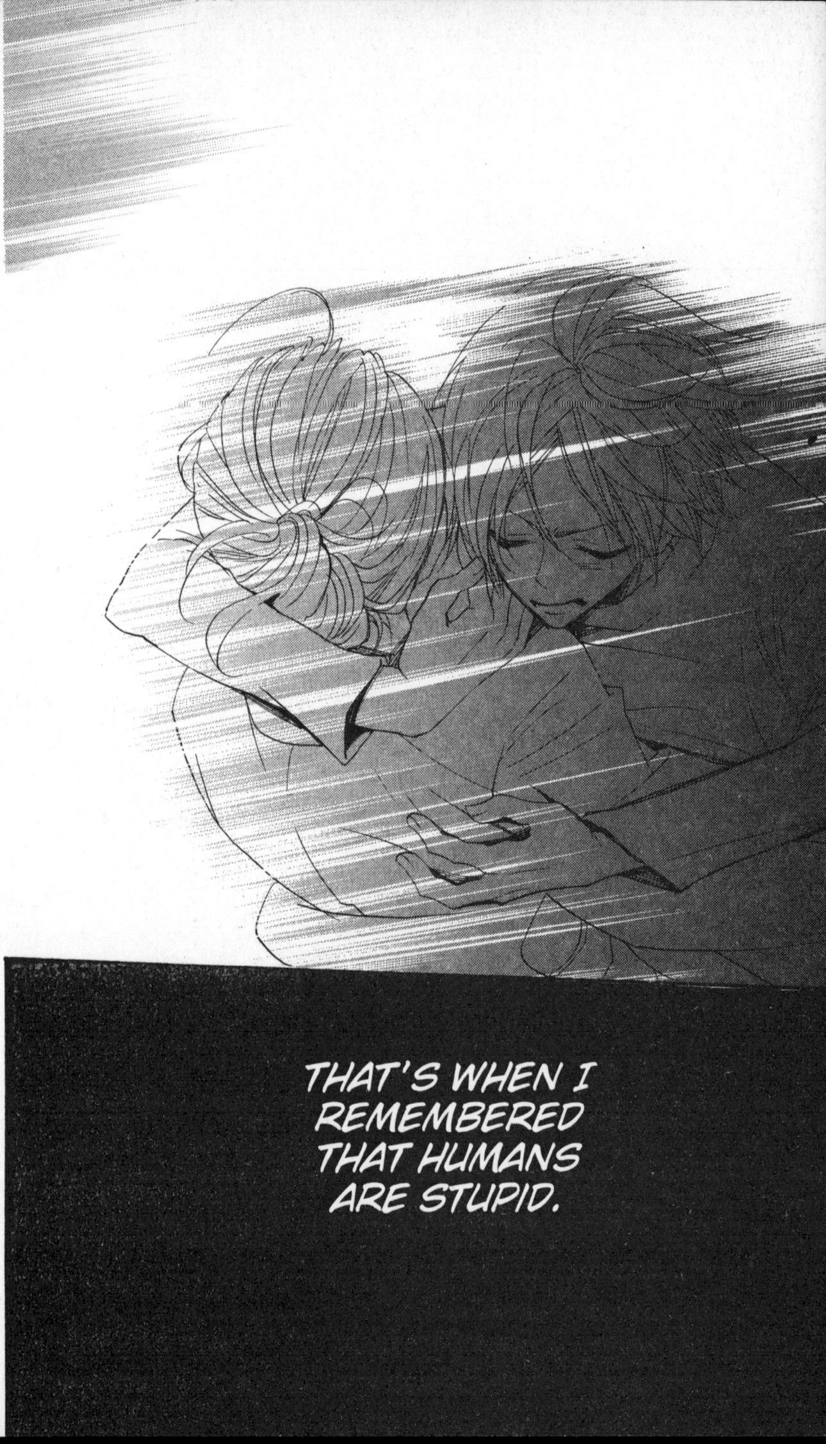
THAT'S WHEN I REMEMBERED THAT HUMANS ARE STUPID.

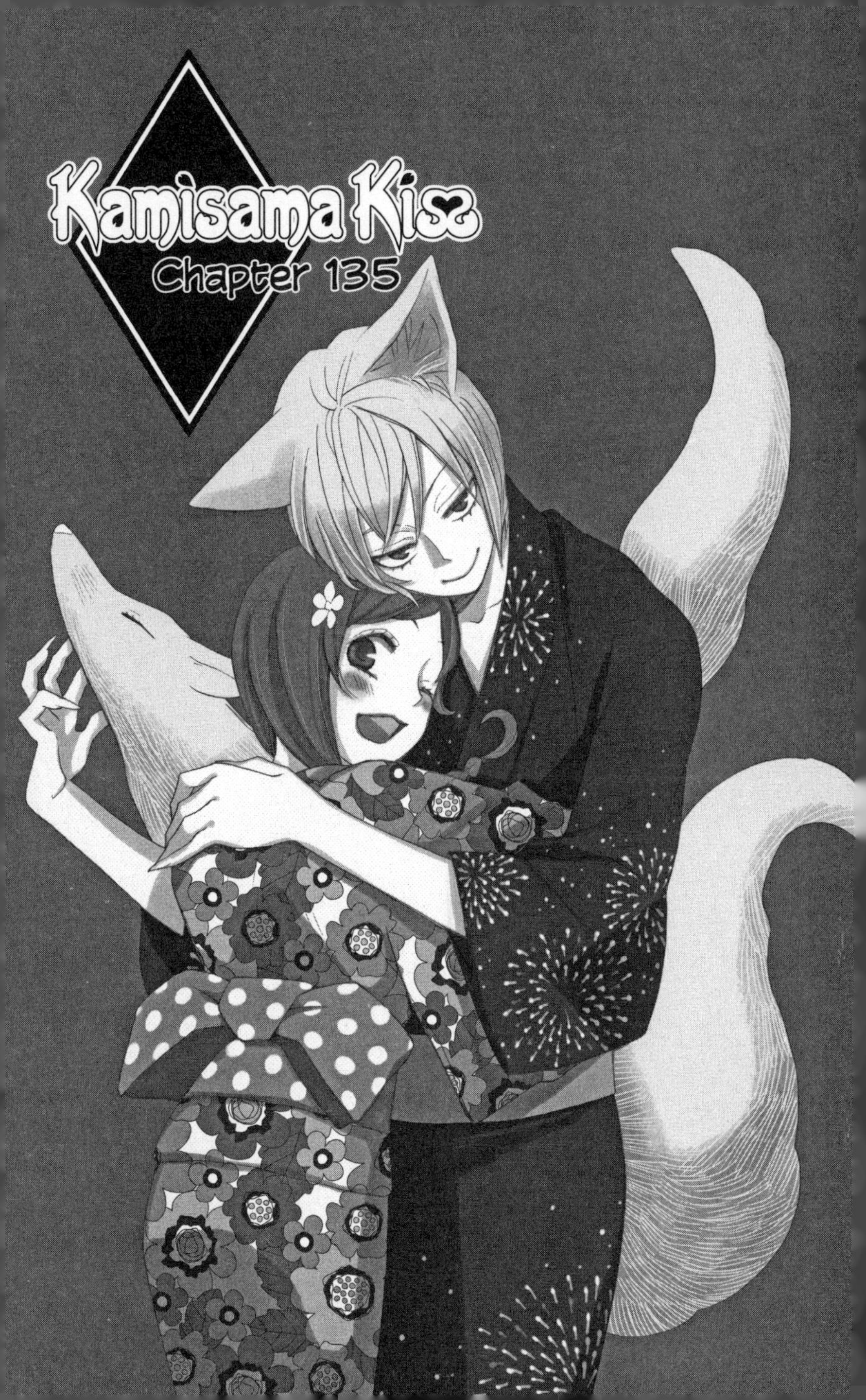
Kamisama Kiss
Chapter 135

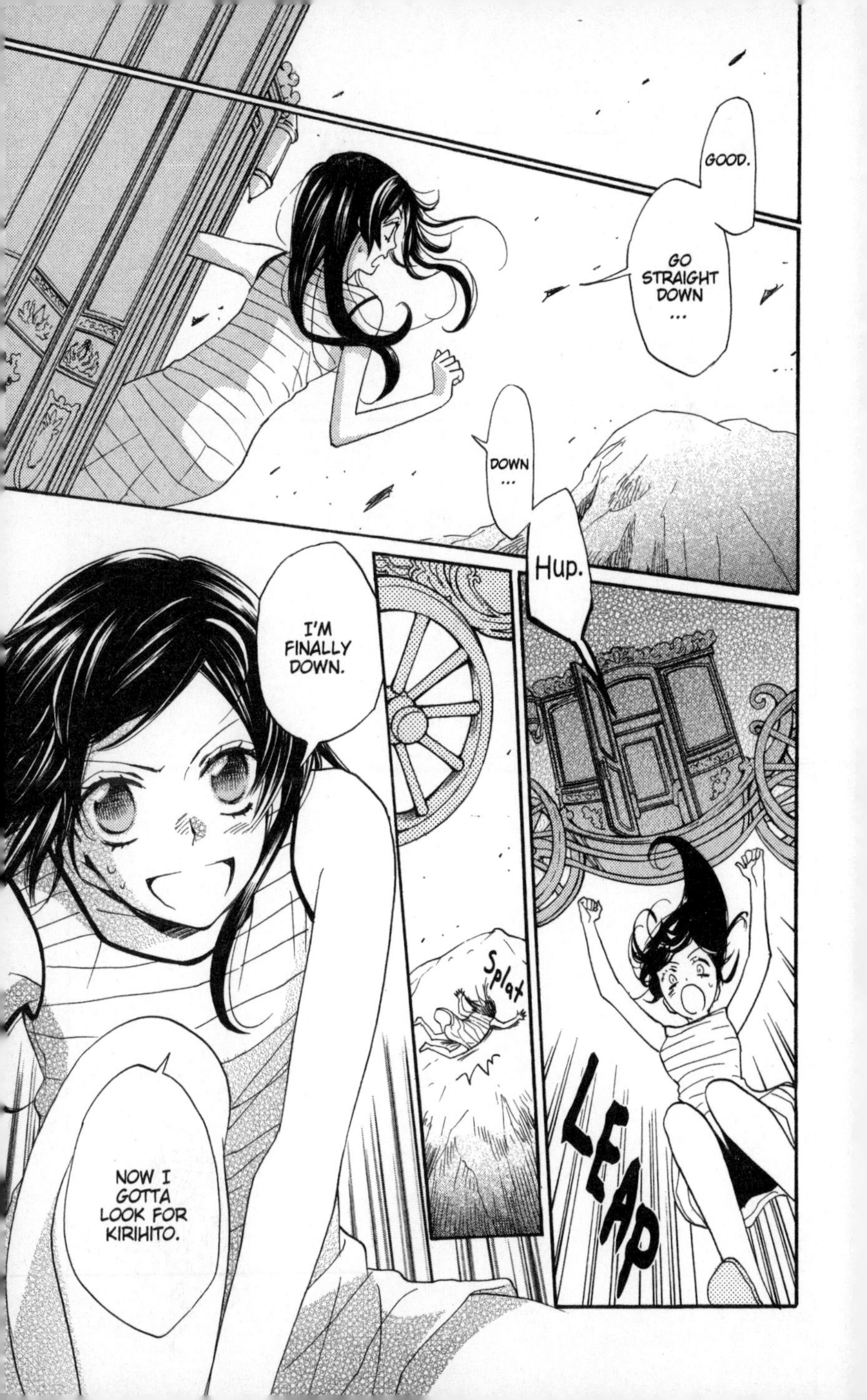
GOOD.
GO STRAIGHT DOWN ...
DOWN ...
Hup.
LEAP
Splat
I'M FINALLY DOWN.
NOW I GOTTA LOOK FOR KIRIHITO.

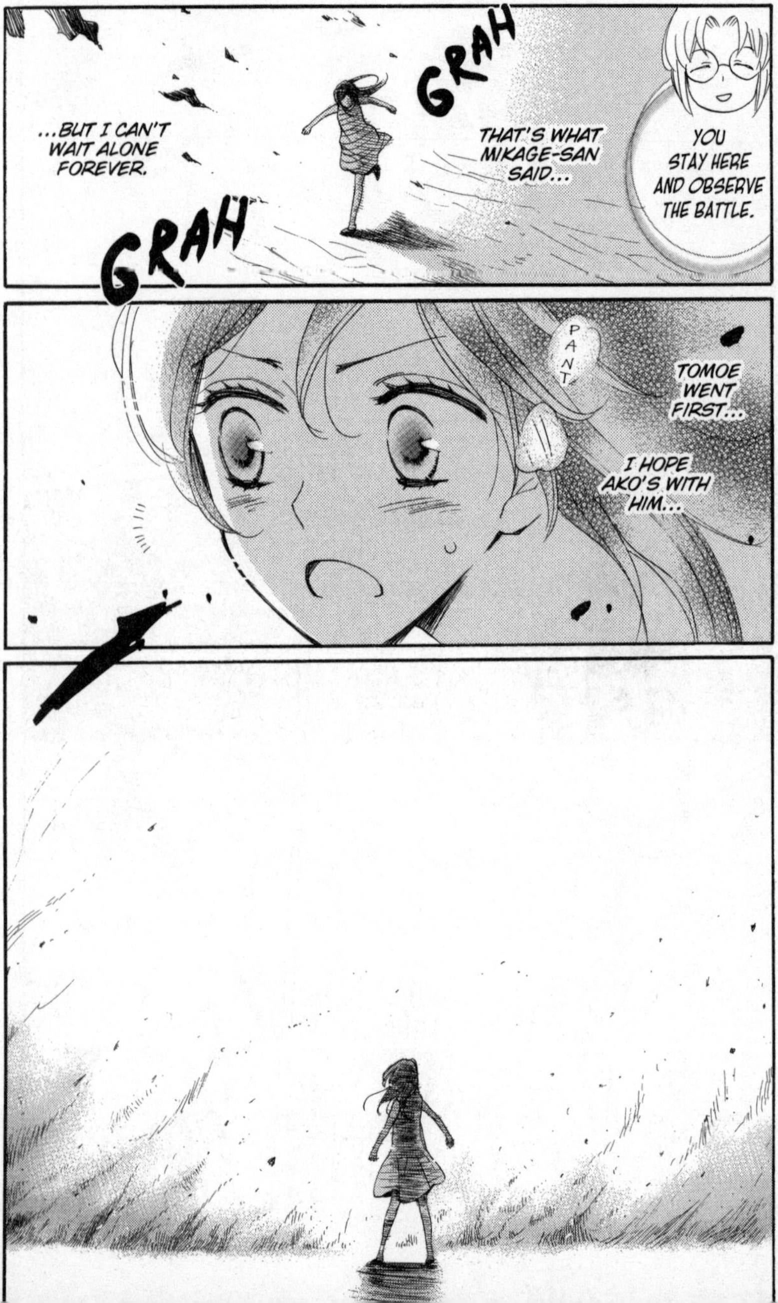
YOU STAY HERE AND OBSERVE THE BATTLE.
THAT'S WHAT MIKAGE-SAN SAID...
GRAH
GRAH
...BUT I CAN'T WAIT ALONE FOREVER.
PANT
TOMOE WENT FIRST...
I HOPE AKO'S WITH HIM...

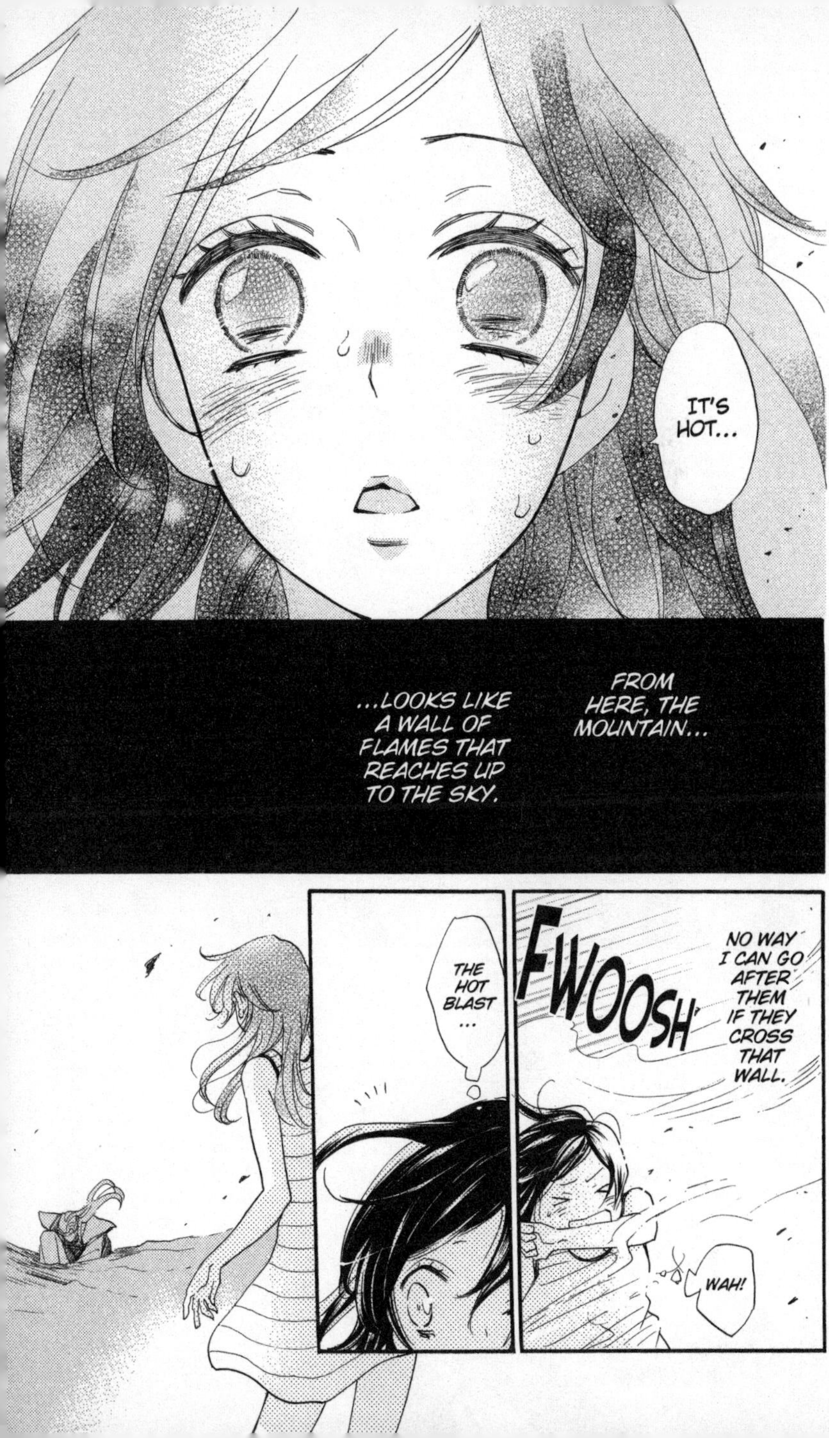
IT'S HOT...
FROM HERE, THE MOUNTAIN...
...LOOKS LIKE A WALL OF FLAMES THAT REACHES UP TO THE SKY.
NO WAY I CAN GO AFTER THEM IF THEY CROSS THAT WALL.
FWOOSH
WAH!
THE HOT BLAST...

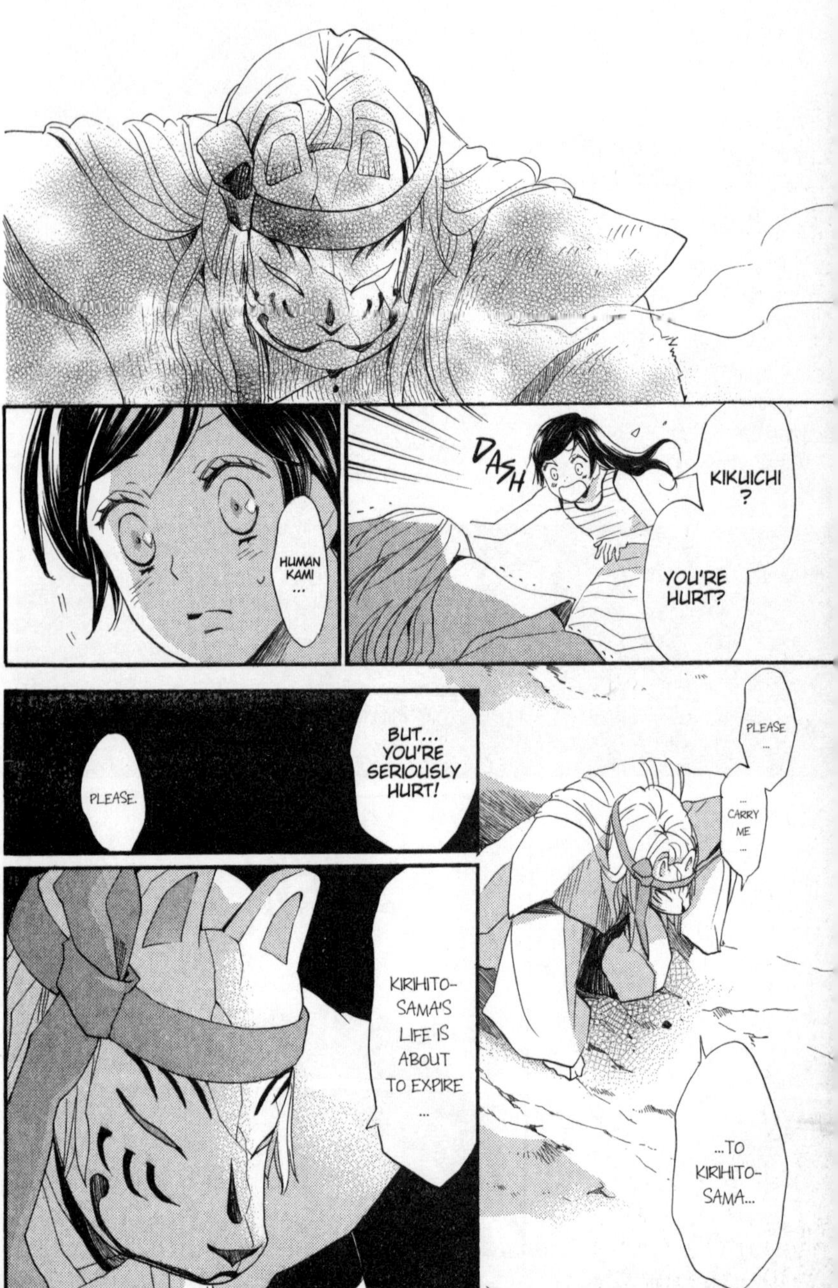
DASH
KIKUICHI?
YOU'RE HURT?
HUMAN KAMI...
PLEASE...
...CARRY ME...
...TO KIRIHITO-SAMA...
BUT... YOU'RE SERIOUSLY HURT!
PLEASE.
KIRIHITO-SAMA'S LIFE IS ABOUT TO EXPIRE...

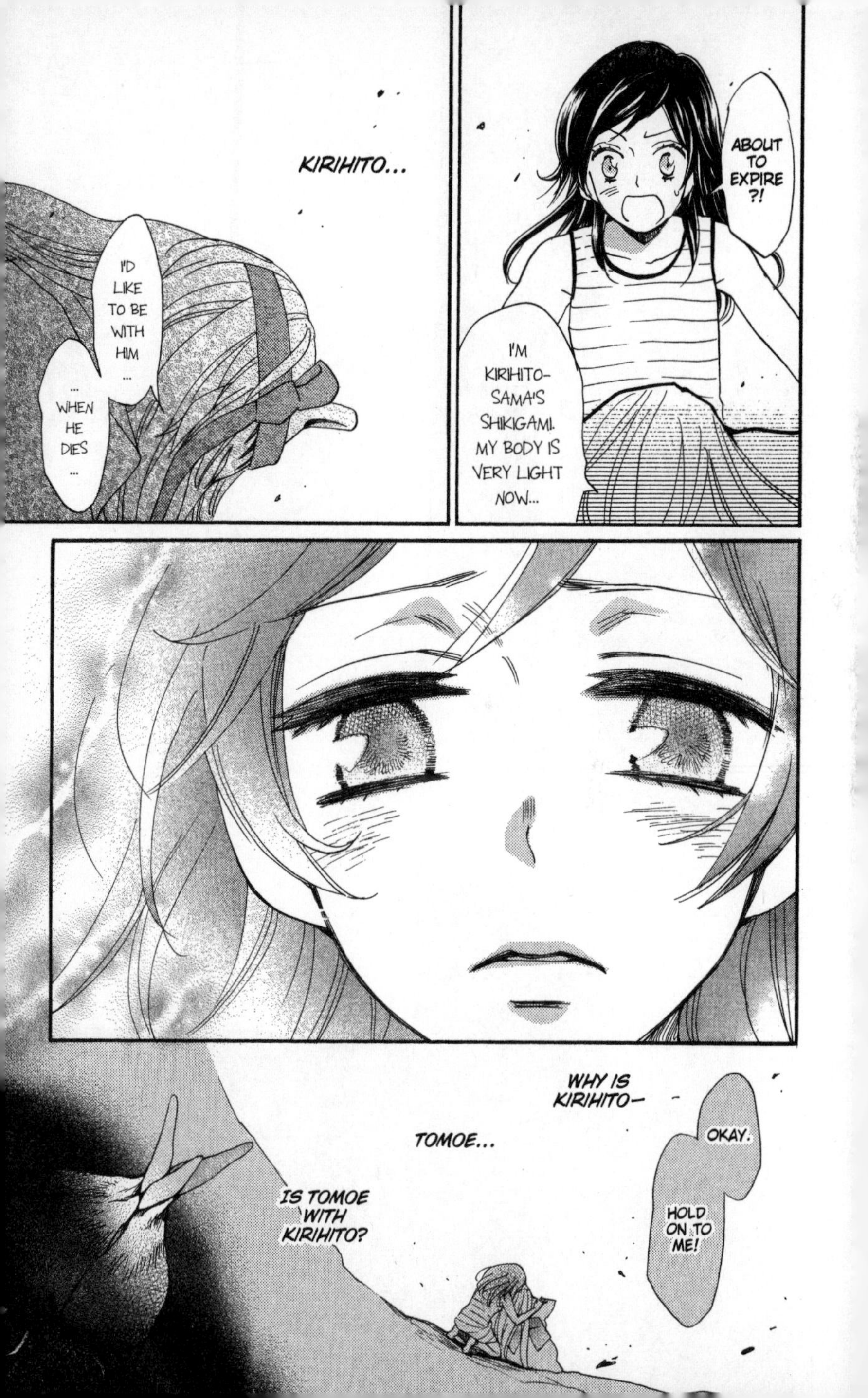
ABOUT TO EXPIRE ?!
I'M KIRIHITO-SAMA'S SHIKIGAMI. MY BODY IS VERY LIGHT NOW...
KIRIHITO...
I'D LIKE TO BE WITH HIM ...
... WHEN HE DIES ...
WHY IS KIRIHITO—
OKAY.
HOLD ON TO ME!
TOMOE...
IS TOMOE WITH KIRIHITO?

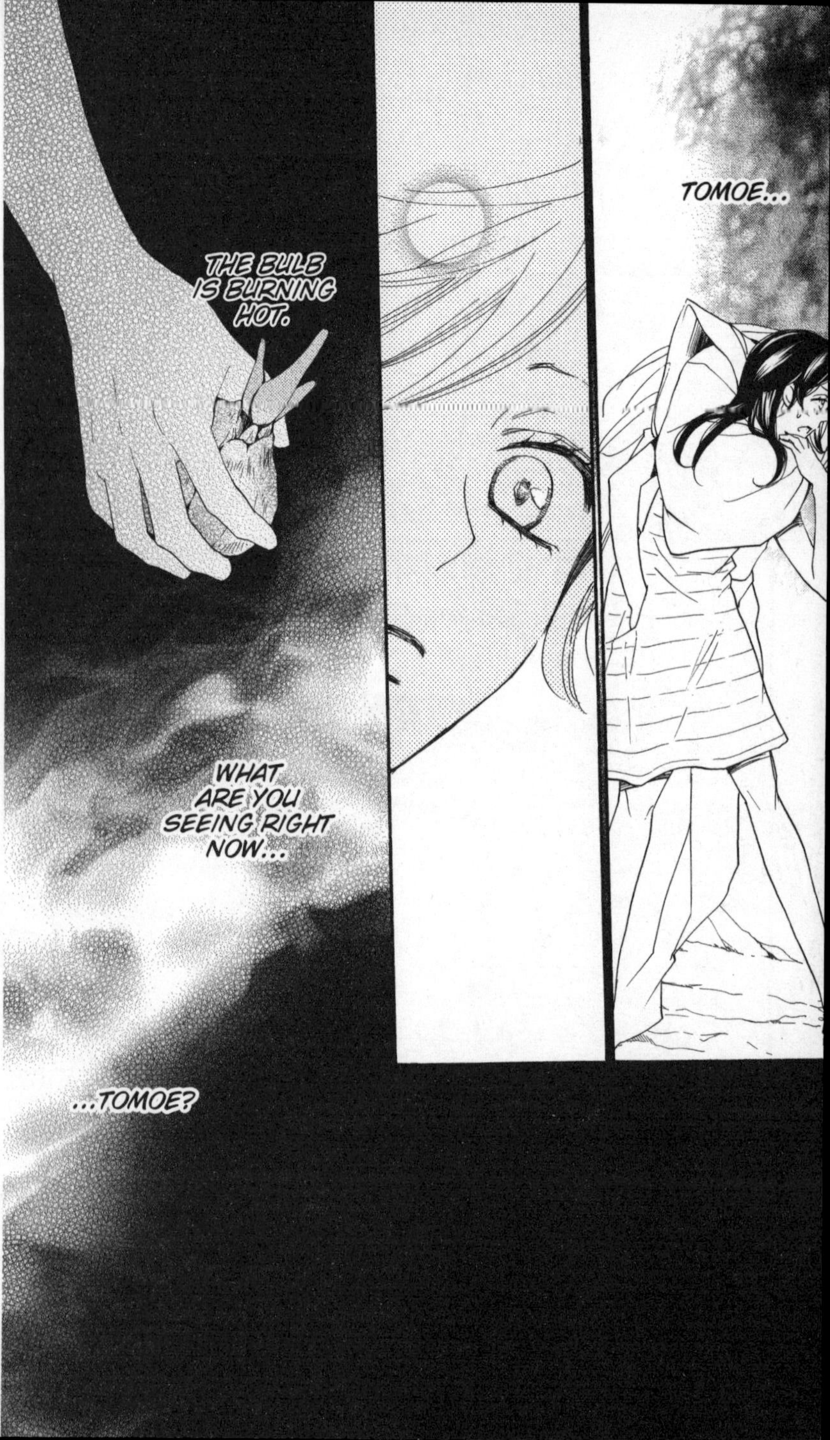
TOMOE...
THE BULB IS BURNING HOT.
WHAT ARE YOU SEEING RIGHT NOW...
...TOMOE?

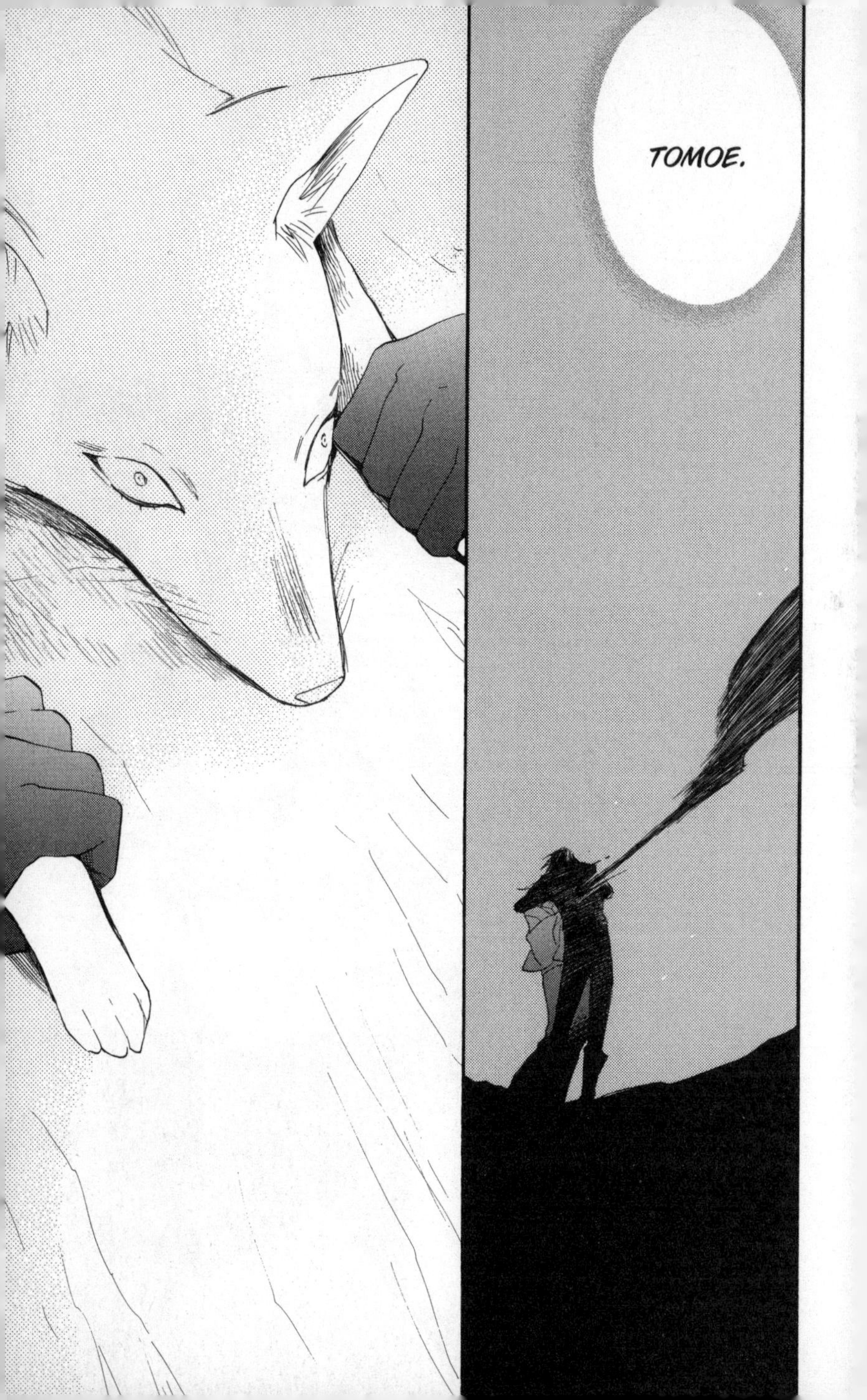
TOMOE.

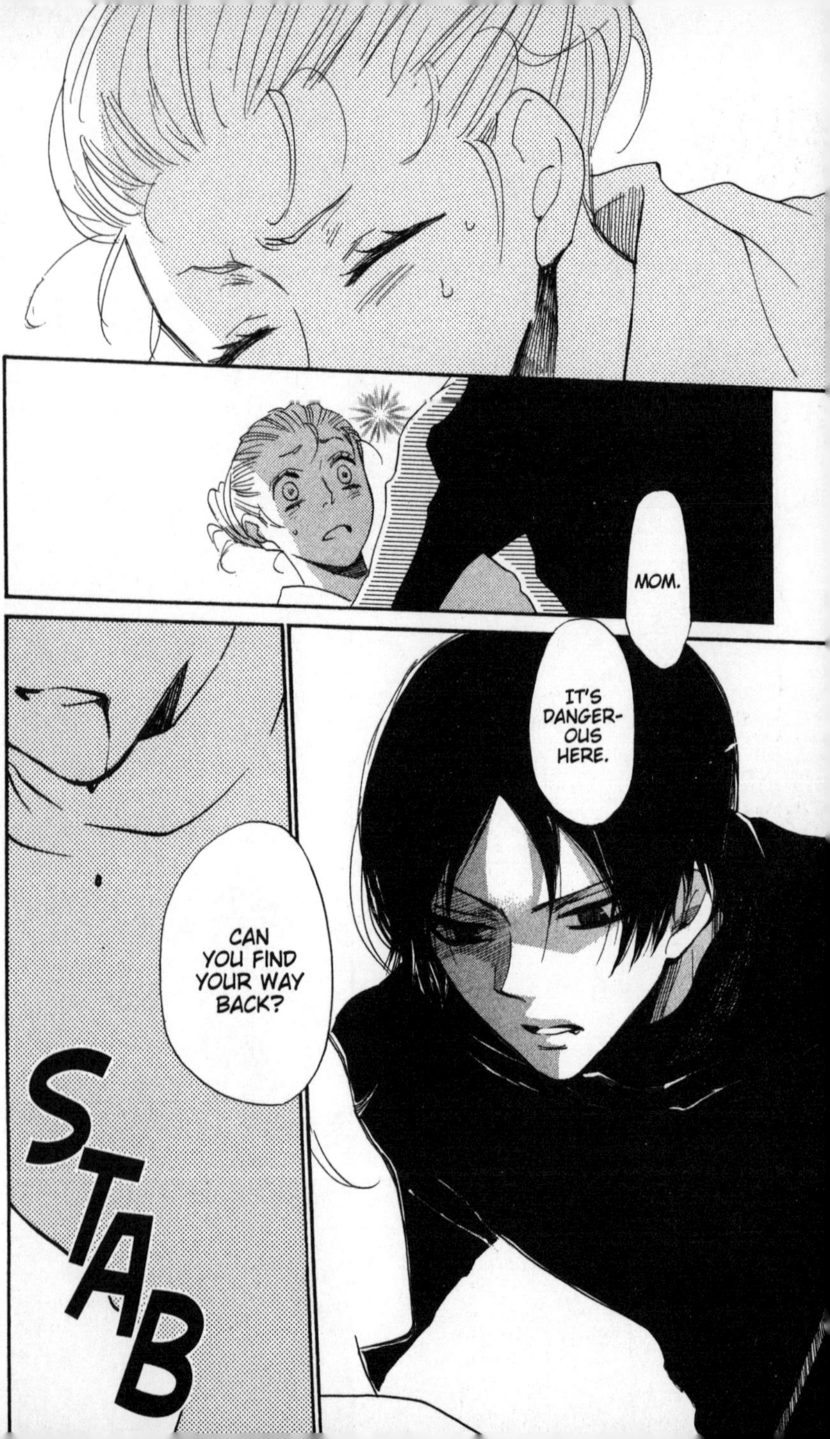
MOM.
IT'S DANGER-OUS HERE.
CAN YOU FIND YOUR WAY BACK?
STAB

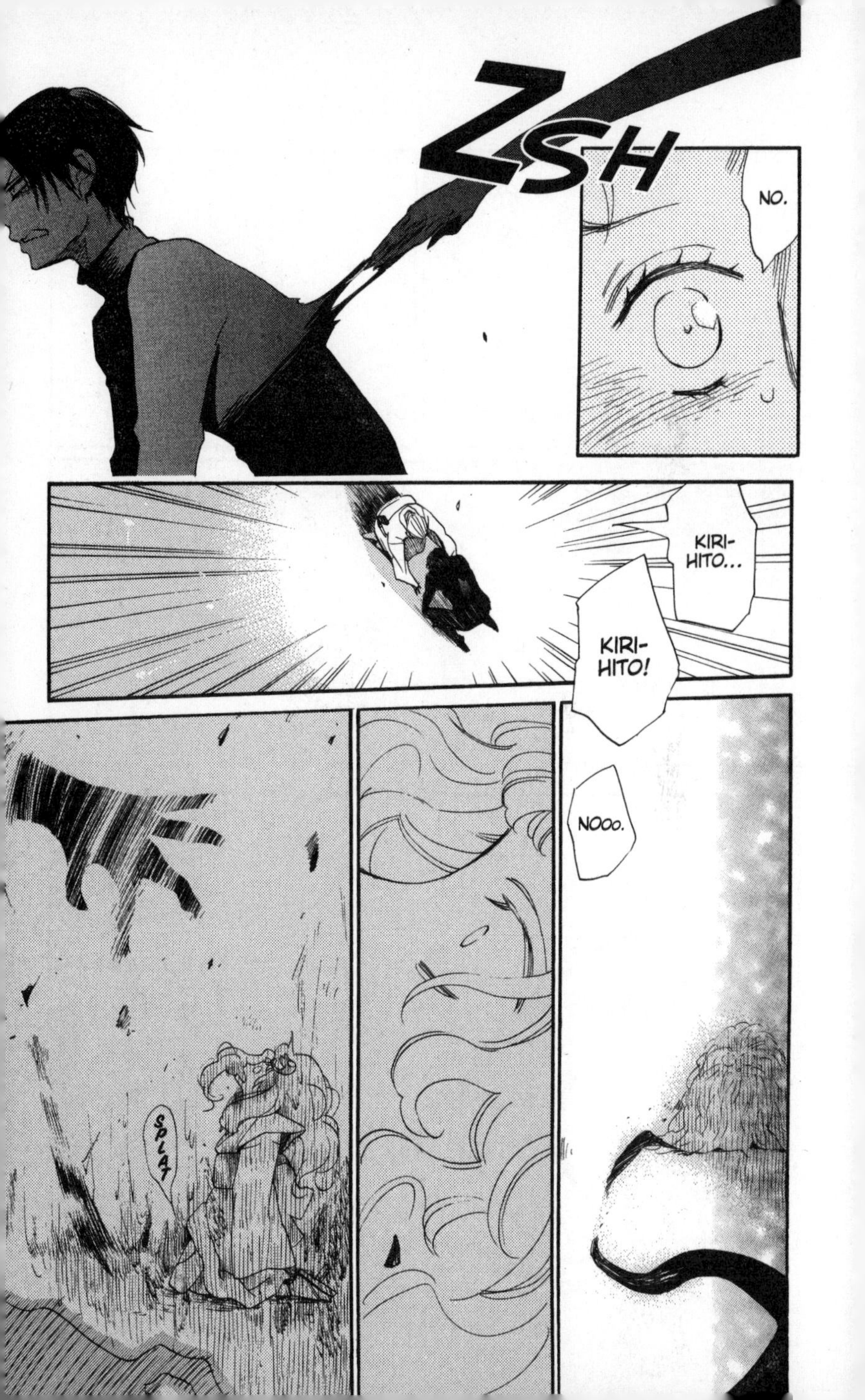
NO.
ZSH
KIRI-HITO...
KIRI-HITO!
NOOO.
SPLAT

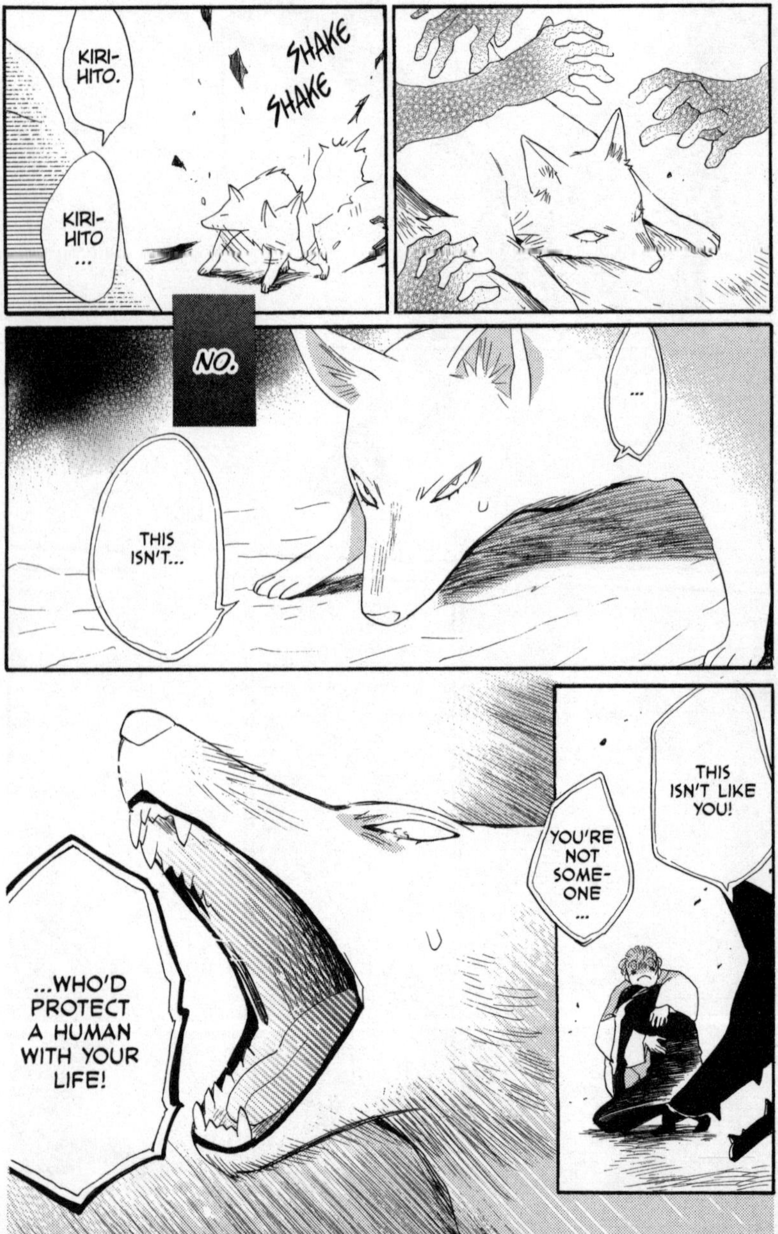
SHAKE
SHAKE
KIRI-HITO.
KIRI-HITO...
...
NO.
THIS ISN'T...
THIS ISN'T LIKE YOU!
YOU'RE NOT SOMEONE...
...WHO'D PROTECT A HUMAN WITH YOUR LIFE!

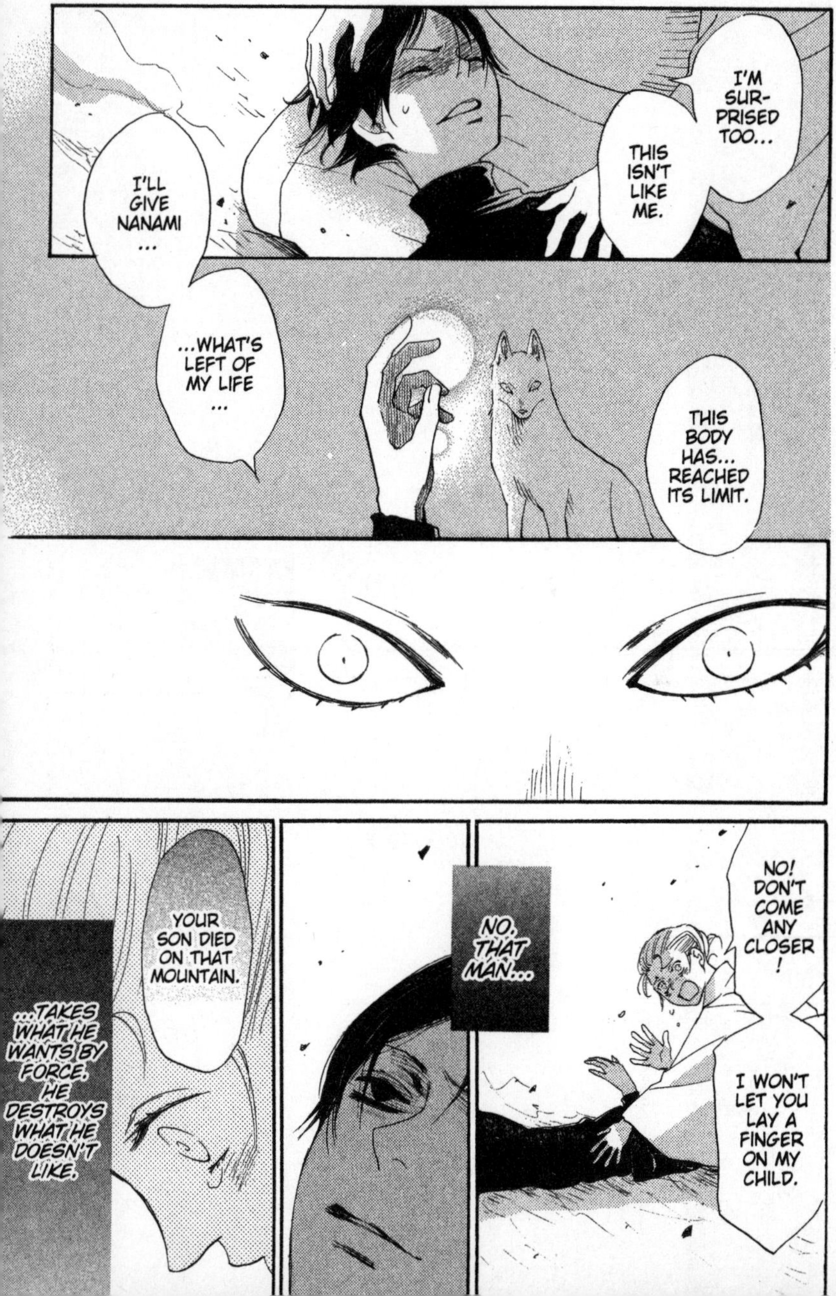
I'M SURPRISED TOO...
THIS ISN'T LIKE ME.
I'LL GIVE NANAMI ...
...WHAT'S LEFT OF MY LIFE ...
THIS BODY HAS... REACHED ITS LIMIT.
NO! DON'T COME ANY CLOSER!
I WON'T LET YOU LAY A FINGER ON MY CHILD.
NO. THAT MAN...
YOUR SON DIED ON THAT MOUNTAIN.
...TAKES WHAT HE WANTS BY FORCE. HE DESTROYS WHAT HE DOESN'T LIKE.

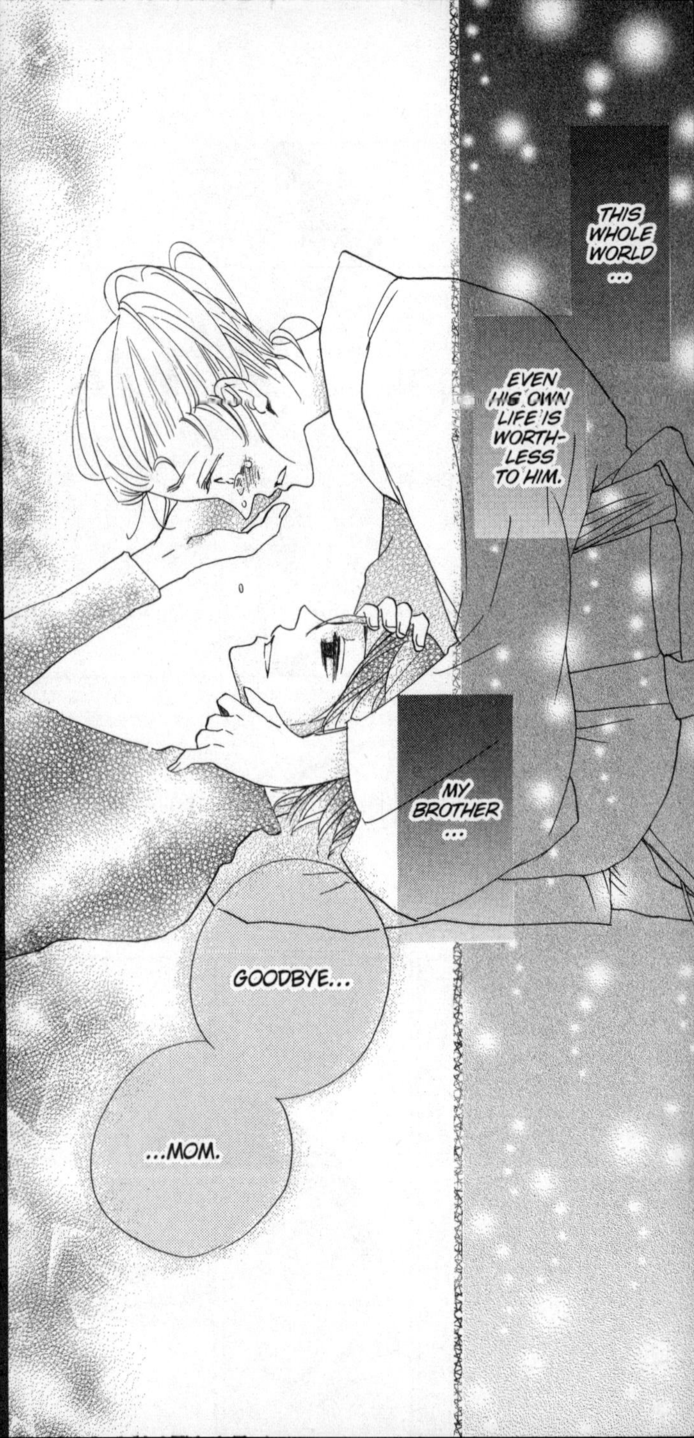
THIS WHOLE WORLD ...
EVEN HIS OWN LIFE IS WORTHLESS TO HIM.
MY BROTHER ...
GOODBYE...
...MOM.

...ISN'T ...

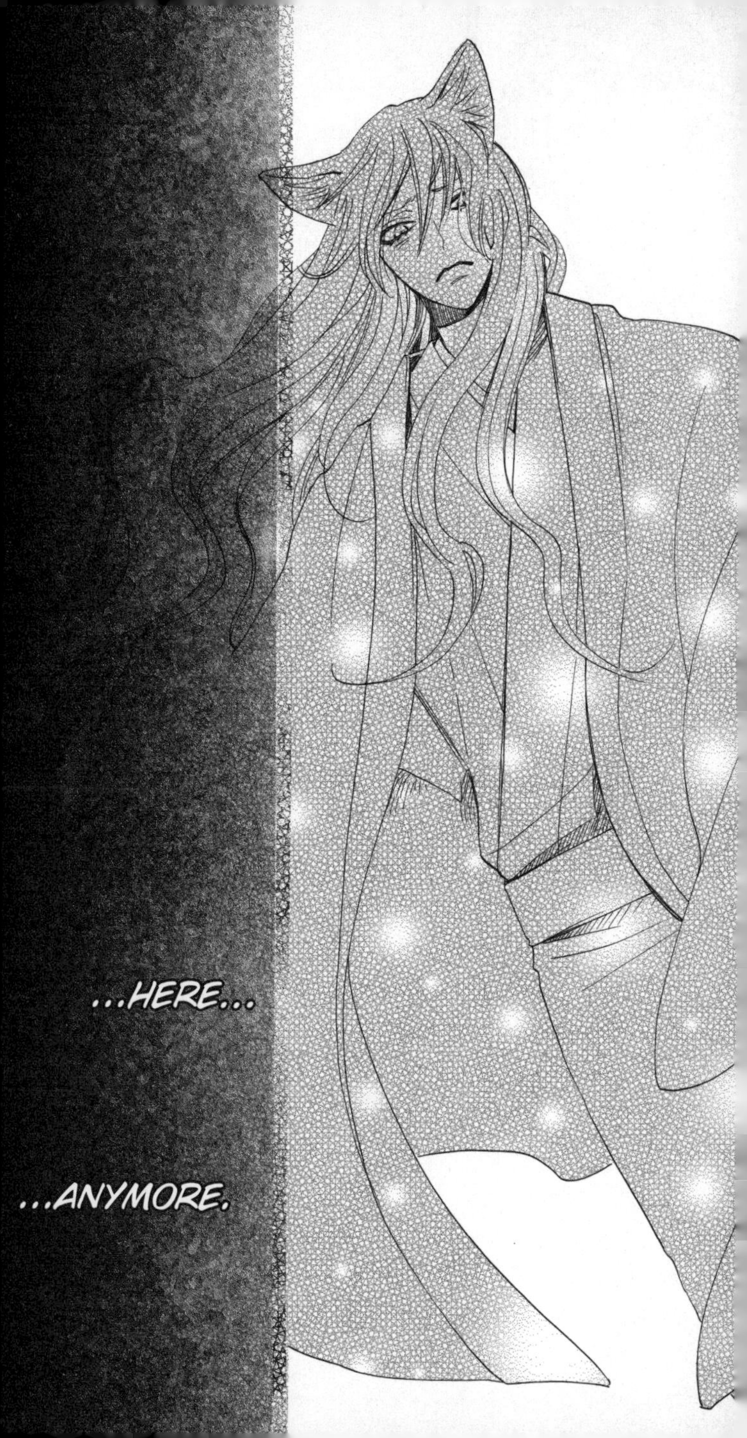
...HERE...
...ANYMORE.

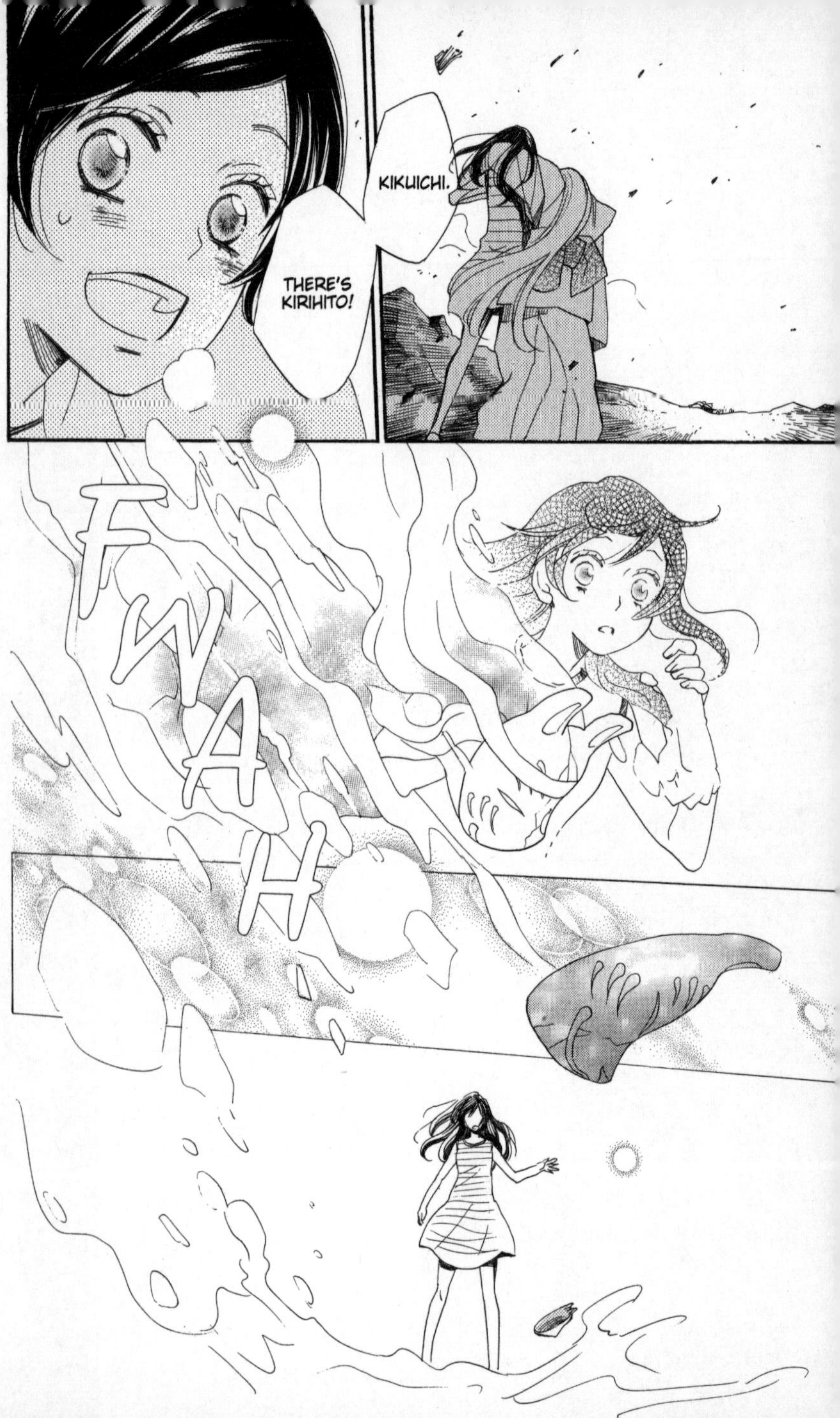
KIKUICHI.
THERE'S KIRIHITO!
FWAH

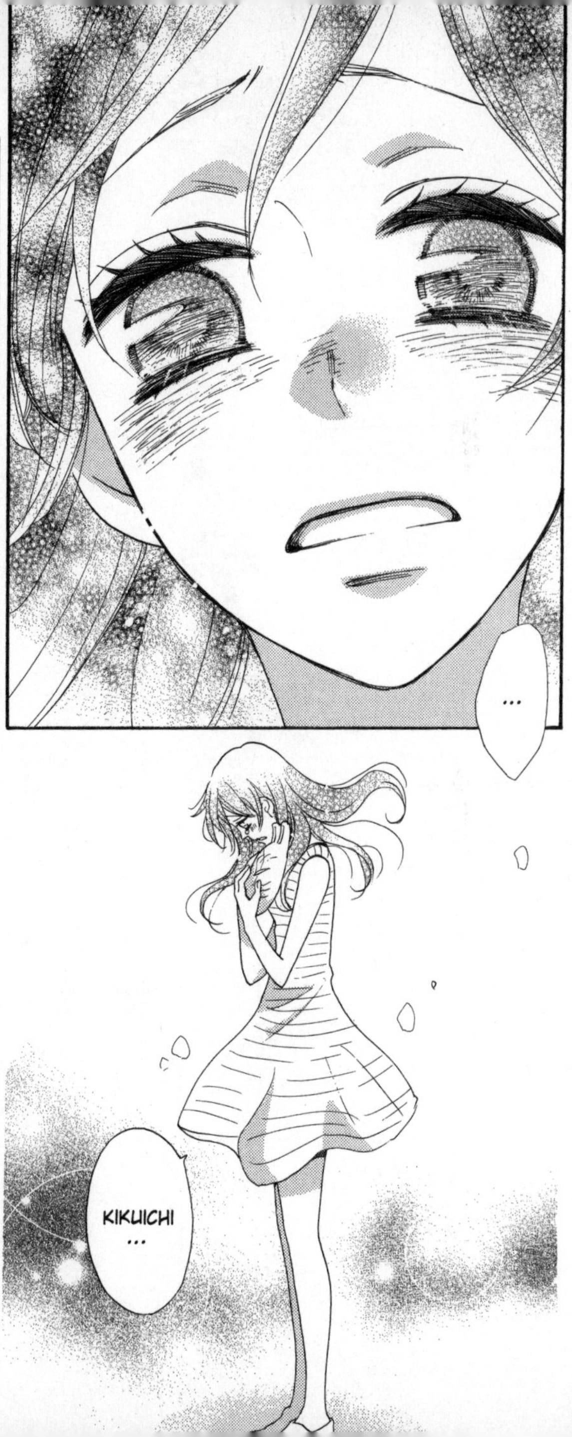
...
KIKUICHI ...

I got my second driver's license, since I let my old license expire by mistake. When I attended driver's school again and studied things, I realized I'd forgotten a lot and there were plenty of "Oh, that's how you do it?" moments. So maybe studying again was a good thing.

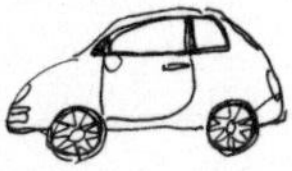

I enjoy driving! I love it when I drive in Tokyo at night because there are so few cars. ☺ Going to the *Hana to Yume* editorial department is easy too.

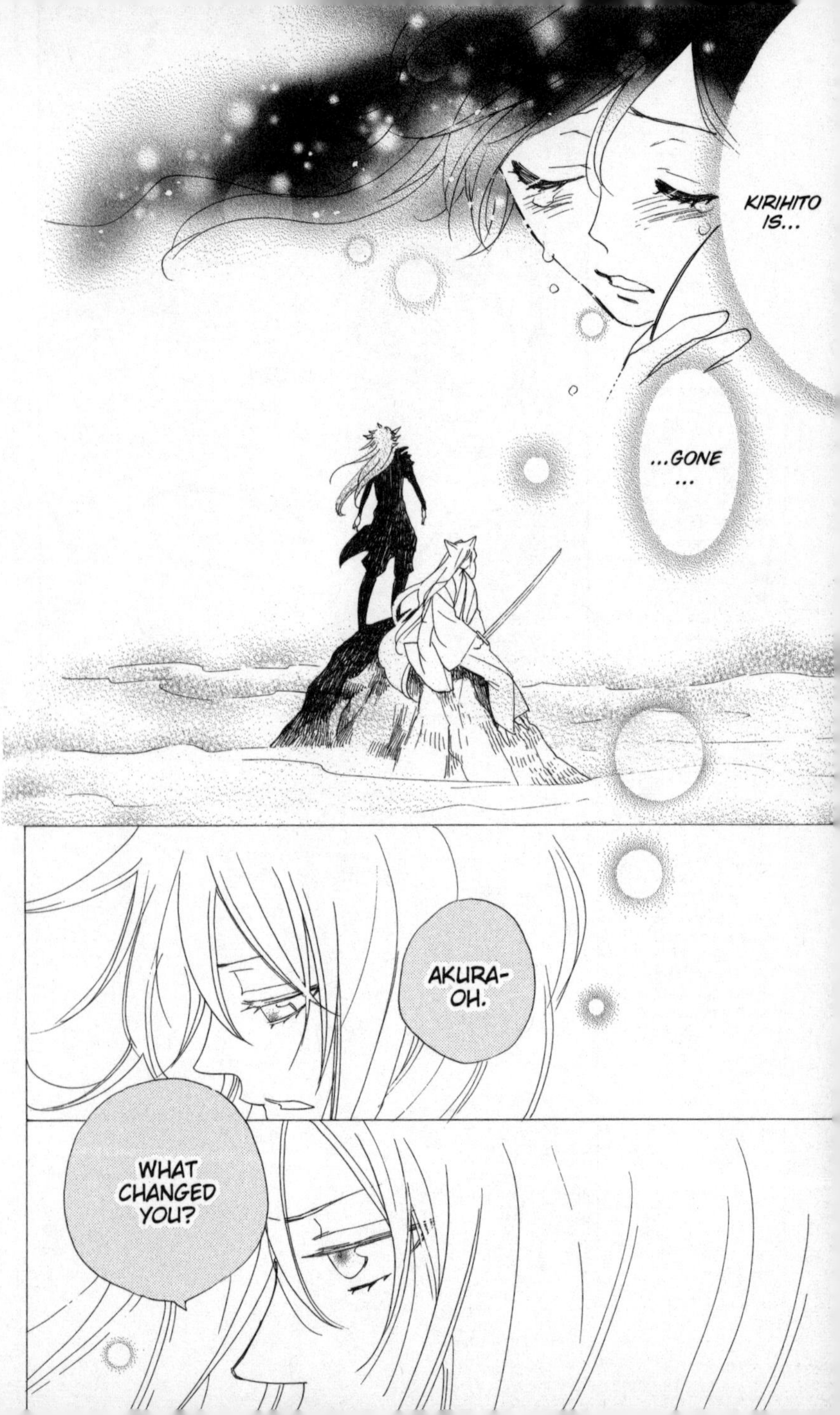
KIRIHITO IS...
...GONE ...
AKURA-OH.
WHAT CHANGED YOU?

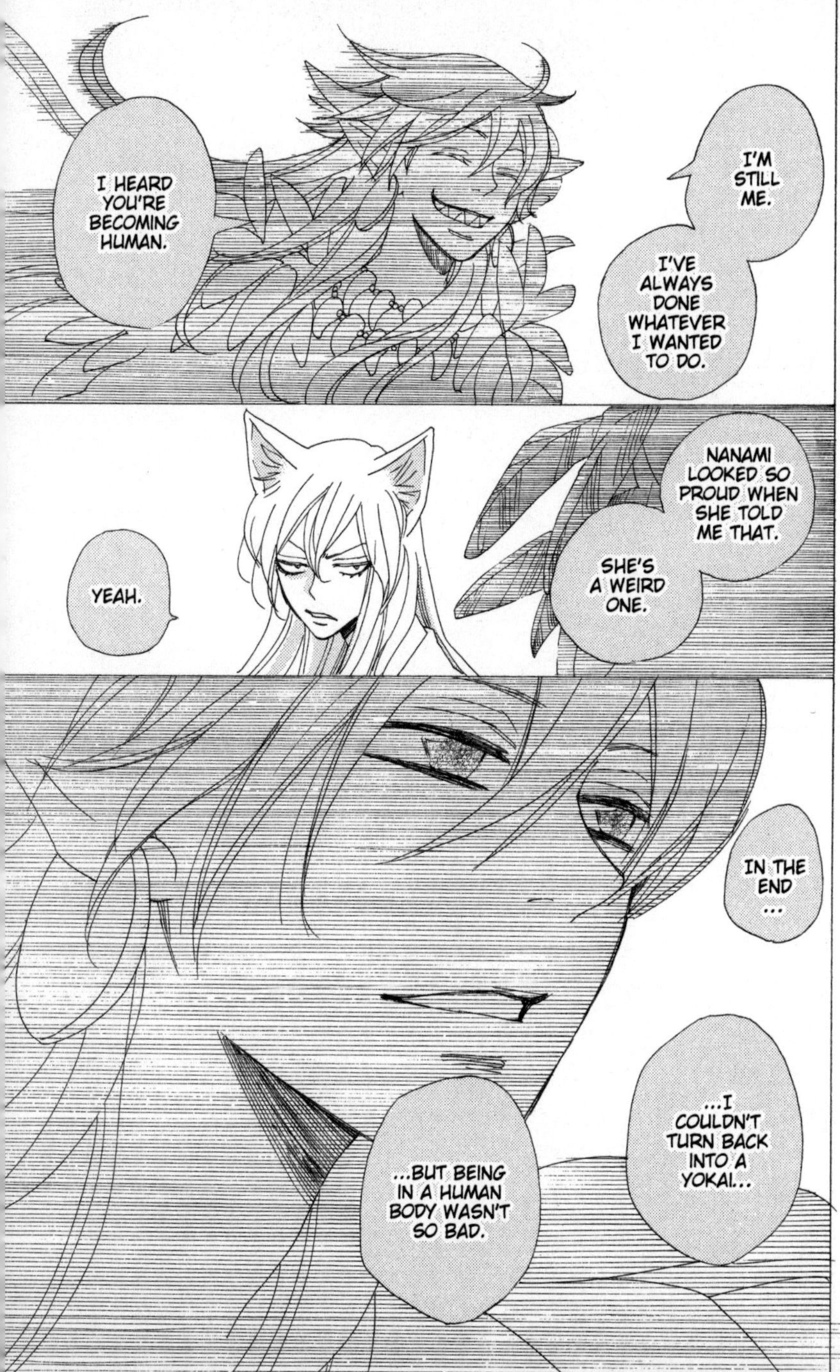
I'M STILL ME.
I'VE ALWAYS DONE WHATEVER I WANTED TO DO.
I HEARD YOU'RE BECOMING HUMAN.
NANAMI LOOKED SO PROUD WHEN SHE TOLD ME THAT.
SHE'S A WEIRD ONE.
YEAH.
IN THE END...
...I COULDN'T TURN BACK INTO A YOKAI...
...BUT BEING IN A HUMAN BODY WASN'T SO BAD.

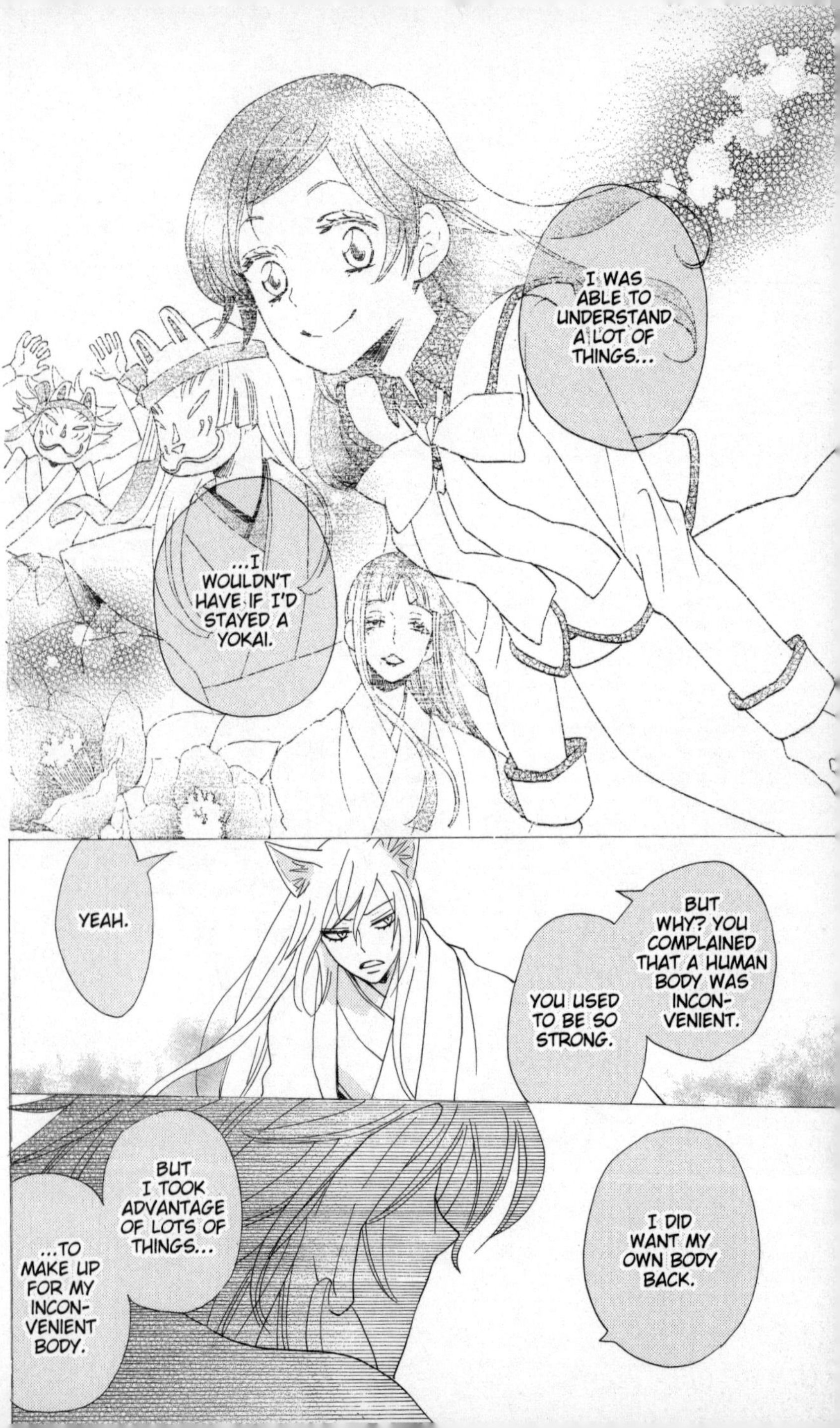
I WAS ABLE TO UNDERSTAND A LOT OF THINGS...
...I WOULDN'T HAVE IF I'D STAYED A YOKAI.
BUT WHY? YOU COMPLAINED THAT A HUMAN BODY WAS INCON-VENIENT.
YOU USED TO BE SO STRONG.
YEAH.
I DID WANT MY OWN BODY BACK.
BUT I TOOK ADVANTAGE OF LOTS OF THINGS...
...TO MAKE UP FOR MY INCON-VENIENT BODY.

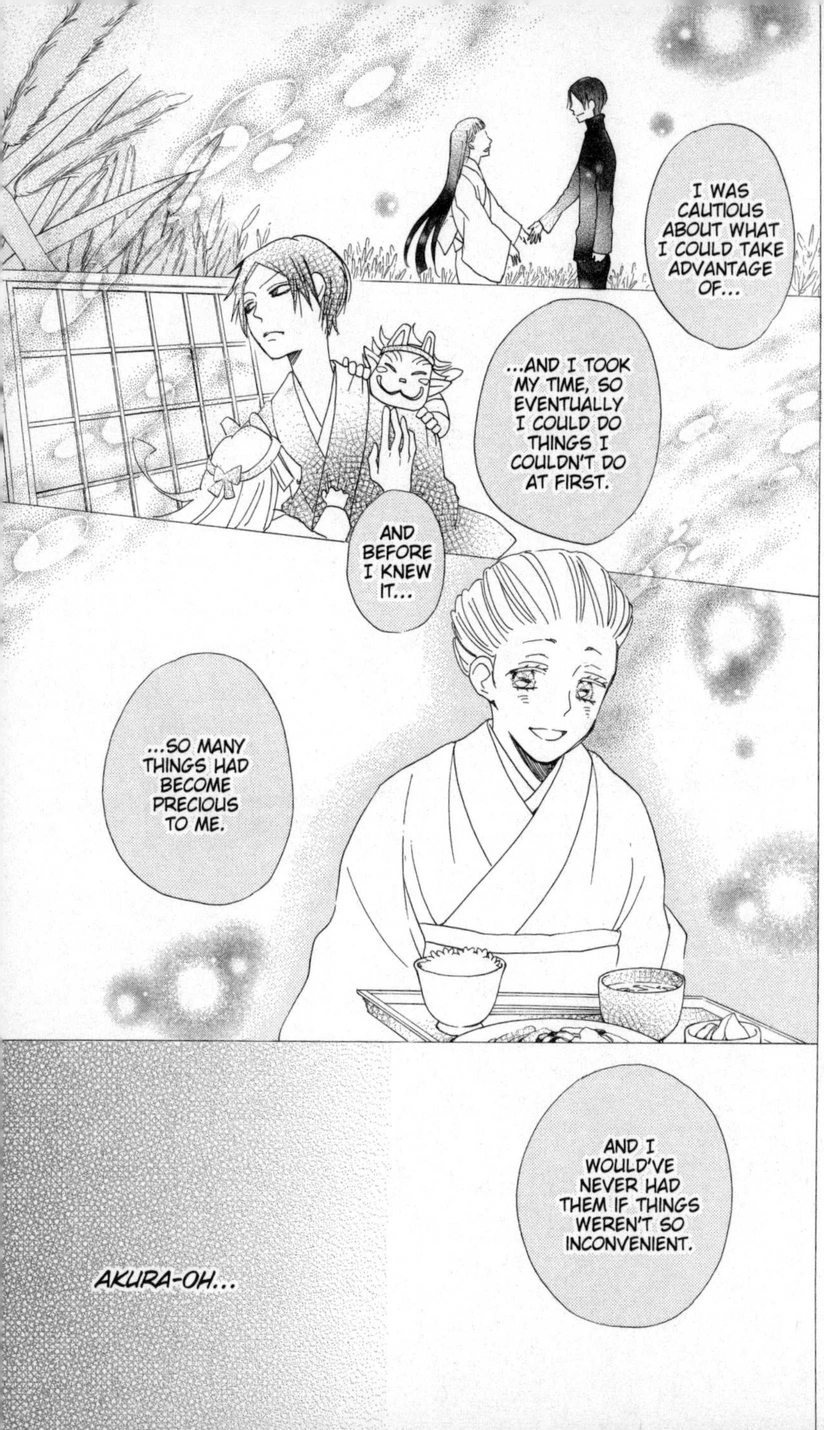
I WAS CAUTIOUS ABOUT WHAT I COULD TAKE ADVANTAGE OF...
...AND I TOOK MY TIME, SO EVENTUALLY I COULD DO THINGS I COULDN'T DO AT FIRST.
AND BEFORE I KNEW IT...
...SO MANY THINGS HAD BECOME PRECIOUS TO ME.
AND I WOULD'VE NEVER HAD THEM IF THINGS WEREN'T SO INCONVENIENT.
AKURA-OH...

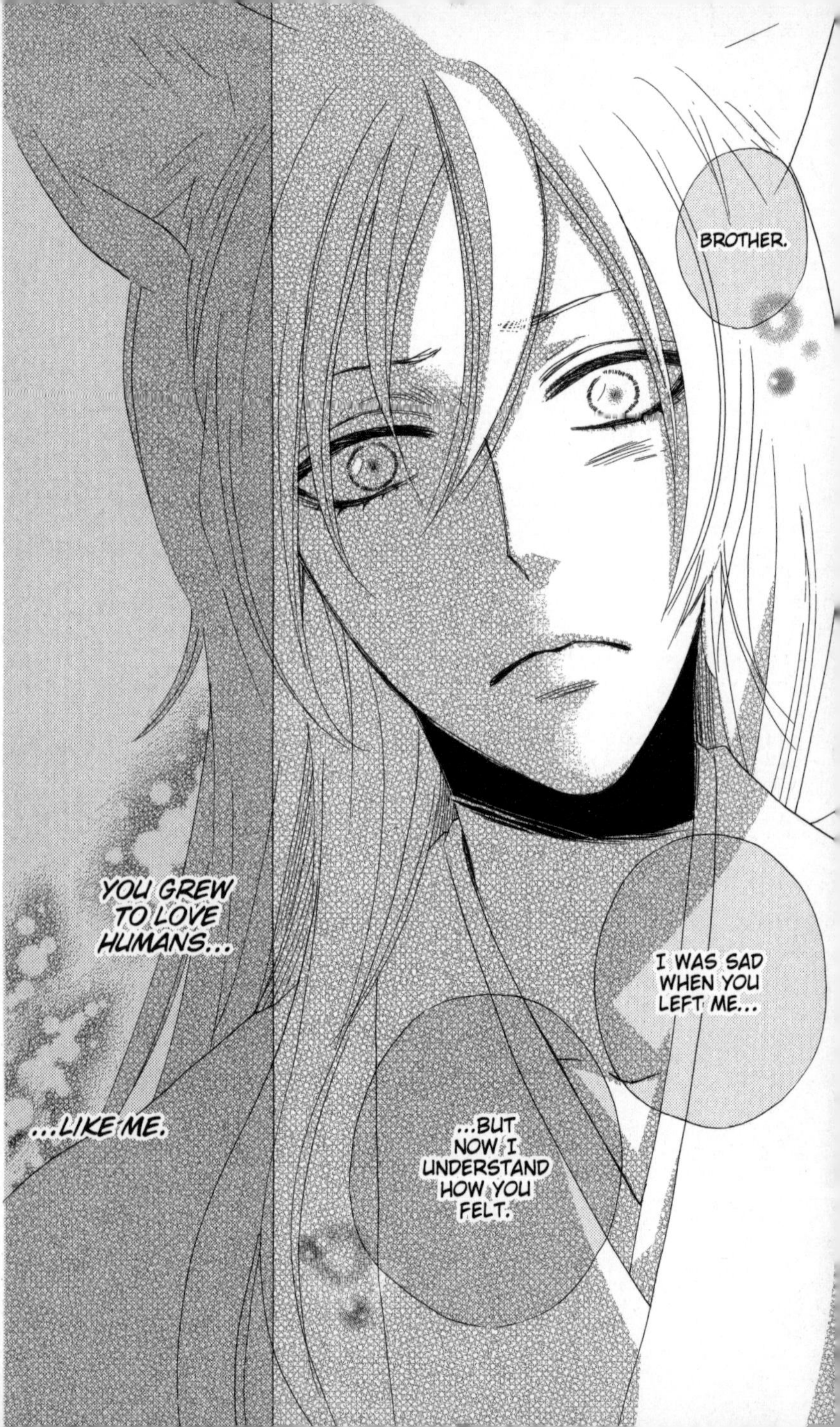
BROTHER.
I WAS SAD WHEN YOU LEFT ME...
...BUT NOW I UNDERSTAND HOW YOU FELT.
YOU GREW TO LOVE HUMANS...
...LIKE ME.

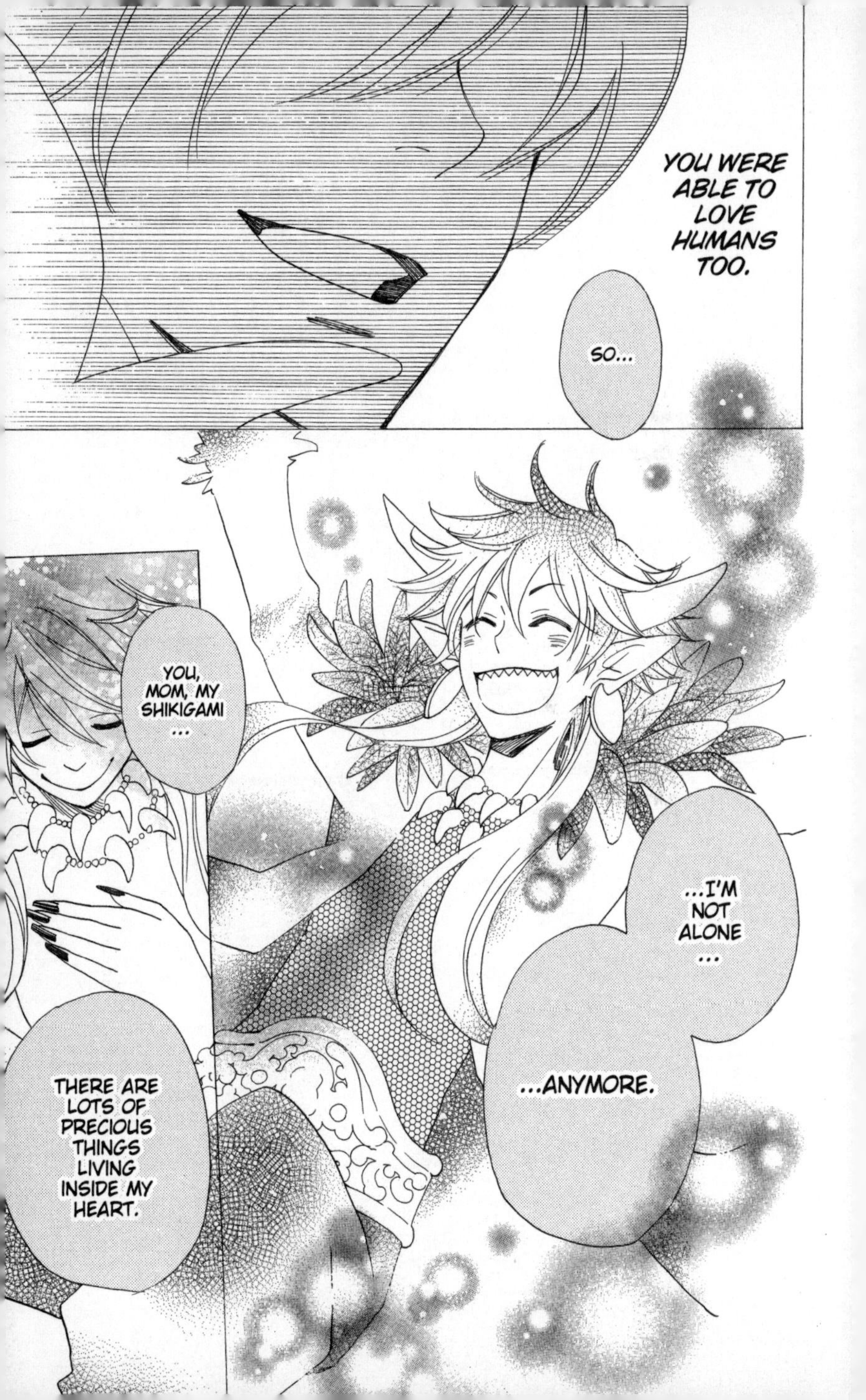
YOU WERE ABLE TO LOVE HUMANS TOO.
SO...
...I'M NOT ALONE ...
...ANYMORE.
YOU, MOM, MY SHIKIGAMI ...
THERE ARE LOTS OF PRECIOUS THINGS LIVING INSIDE MY HEART.

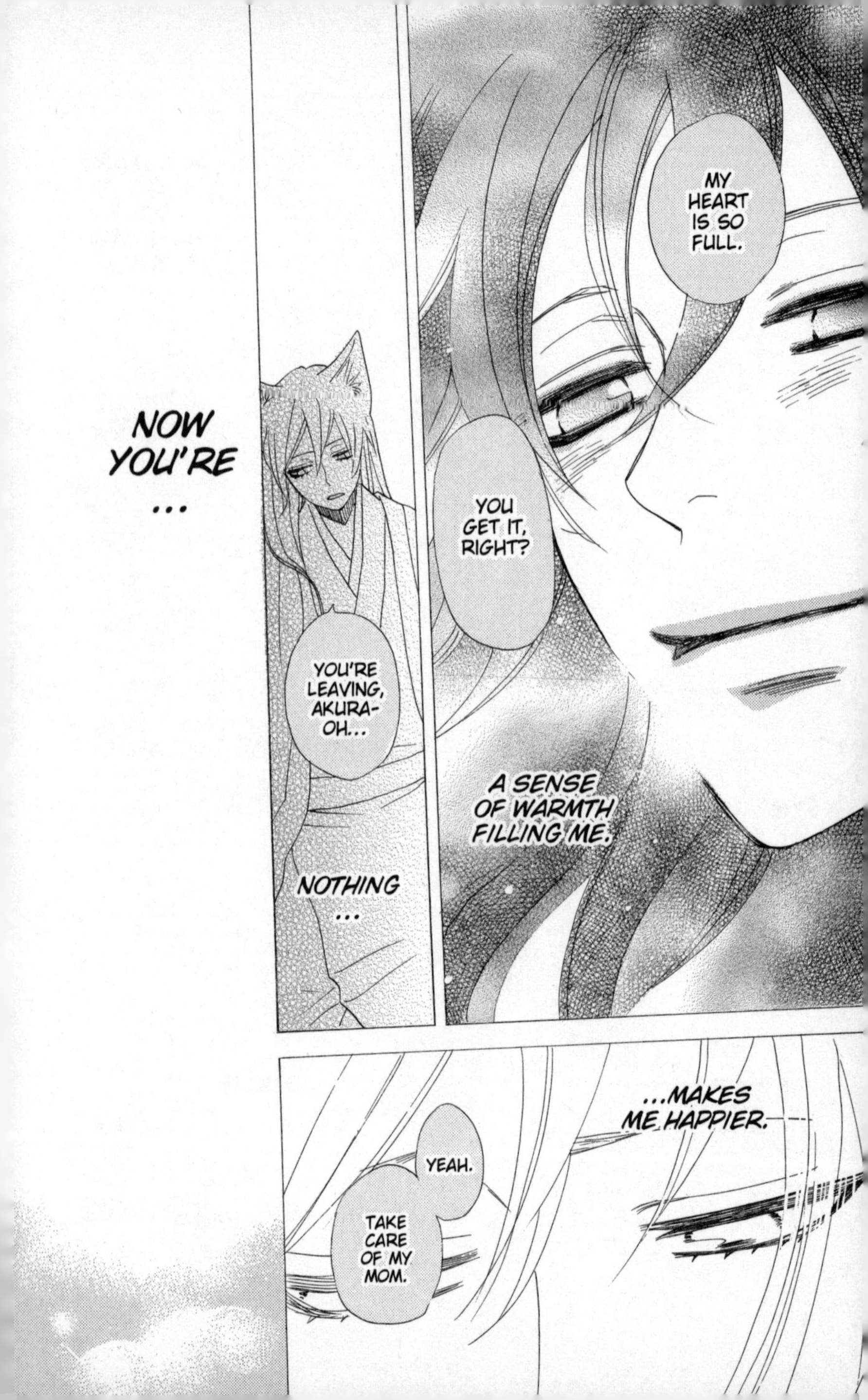
MY HEART IS SO FULL.
YOU GET IT, RIGHT?
A SENSE OF WARMTH FILLING ME.
YOU'RE LEAVING, AKURA-OH...
NOTHING ...
NOW YOU'RE ...
...MAKES ME HAPPIER.
YEAH.
TAKE CARE OF MY MOM.

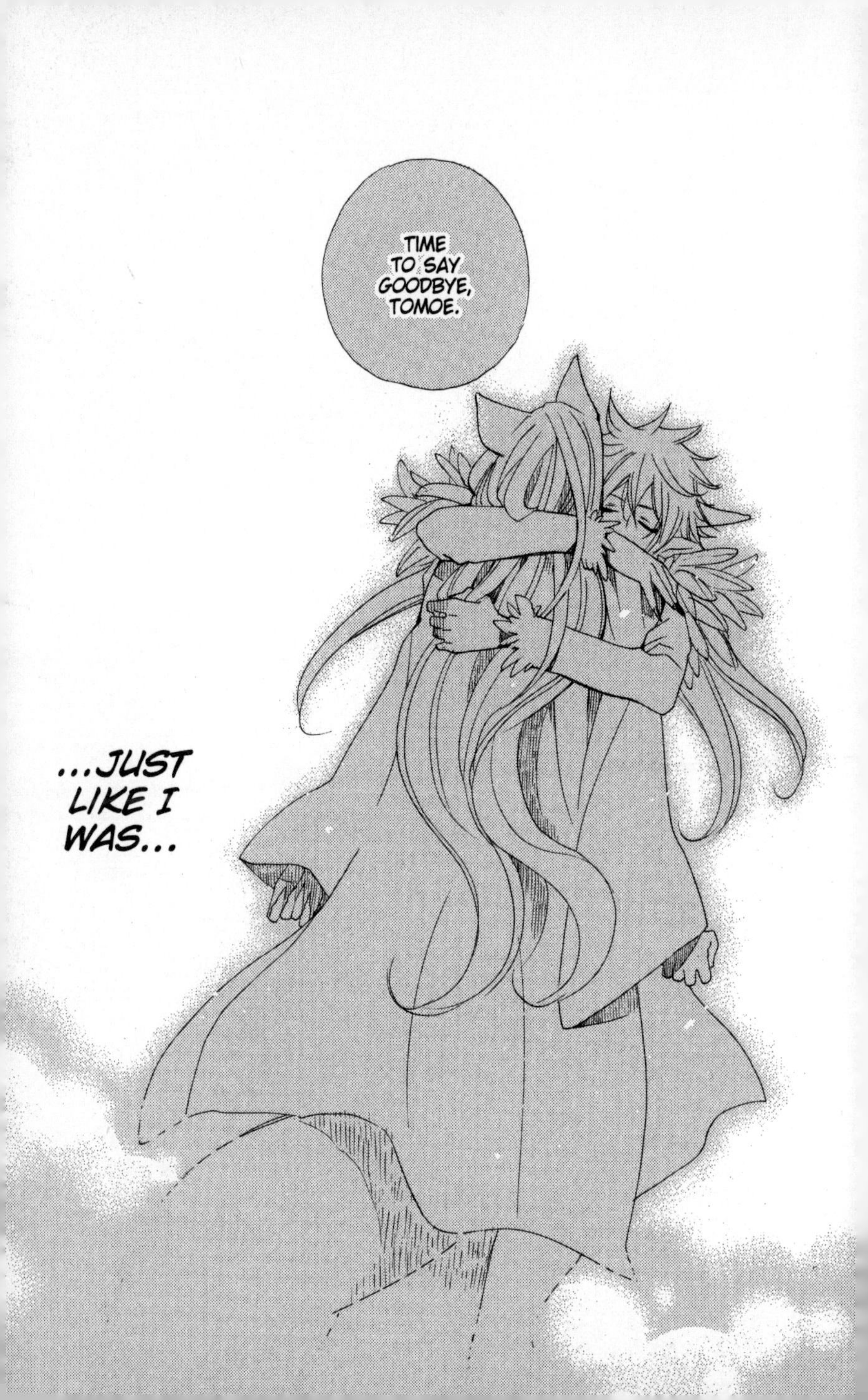
TIME TO SAY GOODBYE, TOMOE.
...JUST LIKE I WAS...

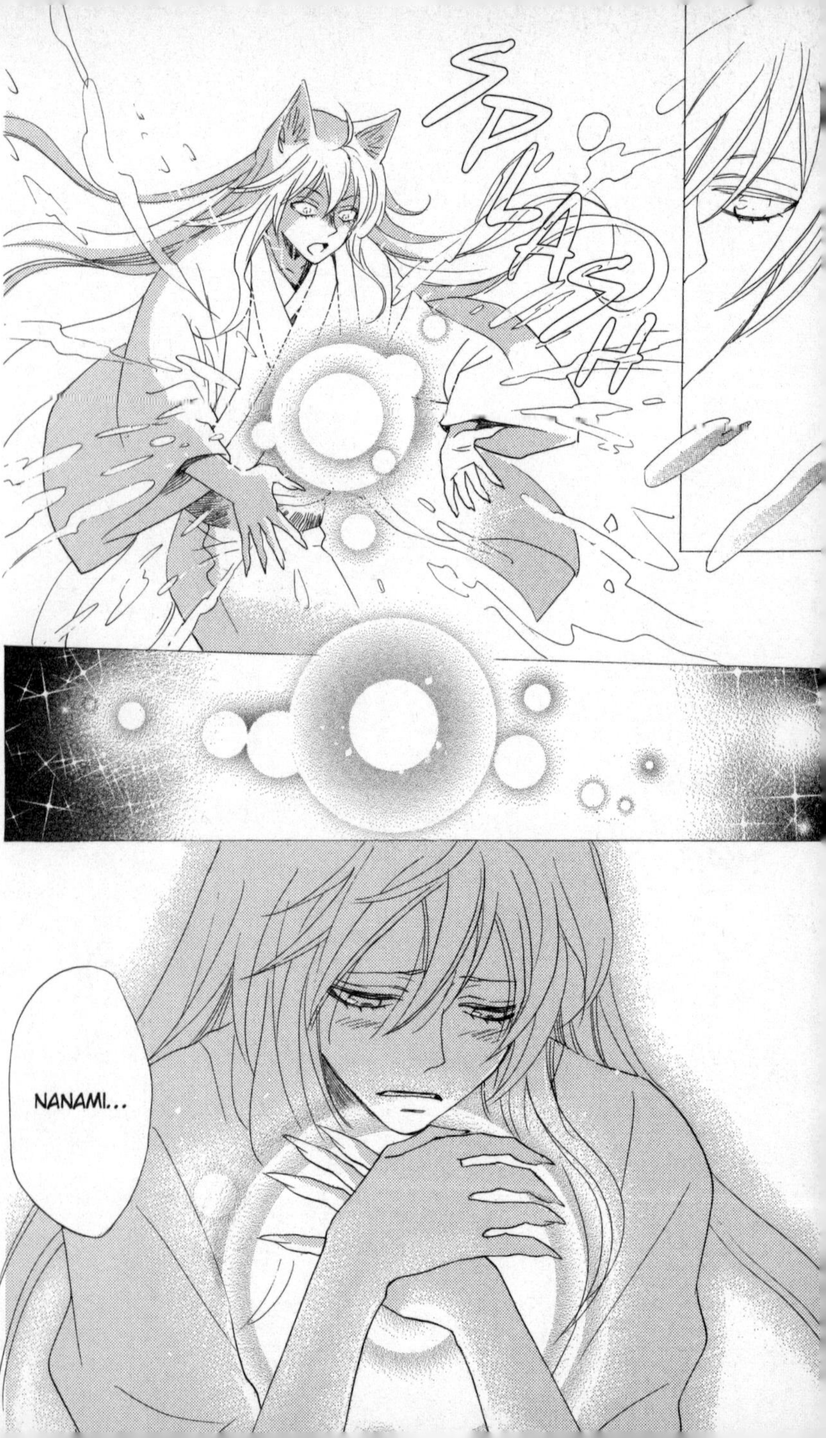
SPLASH
NANAMI...

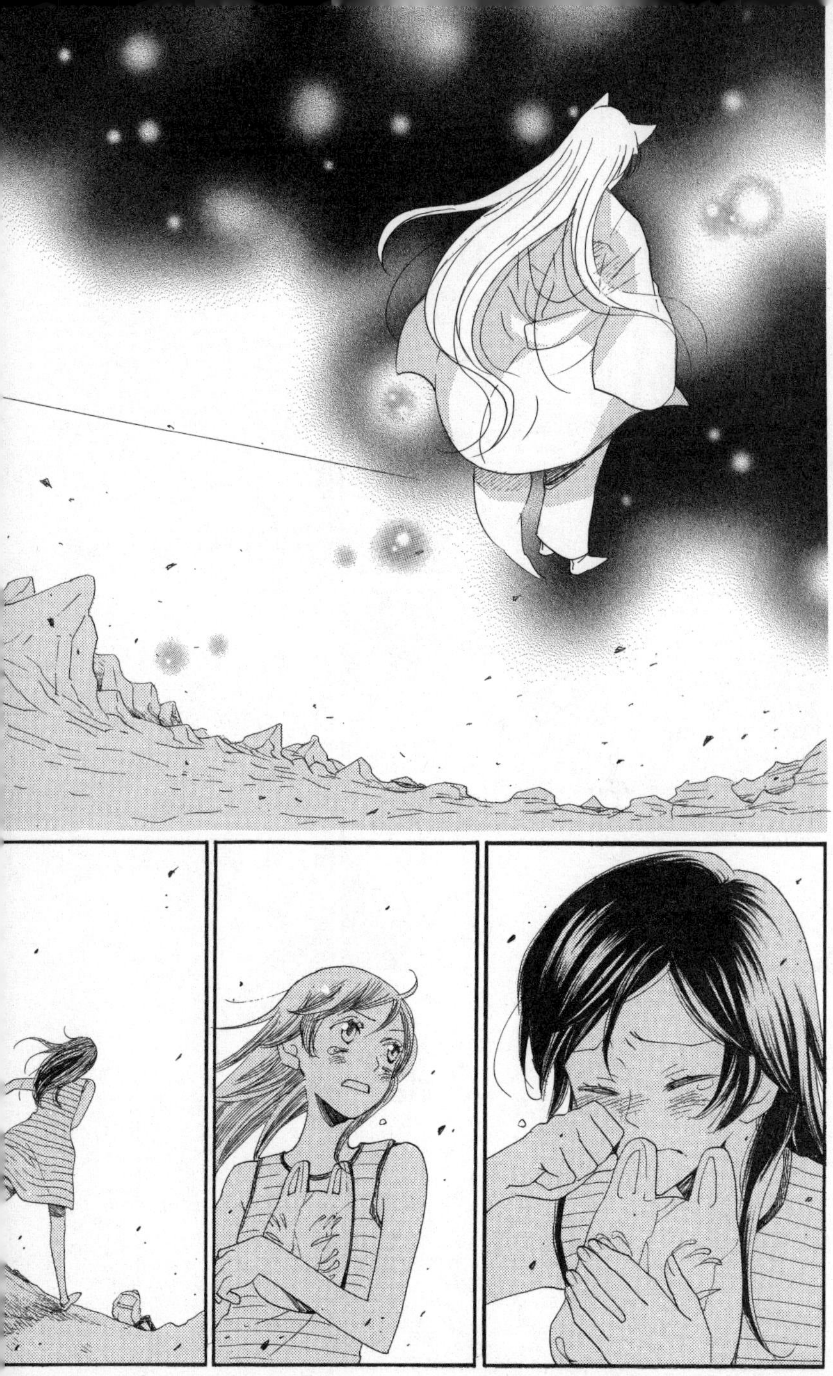

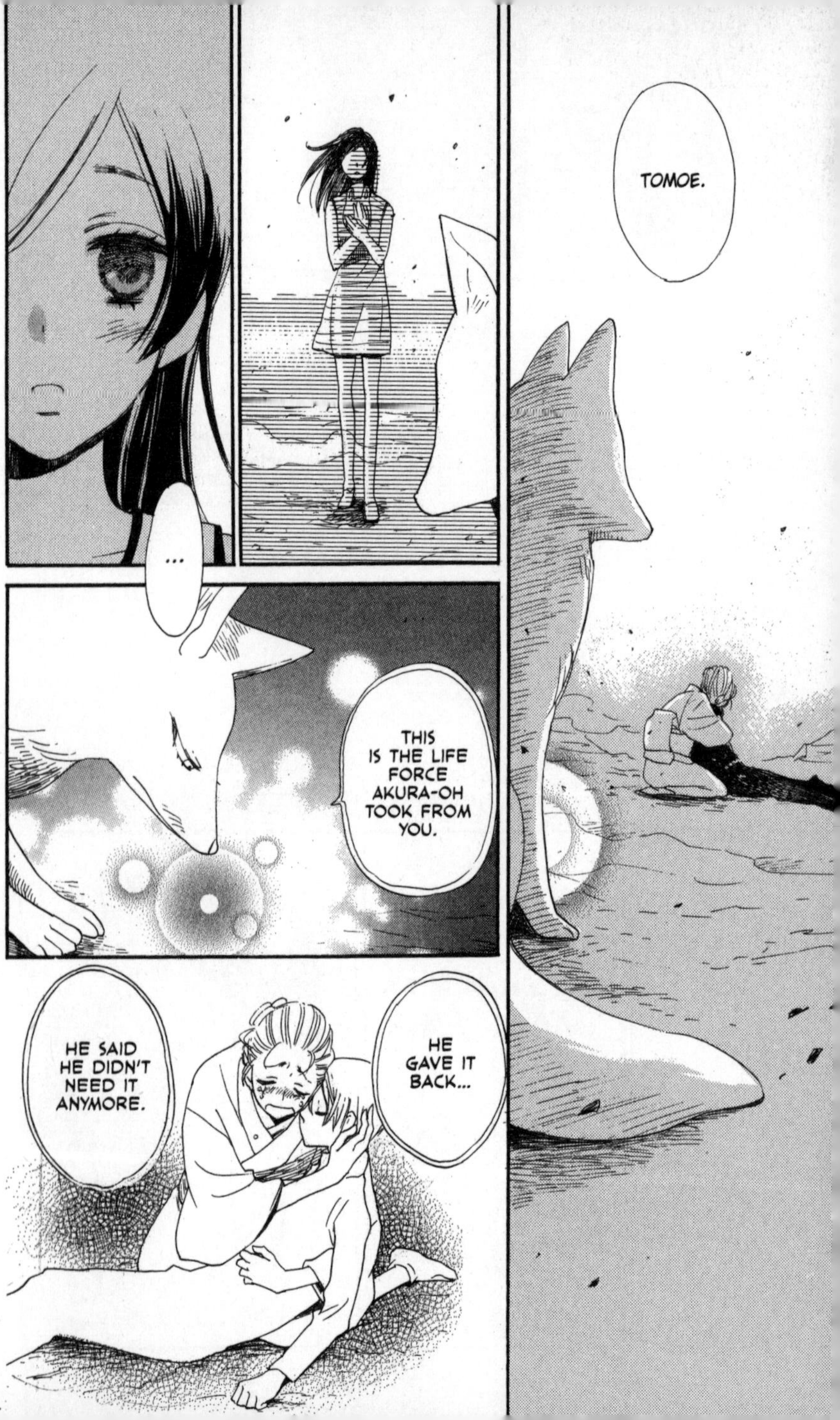
TOMOE.
...
THIS IS THE LIFE FORCE AKURA-OH TOOK FROM YOU.
HE GAVE IT BACK...
HE SAID HE DIDN'T NEED IT ANYMORE.

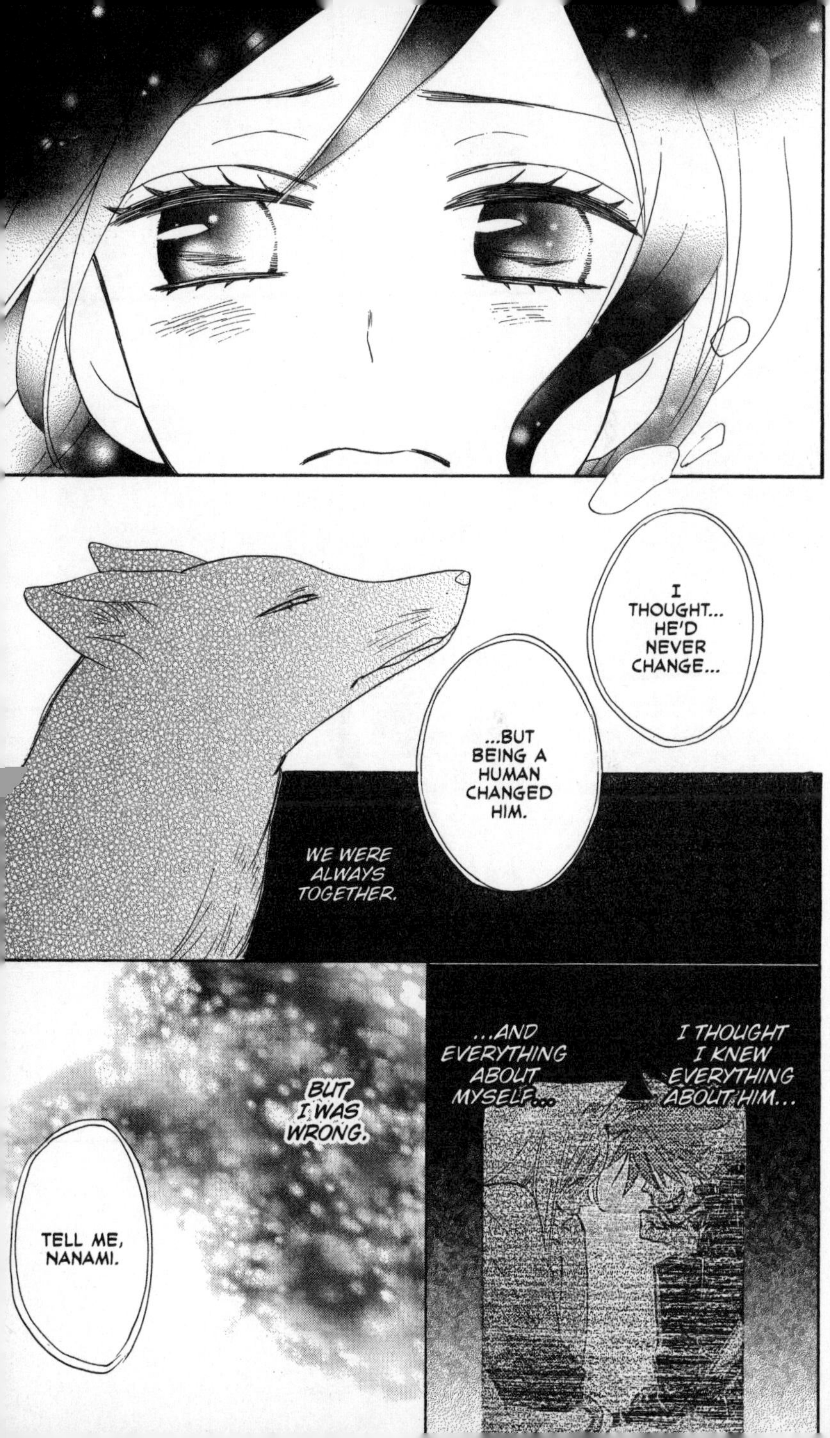
I THOUGHT... HE'D NEVER CHANGE...
...BUT BEING A HUMAN CHANGED HIM.
WE WERE ALWAYS TOGETHER.
I THOUGHT I KNEW EVERYTHING ABOUT HIM...
...AND EVERYTHING ABOUT MYSELF...
BUT I WAS WRONG.
TELL ME, NANAMI.

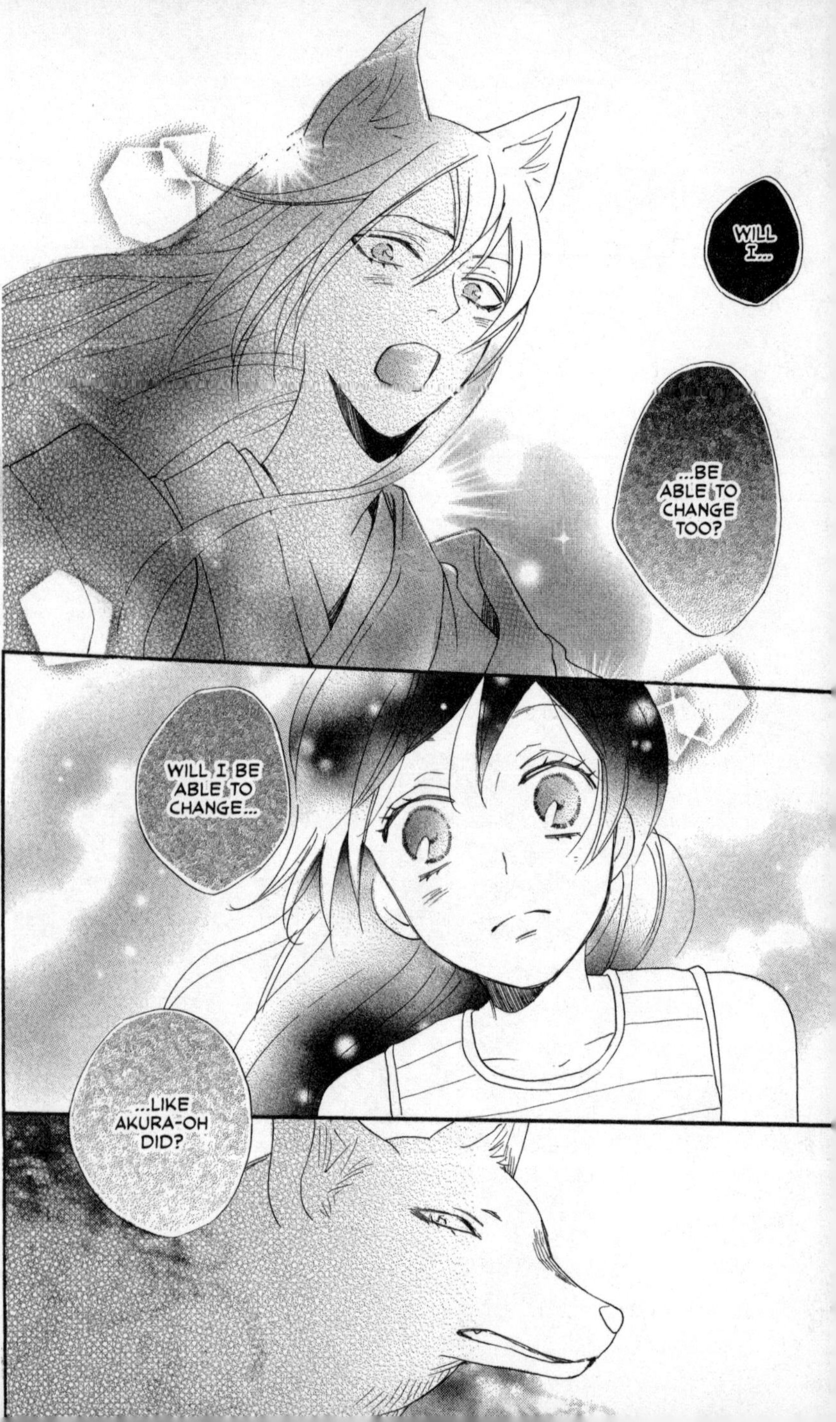
WILL I...
...BE ABLE TO CHANGE TOO?
WILL I BE ABLE TO CHANGE...
...LIKE AKURA-OH DID?

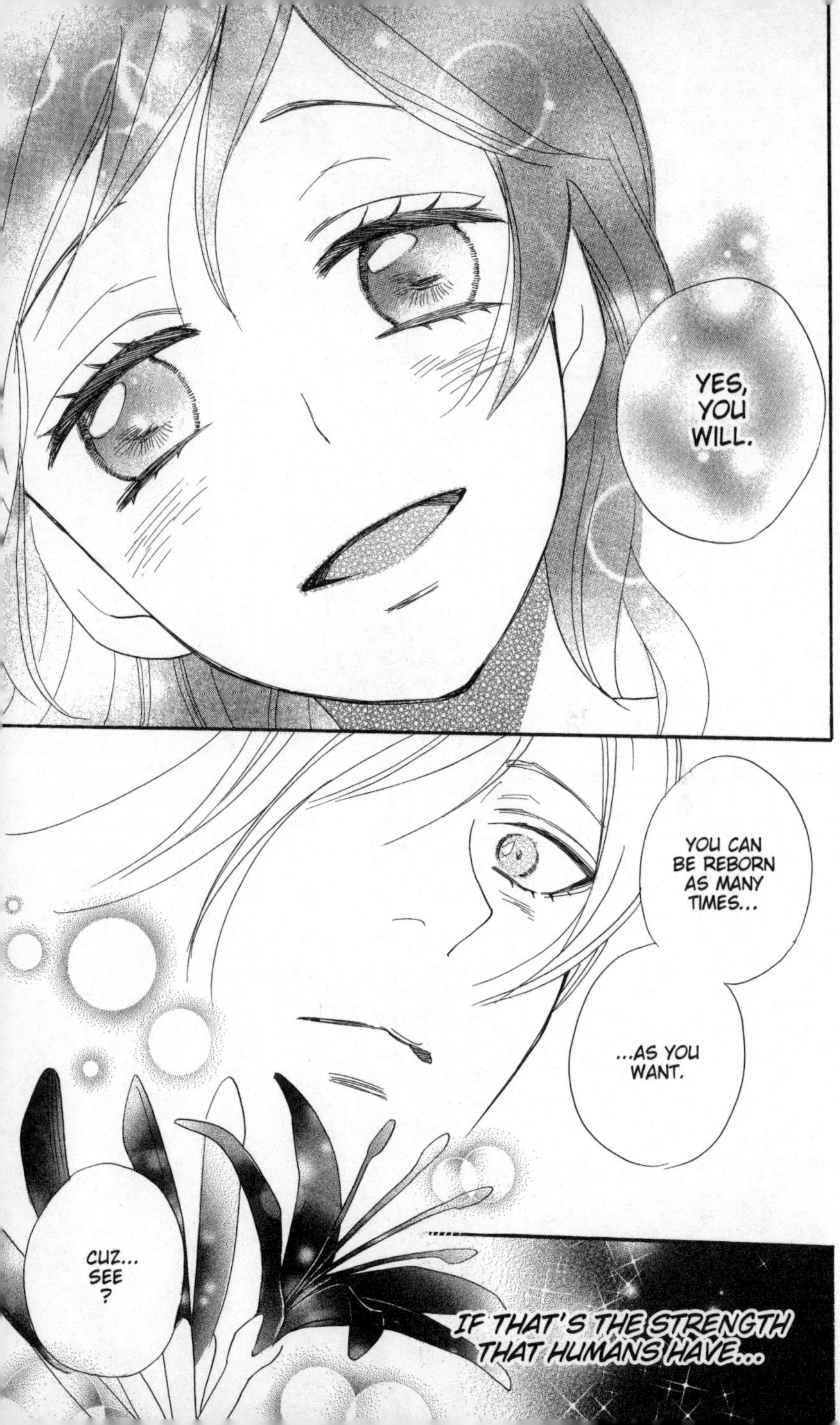
YES, YOU WILL.
YOU CAN BE REBORN AS MANY TIMES...
...AS YOU WANT.
CUZ... SEE?
IF THAT'S THE STRENGTH THAT HUMANS HAVE...

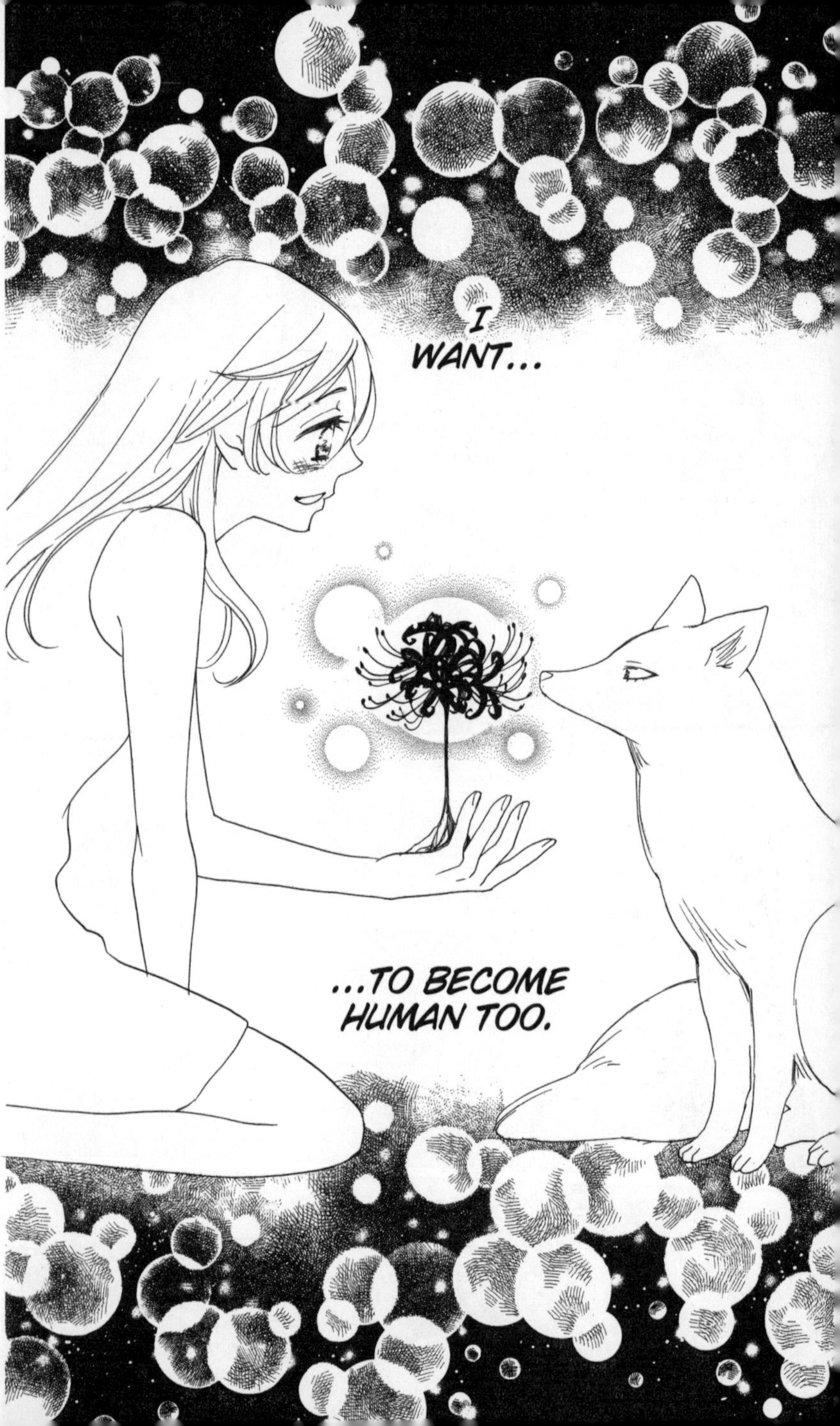
I WANT...
...TO BECOME HUMAN TOO.

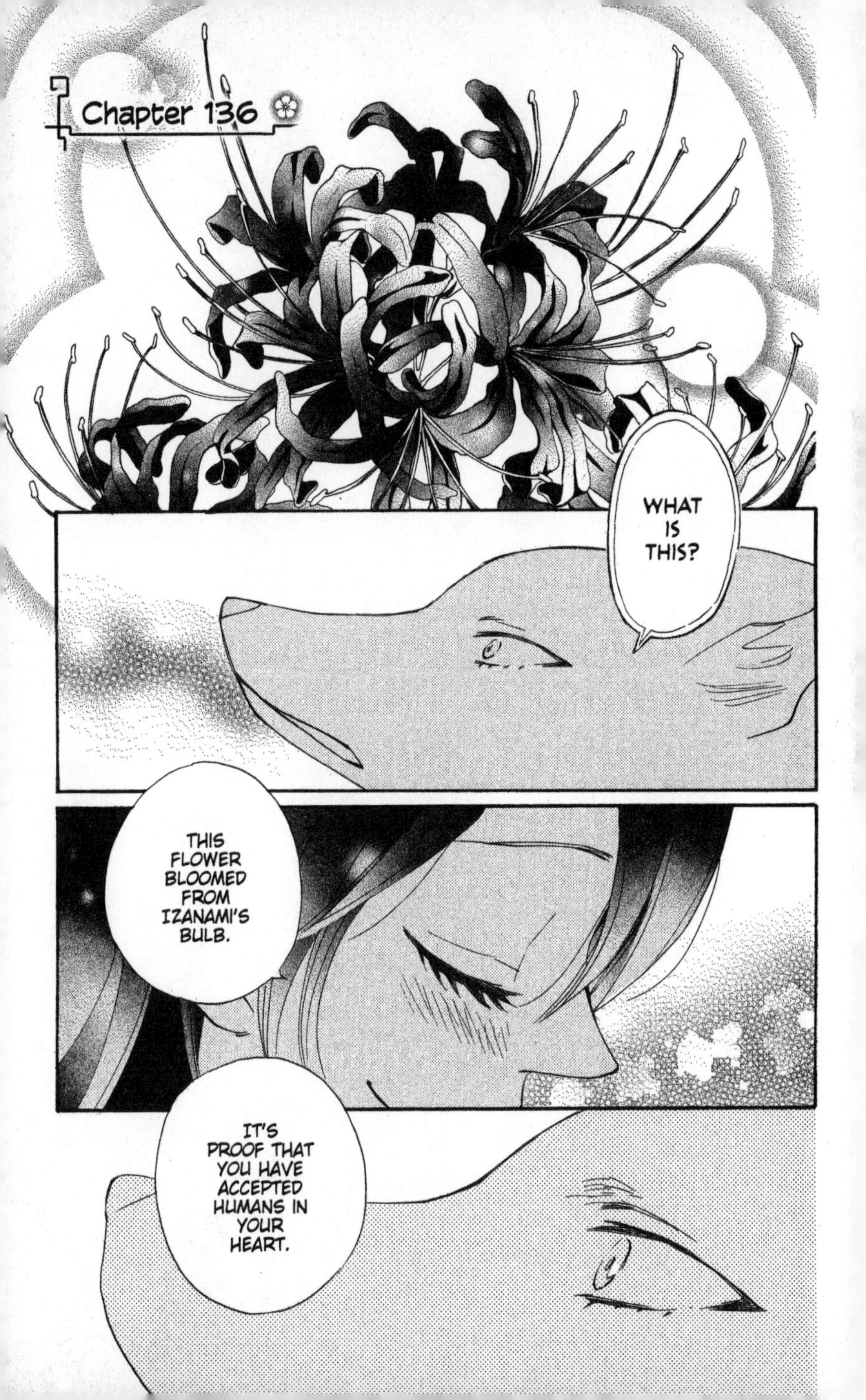
Chapter 136
WHAT IS THIS?
THIS FLOWER BLOOMED FROM IZANAMI'S BULB.
IT'S PROOF THAT YOU HAVE ACCEPTED HUMANS IN YOUR HEART.

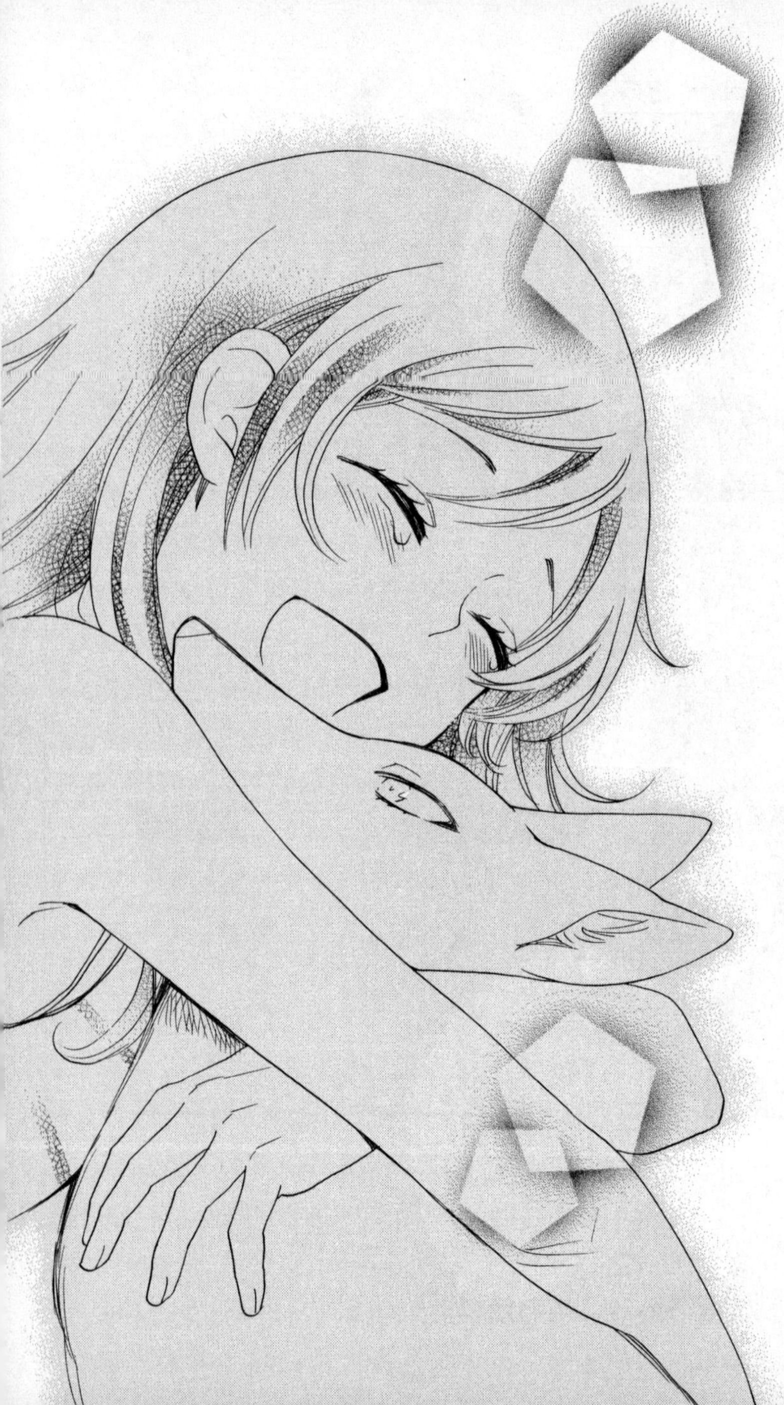

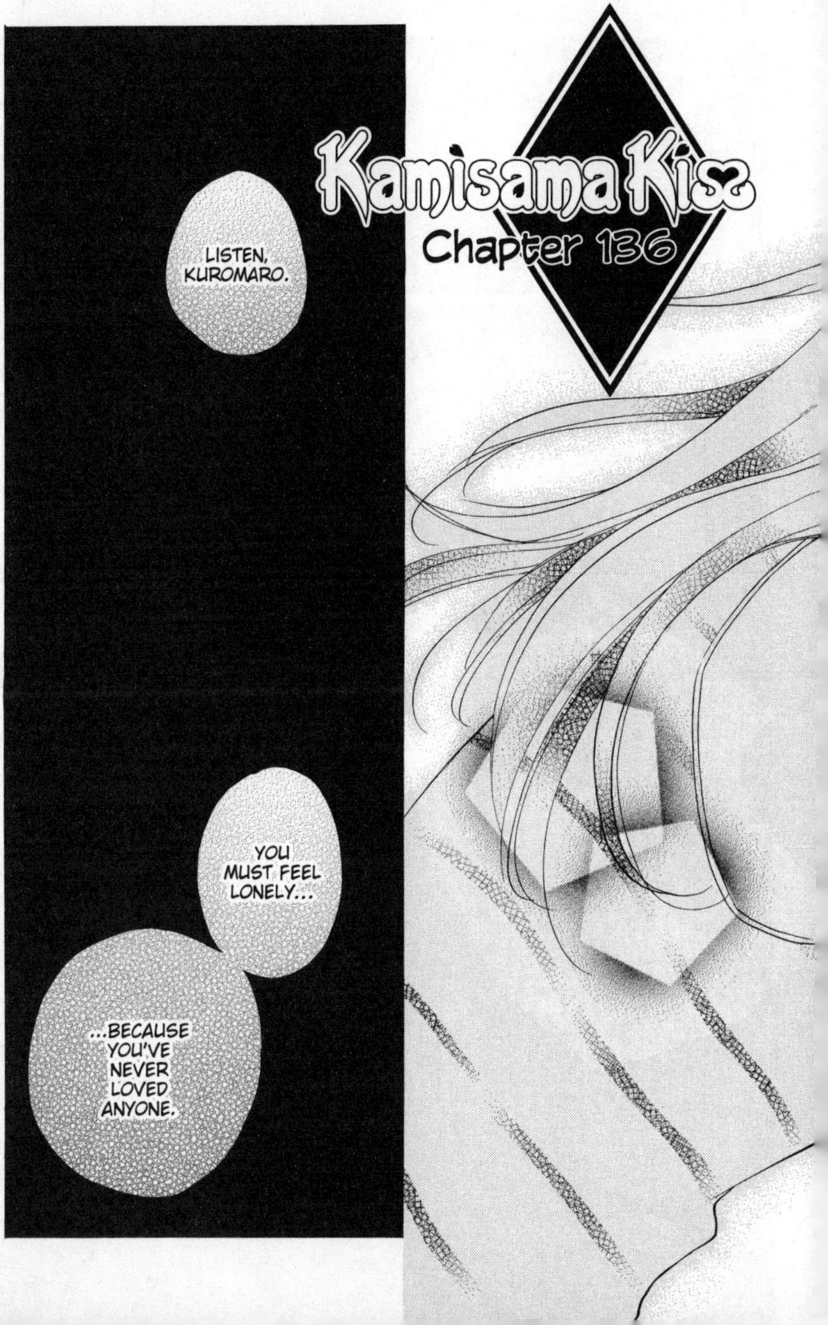
Kamisama Kiss
Chapter 136
LISTEN, KUROMARO.
YOU MUST FEEL LONELY...
...BECAUSE YOU'VE NEVER LOVED ANYONE.

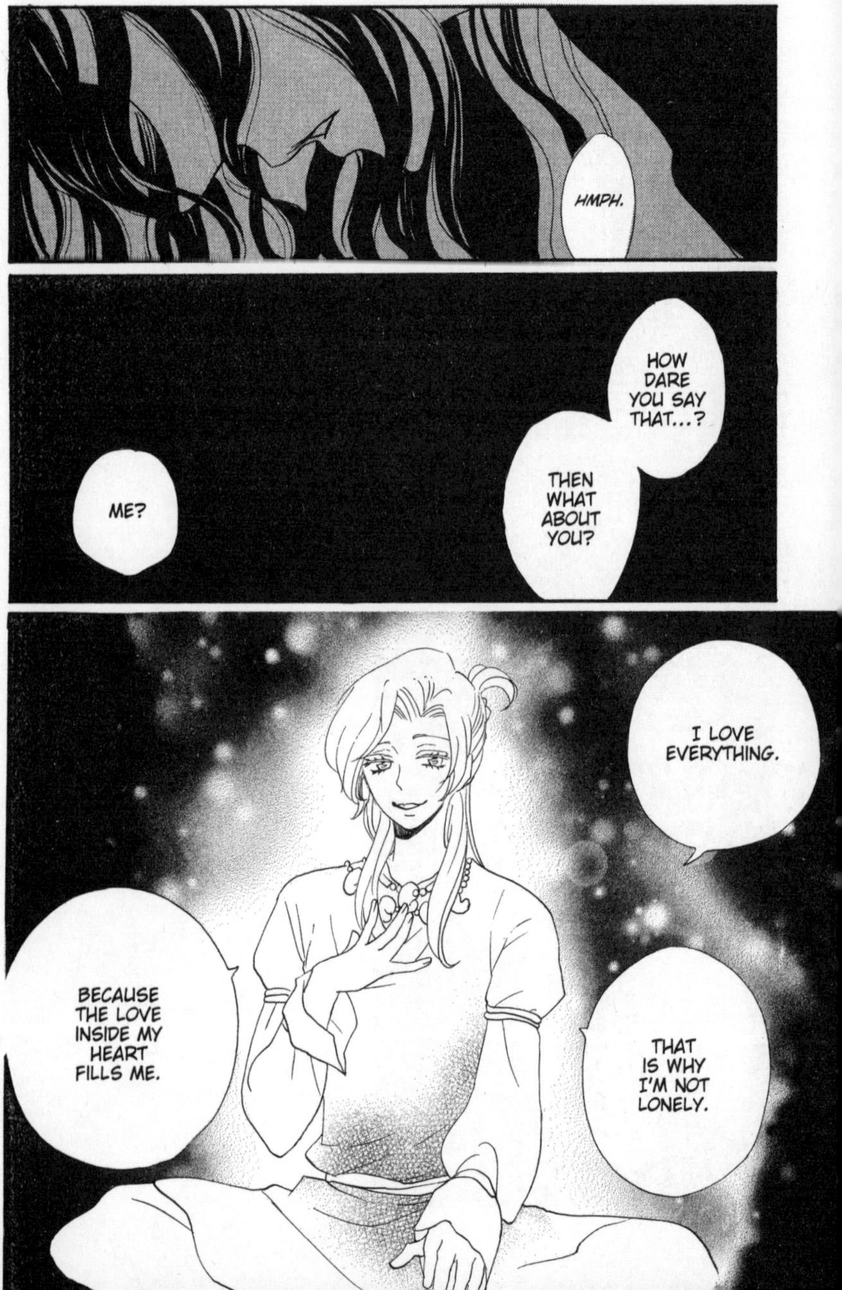
HMPH.
HOW DARE YOU SAY THAT...?
THEN WHAT ABOUT YOU?
ME?
I LOVE EVERYTHING.
BECAUSE THE LOVE INSIDE MY HEART FILLS ME.
THAT IS WHY I'M NOT LONELY.

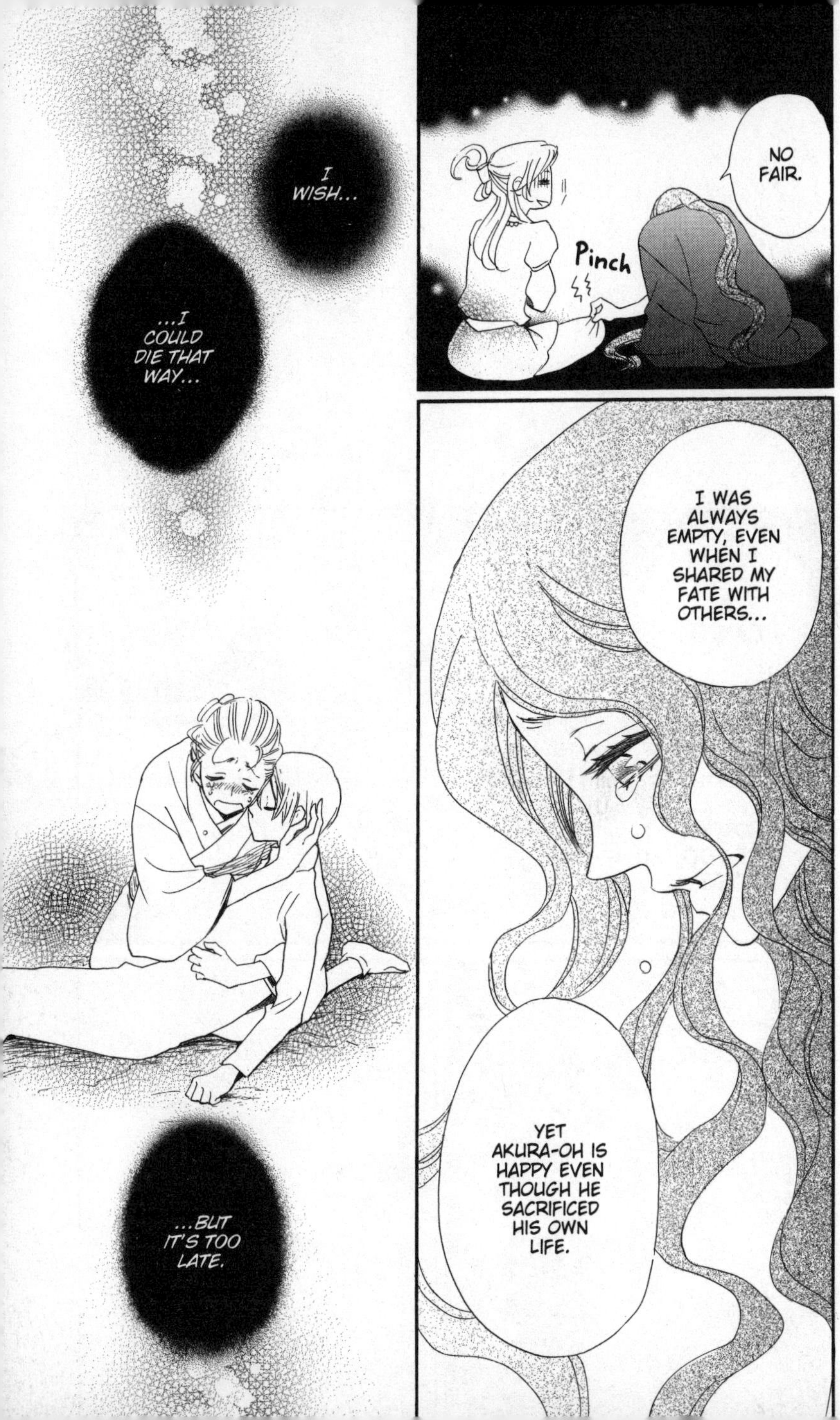
NO FAIR.
Pinch
I WAS ALWAYS EMPTY, EVEN WHEN I SHARED MY FATE WITH OTHERS...
YET AKURA-OH IS HAPPY EVEN THOUGH HE SACRIFICED HIS OWN LIFE.
I WISH...
...I COULD DIE THAT WAY...
...BUT IT'S TOO LATE.

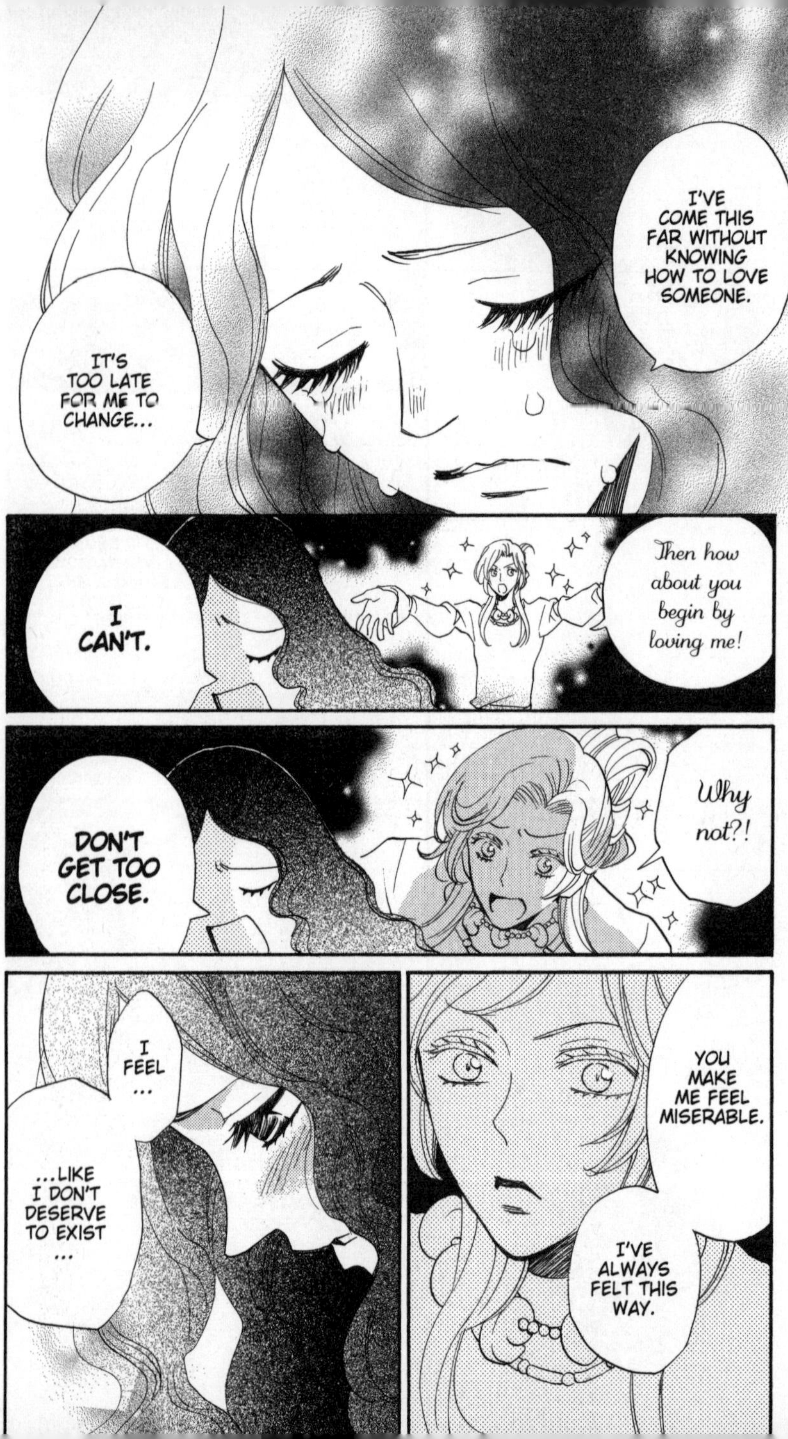
I'VE COME THIS FAR WITHOUT KNOWING HOW TO LOVE SOMEONE.
IT'S TOO LATE FOR ME TO CHANGE...
Then how about you begin by loving me!
I CAN'T.
Why not?!
DON'T GET TOO CLOSE.
YOU MAKE ME FEEL MISERABLE.
I'VE ALWAYS FELT THIS WAY.
I FEEL...
...LIKE I DON'T DESERVE TO EXIST...

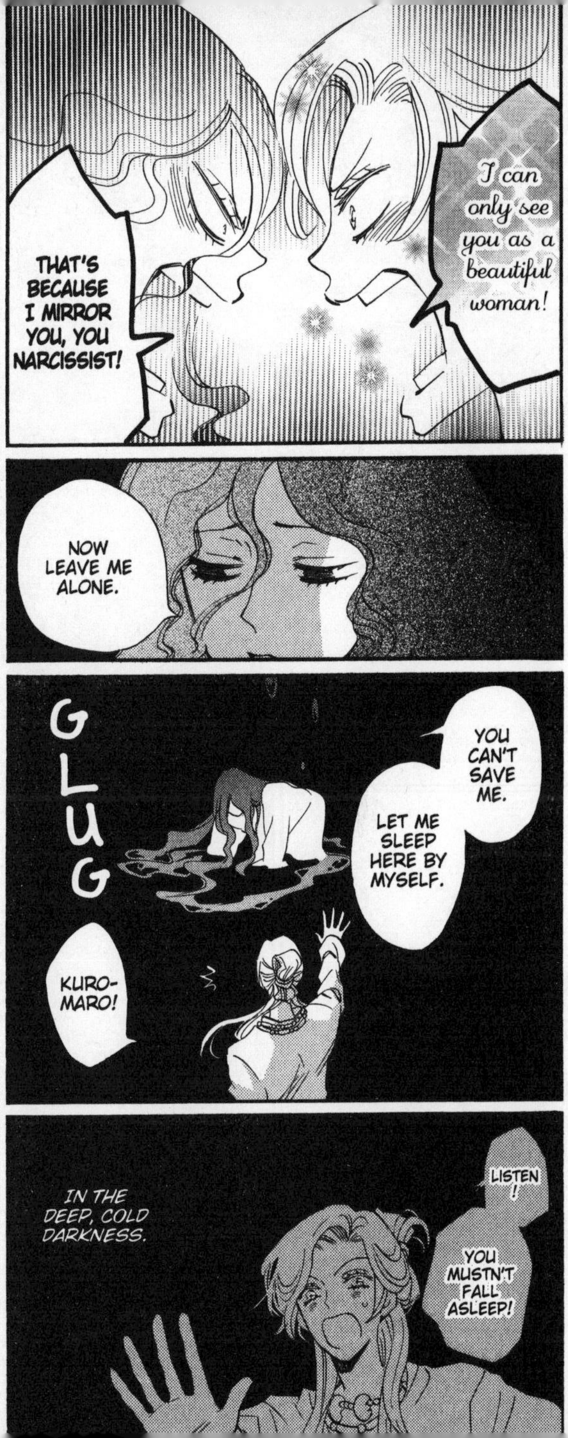
I can only see you as a beautiful woman!
THAT'S BECAUSE I MIRROR YOU, YOU NARCISSIST!
NOW LEAVE ME ALONE.
YOU CAN'T SAVE ME.
LET ME SLEEP HERE BY MYSELF.
GLUG
KURO-MARO!
LISTEN!
YOU MUSTN'T FALL ASLEEP!
IN THE DEEP, COLD DARKNESS.

(continued from previous sidebar)

I went on a Yokohama drive with Ms. Momoya of ZERO-SUM magazine.

We had lunch in Chinatown..

Come on! Come on!

I'll give you some extra!

1,000 yen!

...and bought delicious-looking roast chestnuts.

There was a chestnut peeler included. It was so useful, I still have it.

Yokohama Red Brick Warehouse

There were lots of cute shops.

The ice cream we had there was so delicious!

This is good.

Ms. Momoya

We rode the Ferris wheel to enjoy the night view.

It had been quite a while since I last spent a whole day doing fun stuff!

Thanks, Momoya-san!

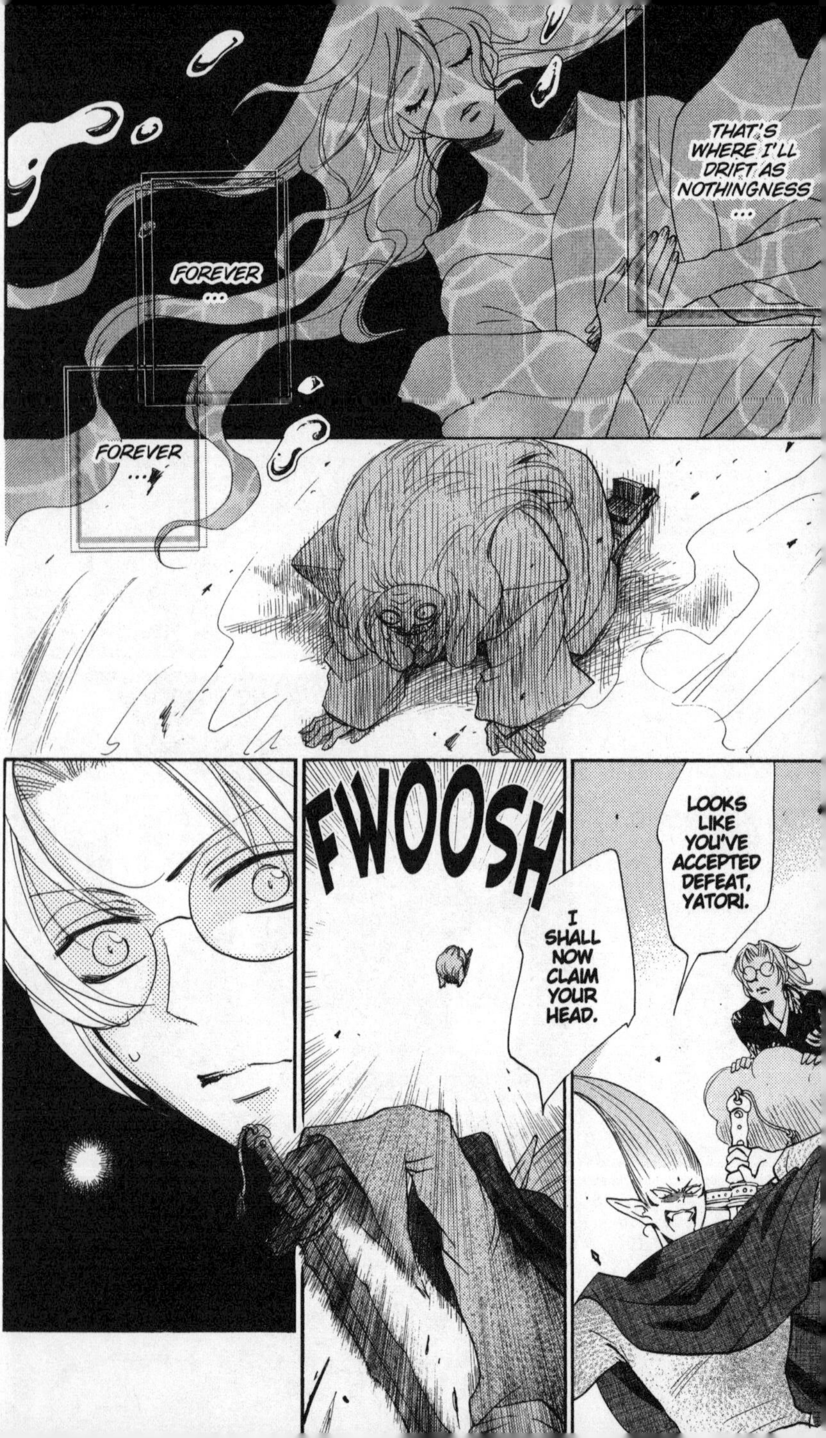
THAT'S WHERE I'LL DRIFT AS NOTHINGNESS ...
FOREVER ...
FOREVER ...
LOOKS LIKE YOU'VE ACCEPTED DEFEAT, YATORI.
I SHALL NOW CLAIM YOUR HEAD.
FWOOSH

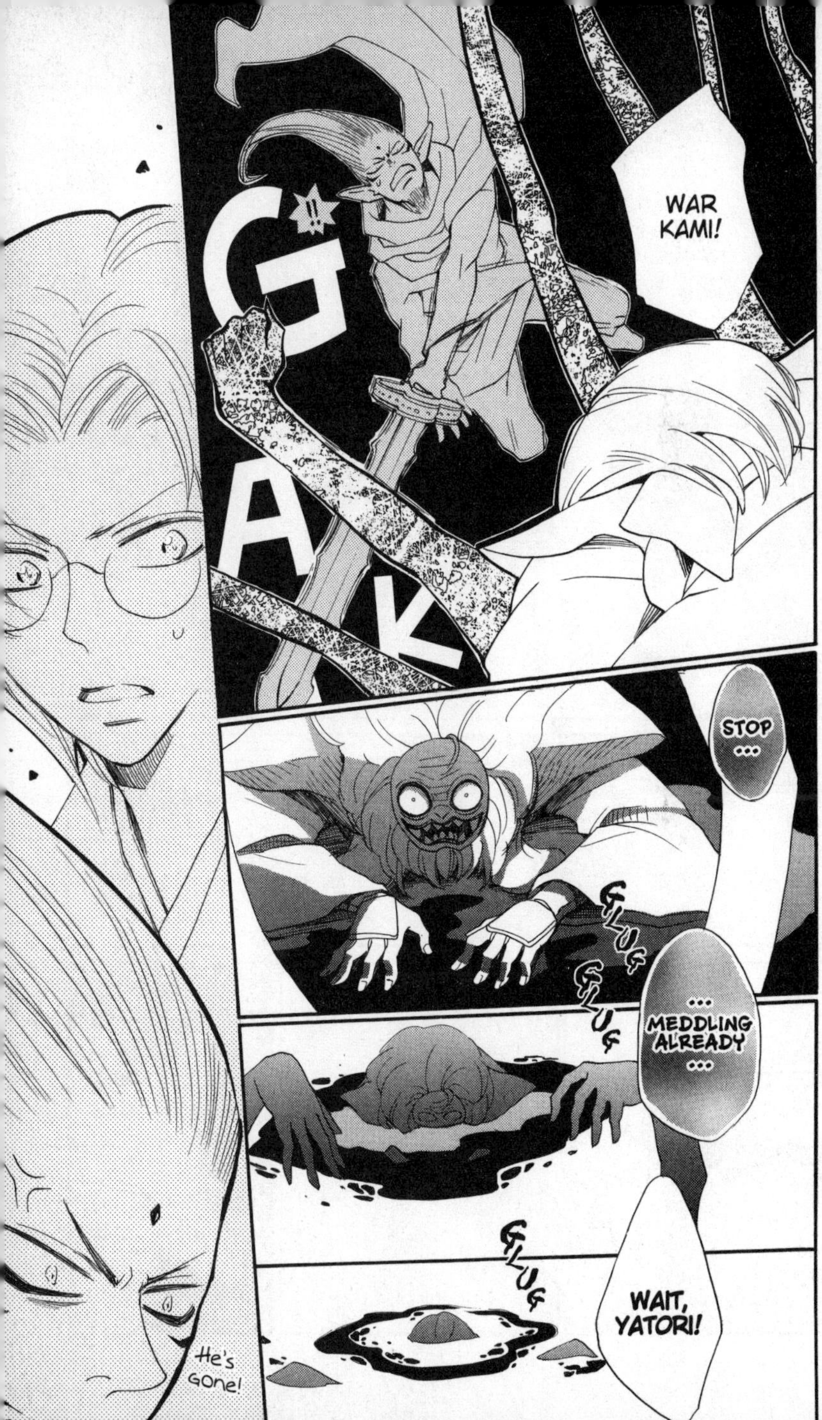

WAR KAMI!
!!
GAK
STOP ...
GLUG
GLUG
... MEDDLING ALREADY ...
GLUG
WAIT, YATORI!
He's gone!

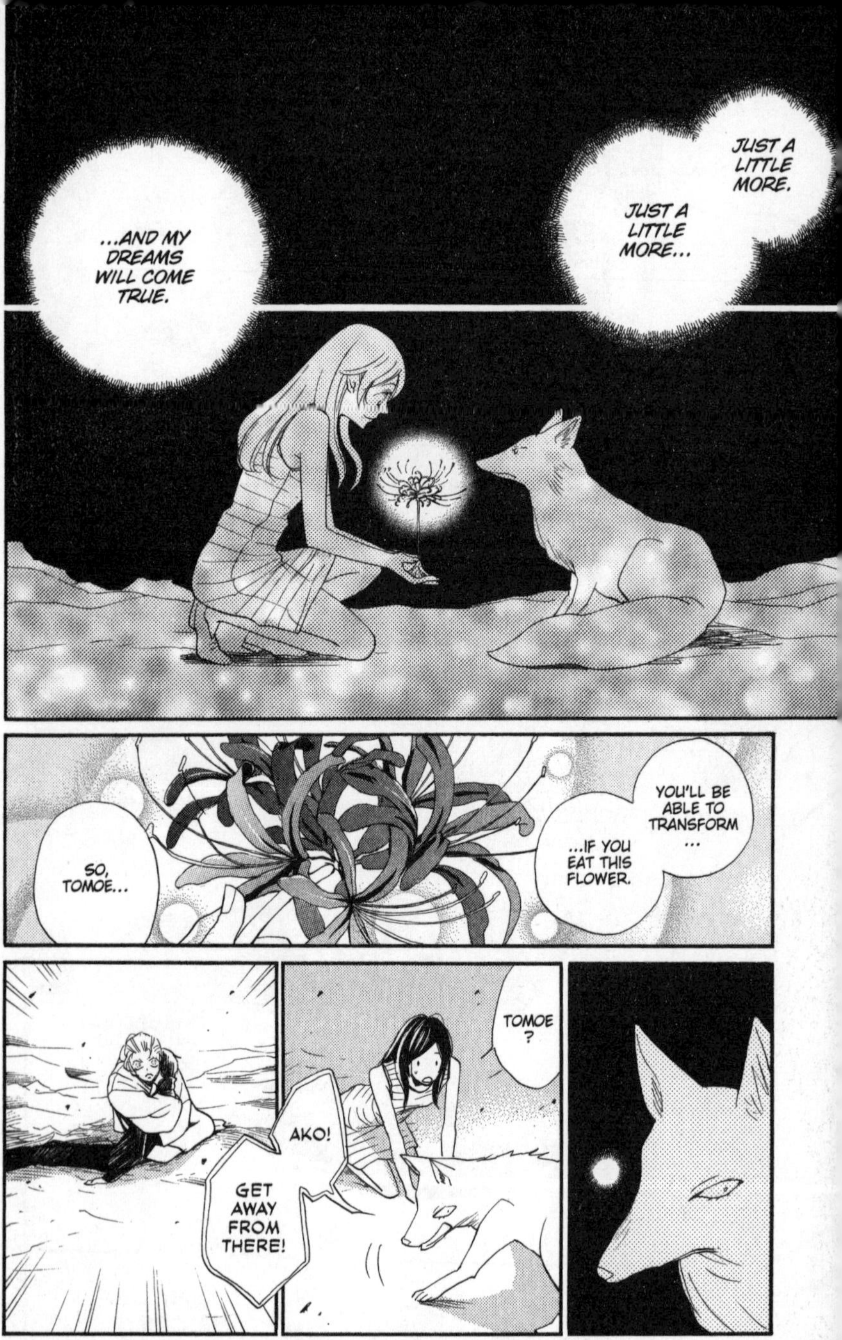
JUST A LITTLE MORE.
JUST A LITTLE MORE...
...AND MY DREAMS WILL COME TRUE.
YOU'LL BE ABLE TO TRANSFORM ...
...IF YOU EAT THIS FLOWER.
SO, TOMOE...
TOMOE ?
AKO!
GET AWAY FROM THERE!

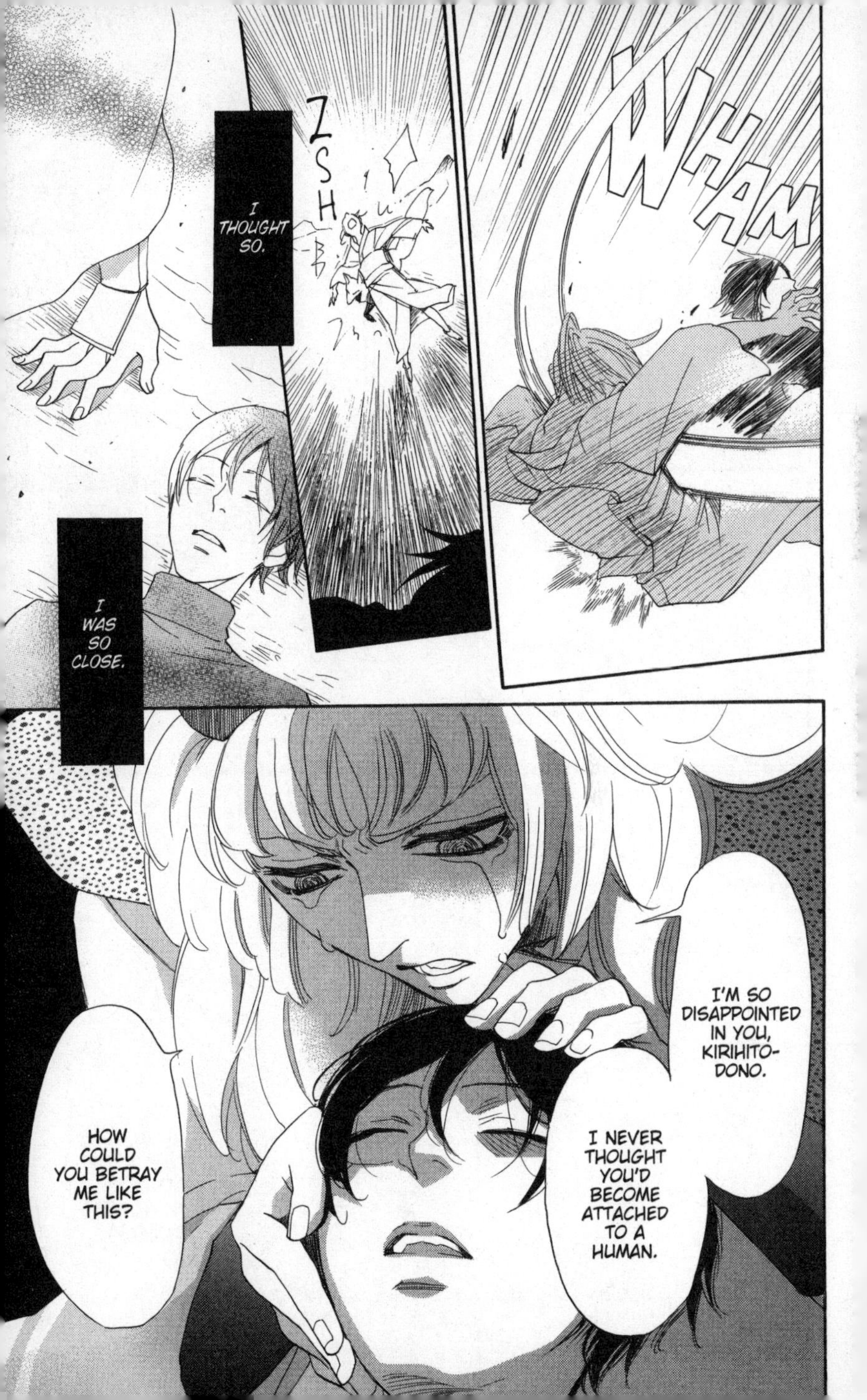
WHAM
ZSH
I THOUGHT SO.
I WAS SO CLOSE.
I'M SO DISAPPOINTED IN YOU, KIRIHITO-DONO.
I NEVER THOUGHT YOU'D BECOME ATTACHED TO A HUMAN.
HOW COULD YOU BETRAY ME LIKE THIS?

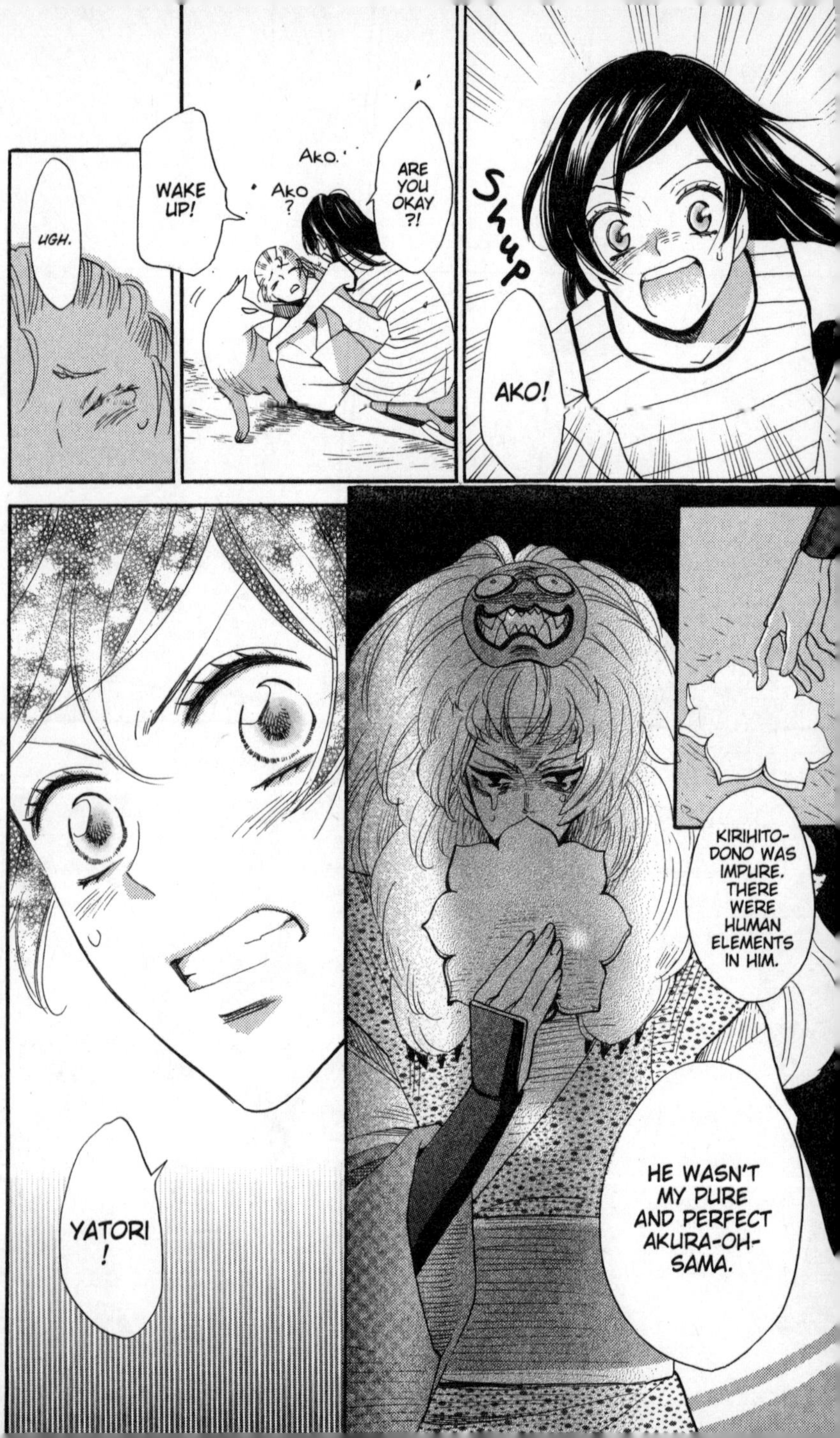
Shup
AKO!
ARE YOU OKAY?!
Ako.
Ako?
WAKE UP!
UGH.
KIRIHITO-DONO WAS IMPURE. THERE WERE HUMAN ELEMENTS IN HIM.
HE WASN'T MY PURE AND PERFECT AKURA-OH-SAMA.
YATORI!

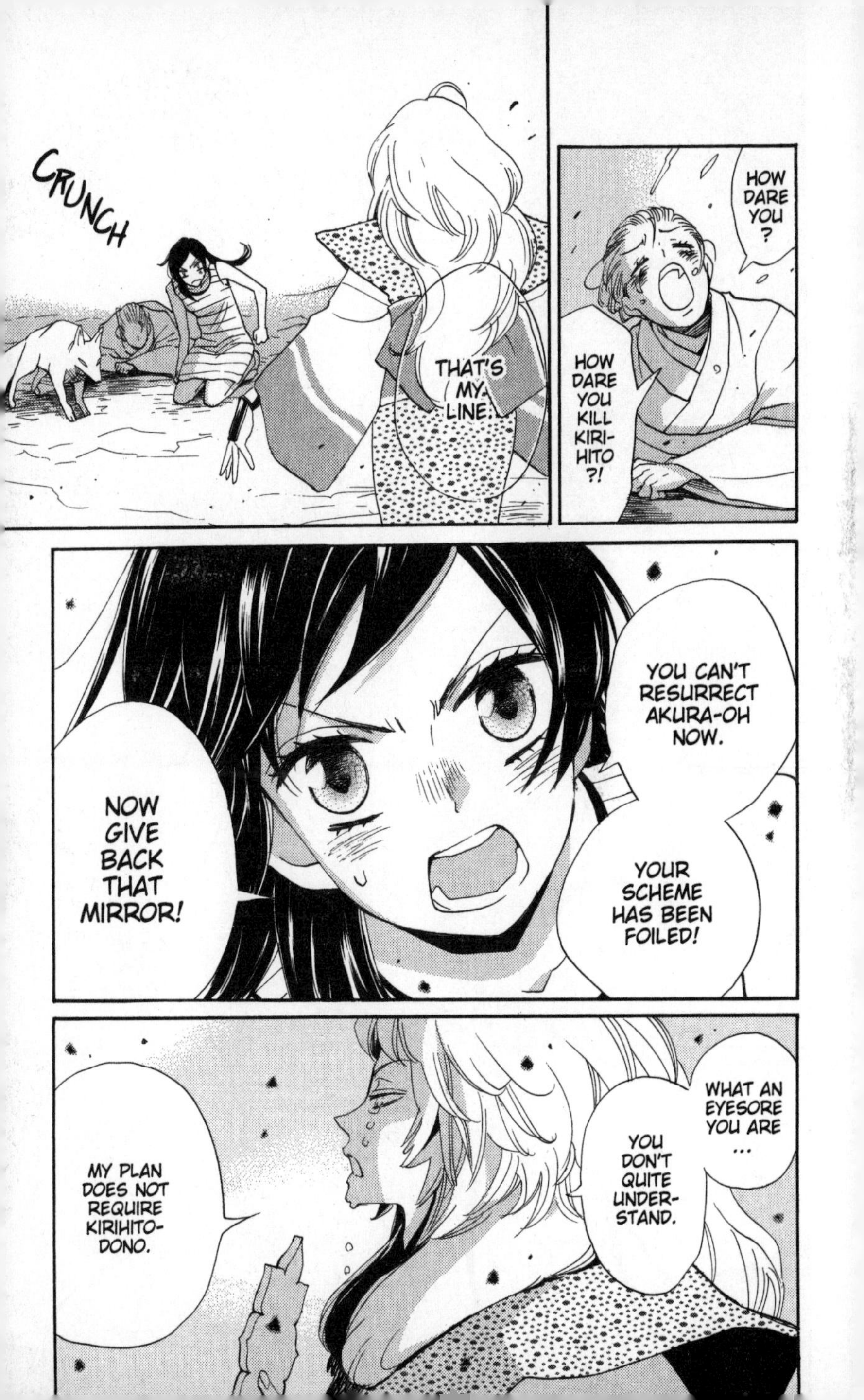
HOW DARE YOU?
HOW DARE YOU KILL KIRIHITO?!
CRUNCH
THAT'S MY LINE.
YOU CAN'T RESURRECT AKURA-OH NOW.
YOUR SCHEME HAS BEEN FOILED!
NOW GIVE BACK THAT MIRROR!
WHAT AN EYESORE YOU ARE...
YOU DON'T QUITE UNDER-STAND.
MY PLAN DOES NOT REQUIRE KIRIHITO-DONO.

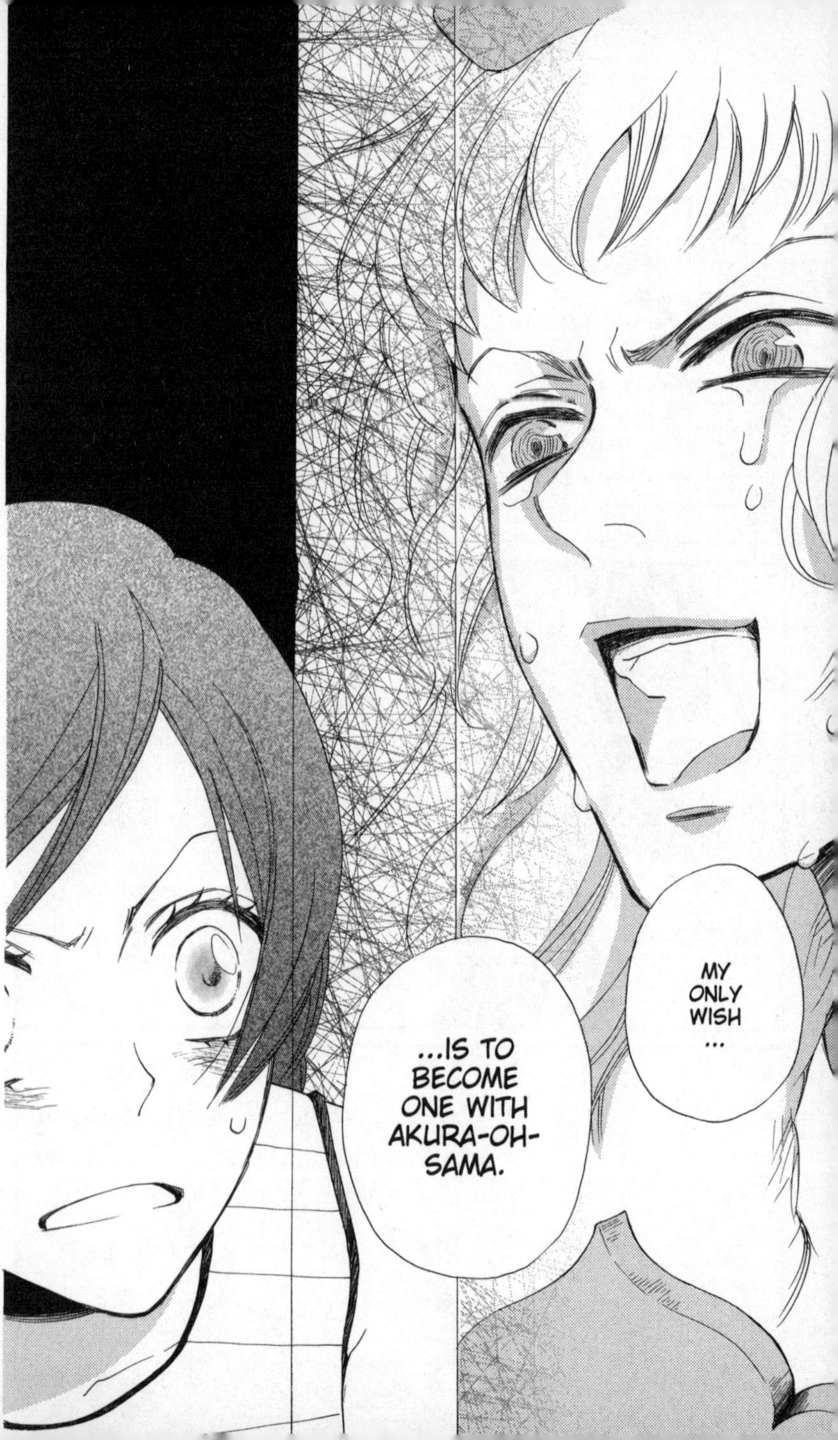
MY ONLY WISH ...
...IS TO BECOME ONE WITH AKURA-OH-SAMA.

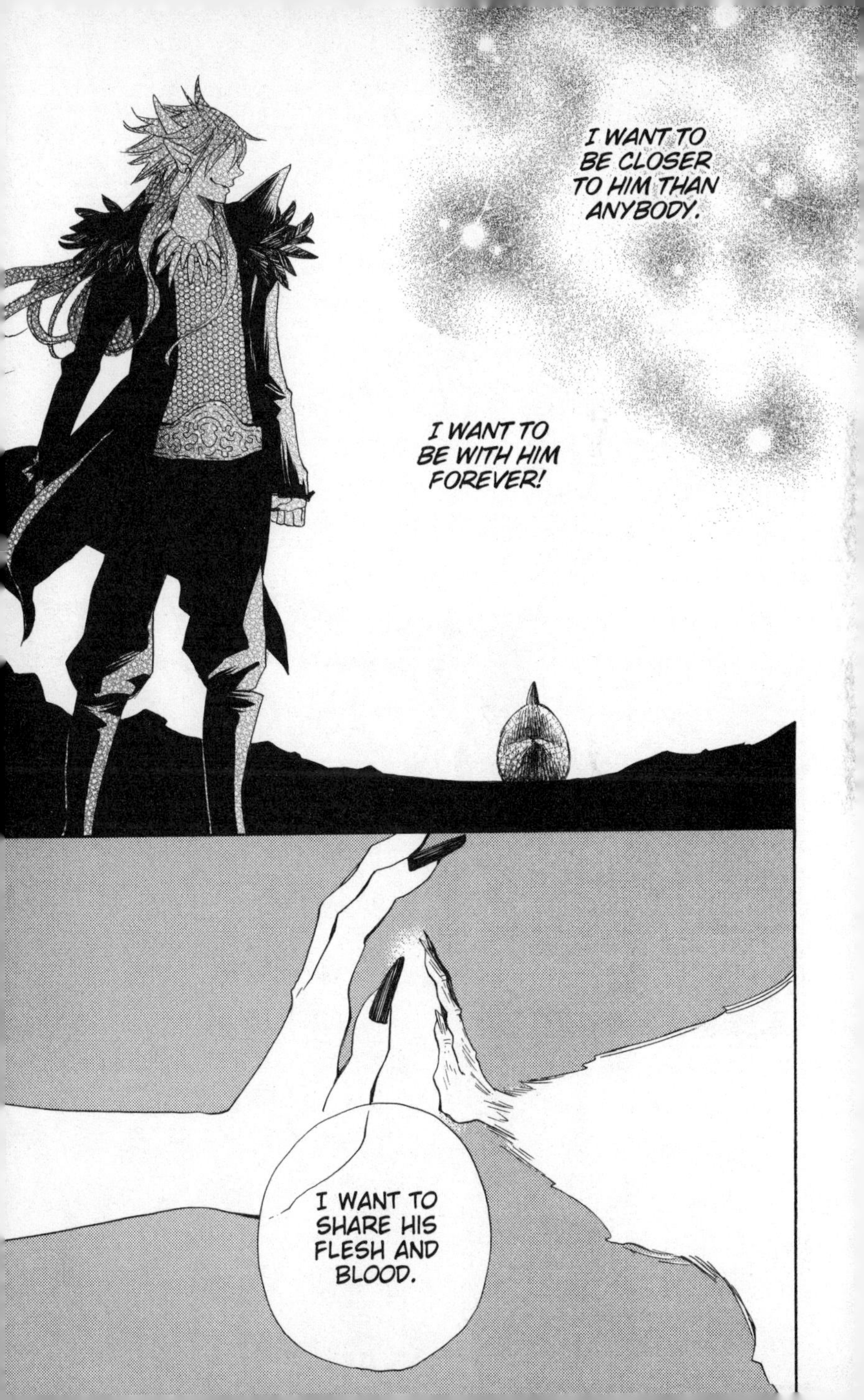
I WANT TO BE CLOSER TO HIM THAN ANYBODY.
I WANT TO BE WITH HIM FOREVER!
I WANT TO SHARE HIS FLESH AND BLOOD.

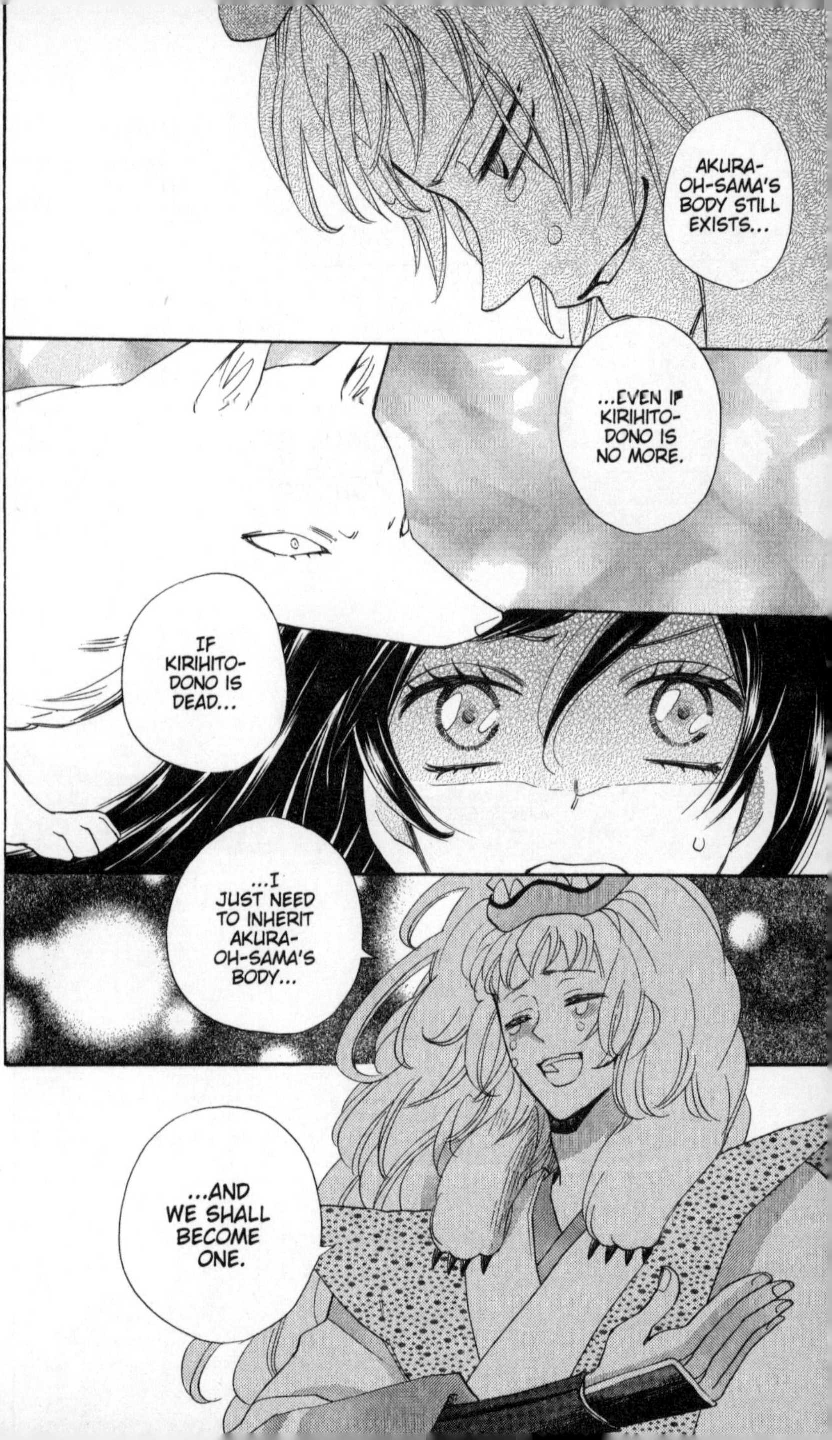
AKURA-OH-SAMA'S BODY STILL EXISTS...
...EVEN IF KIRIHITO-DONO IS NO MORE.
IF KIRIHITO-DONO IS DEAD...
...I JUST NEED TO INHERIT AKURA-OH-SAMA'S BODY...
...AND WE SHALL BECOME ONE.

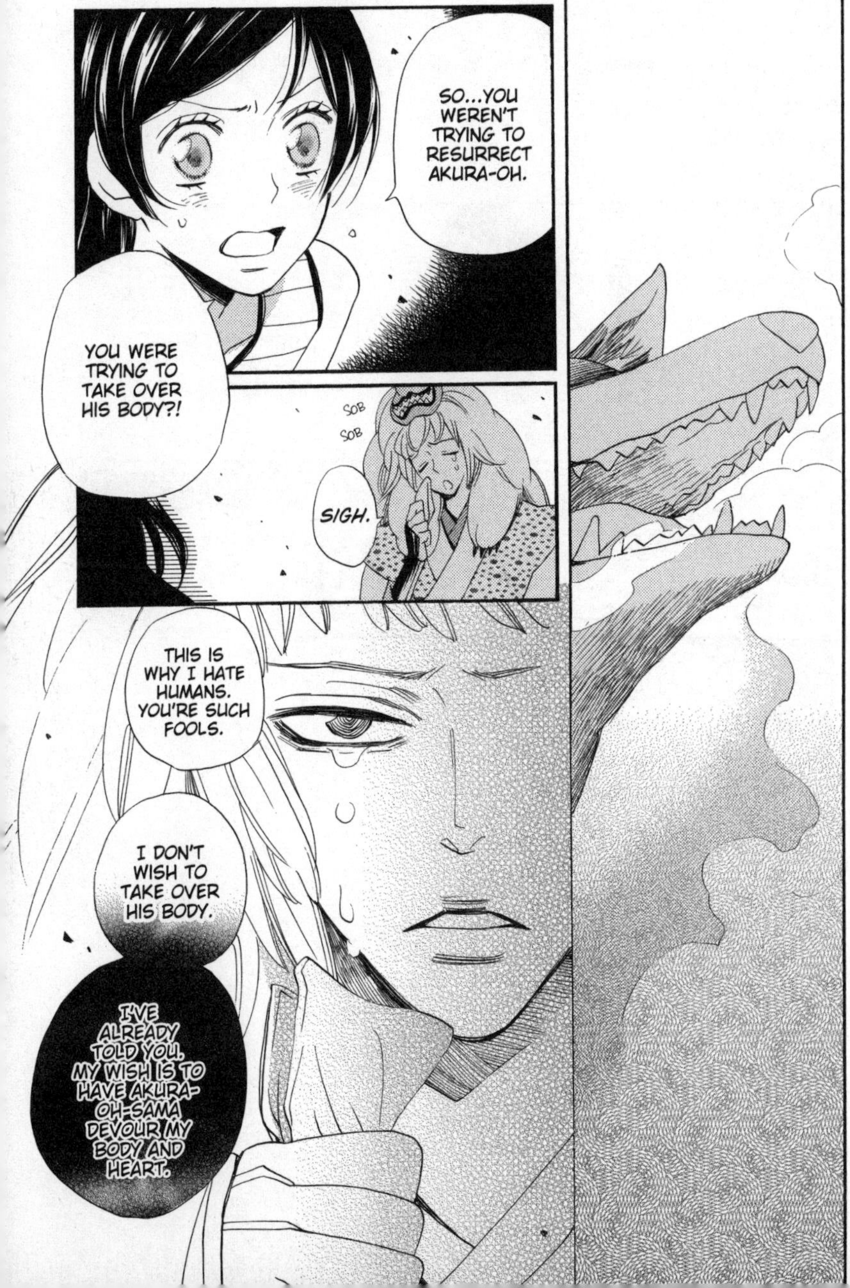
SO...YOU WEREN'T TRYING TO RESURRECT AKURA-OH.
YOU WERE TRYING TO TAKE OVER HIS BODY?!
SOB SOB
SIGH.
THIS IS WHY I HATE HUMANS. YOU'RE SUCH FOOLS.
I DON'T WISH TO TAKE OVER HIS BODY.
I'VE ALREADY TOLD YOU. MY WISH IS TO HAVE AKURA-OH-SAMA DEVOUR MY BODY AND HEART.

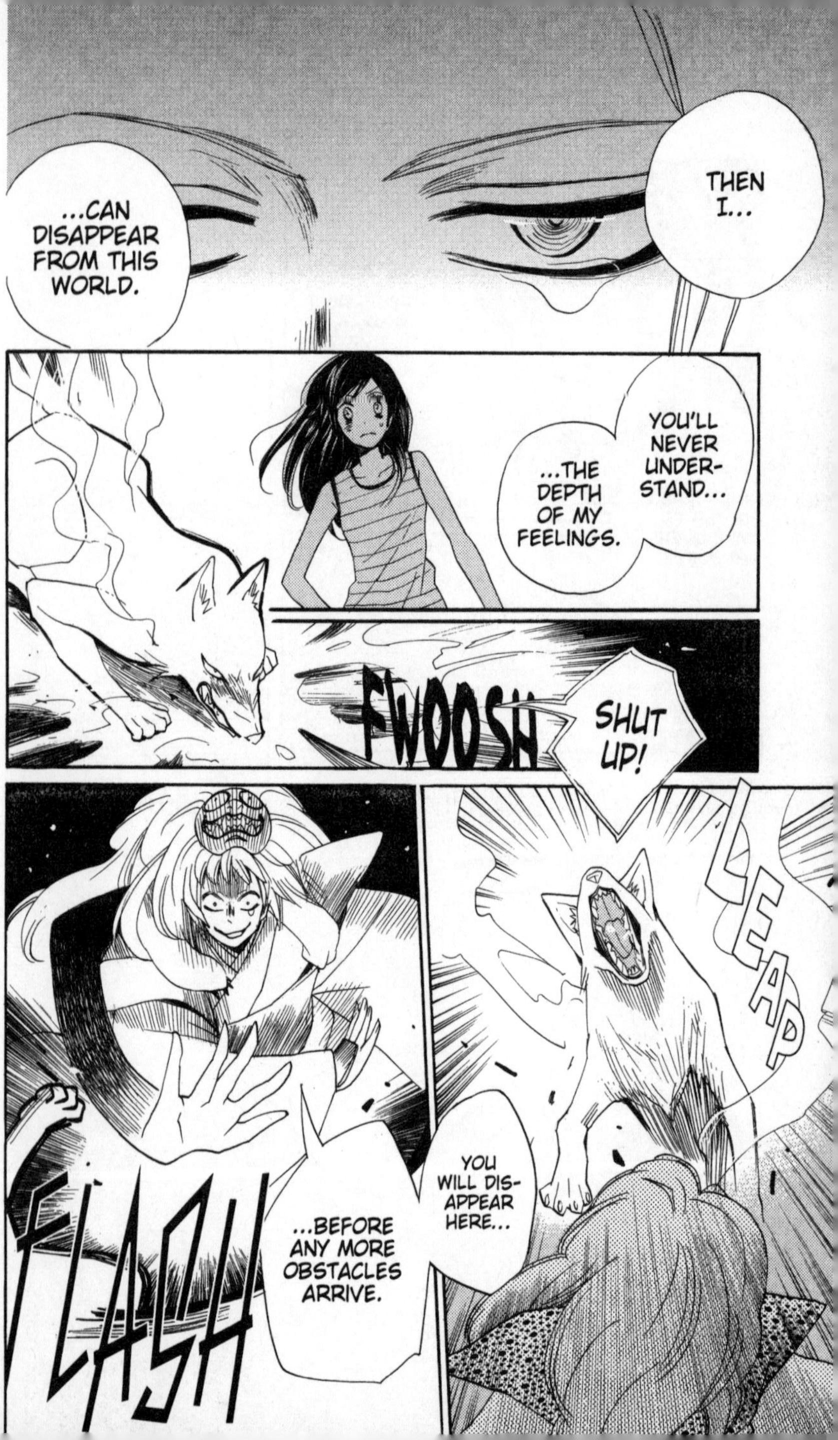
THEN I...
...CAN DISAPPEAR FROM THIS WORLD.
YOU'LL NEVER UNDER-STAND...
...THE DEPTH OF MY FEELINGS.
SHUT UP!
FWOOSH
LEAP
YOU WILL DIS-APPEAR HERE...
...BEFORE ANY MORE OBSTACLES ARRIVE.
FLASH

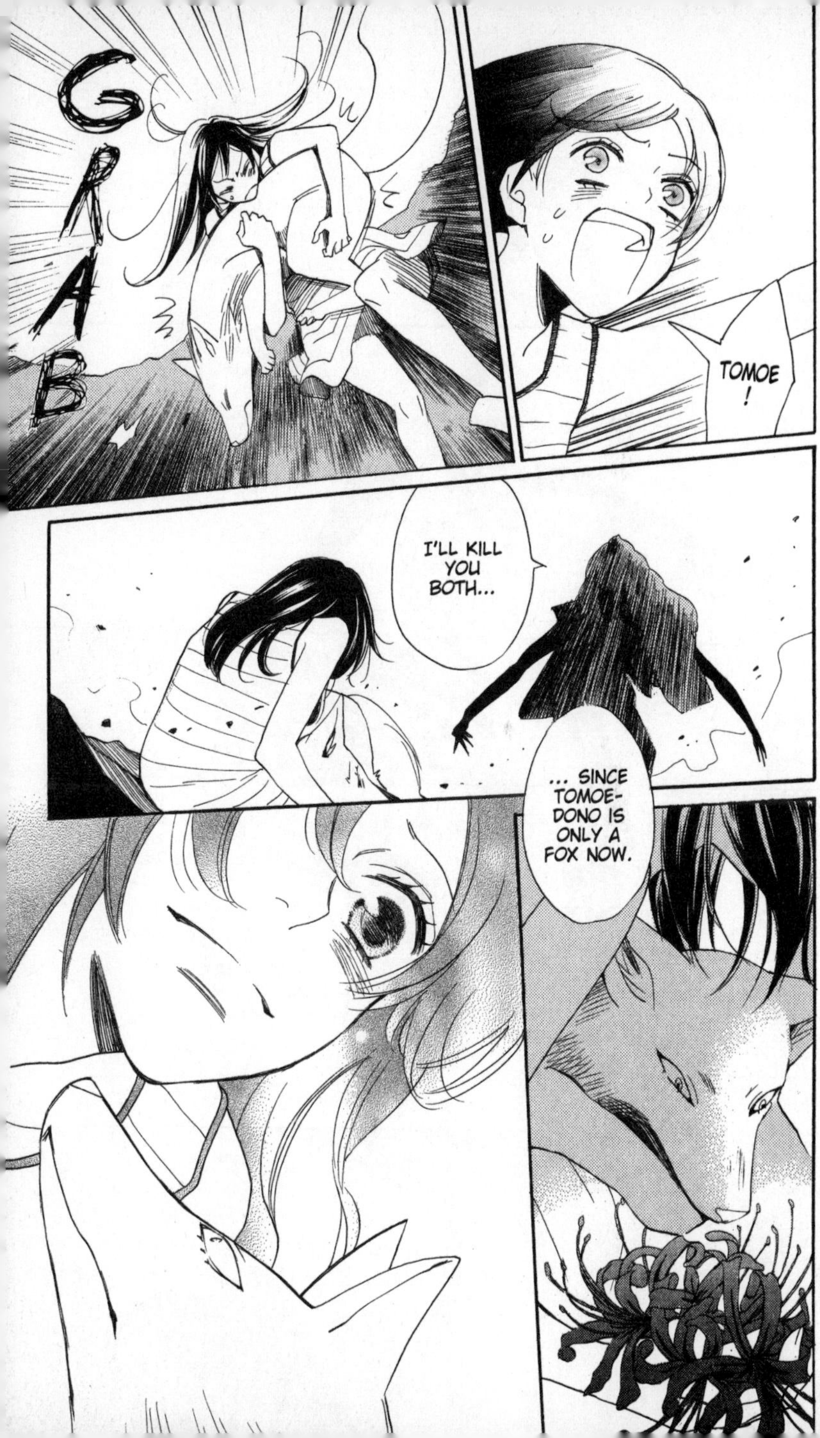
TOMOE!
GRAB
I'LL KILL YOU BOTH...
... SINCE TOMOE-DONO IS ONLY A FOX NOW.

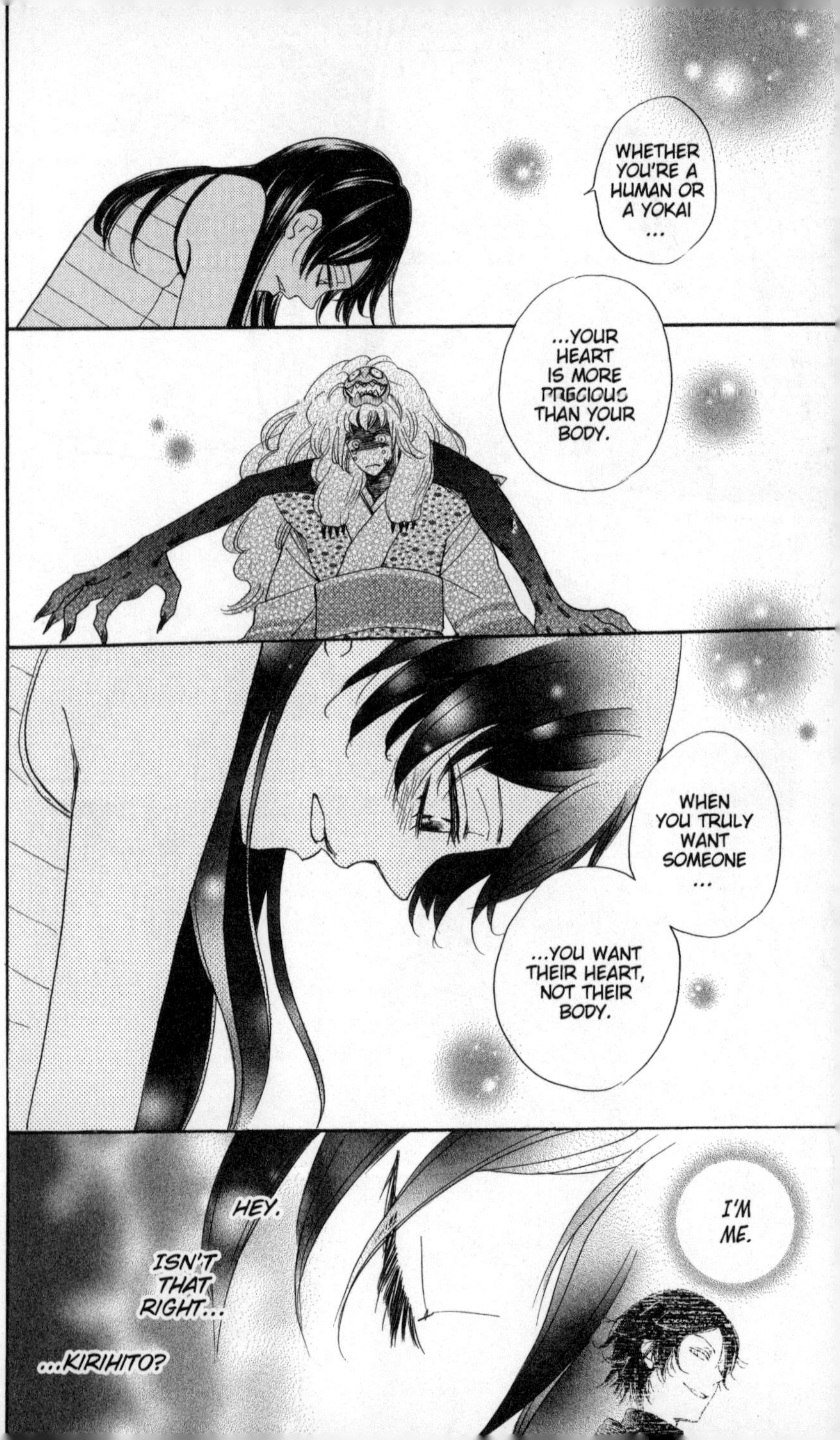
WHETHER YOU'RE A HUMAN OR A YOKAI ...
...YOUR HEART IS MORE PRECIOUS THAN YOUR BODY.
WHEN YOU TRULY WANT SOMEONE ...
...YOU WANT THEIR HEART, NOT THEIR BODY.
I'M ME.
HEY.
ISN'T THAT RIGHT...
...KIRIHITO?

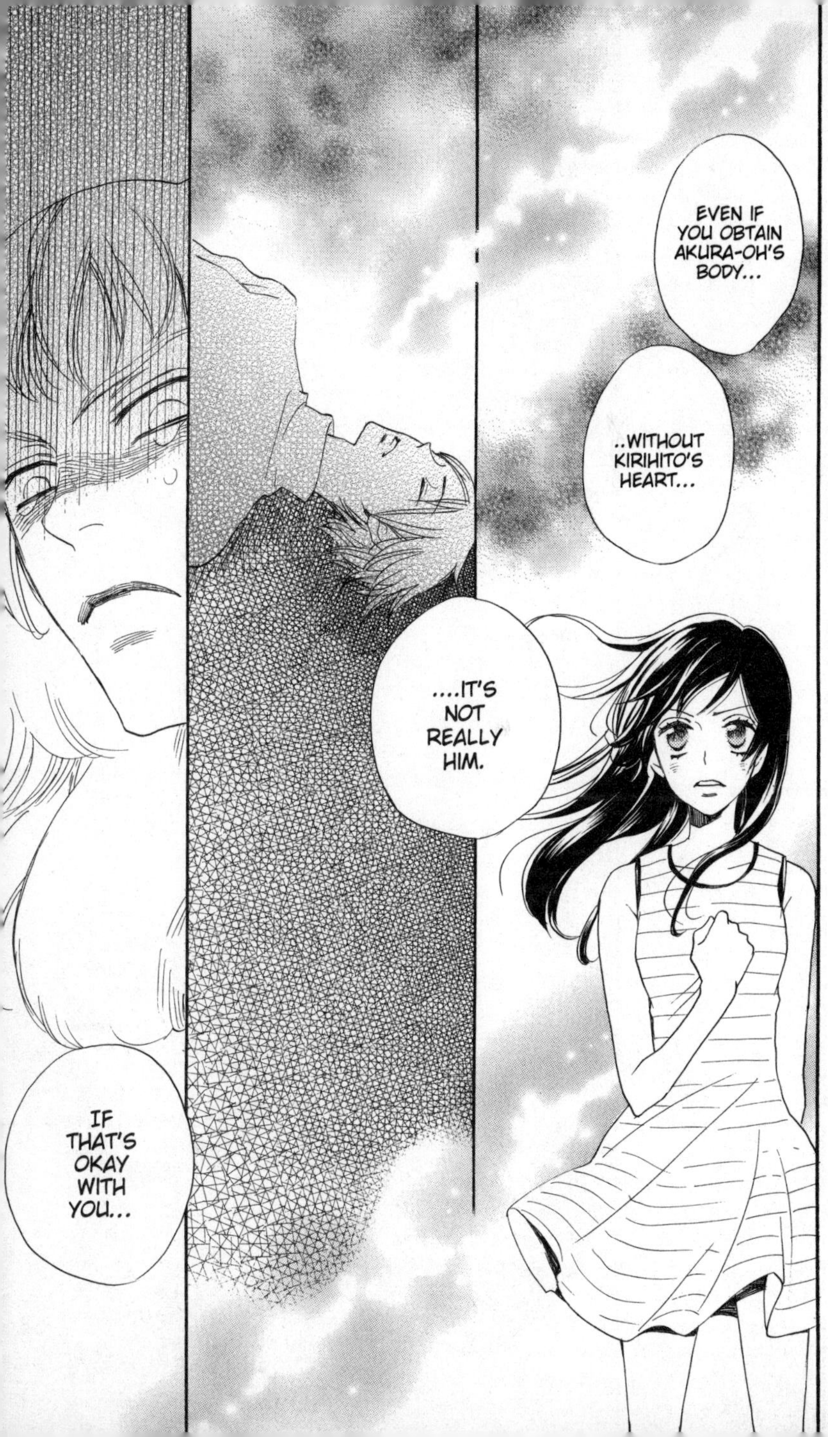
EVEN IF YOU OBTAIN AKURA-OH'S BODY...
..WITHOUT KIRIHITO'S HEART...
....IT'S NOT REALLY HIM.
IF THAT'S OKAY WITH YOU...

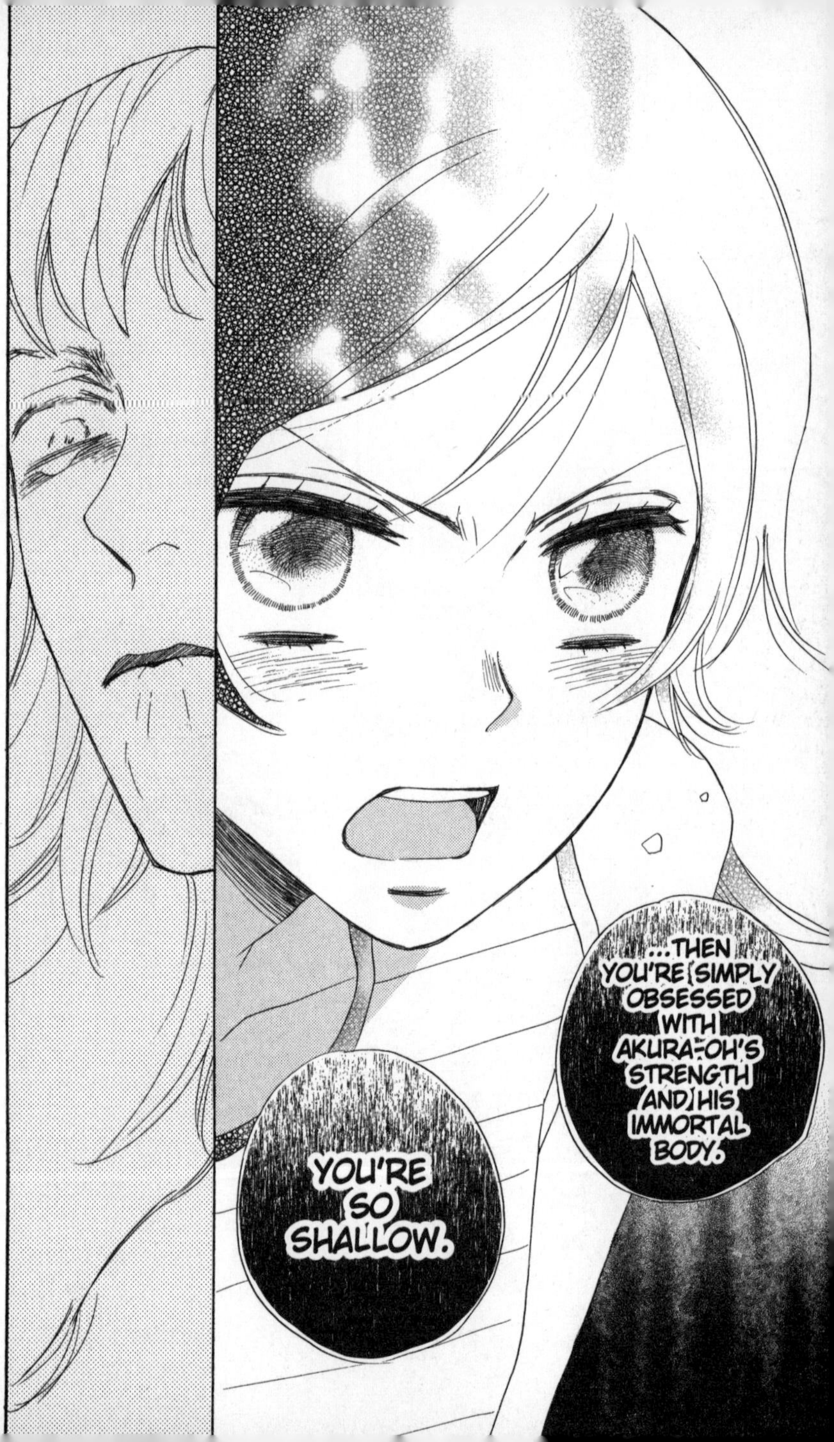
...THEN YOU'RE SIMPLY OBSESSED WITH AKURA-OH'S STRENGTH AND HIS IMMORTAL BODY.
YOU'RE SO SHALLOW.

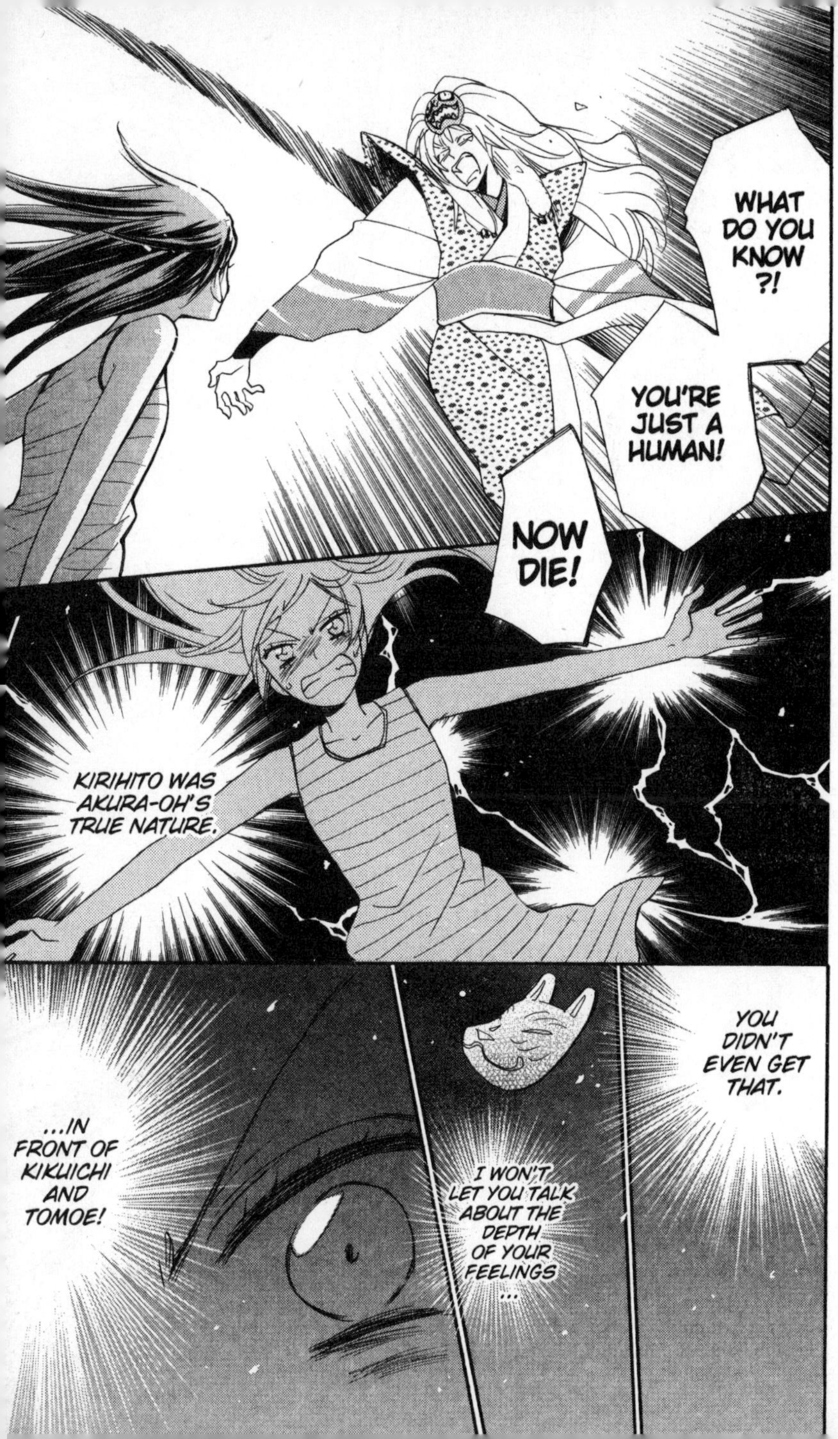
WHAT DO YOU KNOW ?!
YOU'RE JUST A HUMAN!
NOW DIE!
KIRIHITO WAS AKURA-OH'S TRUE NATURE.
YOU DIDN'T EVEN GET THAT.
I WON'T LET YOU TALK ABOUT THE DEPTH OF YOUR FEELINGS ...
...IN FRONT OF KIKUICHI AND TOMOE!

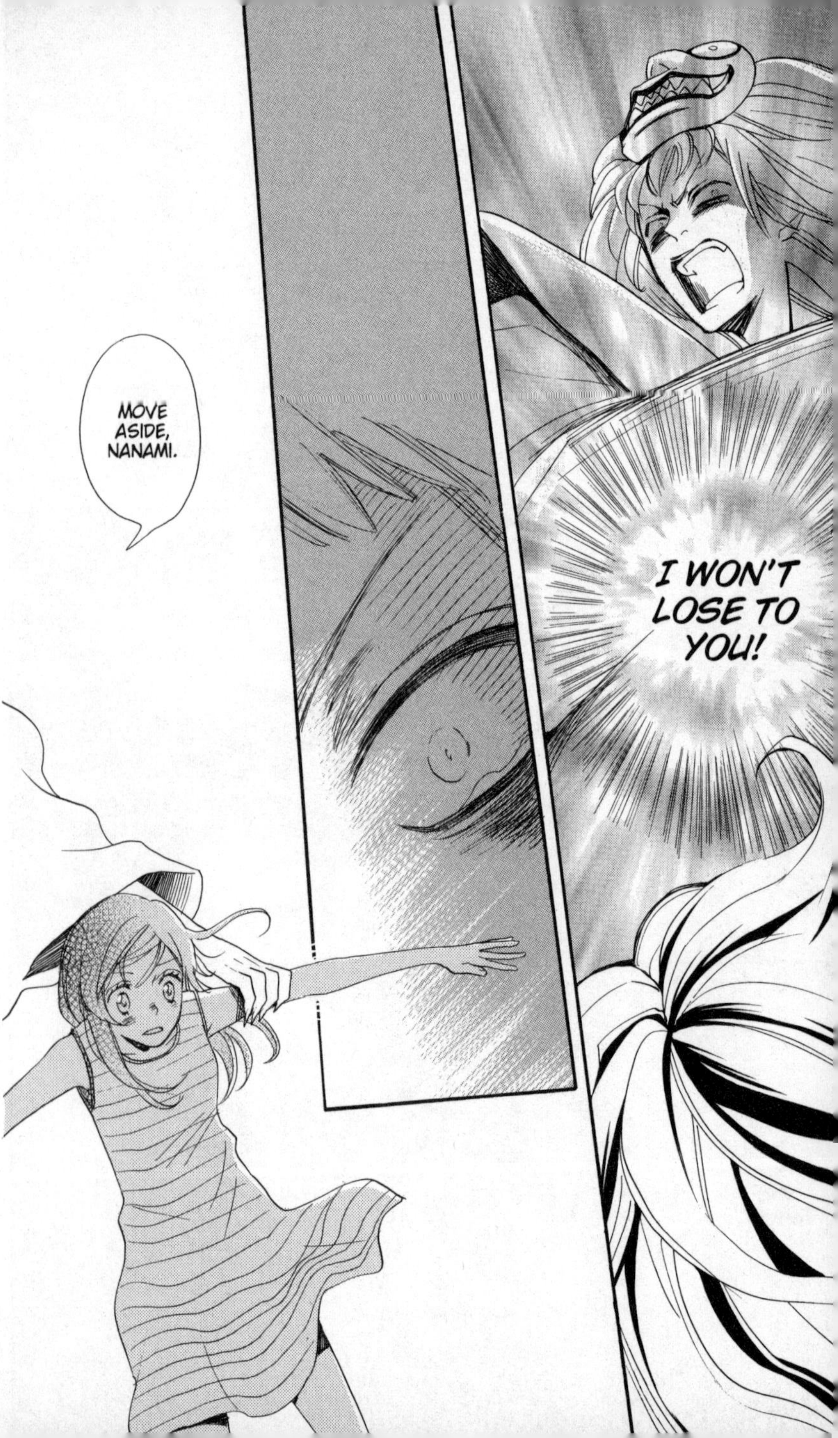
I WON'T LOSE TO YOU!
MOVE ASIDE, NANAMI.

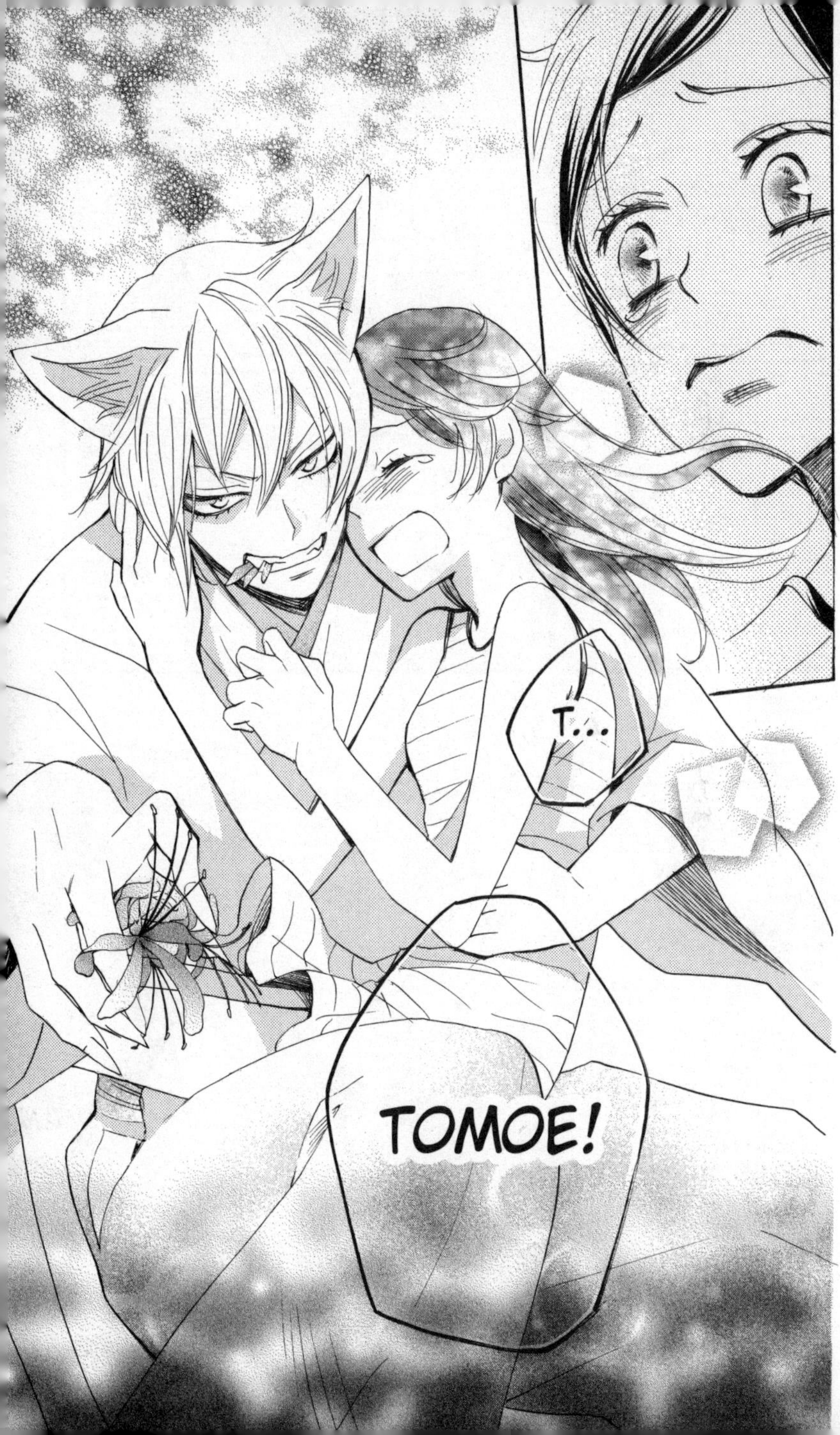
T...
TOMOE!

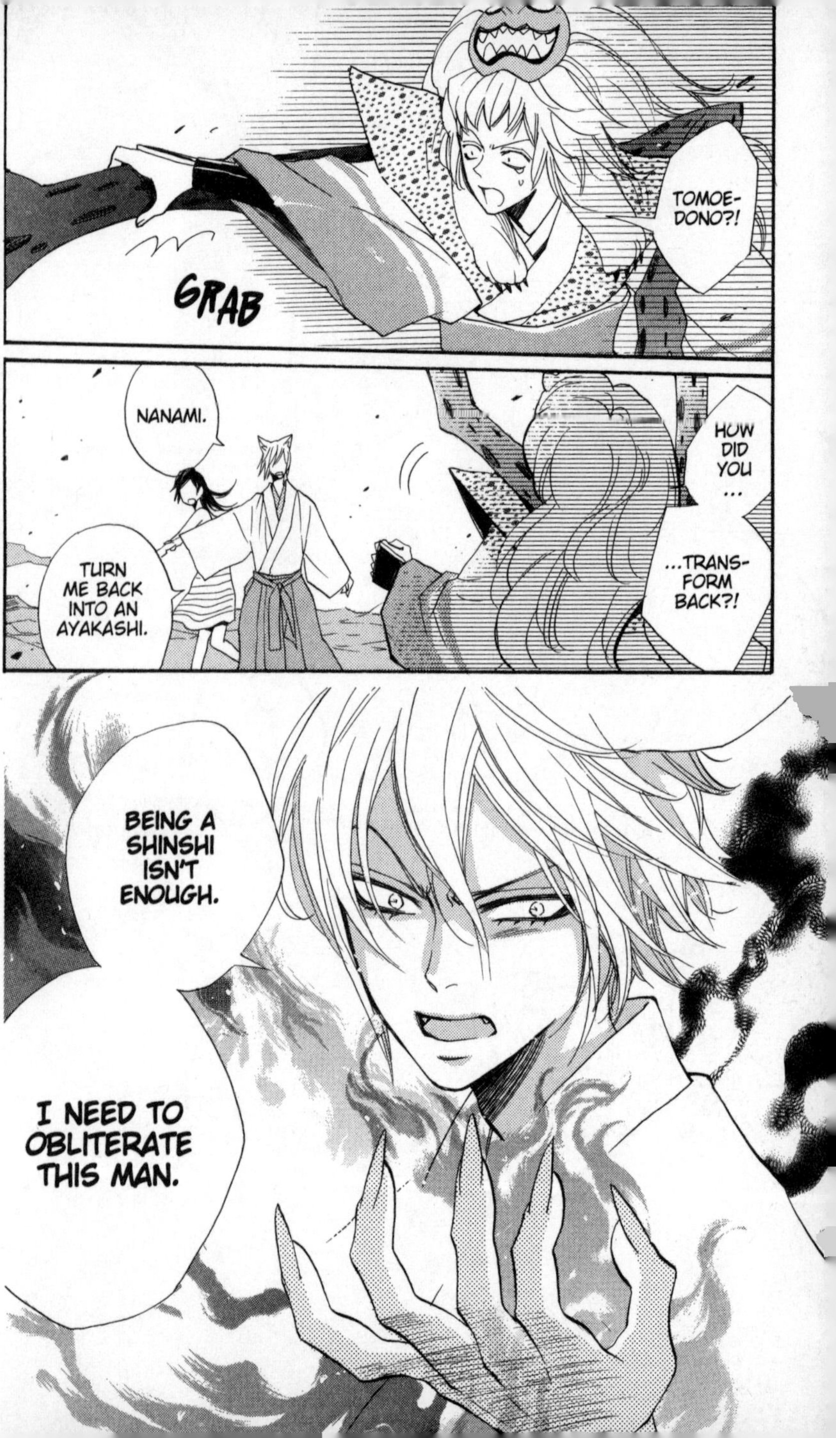
TOMOE-DONO?!
GRAB
HOW DID YOU ...
...TRANS-FORM BACK?!
NANAMI.
TURN ME BACK INTO AN AYAKASHI.
BEING A SHINSHI ISN'T ENOUGH.
I NEED TO OBLITERATE THIS MAN.

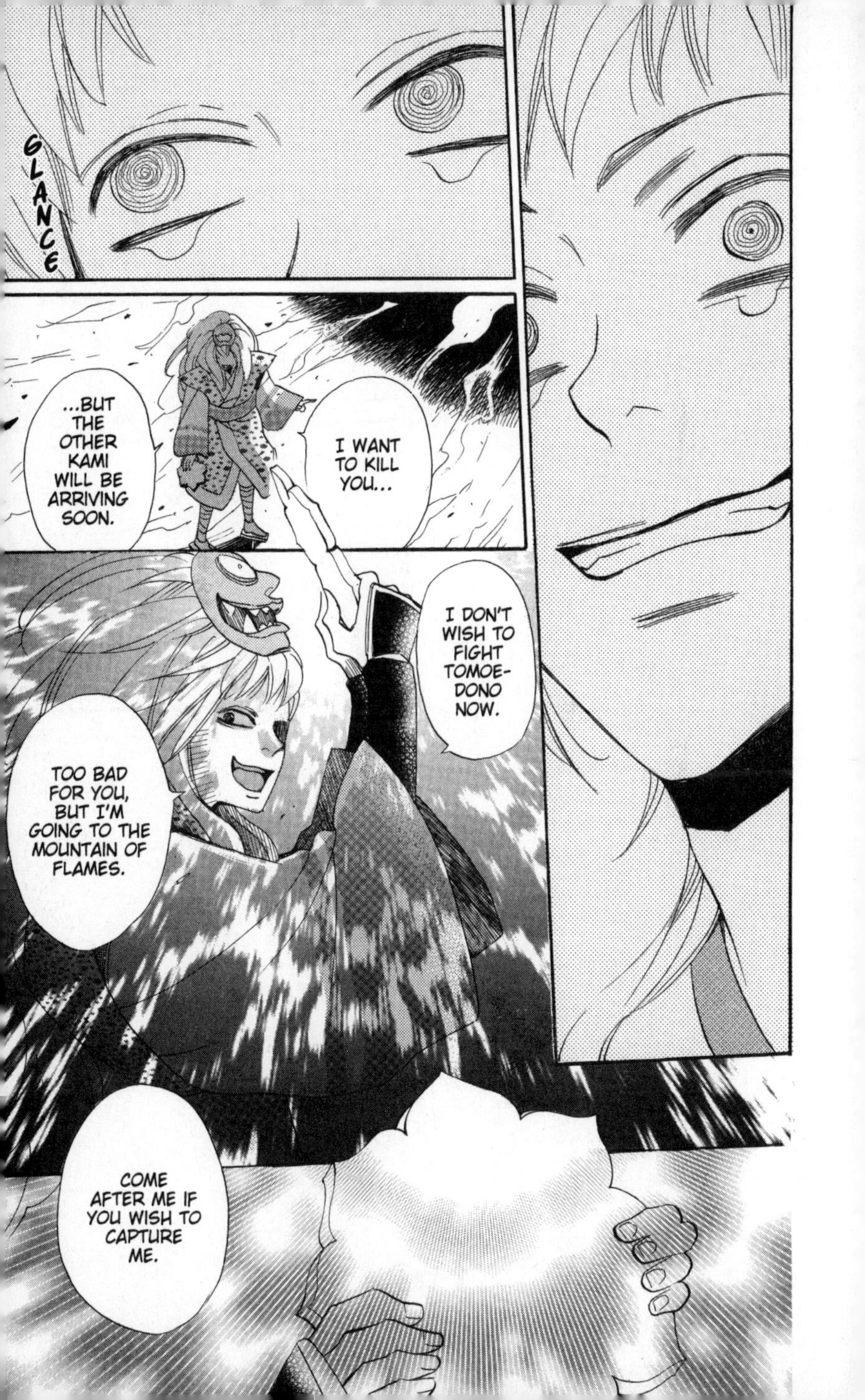
GLANCE
I WANT TO KILL YOU...
...BUT THE OTHER KAMI WILL BE ARRIVING SOON.
I DON'T WISH TO FIGHT TOMOE-DONO NOW.
TOO BAD FOR YOU, BUT I'M GOING TO THE MOUNTAIN OF FLAMES.
COME AFTER ME IF YOU WISH TO CAPTURE ME.

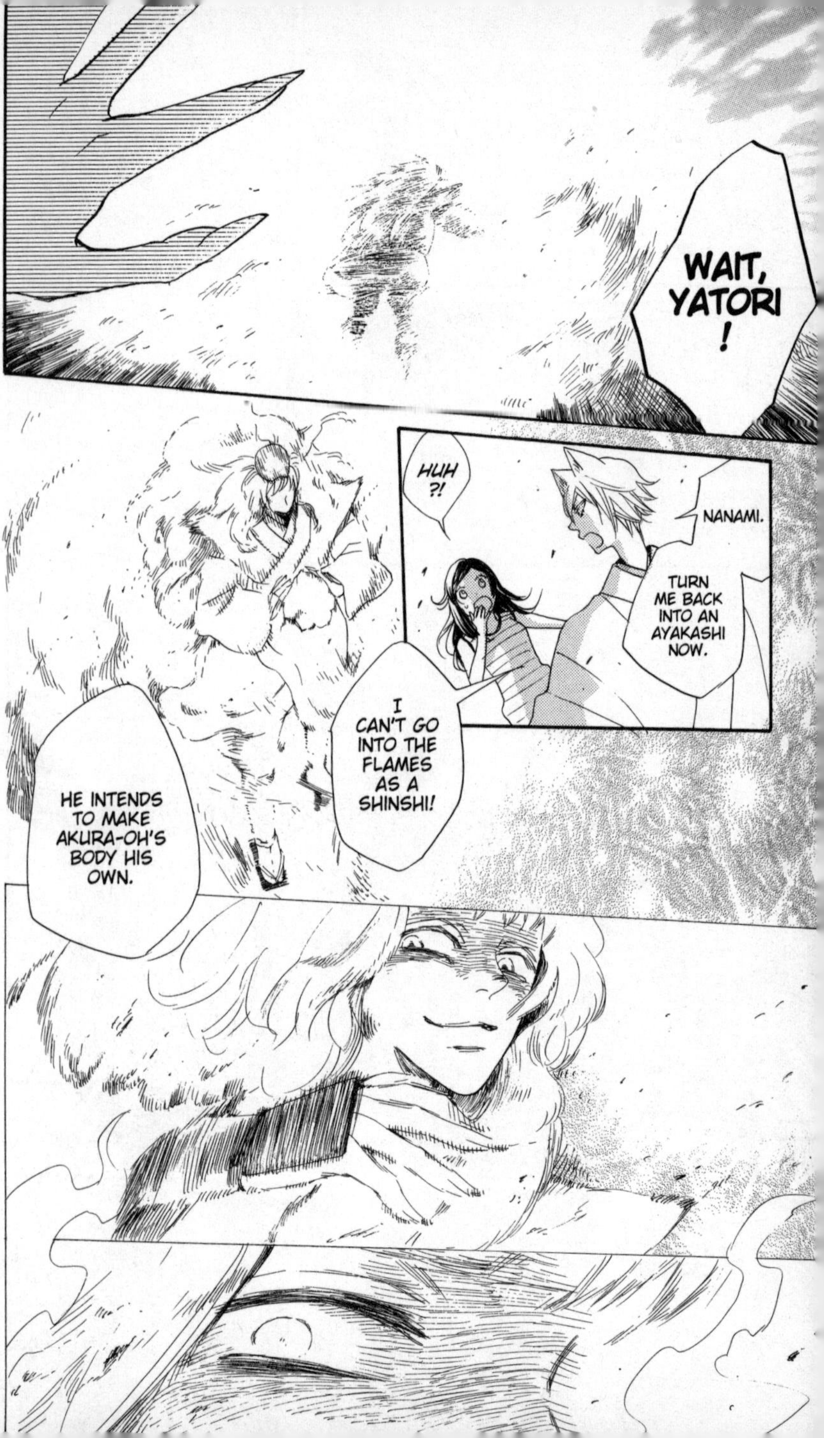
WAIT, YATORI!
NANAMI.
TURN ME BACK INTO AN AYAKASHI NOW.
HUH?!
I CAN'T GO INTO THE FLAMES AS A SHINSHI!
HE INTENDS TO MAKE AKURA-OH'S BODY HIS OWN.

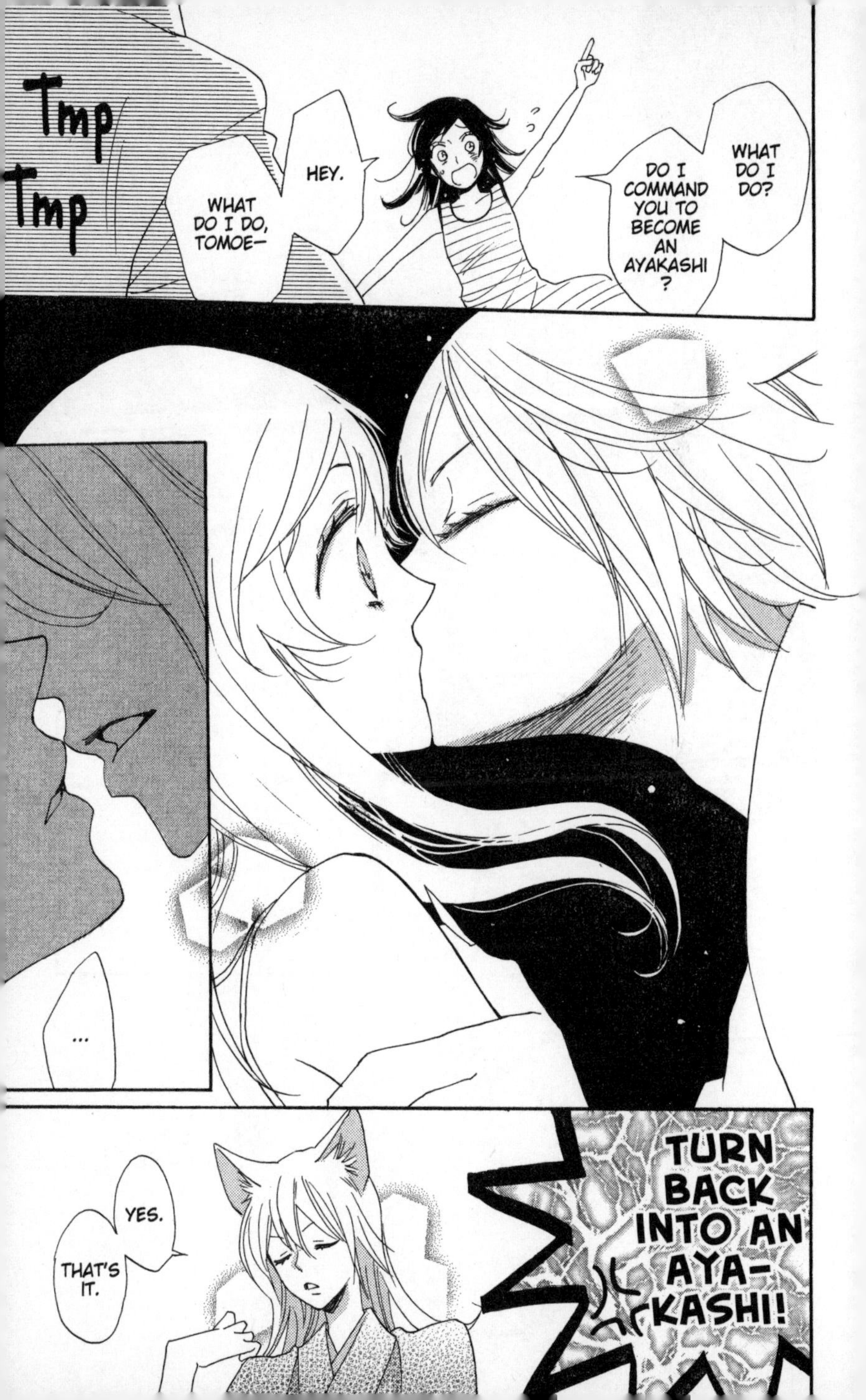
WHAT DO I DO?
DO I COMMAND YOU TO BECOME AN AYAKASHI?
HEY.
WHAT DO I DO, TOMOE—
Tmp Tmp
...
TURN BACK INTO AN AYA-KASHI!
YES.
THAT'S IT.

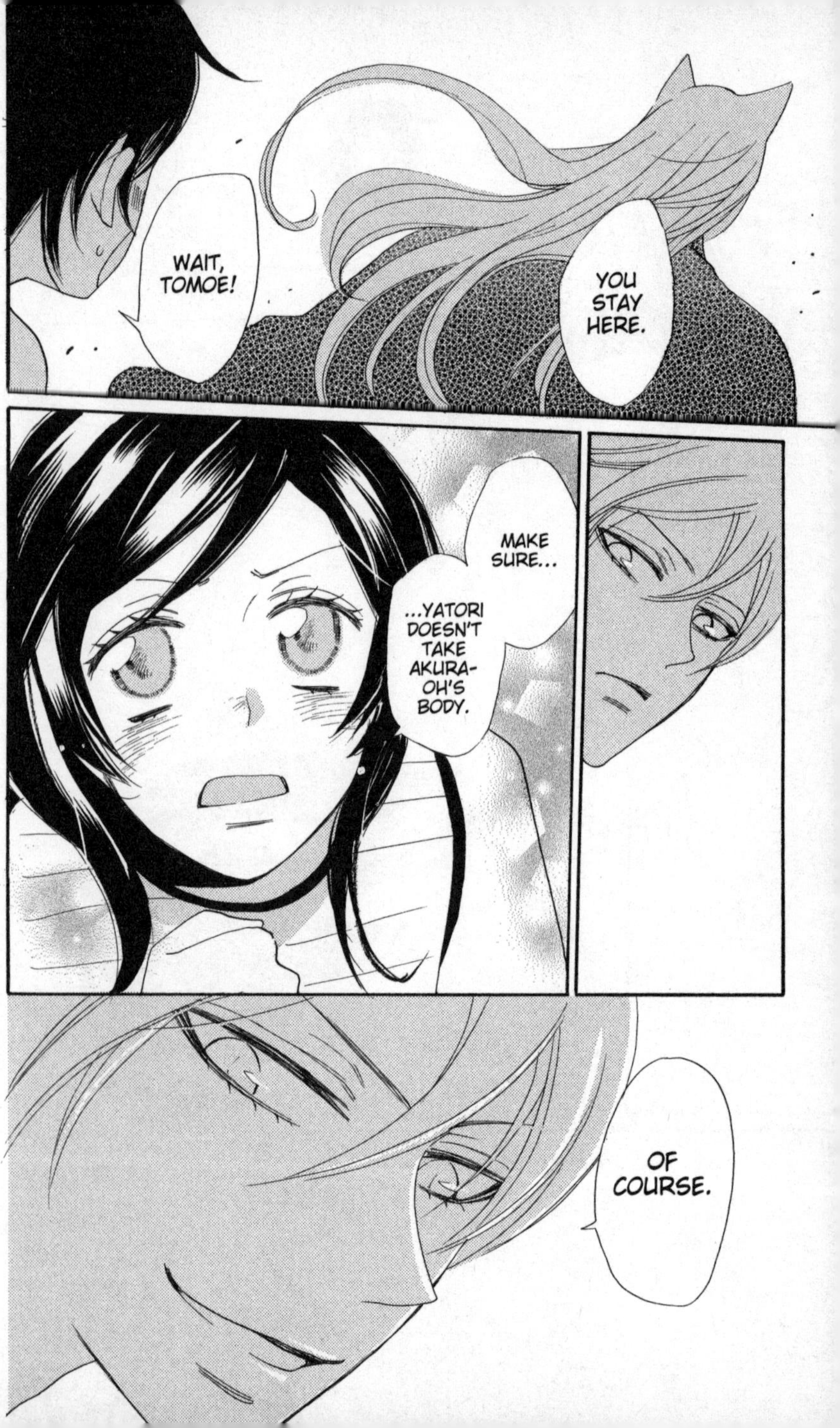
YOU STAY HERE.
WAIT, TOMOE!
MAKE SURE...
...YATORI DOESN'T TAKE AKURA-OH'S BODY.
OF COURSE.

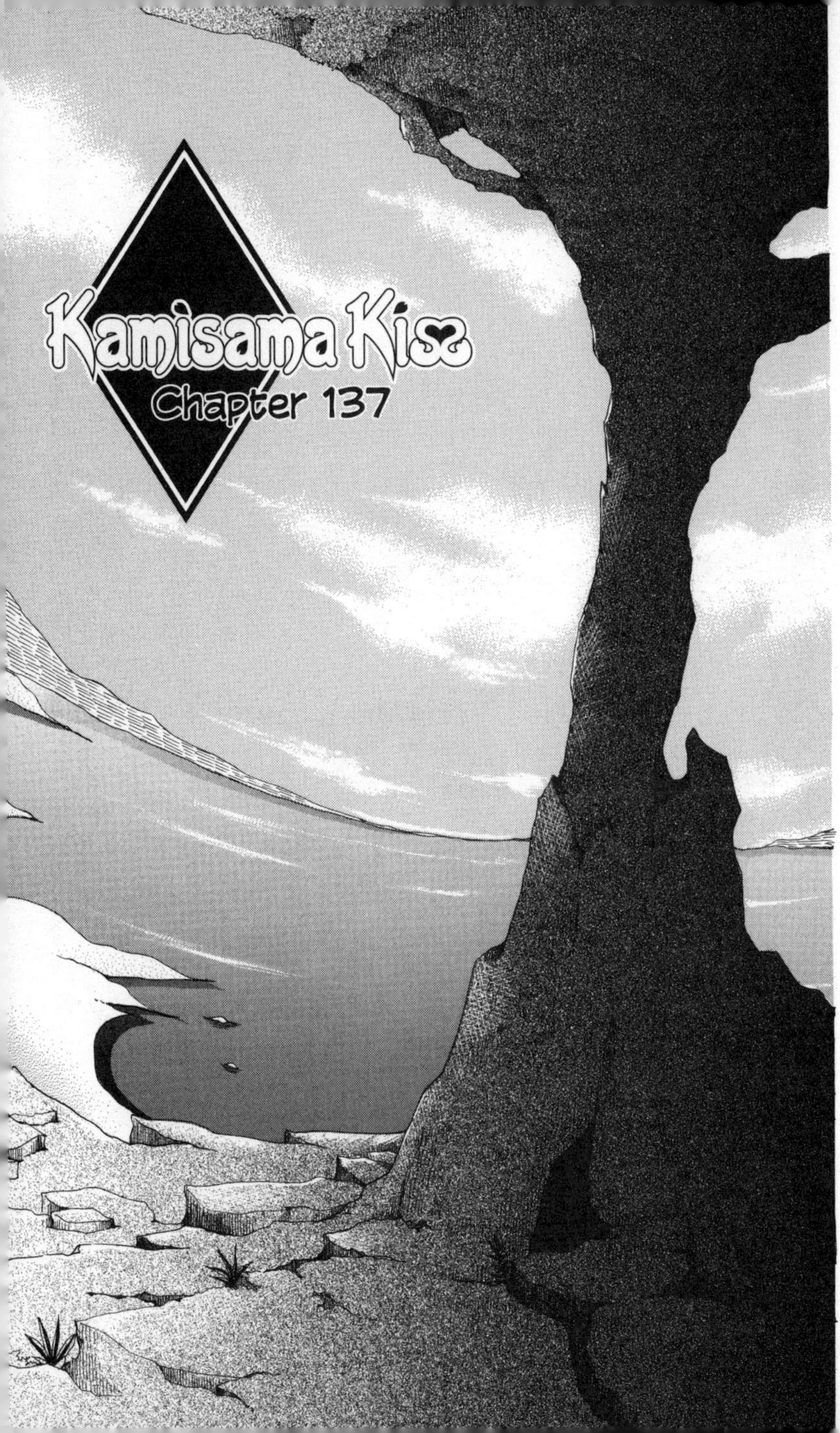
Kamisama Kiss
Chapter 137

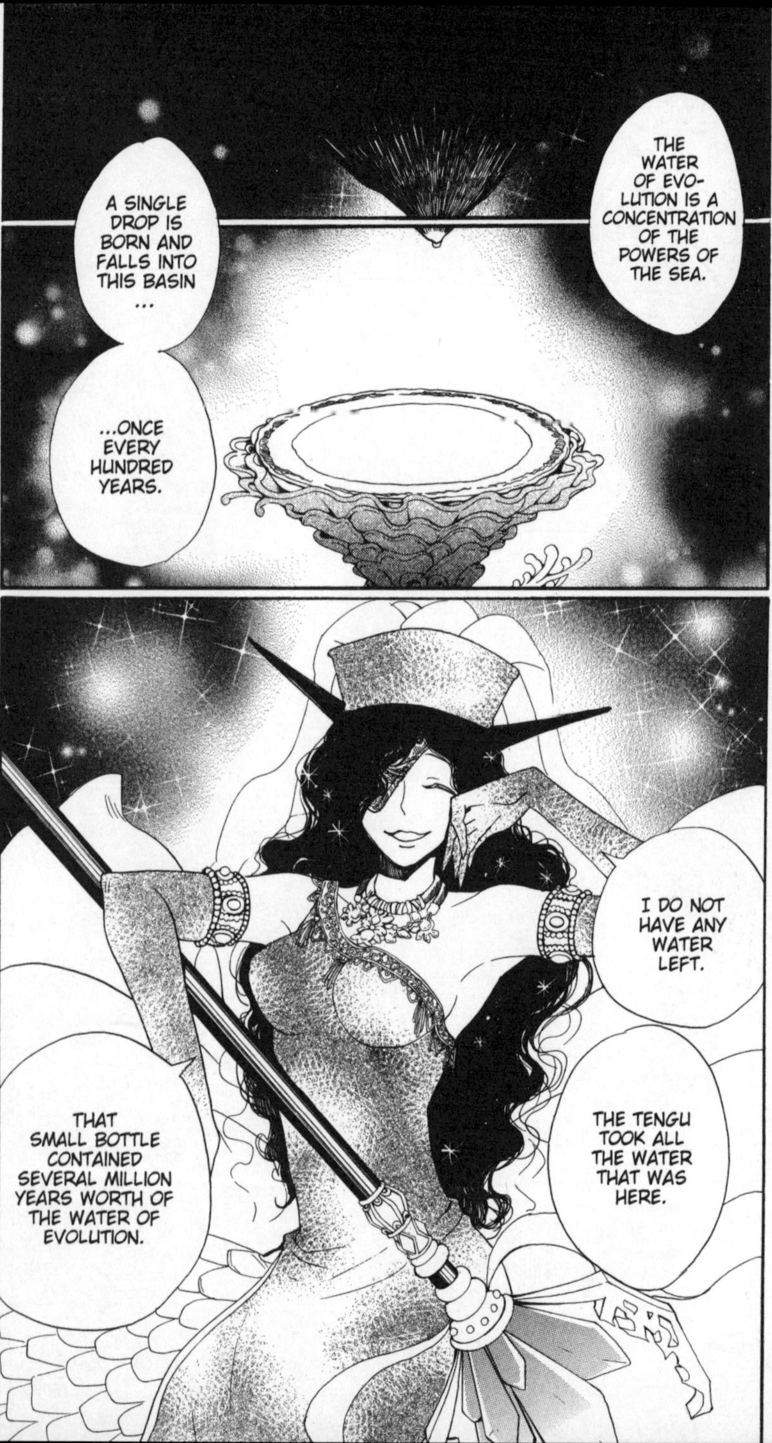
THE WATER OF EVO-LUTION IS A CONCENTRATION OF THE POWERS OF THE SEA.
A SINGLE DROP IS BORN AND FALLS INTO THIS BASIN ...
...ONCE EVERY HUNDRED YEARS.
I DO NOT HAVE ANY WATER LEFT.
THE TENGU TOOK ALL THE WATER THAT WAS HERE.
THAT SMALL BOTTLE CONTAINED SEVERAL MILLION YEARS WORTH OF THE WATER OF EVOLUTION.

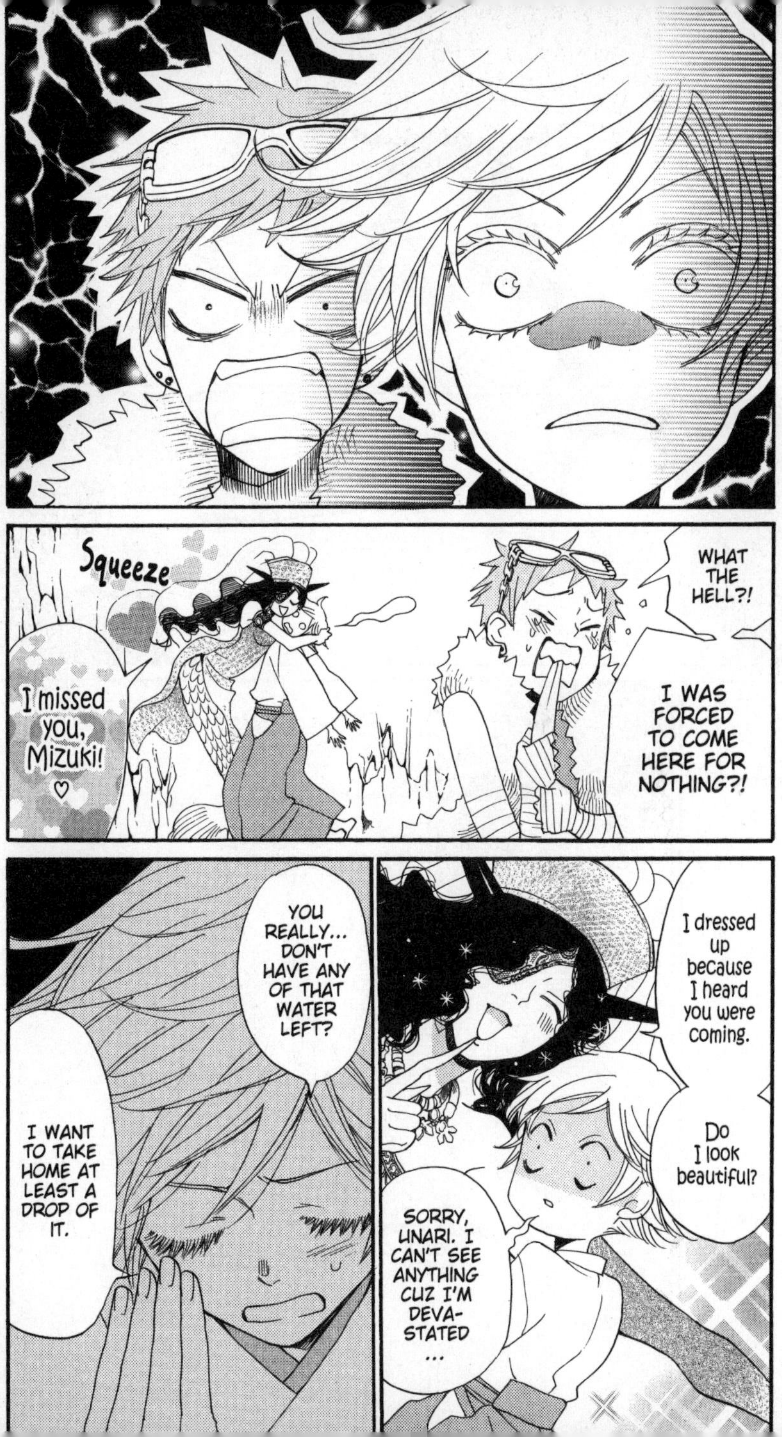
WHAT THE HELL?!
I WAS FORCED TO COME HERE FOR NOTHING?!
Squeeze
I missed you, Mizuki! ♡
I dressed up because I heard you were coming.
Do I look beautiful?
SORRY, UNARI. I CAN'T SEE ANYTHING CUZ I'M DEVA-STATED ...
YOU REALLY... DON'T HAVE ANY OF THAT WATER LEFT?
I WANT TO TAKE HOME AT LEAST A DROP OF IT.

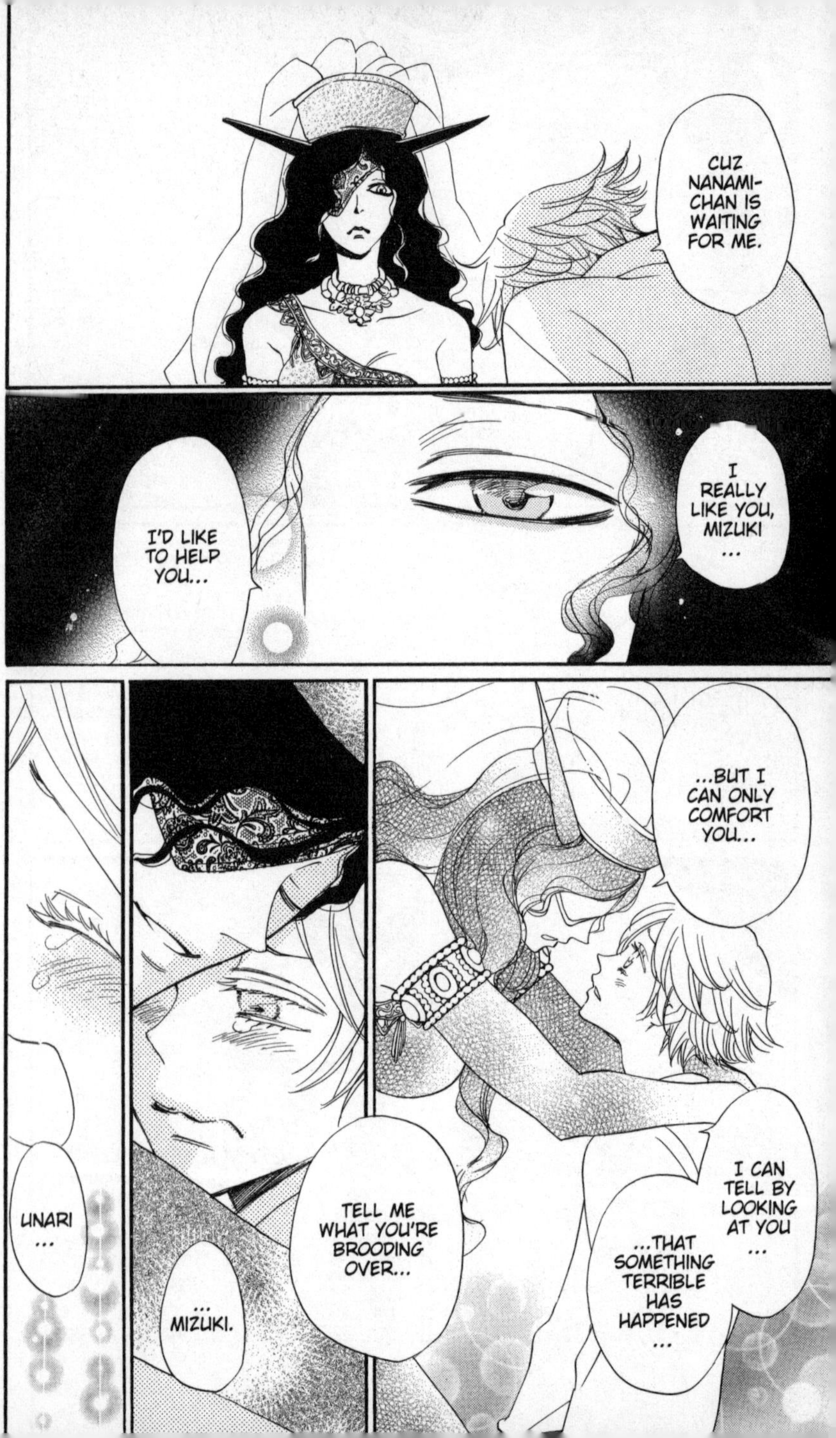
CUZ NANAMI-CHAN IS WAITING FOR ME.
I REALLY LIKE YOU, MIZUKI ...
I'D LIKE TO HELP YOU...
...BUT I CAN ONLY COMFORT YOU...
I CAN TELL BY LOOKING AT YOU ...
...THAT SOMETHING TERRIBLE HAS HAPPENED ...
TELL ME WHAT YOU'RE BROODING OVER...
... MIZUKI.
UNARI ...

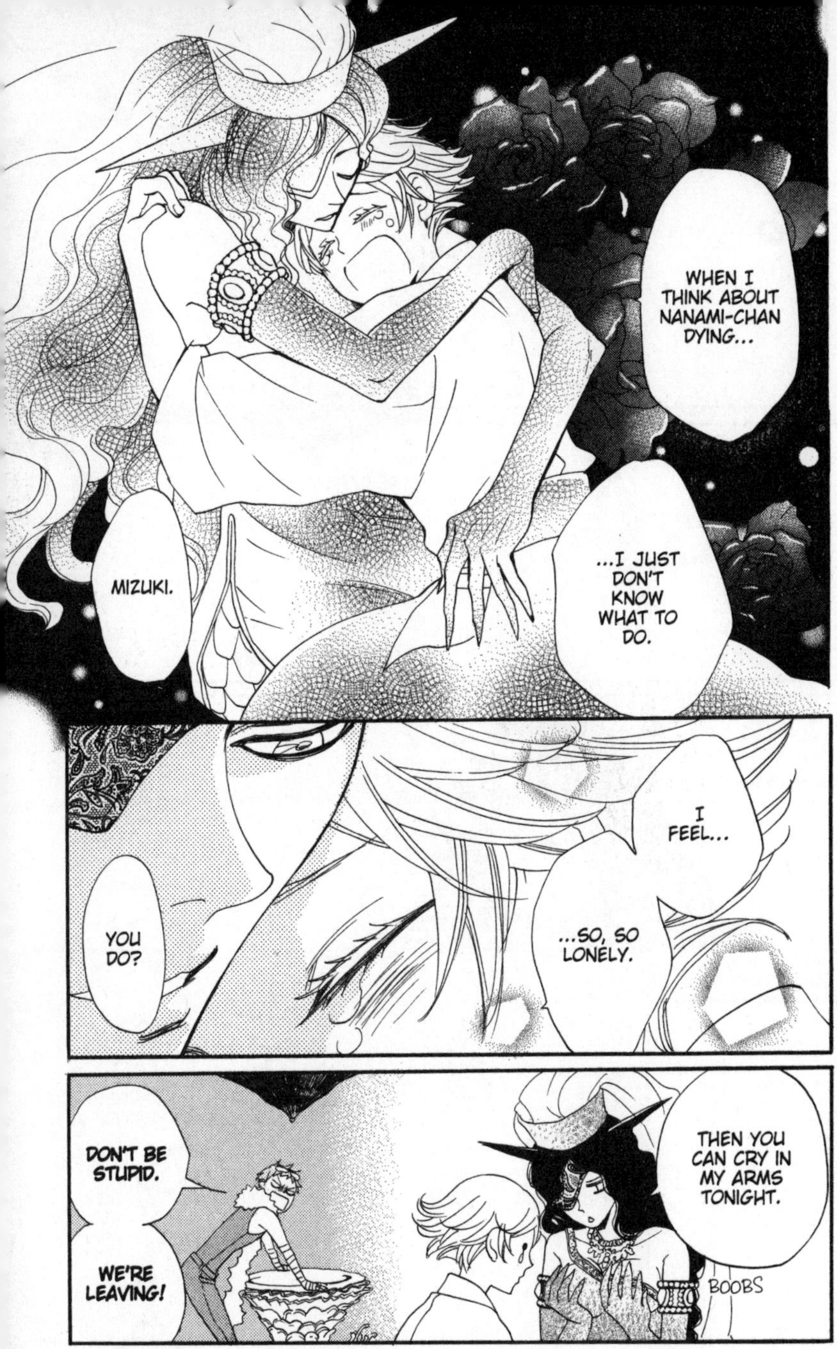
WHEN I THINK ABOUT NANAMI-CHAN DYING...
...I JUST DON'T KNOW WHAT TO DO.
MIZUKI.
I FEEL...
...SO, SO LONELY.
YOU DO?
THEN YOU CAN CRY IN MY ARMS TONIGHT.
BOOBS
DON'T BE STUPID.
WE'RE LEAVING!

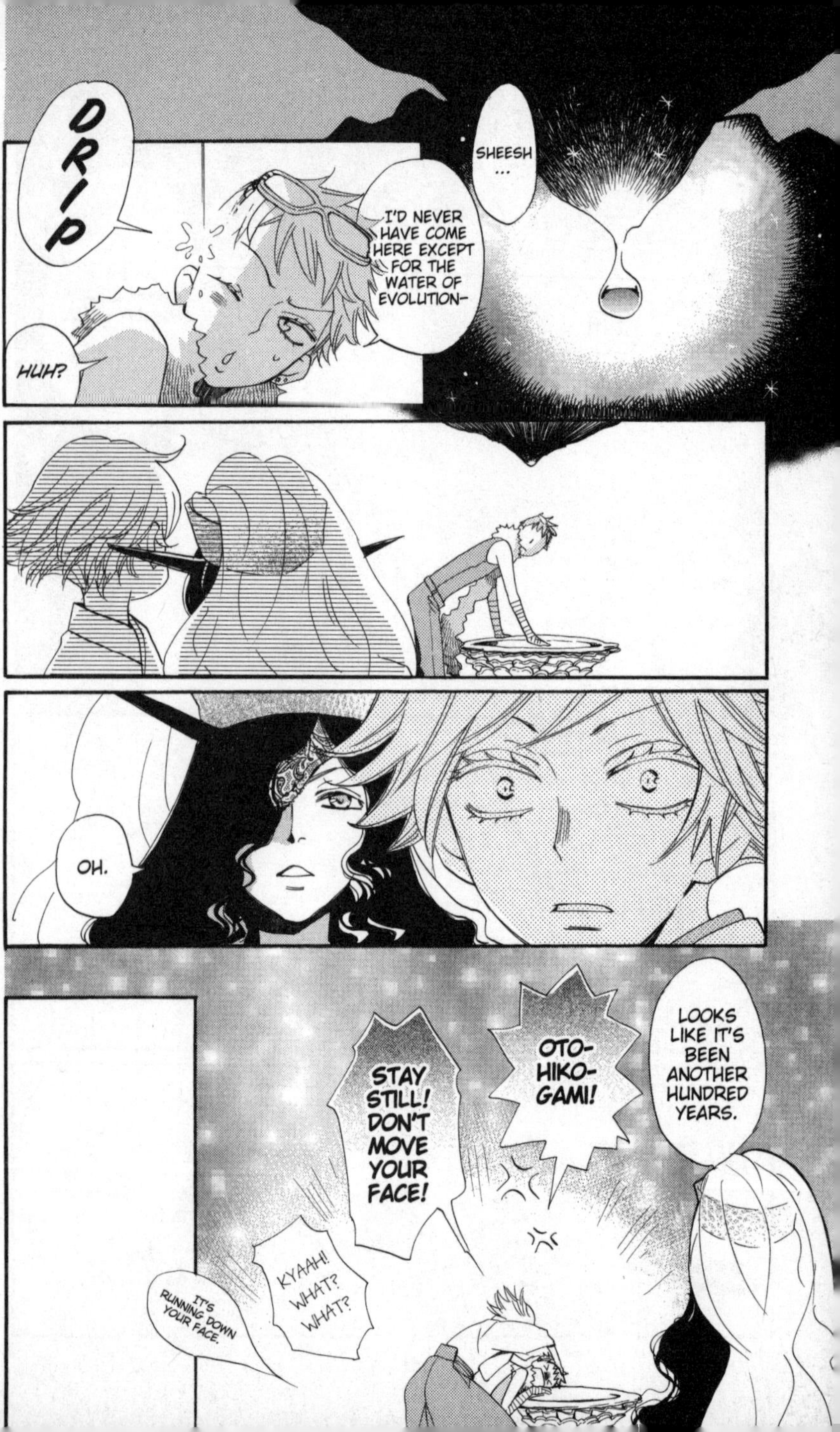
SHEESH ...
I'D NEVER HAVE COME HERE EXCEPT FOR THE WATER OF EVOLUTION-
DRIP
HUH?
OH.
LOOKS LIKE IT'S BEEN ANOTHER HUNDRED YEARS.
OTO-HIKO-GAMI!
STAY STILL! DON'T MOVE YOUR FACE!
KYAAH! WHAT? WHAT?
IT'S RUNNING DOWN YOUR FACE.

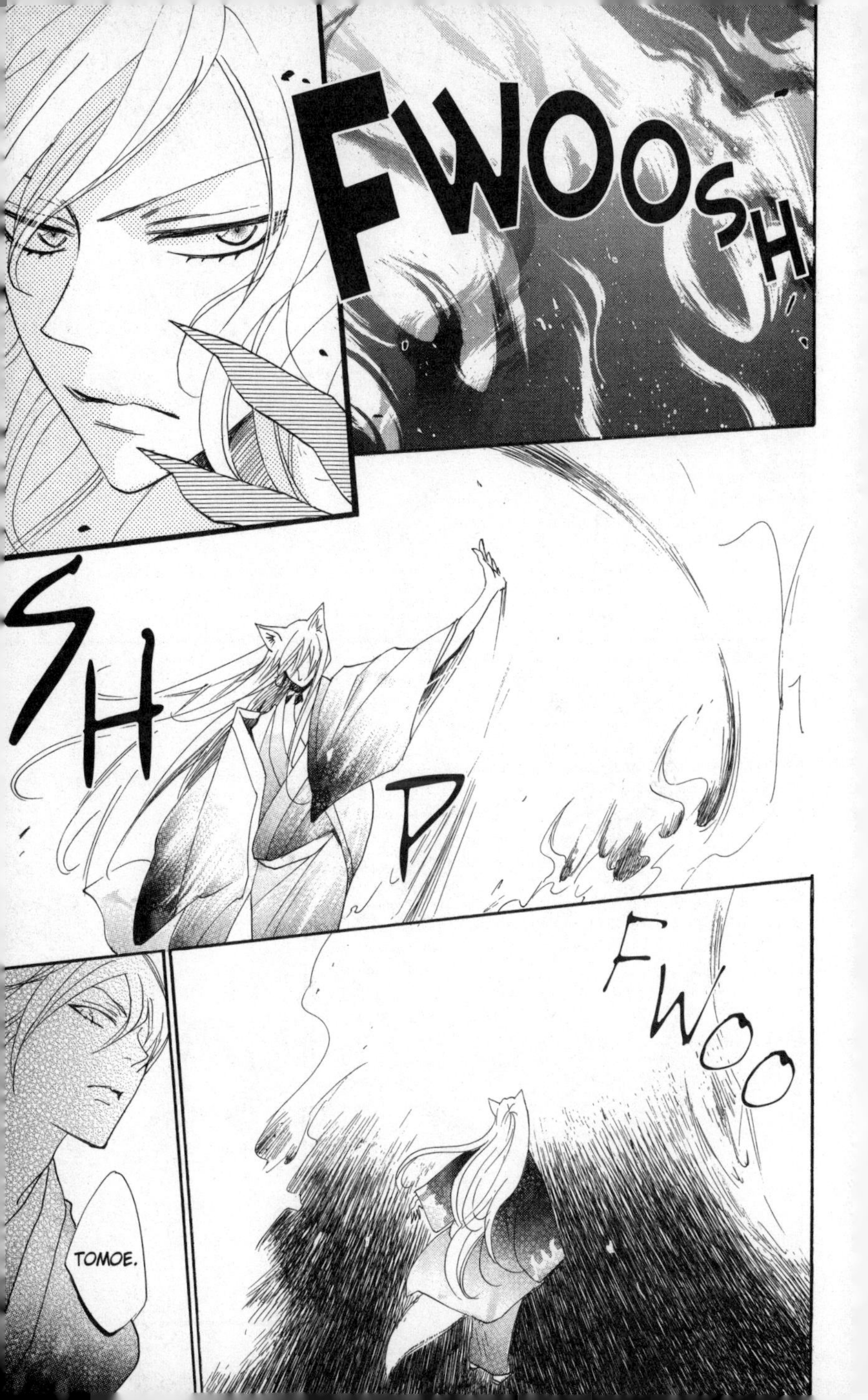
FWOOSH
SHP
FWOO
TOMOE.

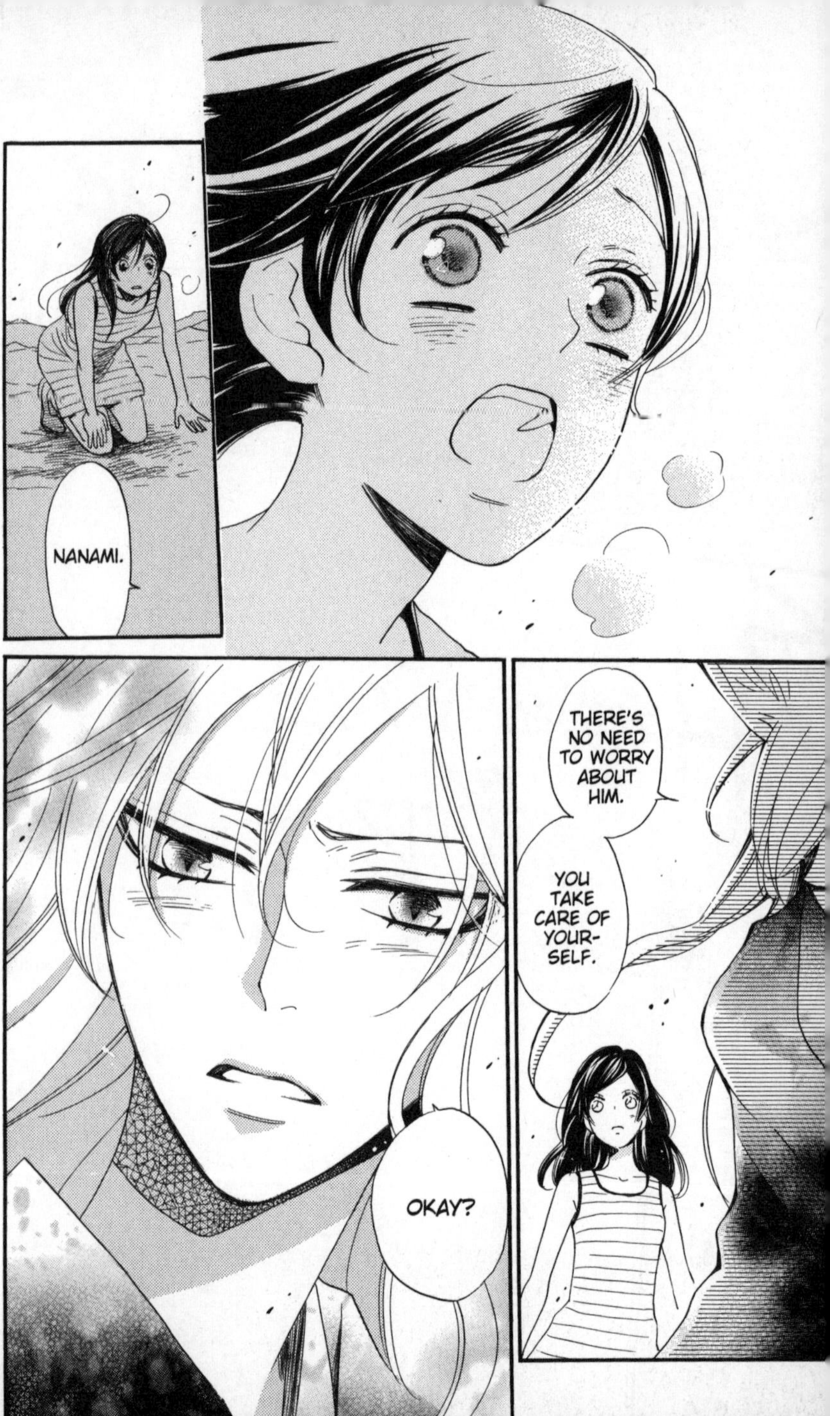
NANAMI.
THERE'S NO NEED TO WORRY ABOUT HIM.
YOU TAKE CARE OF YOUR-SELF.
OKAY?

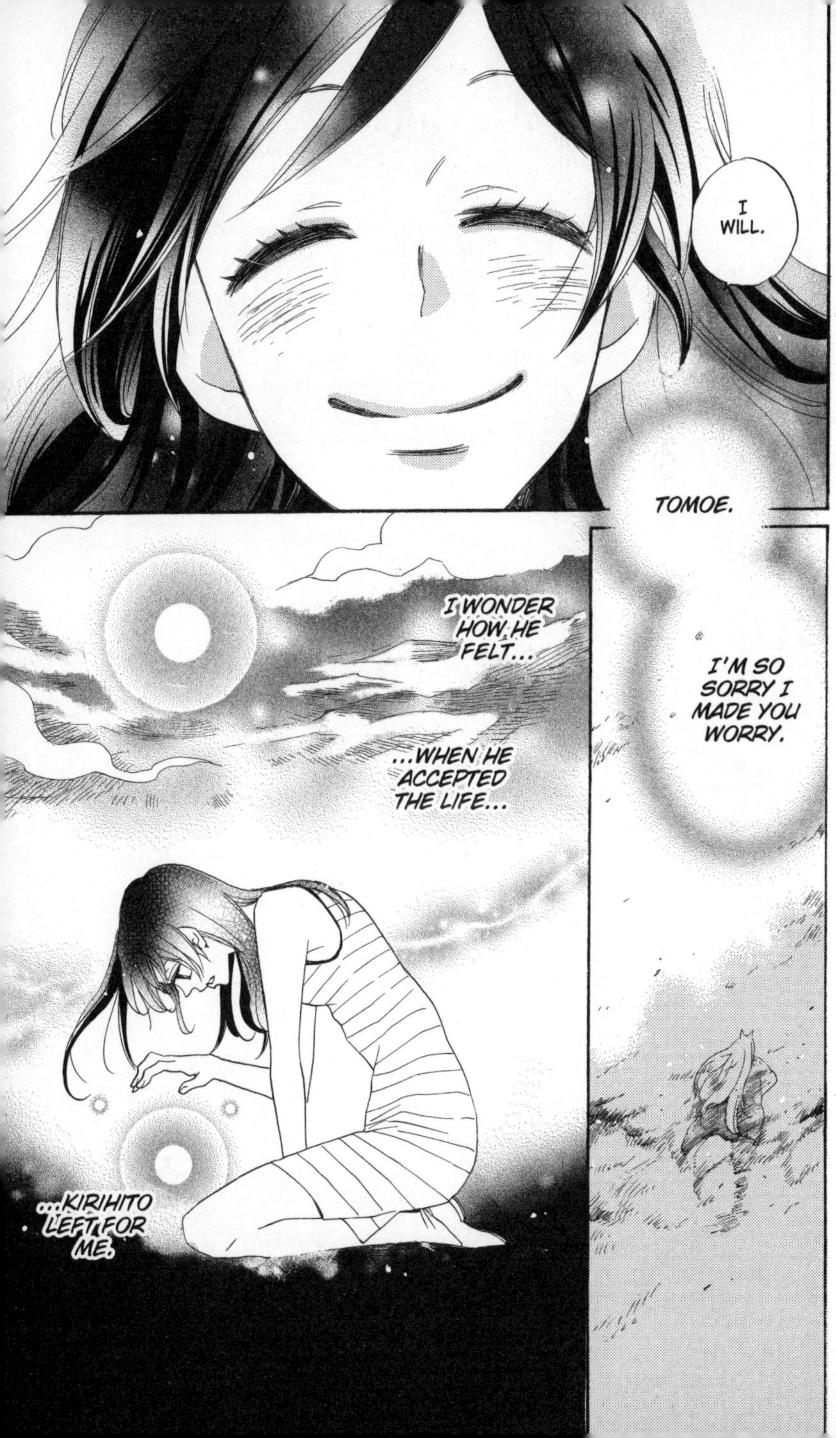
I WILL.
TOMOE.
I'M SO SORRY I MADE YOU WORRY.
I WONDER HOW HE FELT...
...WHEN HE ACCEPTED THE LIFE...
...KIRIHITO LEFT FOR ME.

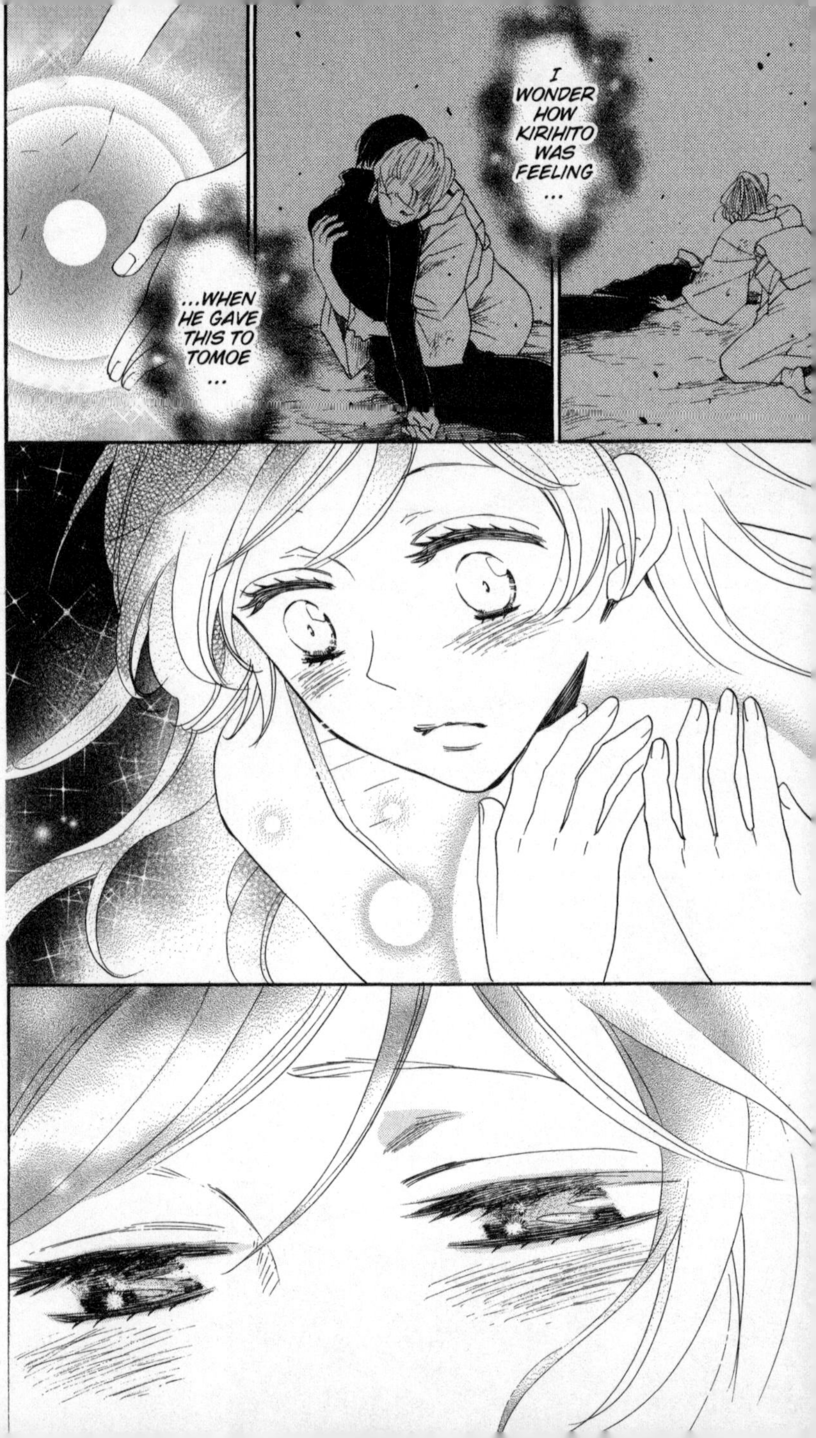
I WONDER HOW KIRIHITO WAS FEELING ...
...WHEN HE GAVE THIS TO TOMOE ...

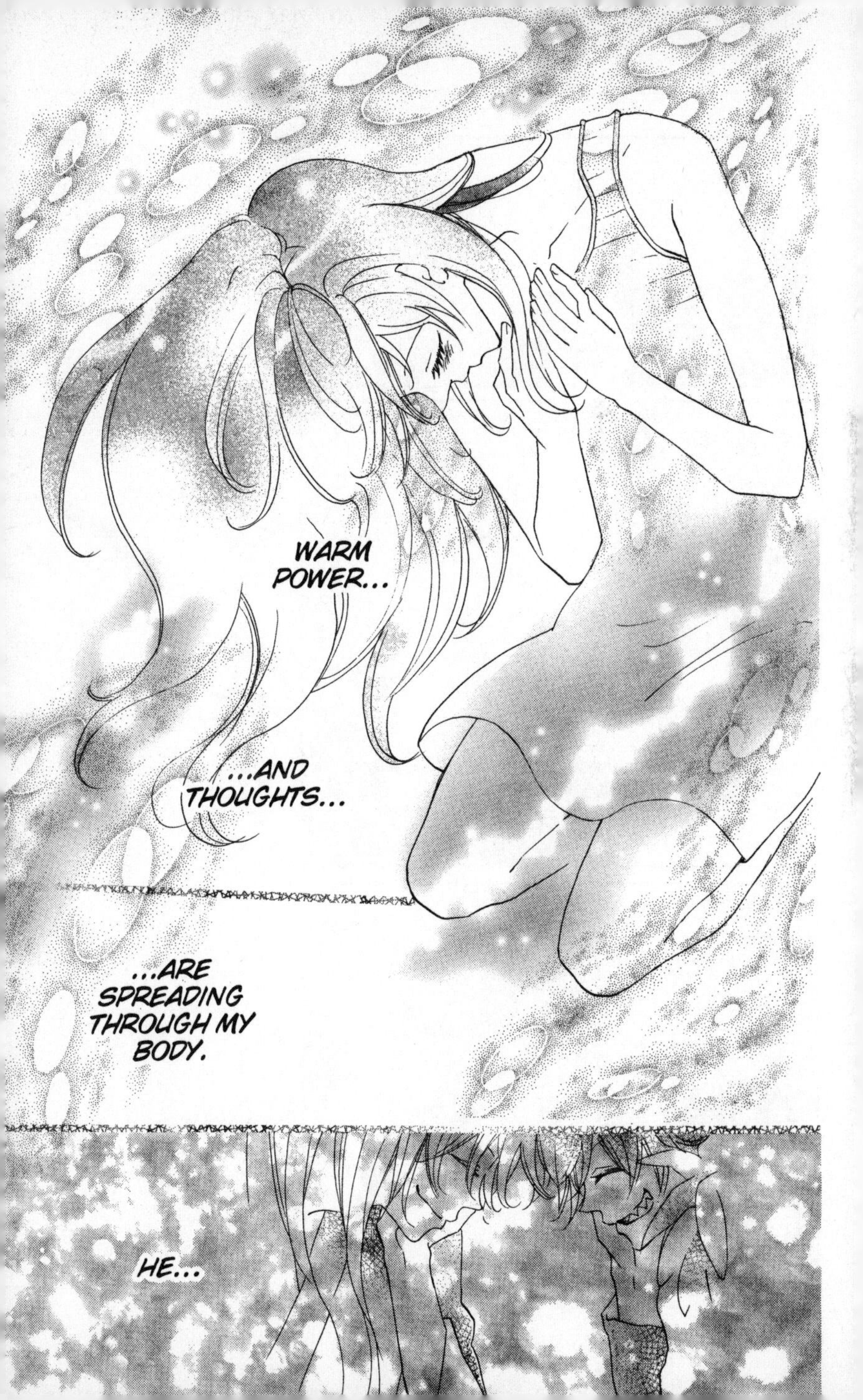
WARM POWER...
...AND THOUGHTS...
...ARE SPREADING THROUGH MY BODY.
HE...

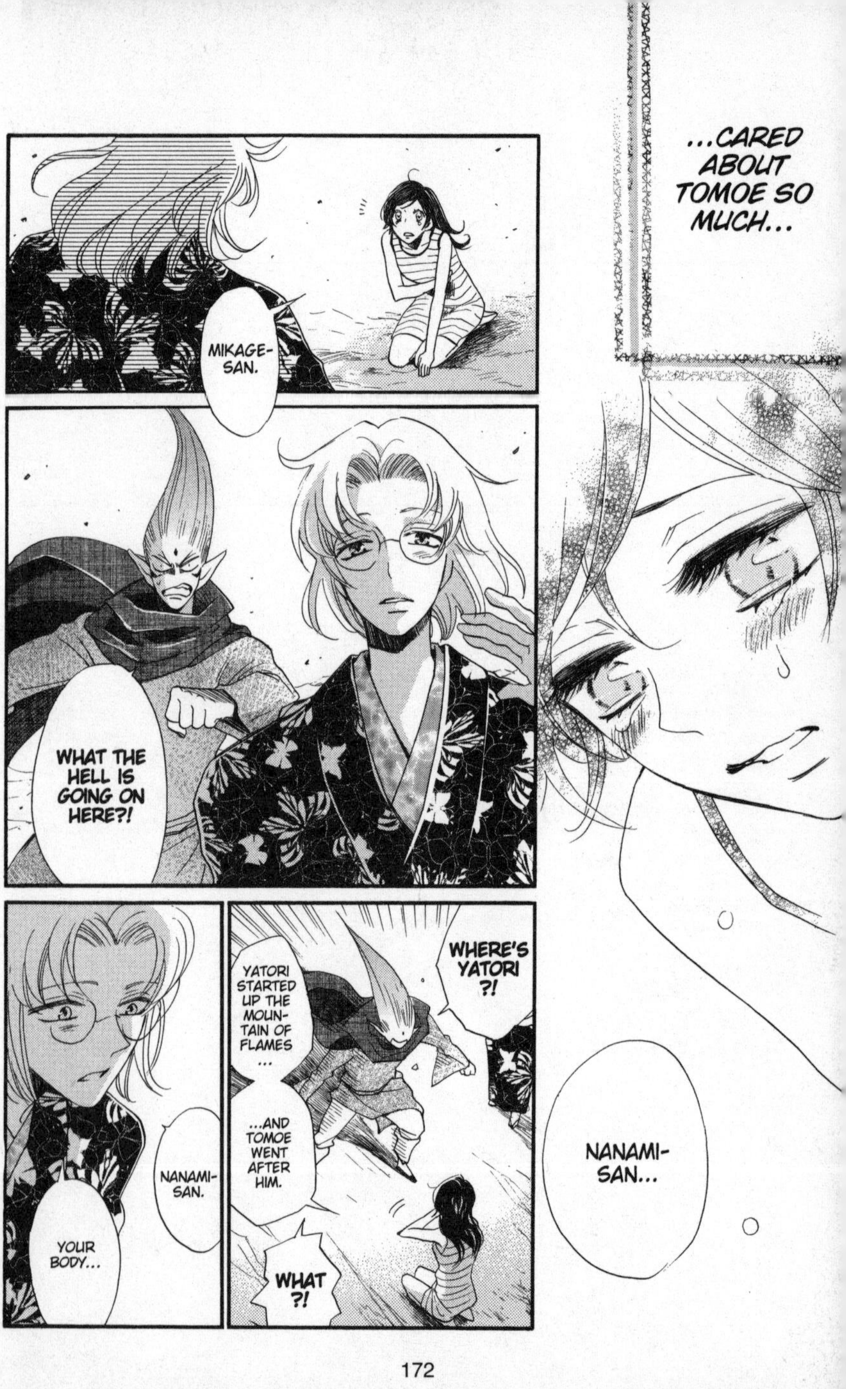
...CARED ABOUT TOMOE SO MUCH...
NANAMI-SAN...
MIKAGE-SAN.
WHAT THE HELL IS GOING ON HERE?!
WHERE'S YATORI?!
YATORI STARTED UP THE MOUNTAIN OF FLAMES...
...AND TOMOE WENT AFTER HIM.
WHAT?!
NANAMI-SAN.
YOUR BODY...

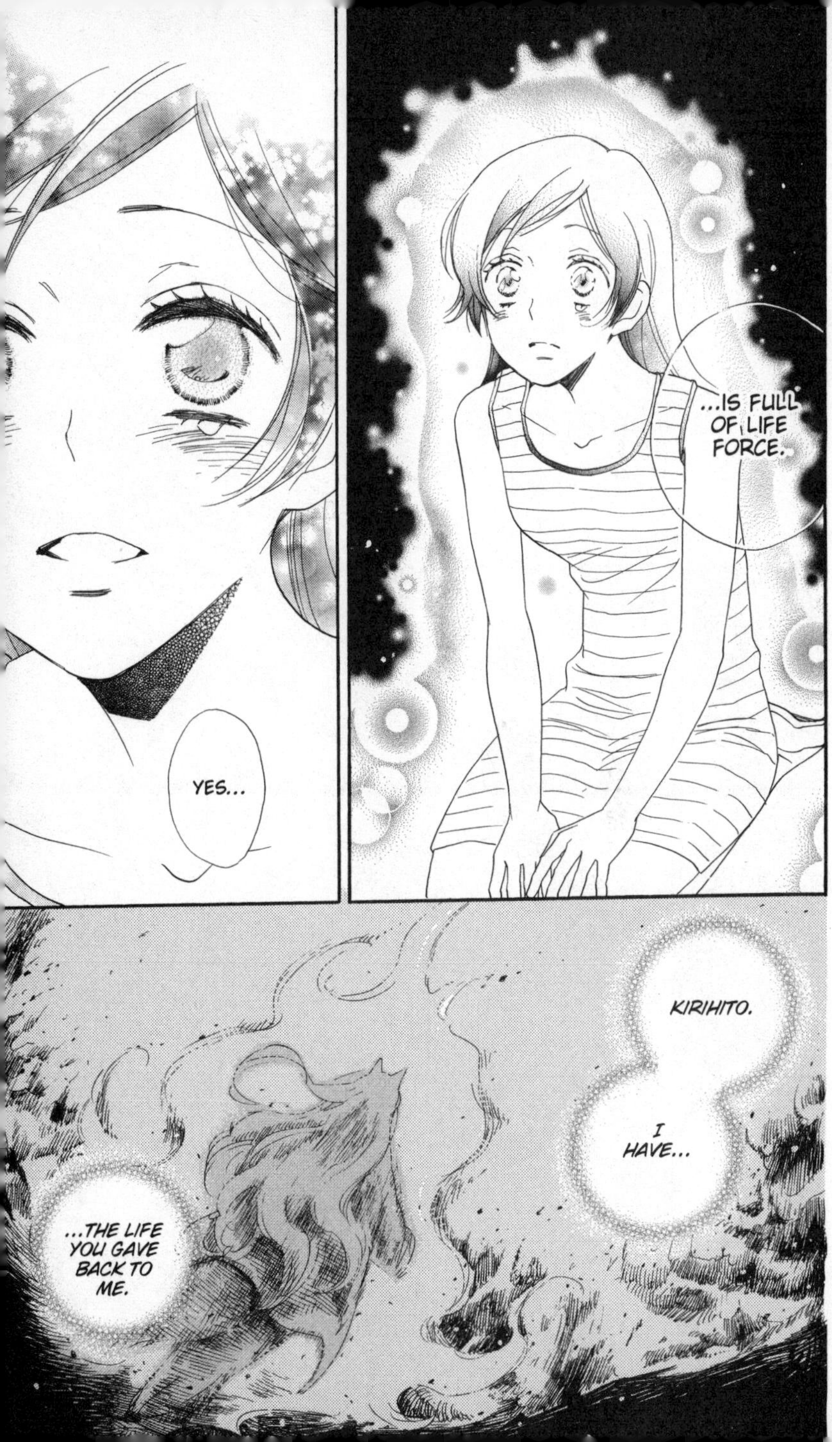
...IS FULL OF LIFE FORCE.
YES...
KIRIHITO.
I HAVE...
...THE LIFE YOU GAVE BACK TO ME.

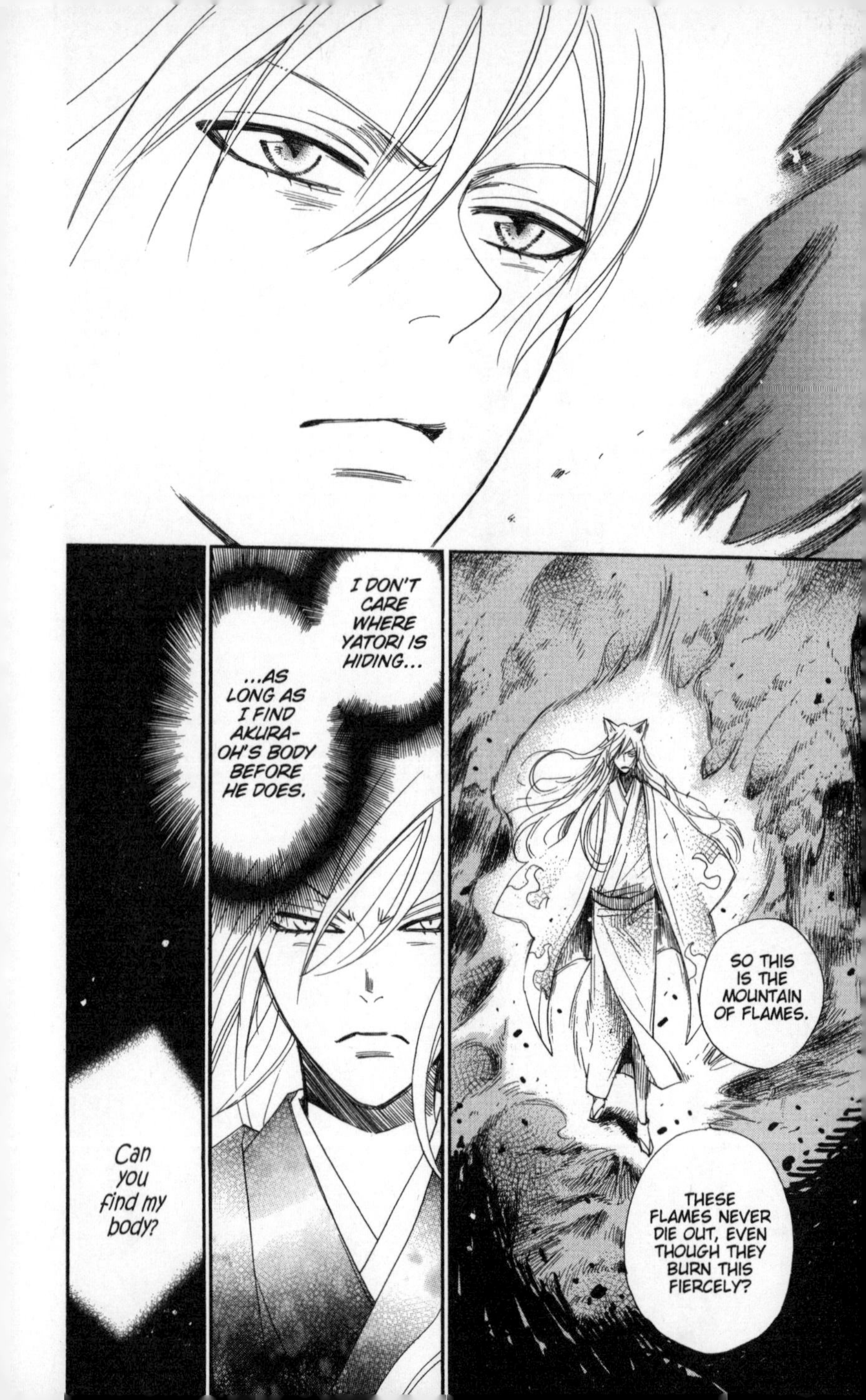
SO THIS IS THE MOUNTAIN OF FLAMES.
THESE FLAMES NEVER DIE OUT, EVEN THOUGH THEY BURN THIS FIERCELY?
I DON'T CARE WHERE YATORI IS HIDING...
...AS LONG AS I FIND AKURA-OH'S BODY BEFORE HE DOES.
Can you find my body?

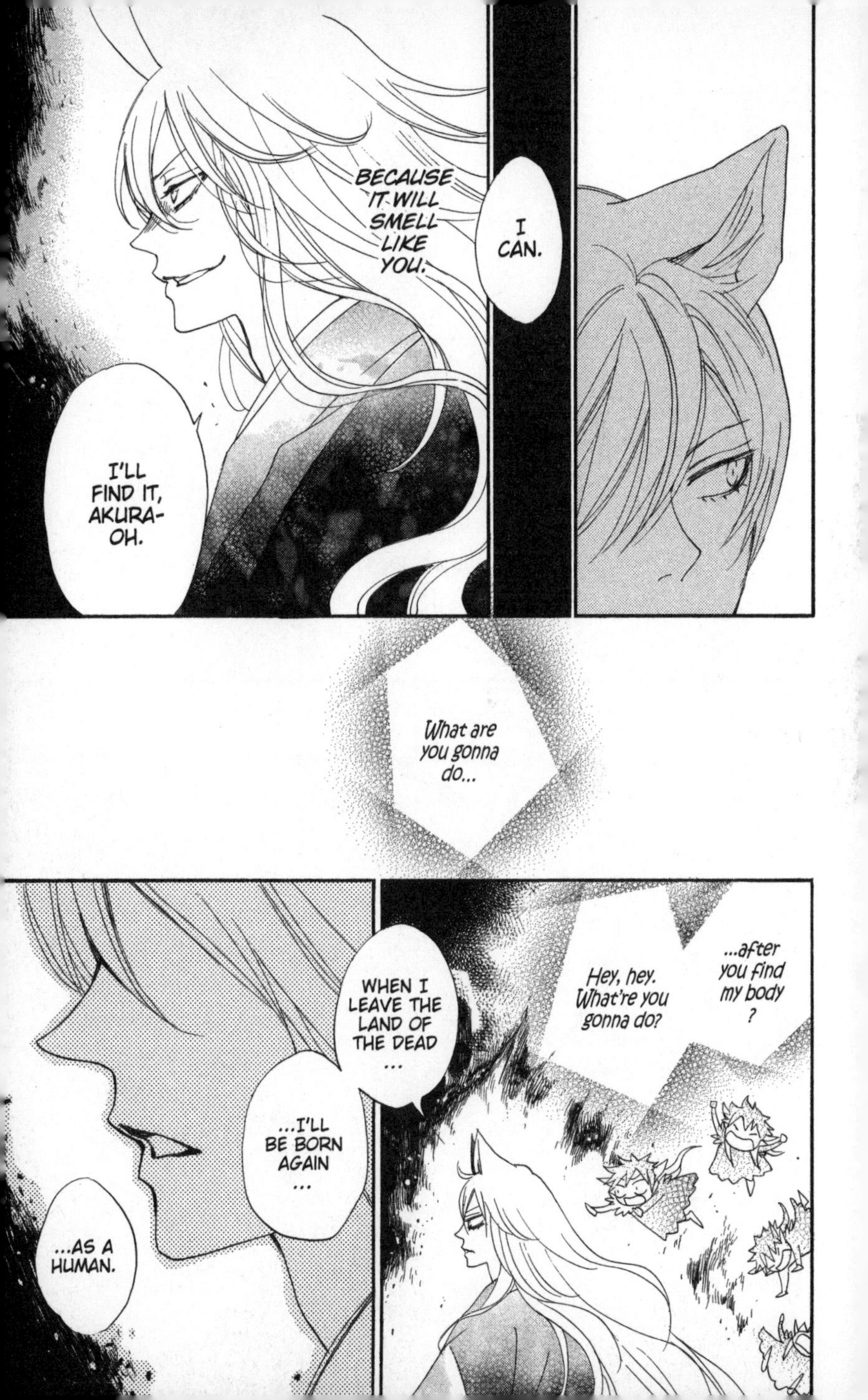
I CAN.
BECAUSE IT WILL SMELL LIKE YOU.
I'LL FIND IT, AKURA-OH.
What are you gonna do...
...after you find my body ?
Hey, hey. What're you gonna do?
WHEN I LEAVE THE LAND OF THE DEAD ...
...I'LL BE BORN AGAIN ...
...AS A HUMAN.

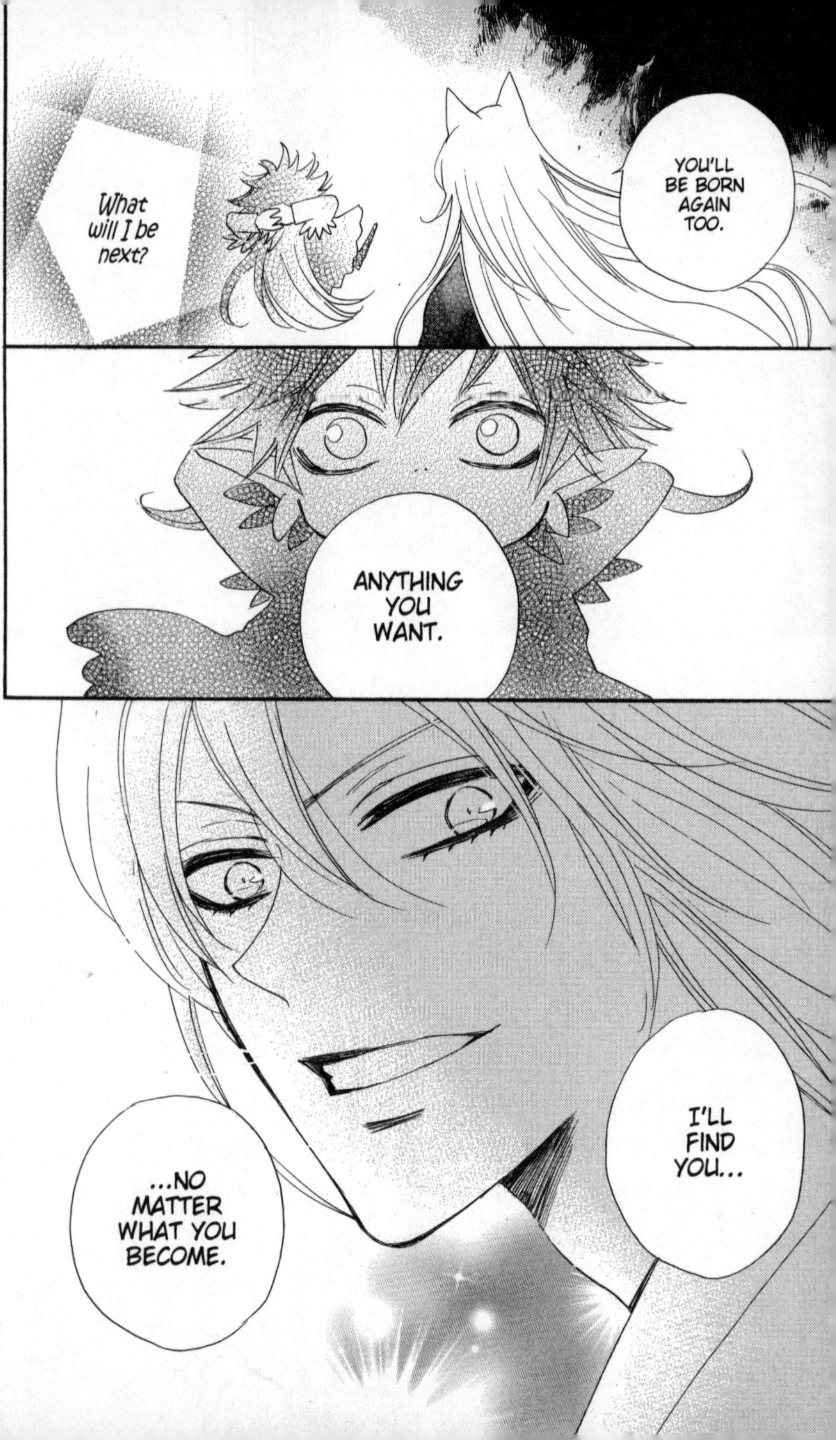
YOU'LL BE BORN AGAIN TOO.
What will I be next?
ANYTHING YOU WANT.
I'LL FIND YOU...
...NO MATTER WHAT YOU BECOME.

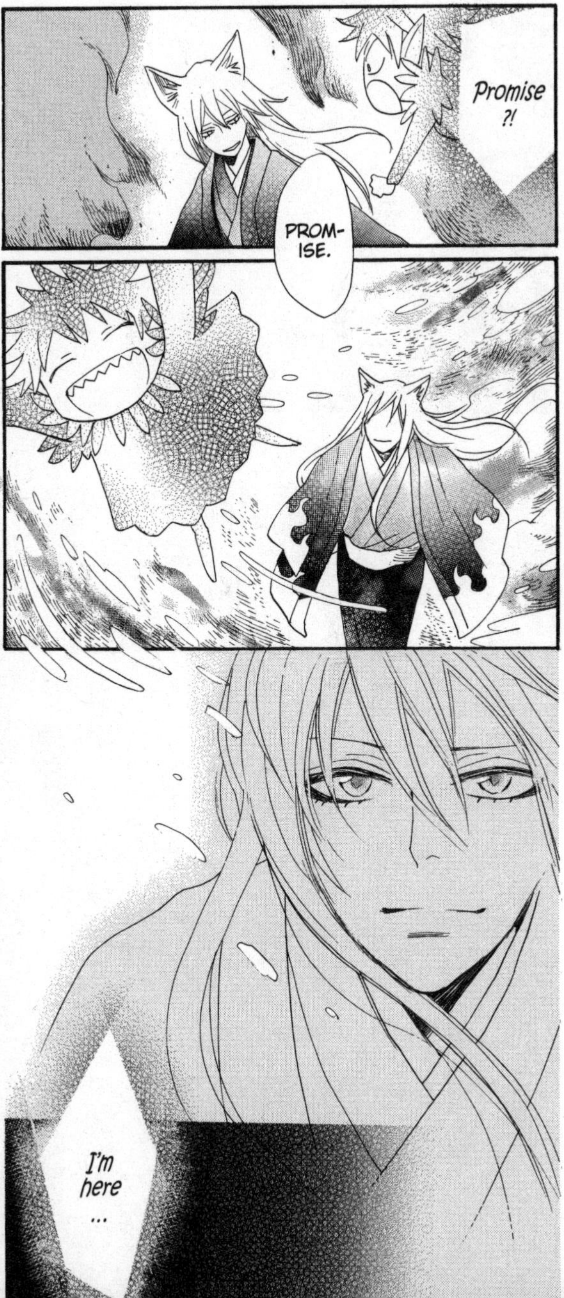
Promise ?!
PROM-ISE.
I'm here ...

Thank you for reading this far!

If you have any comments and thoughts about volume 23, do let me hear from you!

The address is...

Julietta Suzuki
c/o Shojo Beat
VIZ Media, LLC
P.O. Box 77010
San Francisco
CA 94107

Now then.

I hope we'll be able to meet again in the next volume.

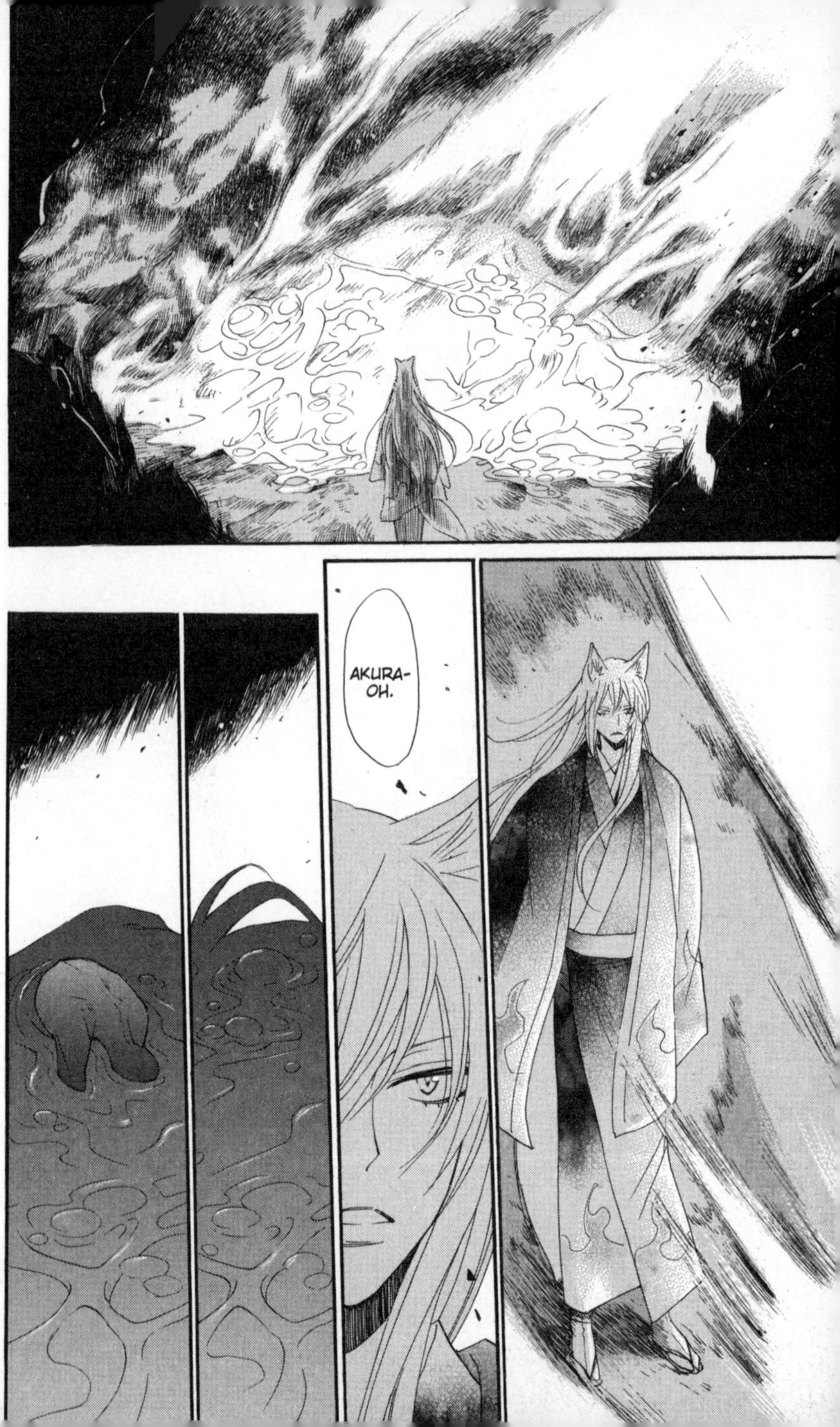
AKURA-OH.

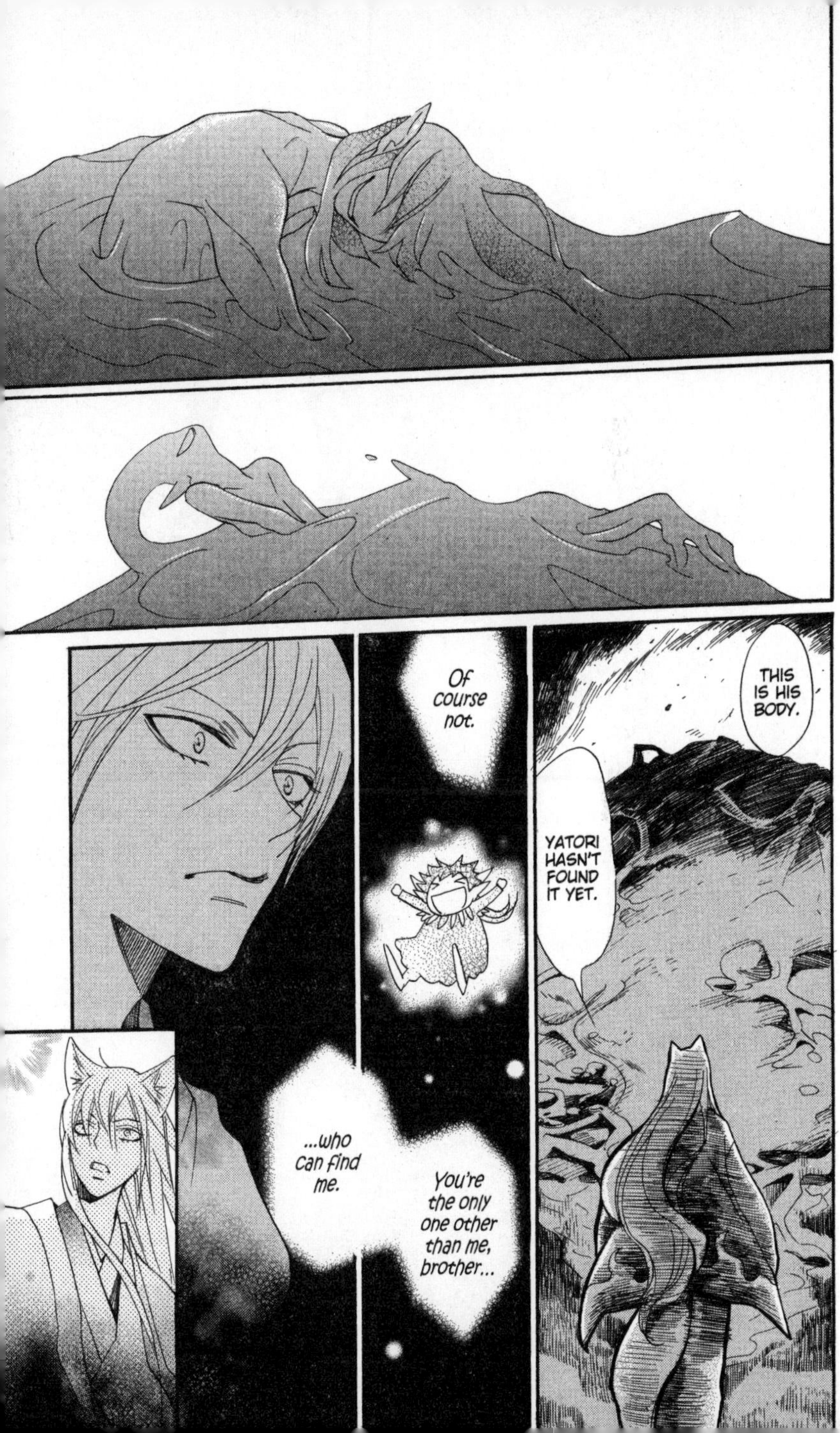
THIS IS HIS BODY.
YATORI HASN'T FOUND IT YET.
Of course not.
You're the only one other than me, brother...
...who can find me.

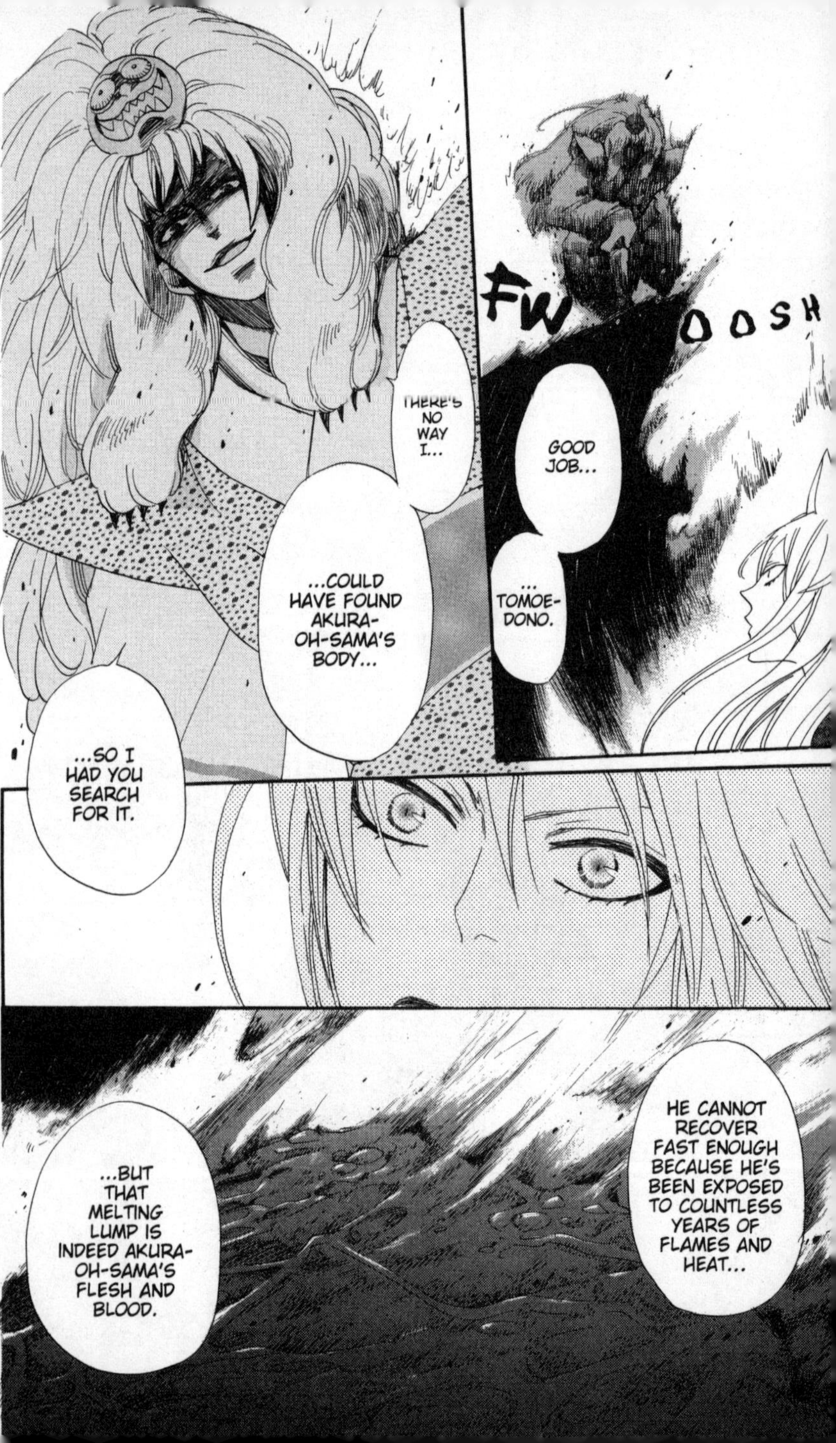
FWOOSH
GOOD JOB...
...TOMOE-DONO.
THERE'S NO WAY I...
...COULD HAVE FOUND AKURA-OH-SAMA'S BODY...
...SO I HAD YOU SEARCH FOR IT.
HE CANNOT RECOVER FAST ENOUGH BECAUSE HE'S BEEN EXPOSED TO COUNTLESS YEARS OF FLAMES AND HEAT...
...BUT THAT MELTING LUMP IS INDEED AKURA-OH-SAMA'S FLESH AND BLOOD.

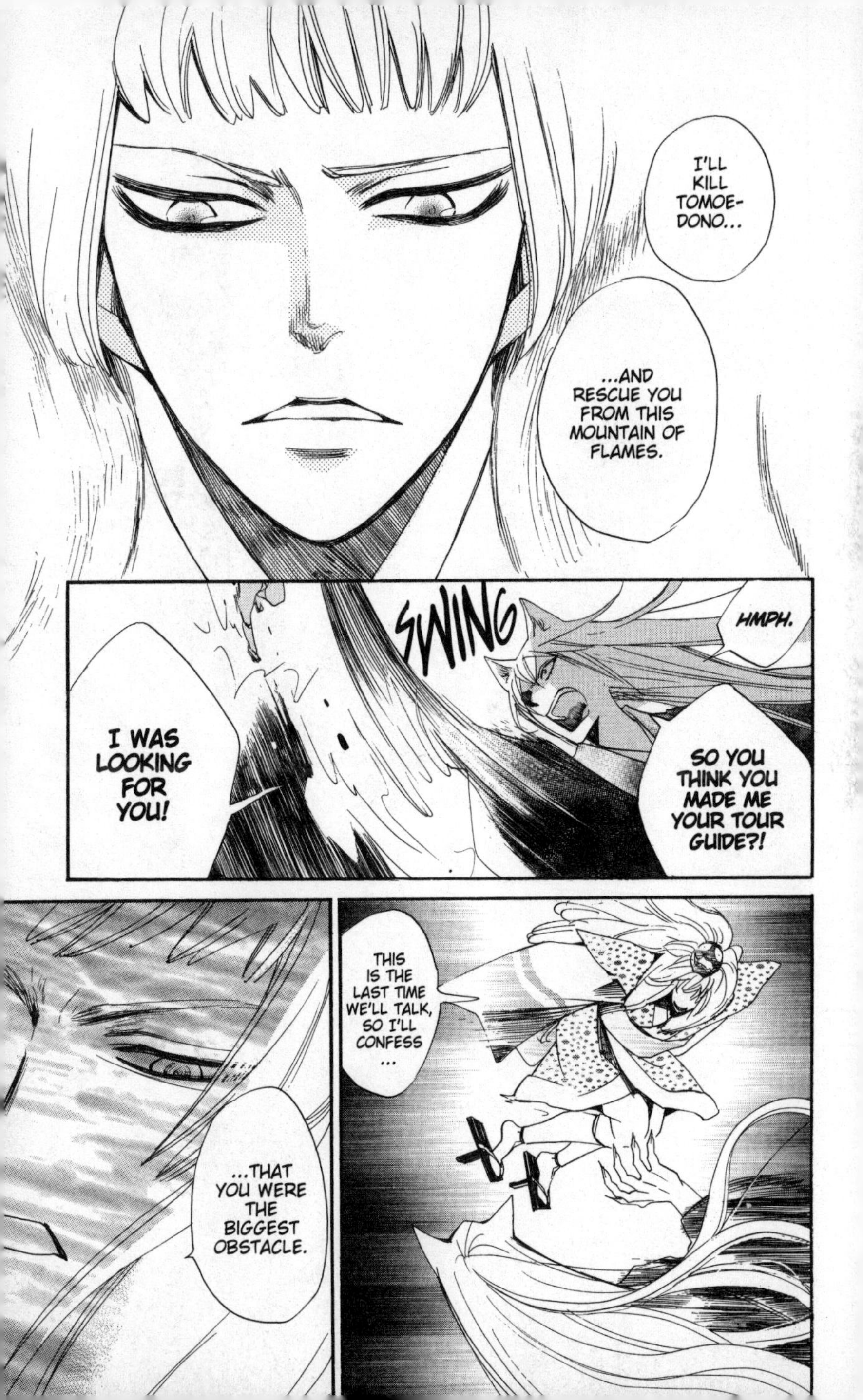
I'LL KILL TOMOE-DONO...
...AND RESCUE YOU FROM THIS MOUNTAIN OF FLAMES.
HMPH.
SWING
SO YOU THINK YOU MADE ME YOUR TOUR GUIDE?!
I WAS LOOKING FOR YOU!
THIS IS THE LAST TIME WE'LL TALK, SO I'LL CONFESS...
...THAT YOU WERE THE BIGGEST OBSTACLE.

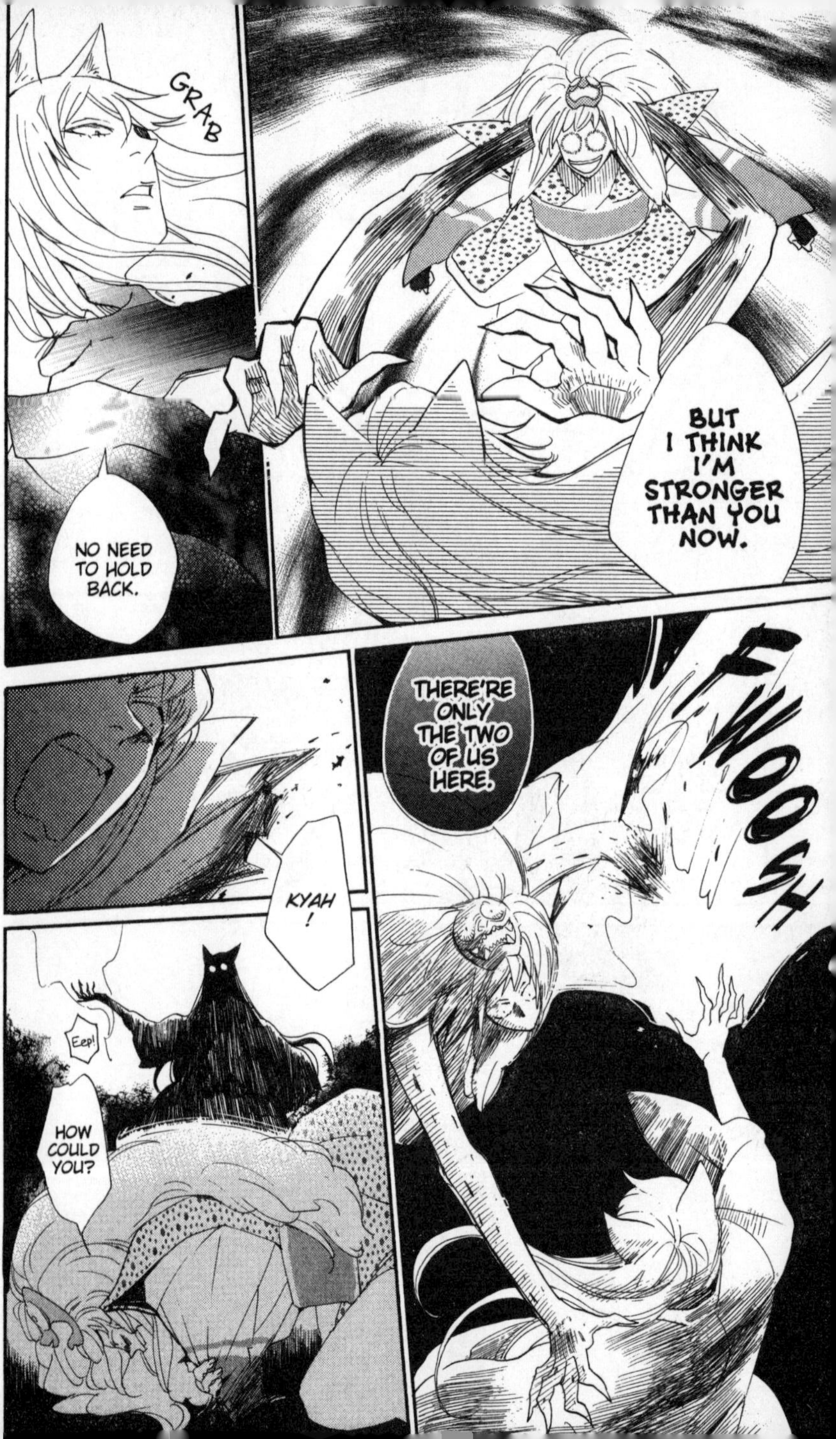
BUT I THINK I'M STRONGER THAN YOU NOW.
GRAB
NO NEED TO HOLD BACK.
FWOOSH
THERE'RE ONLY THE TWO OF US HERE.
KYAH!
Eep!
HOW COULD YOU?

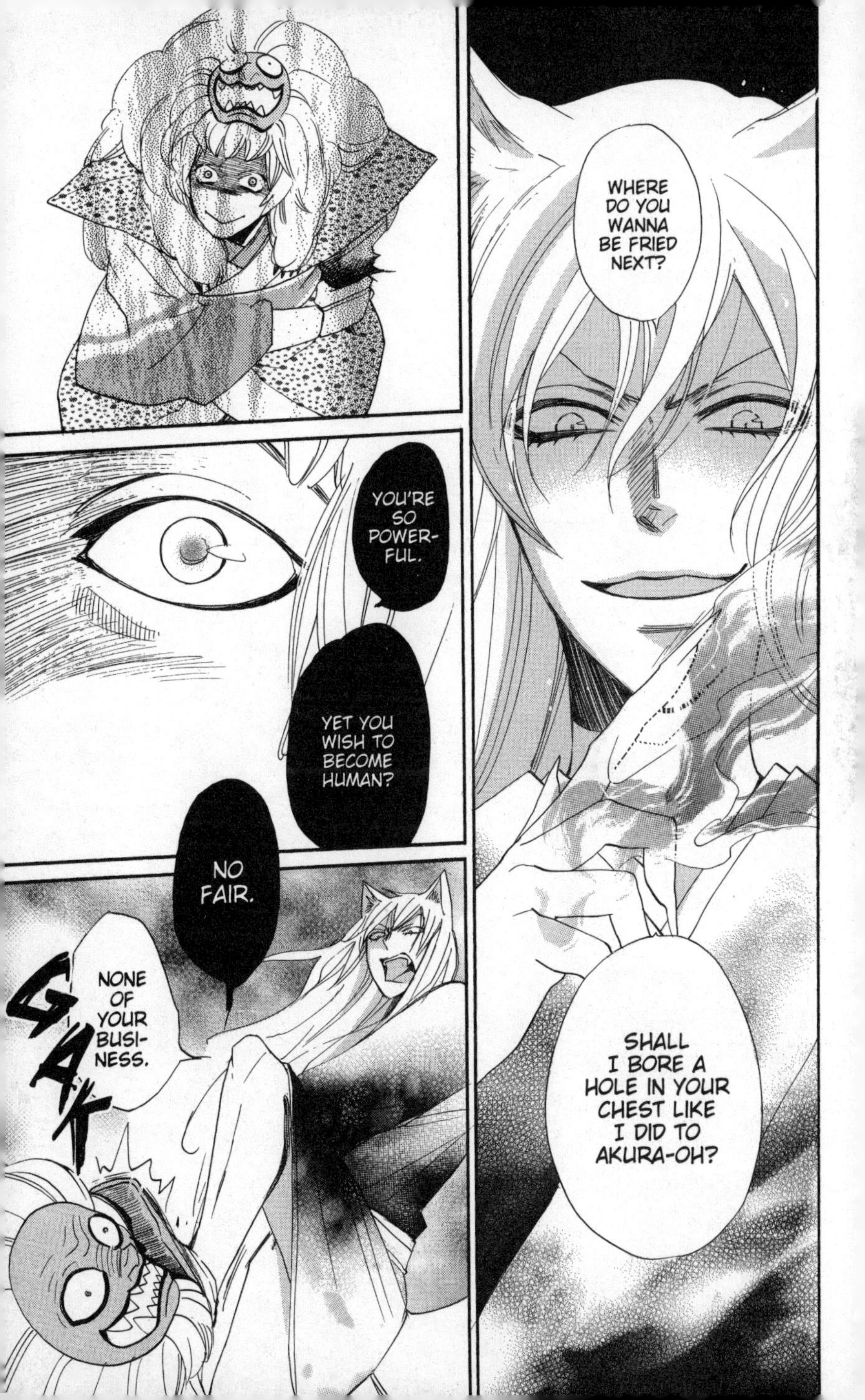
WHERE DO YOU WANNA BE FRIED NEXT?
SHALL I BORE A HOLE IN YOUR CHEST LIKE I DID TO AKURA-OH?
YOU'RE SO POWER-FUL.
YET YOU WISH TO BECOME HUMAN?
NO FAIR.
NONE OF YOUR BUSI-NESS.
GAK

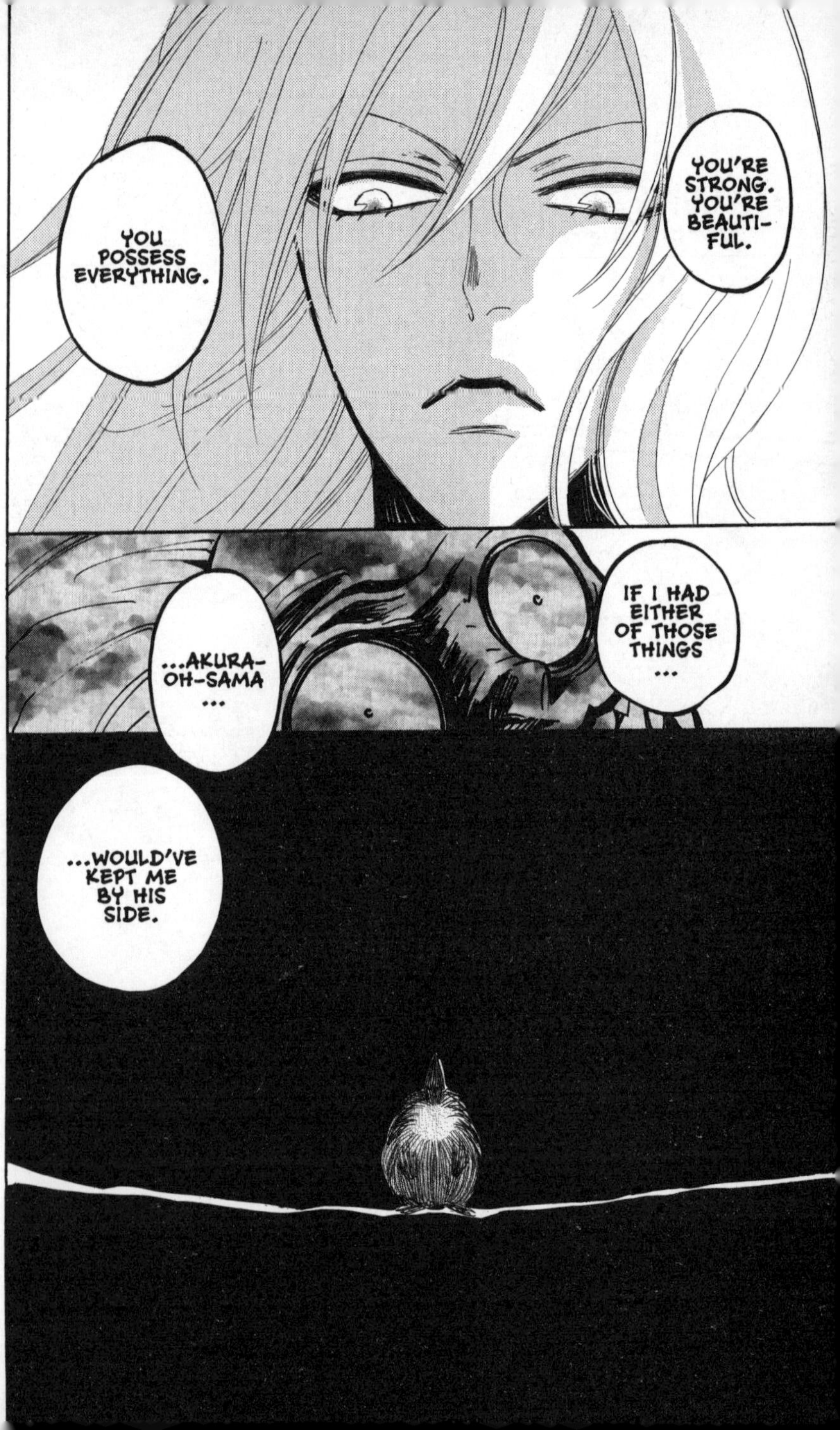
YOU'RE STRONG. YOU'RE BEAUTI-FUL.
YOU POSSESS EVERYTHING.
IF I HAD EITHER OF THOSE THINGS...
...AKURA-OH-SAMA...
...WOULD'VE KEPT ME BY HIS SIDE.

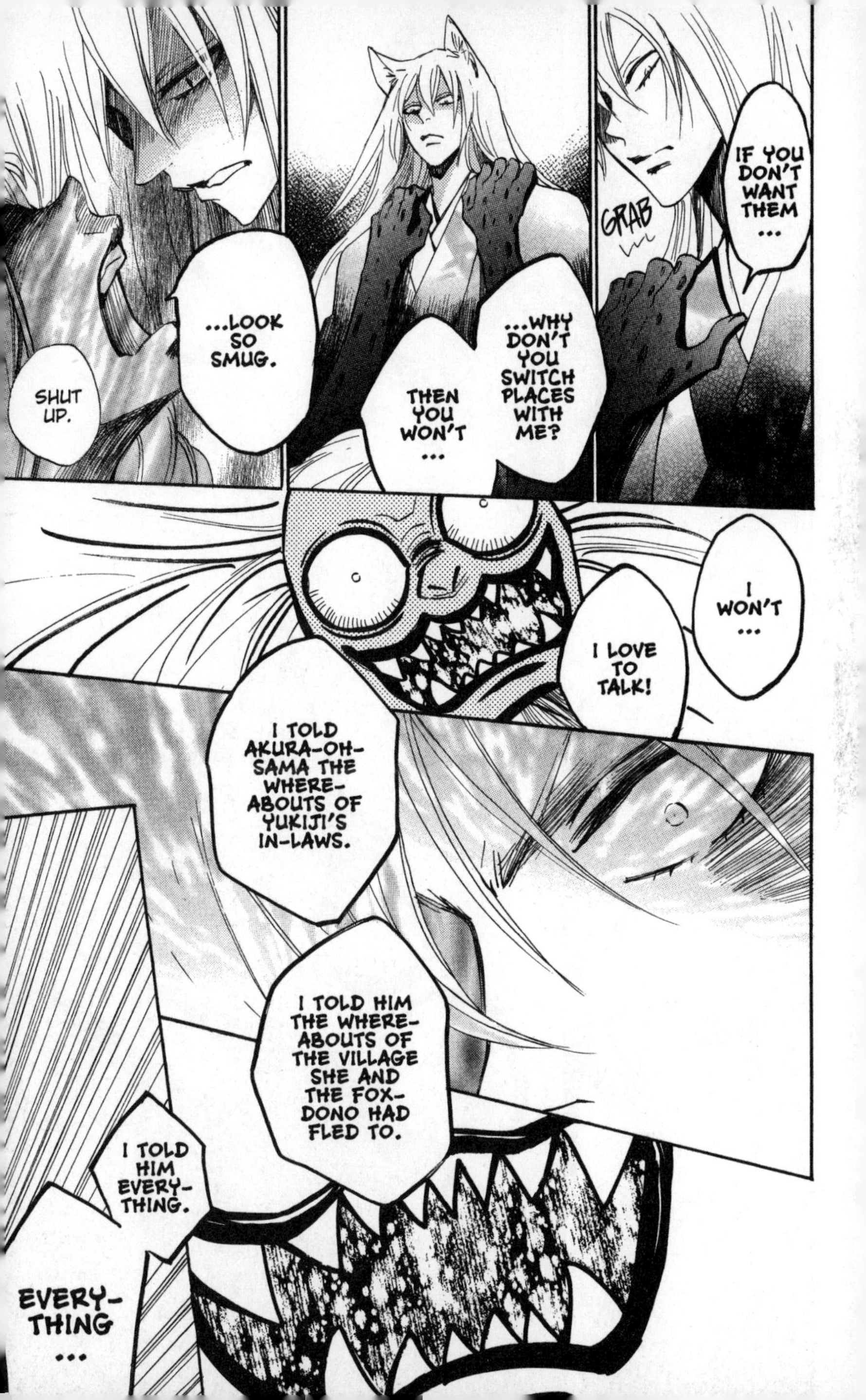
IF YOU DON'T WANT THEM ...
GRAB
...WHY DON'T YOU SWITCH PLACES WITH ME?
THEN YOU WON'T ...
...LOOK SO SMUG.
SHUT UP.
I WON'T ...
I LOVE TO TALK!
I TOLD AKURA-OH-SAMA THE WHERE-ABOUTS OF YUKIJI'S IN-LAWS.
I TOLD HIM THE WHERE-ABOUTS OF THE VILLAGE SHE AND THE FOX-DONO HAD FLED TO.
I TOLD HIM EVERY-THING.
EVERY-THING ...

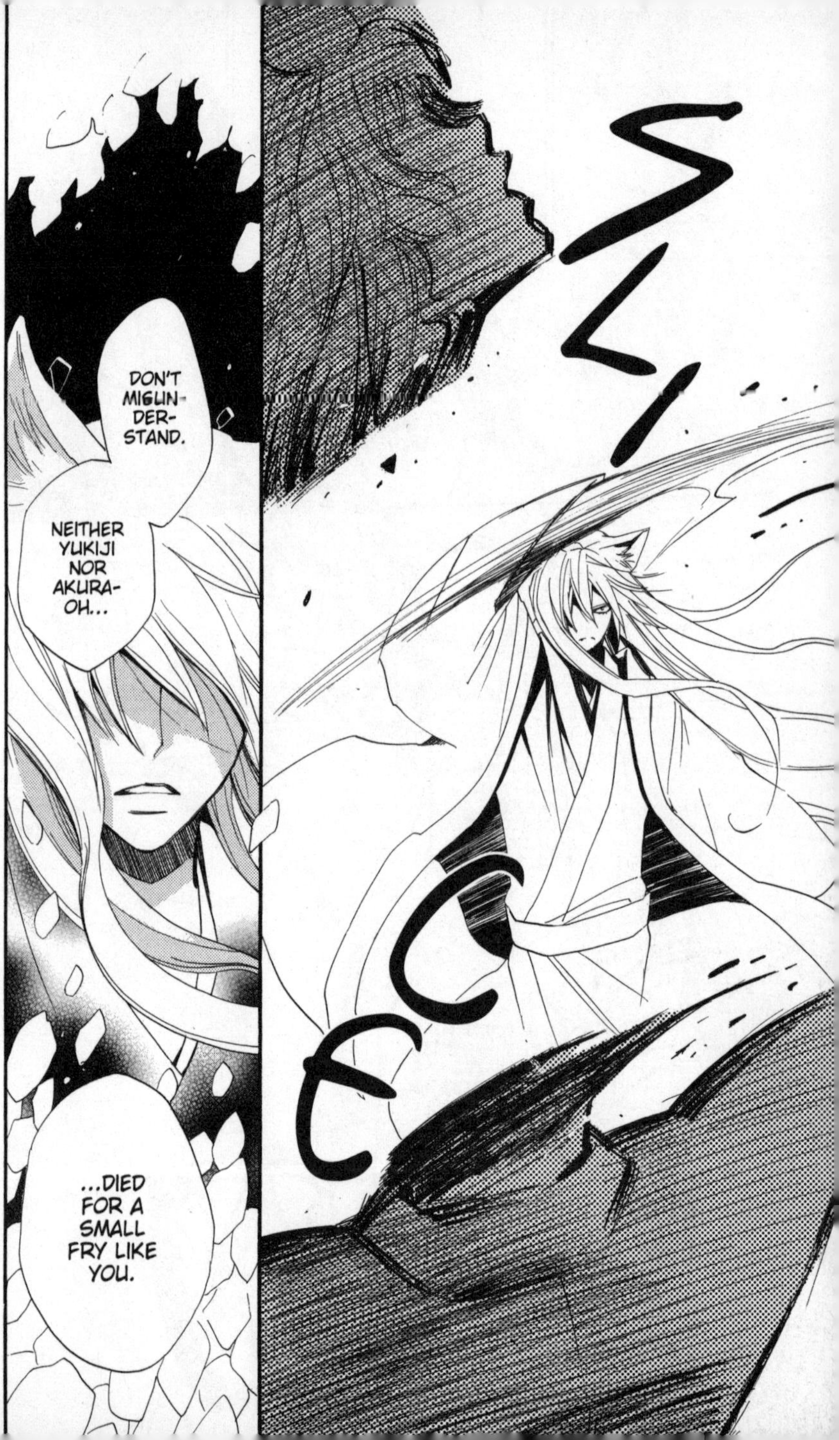
DON'T MISUN-DER-STAND.
NEITHER YUKIJI NOR AKURA-OH...
...DIED FOR A SMALL FRY LIKE YOU.

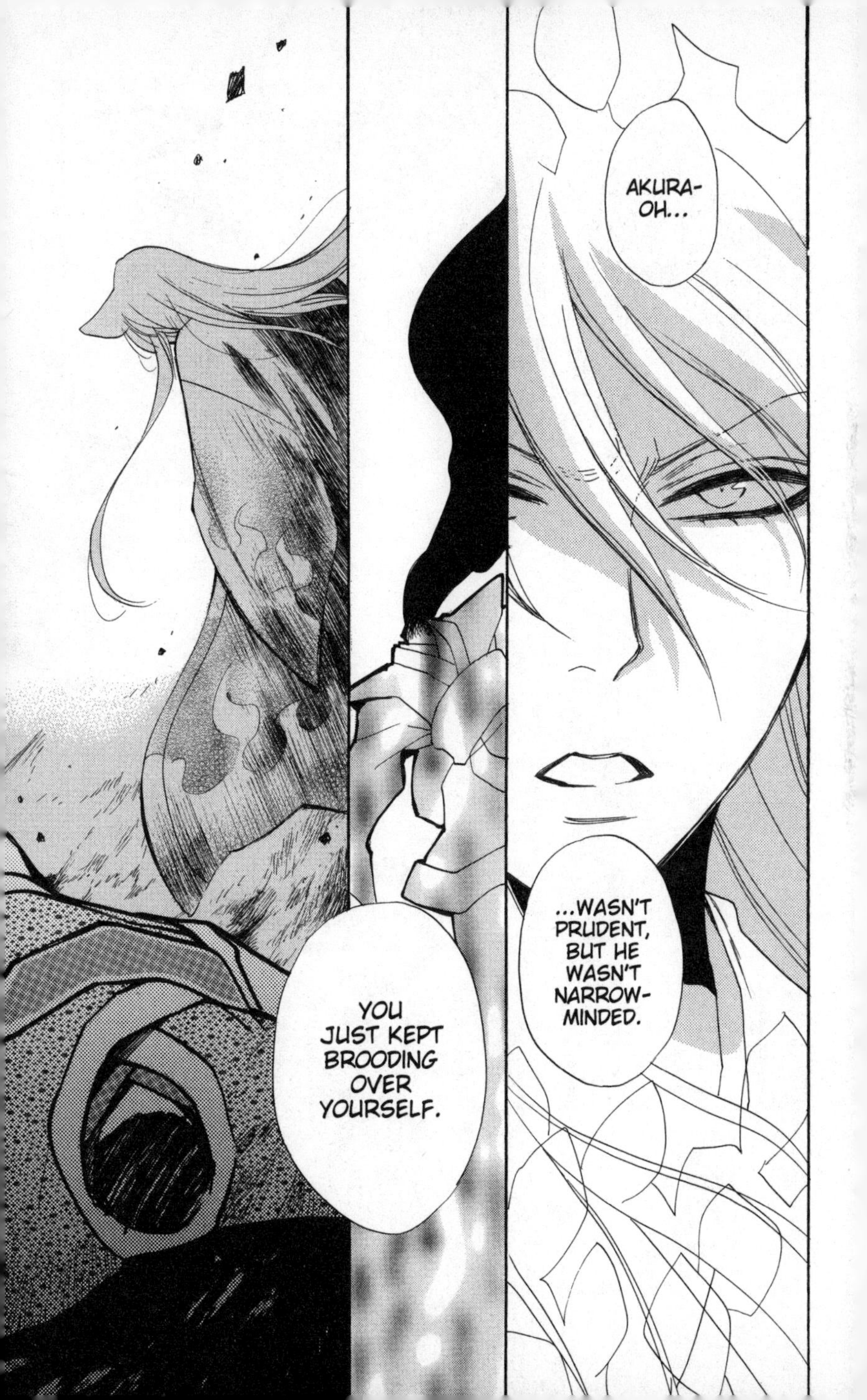
AKURA-OH...
...WASN'T PRUDENT, BUT HE WASN'T NARROW-MINDED.
YOU JUST KEPT BROODING OVER YOURSELF.

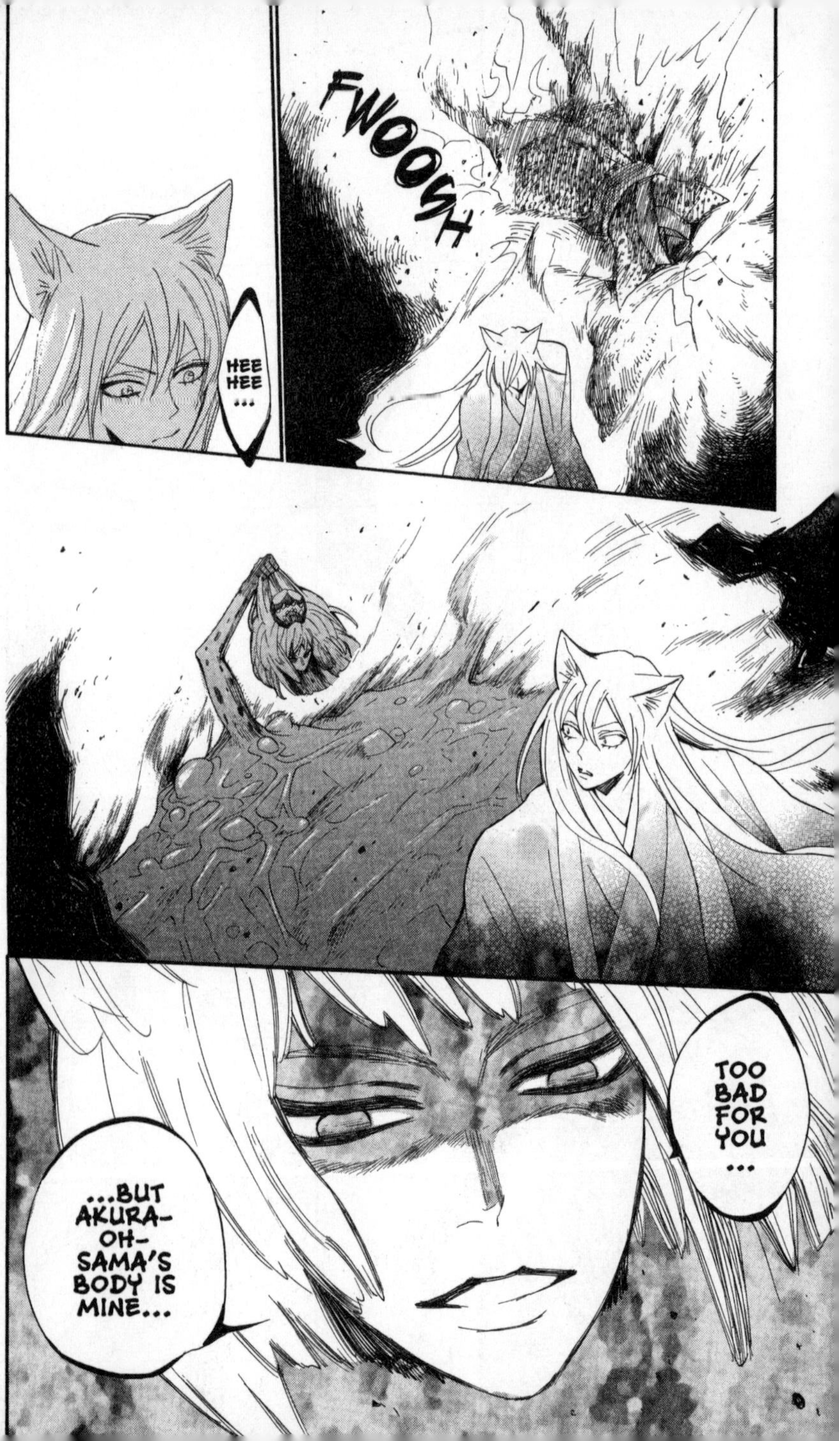
FWOOSH
HEE HEE...
TOO BAD FOR YOU...
...BUT AKURA-OH-SAMA'S BODY IS MINE...

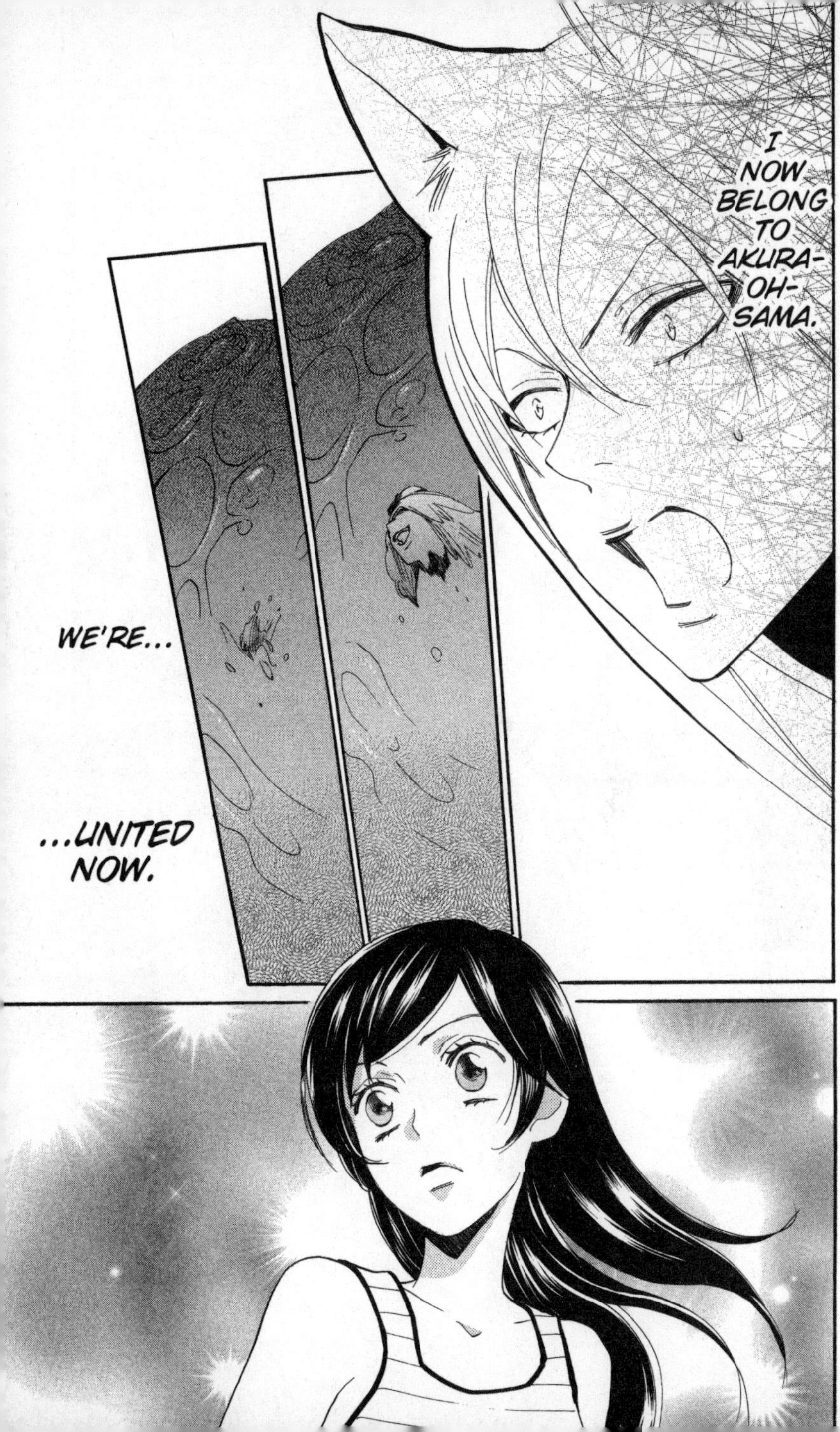
I NOW BELONG TO AKURA-OH-SAMA.
WE'RE...
...UNITED NOW.

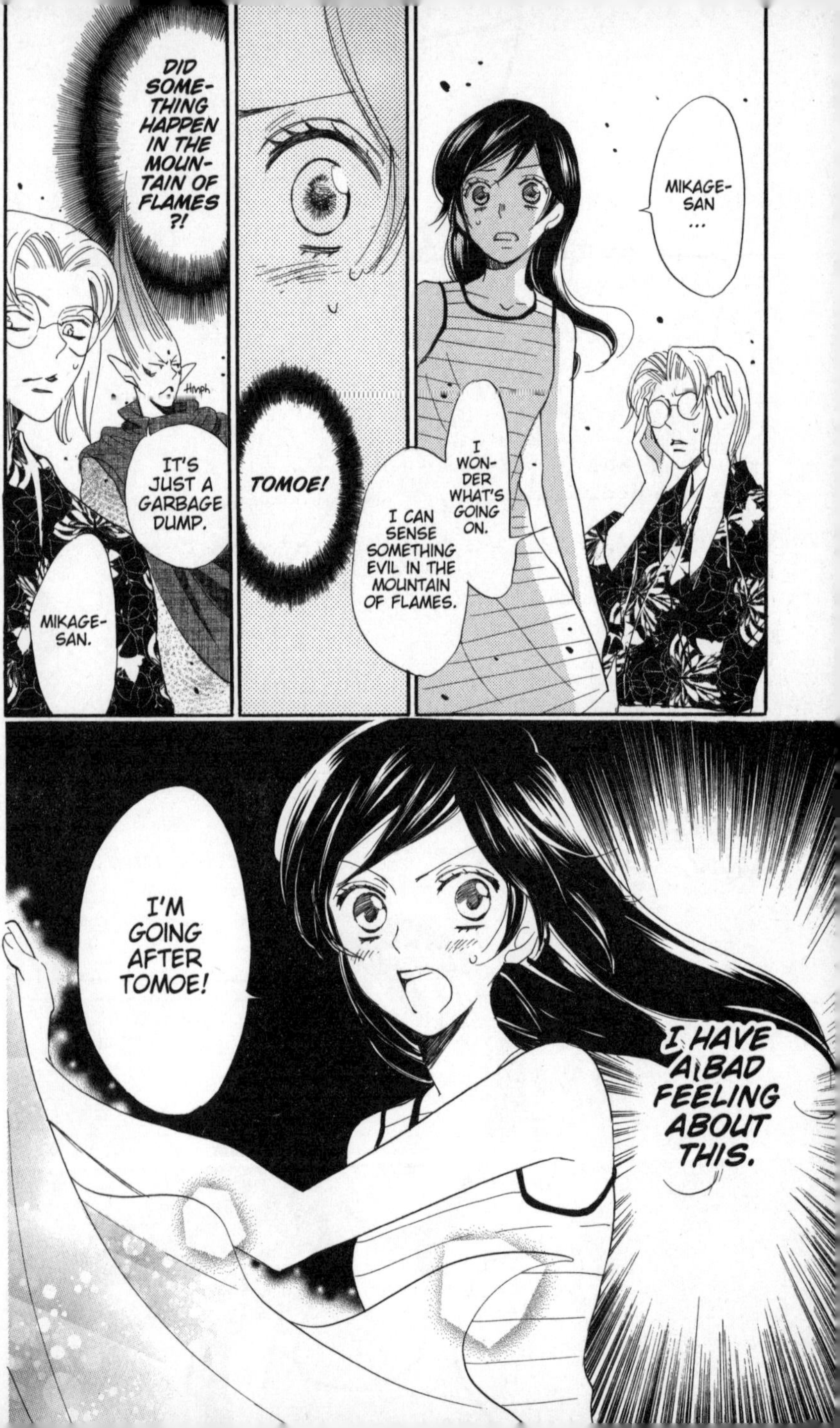
MIKAGE-SAN ...
I WONDER WHAT'S GOING ON.
I CAN SENSE SOMETHING EVIL IN THE MOUNTAIN OF FLAMES.
TOMOE!
DID SOMETHING HAPPEN IN THE MOUNTAIN OF FLAMES?!
Hmph
IT'S JUST A GARBAGE DUMP.
MIKAGE-SAN.
I HAVE A BAD FEELING ABOUT THIS.
I'M GOING AFTER TOMOE!

The Otherworld

Ayakashi is an archaic term for yokai.

Kami are Shinto deities or spirits. The word can be used for a range of creatures, from nature spirits to strong and dangerous gods.

Onibi-warashi are like will-o'-the-wisps.

Shikigami are spirits that are summoned and employed by onmyoji (yin-yang sorcerers).

Shinshi are birds, beasts, insects or fish that have a special relationship with a kami.

Tochigami (or *jinushigami*) are deities of a specific area of land.

Yokai are demons, monsters or goblins.

Honorifics

-chan is a diminutive most often used with babies, children or teenage girls.

-dono roughly means "my lord," although not in the aristocratic sense.

-kun is used by persons of superior rank to their juniors. It can sometimes have a familiar connotation.

-san is a standard honorific similar to Mr., Mrs., Miss or Ms.

-sama is used with people of much higher rank.

Julietta Suzuki's debut manga *Hoshi ni Naru Hi* (The Day One Becomes a Star) appeared in the 2004 *Hana to Yume Plus*. Her other books include *Akuma to Dolce* (The Devil and Sweets) and *Karakuri Odette*. Born in December in Fukuoka Prefecture, she enjoys having movies play in the background while she works on her manga.

KAMISAMA KISS
VOL. 23
Shojo Beat Edition

STORY AND ART BY
Julietta Suzuki

English Translation & Adaptation/Tomo Kimura
Touch-up Art & Lettering/Joanna Estep
Design/Yukiko Whitley
Editor/Pancha Diaz

KAMISAMA HAJIMEMASHITA by Julietta Suzuki

First published in Japan in 2015 by HAKUSENSHA, Inc., Tokyo.
English language translation rights arranged with
HAKUSENSHA, Inc., Tokyo.

Printed in the U.S.A.

Published by VIZ Media, LLC
P.O. Box 77010
San Francisco, CA 94107

10 9 8 7 6 5 4 3 2 1
First printing, February 2017

www.viz.com
www.shojobeat.com

PARENTAL ADVISORY
KAMISAMA KISS is rated T for Teen and is recommended for ages 13 and up. This volume contains fantasy violence.
ratings.viz.com

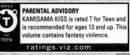

IDOL dreams

STORY & ART BY
ARINA TANEMURA

At age 31, office worker Chikage Deguchi feels she missed her chances at love and success. When word gets out that she's a virgin, Chikage is humiliated and wishes she could turn back time to when she was still young and popular. She takes an experimental drug that changes her appearance back to when she was 15. Now Chikage is determined to pursue everything she missed out on all those years ago—including becoming a star!

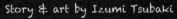

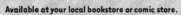